Anonymous

Gold and the gospel.

The Ulster prize essays on the scriptural duty of giving in proportion to means and income

Anonymous

Gold and the gospel.
The Ulster prize essays on the scriptural duty of giving in proportion to means and income

ISBN/EAN: 9783337714659

Printed in Europe, USA, Canada, Australia, Japan

Cover: Foto ©ninafisch / pixelio.de

More available books at **www.hansebooks.com**

GOLD AND THE GOSPEL.

THE

Ulster Prize Essays

ON

THE SCRIPTURAL DUTY OF
GIVING IN PROPORTION TO MEANS AND INCOME.

THIRTY-FIRST THOUSAND.

LONDON:
JAMES NISBET AND CO. 21 BERNERS STREET.
MDCCCLXIX.

TO

SIR CULLING E. EARDLEY, BART.

PRESIDENT OF THE COUNCIL OF THE EVANGELICAL ALLIANCE,

This Volume,

EXEMPLIFYING SO MUCH CATHOLIC CO-OPERATION,

IS

WITH PERMISSION

MOST RESPECTFULLY DEDICATED.

"The general adoption of the principles of the volume before us would change the condition of the Church and of the world. The discovery of the law of gravitation, and the application of steam to its manifold uses in modern society, have not produced a greater change on the philosophy and physical condition of mankind than the practice of the views of pecuniary contribution here submitted to the public would effect on the life, energy, and usefulness of the Church of Christ."—*Free Church of Scotland Magazine.*

ORIGINAL ADVERTISEMENT.

SEVERAL treatises have recently been published on the subject of Christian Liberality, and in these the fearful prevalence of Covetousness has been ably exposed. But, after all, it is to be feared that no satisfactory method of bringing home to the consciences of individuals the guilt of this insidious evil has been elicited. *The measure of liberality* is still left to the decision of the selfish, and though covetousness is a sin of the deepest dye, and excludes from the kingdom of heaven, the question, " Who is covetous ?" still receives no definite answer.

There is still, therefore, the most urgent necessity for further inquiry on the subject ; and if the Holy Scriptures are indeed an all-sufficient rule of faith and practice, "that the man of God may be perfect, thoroughly furnished unto all good works ;" we may expect to find in them some measure or standard of Christian almsgiving if not by direct precept, yet by fair and conclusive inference, the general adoption of which would be of essential advantage to the piety and usefulness of the Church of Christ.

In reading the biography of the most eminently pious and useful in different ages, one must have been often struck with the fact that almost all of them devoted a regular proportion of their income to the Lord in pious and charitable uses. We might mention many whose names are familiar, whose writings are venerated, and whose memory is precious ; *e. g.* the Lord Chief Justice Hale, the Hon. Robert Boyle, Archbishop Tillotson, the Revs. Drs. Hammond, Annesley, Watts, and Doddridge, the Revs. R. Baxter, J. Wesley, T. Gouge, Brand, and R. Treffry, jun., together with the excellent Countess of Huntingdon, Mrs. Rowe, and Mrs. Bury. None of these gave less than one-tenth of their annual means or income, while several of them gave much more, and some of them gave all they had away, beyond the scriptural provision—"food and raiment."

R. Baxter, that great and exemplary master of practical theology, says in his Directory on this subject, "that on the whole he believes it is the duty of Christians generally to devote some fixed proportion of their income to the Lord ; that the one-tenth is as likely a proportion as can be prescribed, and that the devoting that amount to the Lord is a matter that we have more than human direction for." Whilst an able living expositor of Scripture says, "that he thinks it may be demonstrated from the Scriptures, that no one believing them can consistently give *less* than a tenth of his income annually to the cause of God, however much more he may give."

A few friends in the North of Ireland, of Evangelical views, desirous to obtain for cheap and gratuitous circulation, an able and persuasive statement of the Scriptural argument in favour of "*Giving in proportion to means and income*," with special reference to Prov. iii. 9, 10, Gen. xxviii. 22, and 1 Cor. xvi. 2, *hereby offer a Prize of* 50*l.* for the best, *and of* 20*l.* for the second best Essay on that subject, not exceeding 100 pages 8vo. The successful Essays to belong to the Donors.

The manuscripts are to be sent to the Revs. James Morgan, D.D., and Wm. Lupton, Fisherwick Place, Belfast, on or before the 1st February, 1852, and the award will be given on the 1st June, 1852.

The Revs. Drs. Drew and Edgar, of Belfast, and the Revs. Drs. Urwick and Appelbe, of Dublin, and the Rev. Robert G. Cather, A.M., Castledawson, have engaged to act as Arbitrators.

It is intended that the Essays shall eventually be published, and that they shall be dedicated, with permission, to Sir Culling E. Eardley, President of the Council of the Evangelical Alliance.

On behalf of the Donors,

THOMAS SINCLAIR,
W. PAUL.

Belfast, 28th August, 1851.

PREFACE TO THE FIRST EDITION.

It may not be uninteresting to the Christian public to know the origin of these Essays.

On the subject of which they treat, several friends, belonging to various denominations, had for many years entertained strong convictions; and eventually it appeared to them desirable that a powerful statement of the principle should be produced, and circulated as widely as possible.

Twenty-one gentlemen, members of different churches, having contributed 5*l*. each to a Prize-fund, it was resolved to offer a Prize of 50*l*. for the best, and another Prize of 20*l*. for the second-best Essay on the Scriptural duty of giving according to means and income. The Essays were restricted to 100 pages.

Five ministers of different denominations kindly consented to act as Adjudicators.

The advertisement (a copy of which is prefixed) appeared in the leading religious journals of the empire; and in due time fifty-one MSS., including one from the United States, were submitted to the Adjudicators.

After seven months' careful and independent investigation, each gave his verdict in favour of a different writer; yet, on consultation, the Adjudicators were agreed, that those chosen in their conjoint capacity treated the subject in a manner so able and interesting, and had so fully exhausted it, that they warmly and unanimously recommended that, subject to the consent of the authors, the five Essays should be published in one volume, without prejudice to any.

On various grounds, this course appeared the most desirable and the most likely to promote the object in view,

1. Each Essay is distinct and self-contained. Without trenching on the province of the other, one gives the logic of the case, another its Scripture, a third its law or precedents, a fourth its sentiment, and the fifth is addressed to its practical details.

2. The authors represent the several divisions of the United Kingdom. Two are Englishmen, two are Irishmen, and one is a Scotchman.

3. They belong to different Christian communities. One is an Episcopalian clergyman, the second is a Presbyterian minister, the third is a Scotch Dissenter, the fourth is an English Nonconformist, and the fifth is a layman. And as the scheme in the first instance originated with Baptists and Wesleyan Methodists, it may so far be regarded as combining the suffrage and sympathy of the largest evangelical denominations in the United Kingdom.

The four ministerial authors generously agreed to accept a moiety of the Prize-fund; and in order to promote the publication of a cheap edition of the Essays, they bespoke a large number for gratuitous distribution. The lay writer not only relinquished his own share in the Prize-fund, but offered the promoters a large contribution towards the expense of publication, and in order to cheapen the forthcoming volume.

At the Conference of the Evangelical Alliance, held at Dublin last year, the idea of bringing out these Essays at a price almost unprecedentedly low, was propounded, and was warmly received. Already two gentlemen,—one in Manchester and one in London,—have each ordered a thousand copies for distribution among ministers of the Church of England. A Presbyterian, a Congregationalist, a Baptist, and a Wesleyan gentleman, have each ordered a thousand copies, for similar distribution amongst their respective churches.

The originators of the scheme are not a little cheered and encouraged by this early success of their effort. Through the medium of Office-bearers in Churches and Sunday-school Teachers, they trust that the work will soon reach its appropriate destination among the masses of the Christian community and the members of our several Congregations. And whilst devoutly thankful for the countenance which the Lord has graciously vouchsafed to their humble undertaking, they would exclaim "Not unto us, O Lord, not unto us, but unto thy name give glory, for thy mercy, and for thy truth's sake."

PREFACE TO THE SECOND EDITION.

THE First Ten Thousand Copies of "Gold and the Gospel" having been disposed of, a Second Edition is now issued, to meet an eager and steady demand, which still continues.

A general Index has been carefully prepared; and the headings of the pages so arranged that the contents may be seen at a glance.

The present Edition is so portable and so cheap, that it is hoped no Christian household will remain without the volume, as a united Catholic testimony on a great and every-day duty.

The incomparable Lecture by the Rev. William Arthur, A.M., a copy of which shall be presented with this Edition, is printed in the same shape, with a view, where desired, to its being eventually bound along with it.

As the only object of the Promoters is to extend the knowledge and practice of the great principle of Proportionate Giving, they offer the Essays and the Lecture to all parties who wish to distribute them amongst their friends, or who unite together to order them of the Publishers, on the following terms, which barely cover the cost of publication, viz. :—

> Ten Copies of Gold and the Gospel
> and
> Ten Ditto of Mr. Arthur's Lecture
> } for £1.

Orders to be sent to Messrs. Nisbet.

More than one great financial movement in the Churches has already sprung out of the sentiment created by the Essays, and still larger fruits are, under the Divine blessing, confidently anticipated from its silent working in the hearts of Christians.

LIST OF ESSAYS.

ESSAY I.

PAGE

THE MEASURE OF CHRISTIAN LIBERALITY . . . i

ESSAY II.

THE SCRIPTURE RULE OF RELIGIOUS CONTRIBUTION . 83

ESSAY III.

THE JEWISH LAW OF TITHE, A GUIDE TO CHRISTIAN
LIBERALITY 179

ESSAY IV.

THE CHRISTIAN WEEKLY OFFERING 263

ESSAY V.

THE CHRISTIAN STEWARD 337

AN ESSAY

ON THE

Measure of Christian Liberality.

BY THE

REV. HENRY CONSTABLE, A.M.

CURATE OF ATHNOWEN, DIOCESE OF CORK.

PREFACE.

It is the object of the following Essay to establish that God has at all times laid down a standard by which man is to regulate his liberality in his cause, and that this standard has been the same for all dispensations. The writer is free to confess that, when led on the present occasion to consider this subject with attention, he was disposed to view it in a somewhat different light from that in which he has presented it here. He was inclined to think, that while Holy Scripture required of the Christian to honour God with a portion of his substance, that portion was left undetermined, and each was permitted to give just as his own conscience and judgment suggested. The more he considered the matter, however, in the light of reason and of Scripture, the more inclined he became to doubt the correctness of his opinion; until, at length, he came to the conclusion, that in this, as in other respects, God has laid down a rule by which Christians ought to walk. It may be that the arguments, almost wholly drawn from Scripture, which have convinced his own mind, may have the same effect on others. If they shall lead even a single worldling to perceive that he is not, in the disposition of his property, free from the claims of Him who is, in fact, the sole great Proprietor of all, or if they shall induce any, who heretofore may have satisfied themselves with giving in the noblest of all causes some miserable portion wholly unworthy of Him to whom it is offered, to feel that more is required at their hands, he will not have written in vain. For the sake of convenience the Essay has been divided into the following chapters:—

    Chap. 1. God is the owner of all things.
         2. God is the disposer of all things.
         3. Man's use of God's goods has always been limited.
         4. It is reasonable to think this limit should be a definite one.
         5. A tenth required of mankind from the earliest times.
         6. Abraham and Jacob's tenth.
         7. The Jewish tithe.
         8. The Jewish free-will offering.
         9. A tenth required from Christians.
        10. The Christian's free-will offerings.
        11. The objects on which the Christian is to expend his offerings.
        12. Motives to liberality.
        13. A test of covetousness.

CHAPTER I.

"The earth is the Lord's, and the fulness thereof."
—*Ps.* xxiv. 1.

The leading maxim of a celebrated modern Socialist* is, that "property is a crime." False and ruinous as such a maxim is in the mouths of those who proclaim war against property for the sake of plunder, and seek to overturn the powers that be in order to erect themselves into a tyranny, there is yet a point of view in which it is indisputable by the believer. Man has a right of property towards his fellow-man: he has none towards his God. Viewed in this latter light, no man can say that what he possesses is his own. For here comes in the prior, the inalienable claim of the great Maker and Owner of all things; and in regard of him the wealthiest and the most powerful descend at once from the rank of proprietors to that of the stewards of another's rights.

Such is, unquestionably, man's relation to God, as placed before us in Holy Scripture. "All the earth is mine,"† is the Creator's claim; and who is prepared to deny it? Accordingly, he asserts his right, one by one, to each and every of those things which man prizes most. "Sanctify unto me all the first-born among the children of Israel, both of man and beast, it is mine."‡ Of the land of Canaan—the land of so many promises—the land hardly obtained, after travel, and toil, and warfare, he said, "The land shall not be sold for ever, for the land is mine."§ "Every beast of the forest is mine, and the cattle upon a thousand hills."||

* M. Proudhon.   † Exod. xix. 5.   ‡ Exod. xiii. 2.
§ Lev. xxv. 23. || Ps. l. 10.

"The silver is mine, and the gold is mine, saith the Lord of hosts."* "All souls are mine."†

If we turn to the pages of the New Testament, we shall find the same universal claim made and acted on. "Come and follow me," was the address of Christ to whomsoever he pleased, and whenever he pleased. It implied the forsaking of every earthly calling and possession, and yet was not asked as a favour, but as a right. "Walking by the sea of Galilee,"‡ he sees two brethren following their occupation of fishermen: he saith to them, "Follow me, and they straightway left their nets and followed him."§ Going farther on, he sees two more occupied in the same pursuit. But these were the stay and comfort of a father. Shall he deprive an aged father of his sons? What matter? The Lord had need of them. The higher claim steps in before the lesser. To these, too, the call is given; "and they left the ship and their father, and followed him." But some one may say, These were poor fishermen, and in asking them to forsake all he asked not for much. This were, indeed, poor reasoning, and would indicate a shallow acquaintance with the human heart. A man's all is equally precious to him, whether it be little or great; and so He, who knew the heart, pronounced of the widow's gift,|| that it was more than all the costly offerings of the wealthy, because, though in amount but two mites, it was in fact her all. But Matthew was not a poor man,¶ and he was called from the midst of his gainful occupation. The young man whom Christ commanded to sell all that he had** was noted for his riches. Yet the same summons came to him that was addressed to the humble fishers by the sea of Galilee. How great the difference, however, between these parties! They recognised the claims of their Lord to themselves and their possessions; he refused to do so. They perceived themselves to be but stewards; he held fast by the notion of ownership. They resigned their trust to Him who gave it; he usurped it. They were faithful in that which was another's, and obtained the true riches; he shut himself out by his unfaithfulness from the kingdom of God.

* Hag. ii. 8. † Ezek. xviii. 4. ‡ Matt. iv. 18. § Matt. iv. 20.
|| Mark, xii. 42. ¶ Mark, ii. 14. ** Luke, xviii. 22.

If we would see a picture of man's exact position in this respect drawn by the great Master's hand, we will find it in the remarkable parable of the talents in the twenty-fifth chapter of St. Matthew.* Who are they to whom the talents are given? They are all of them the servants of God. Whose are the talents? They are God's goods. For what are they given? To redound to the glory and praise of the Giver. Have they passed out of his control and thought? No: he exacts of them a strict account. True, to some is given more than to others; but all are in their respective talents on the exact same footing,—that of managers in trust, and under a grave responsibility, of another's goods. It is quite true, indeed, that riches are not the only talents intrusted to man, or spoken of here; but they are certainly among them, and not the least important of them.

Oh, vain man of the world, with thy heart set upon thy treasures, be they great or little, with the firm purpose to use them for thyself, and to call them and think them thine own, in what a light does Scripture place thee! Thou art in its searching eye but the usurper of another's rights—the breaker of a trust which thy God has given thee—the earner of vengeance when he comes to call thee to account. What would you think of him who was intrusted by his friend with property, who, during that friend's absence, appropriated this property to himself, and on his return denied that he had done him wrong? Great would be your indignation, and severe your judgment. And yet thou art thyself the man! God has given you wealth, or the power and opportunity to get wealth; but thou hast said with prosperous and covetous Israel of old,† that it was " thy own power, and the might of thy hand," and the strength of thy intellect, which have done it all. You look not beyond your intellect to Him that gave it to you,—beyond your enterprise to Him that endowed you with it,—beyond your bodily strength to Him that made you strong,— beyond the opportunities of your position to Him that placed you in it. You contract your thought within second causes, and reflect not on the first Great Cause. You bound your vision by

* Matt. xxv. 14–30. † Deut. viii. 17, 18.

the narrow horizon of your own making, and will not look beyond it, lest you should discover that you are, after all, in God's own world,—a servant amid an innumerable ministry,—a steward amid countless multitudes, who render, or must one day render, an account of their stewardship. Oh, reflect but for a moment on what an extended view into the realities of creation will bring before you! Behold the bright throng of angels, creatures of mighty power and transcendent intellect! They are busy; not one of them is idle. They pervade each part of the boundless universe; they visit each planet and star which stud infinite space; millions of them walk this earth. On whose business do they speed? For whom do they exercise their mighty energies? All is done for *God*. With ceaseless praise they behold his works; with ceaseless activity they do his will; proud even to wait upon sinful man, because they are sent by God, Or, cast your eyes even on those, your fellow-creatures upon earth, whom at times you are disposed, perhaps, to regard as fools. Amid your ever-crowding businesses and your fast-succeeding pleasures you have, doubtless, heard of, you have occasionally met with, a peculiar people. Observe them, mark them well. There may be hypocrites among them, but all are not hypocrites. There may be dross, but there is also gold. You will find one idea, to you a strange one, their ruling idea,—it is that *they are not their own;* that all that they are and have, their time, their energies, their knowledge, their riches, their souls and bodies, belong to the God of their redemption. Yes, even here, at this time are, and at all times have been, such a people. Their graces obscured by infirmity and tarnished by sin, they are yet, in the actuating and governing principle of their minds, one with the unsullied angels, in that with them they ascribe to their Lord the undivided right to them and to theirs. Why should you stand upon a different footing? Are you not alike the creatures of God? Is it not from the same bounty on his part that *your* blessings are derived? Is not that bounty the great original fountain whence streams of goodness and love flow to every individual of the race? Cease, then, to speak of your possessions as your own: be wise, and call them what they are—*a trust from your God.*

CHAPTER II.

"Is it not lawful for me to do what I will with mine own?"
—*Matt.* xx. 15.

If God be, in truth, the Owner of all things, as we have seen from Scripture that he is, it follows, as a matter of course, that he is also the disposer of his property. "May I not do what I will with my own?" is the language of ownership; and without this power it is but an empty name. And so St. Paul says of the heir, while under age, and incapable of making disposition of his property, that he "differeth nothing from a servant, though he be Lord of all."* It plainly rests with God, then, in intrusting his property to man, to make what regulations he pleases for its disposal. What those regulations are we will consider farther on, and are now merely insisting on his right to make them. We apprehend, indeed, that there will be few, if any, to dispute this point,—at least when they have calmly reflected on the matter. The owner of property among men, in engaging a steward over his estates, or a manager over his mercantile business, is never thought to exceed his right in defining to such parties the manner in which they are to transact his business. Surely the great Owner of the universe has an equal, or rather a far better, right to do the same. He may indeed, as pleases him, see fit to place greater or less restrictions on human management; to leave man in a greater or less degree to his own judgment; to leave what portion he esteems suitable to man's discretion; or to tie up what portion he thinks fit to be used in a particular way. All that we contend for now is God's perfect right to interfere in what degree he pleases with man's management of his trusts. This point is, indeed, so plain—follows so necessarily from the conclusion of our first chapter, that to insist at further length upon it would be the merest waste of time. It only remains for us to inquire on what terms God has put us in trust with his goods: has he left us at

* Gal. iv. 1.

an absolute freedom in their use? or has he pointed out how we are to use a portion of them, and what that portion is to be?

That God has not resigned to man the absolute disposal even of a portion of his trust we can prove beyond a doubt. The proof arises from this fact, that there is not a single gift of God to man which he does not withdraw at pleasure. I argue upon the assumption, which no Christian disputes, that God's providence directs every event of every man's life; that there is no such thing as chance, and no power independent of God's. Now, let us run over in our minds the various gifts of God to man, and we will see that they have been, and continue to be, taken away from men of every variety and shade of character, the enemies and friends of God alike. The deluge deprived the world of the ungodly of their all, and fire from heaven did the same for the wicked inhabitants of Sodom. Saul had his crown wrested from him, and Israel and Judah were left without home, or possession, or native land, when the decree of God sent them captives to Assyria and Babylon. Abraham, the friend of God, gave up his country, and in intention his son, at the divine command: Lot barely escaped with life from Sodom, but left all his wealth behind: Job in one day lost servants and substance, sons and daughters, was left as naked of worldly goods as when he came from his mother's womb, yet nothing escaped from his lips but the words of pious submission to the great Disposer, "The Lord gave, and the Lord hath taken away; blessed be the name of the Lord."* So in the New Testament, those cases on which we relied as proving God's ownership were, in fact, instances of his disposing of men's possessions, and need not be referred to further. And what are pestilences, and famines, and earthquakes, and other fearful judgments, but heaven-sent witnesses to the truth that God has not ceased to exercise sovereign authority in the disposal of his trust to man, or to control and withdraw that trust, or any portion of it, as seems fit to his discretion?

It may, perhaps, appear at first that I have dwelt too long on these preliminary points; but I have thought it better, where human covetousness and selfishness are so deeply concerned, to

* Job, i. 21.

go to the root of the matter, to lay plainly before the mind God's full right and claim to all which we call ours, that we may be the less disposed to contest what his ordinary providence requires at our hands, viz., the application of a portion of our goods to his especial cause.

CHAPTER III.

"THOU MADEST HIM TO HAVE DOMINION OVER THE WORKS OF THY HANDS."—*Ps.* viii. 6.

I HAVE hitherto considered God's claims in their widest, though at the same time their true and legitimate, extent, and have shown that they extend to the possession and disposal of our all. This should never be lost sight of by us, no matter how little God may seem disposed to insist on his fullest right. That he has insisted, and does at times insist, and may at any time he pleases insist upon it, with ourselves or others, with few, or many, or all, is testified equally in the Book of Providence and the pages of Revelation; while the submission of our minds to this his sovereign authority, and the determination to bend to his will in this respect, if called upon, seems essential to the Christian character, according to that saying of our Lord, "Whosoever he be of you that forsaketh not all that he hath, he cannot be my disciple."*

But there is a wide difference in God's *ordinary providence* between his claims, however rightful, and his requirements from man. He has from time to time, indeed, put forward his fullest claim to man's all, lest it should be forgotten, and at last perhaps denied; just as he has, from time to time, wrought miracles to show, along with other reasons, that he has not resigned to what is called the course of nature his control over her laws. But in his usual course he does not act thus. Of his trust to man he leaves him a large portion to use for his own especial comfort and benefit. Having endowed him with reason and judgment, he has left much at his discretion. Wishing his happiness, he has be-

* Luke, xiv. 33.

stowed his gifts to produce and to increase it; and has given him "richly all things to enjoy." He has, indeed, forbidden the abuse of the smallest portion of his goods; the spending of any, however trifling a proportion, in any way that would militate against his glory or the advancement of his cause in the world; and has, in fact, required as much in that portion which man spends upon himself as in that which he devotes especially to his Maker and Redeemer, that "all should be done with an eye to the glory of God." With these important considerations, which must never be forgotten by the Christian, he has at the same time left him at liberty in the use of a large proportion of his trust.

Thus has God treated his creature man in a liberal spirit. He has not fettered him with restrictions meeting him at every step. Having gifted him with a noble capacity and large susceptibilities of enjoyment, he has placed him in a situation, and allowed him a freedom, which affords ample scope for both. It was not a mockery of his real condition to describe him as made "in God's image"* in the matter of dominion. And truly as well as beautifully has David celebrated the power bestowed by God upon his creature,—" Thou madest him to have dominion over the works of thy hands: thou hast put all things under his feet."†

But what we do contend for now is this, that to man's discretionary use of God's trust to him there is, and has always been, a limit. He may expatiate in a wide field, but not a boundless one. He shall indeed feel himself at freedom in the use and enjoyment of temporal blessings, but there shall be at the same time something to remind him that there is One above him to whom these things, after all, belong, and by whom they have been intrusted to him. The wide ocean might seem to be without a master, rolling its huge billows where it pleased, were it not met by that restraining shore—those bars and doors which He hath placed who said to it, "Thus far shalt thou come, and no farther; and here shall thy proud waves be stayed."‡ And just so might man imagine himself without a superior—the original, not the delegated, lord of this lower world, unless he too were met with a bound beyond which he might not pass; unless, in the disposal

* Gen. i. 26.   † Ps. viii.   ‡ Job, xxxviii. 10, 11.

of his property, there was a portion placed out of his discretion, of which God had said, "This may not be used for thy pleasure, *it is mine.*"

Even in Eden it was so. Even to man just come from his Maker's hands, the voice, scarce silent, that had called all things into being, the impress of Heaven's workmanship still fresh and vivid upon the creation, even to unfallen Adam, this limit was placed. The fruit of his fairest trees, and the seventh part of his time, were hallowed. He might not touch the one, nor infringe upon the other. They were the peculiar property of Him who had placed him in the garden, to dress it and to keep it—the sign and token of his inalienable sovereignty.

If this were the case with sinless man, how much more does sinful man require it? "Who is Lord over us?"* is the suggestion of the natural heart. Deny it, or disguise it as they will, practical independence of God is the darling aim of the natural man, in all his ways, in the use of all his talents, and, among them, of his substance. To use it just as he pleases himself—on his pleasures, on his vanities, subservient to the attainment of power, or, as in the miser's case, to hoard and worship it for itself, is the determination and the habit of the unregenerate mind. *To use it as God pleases*—with a thankful spirit for his own purposes, with as thankful a spirit when expended on objects foreign to himself—this is not in all his thoughts. And this tendency remains in the regenerate. Checked, conquered, crucified, it is still there to his dying day, a lurking, treacherous foe. Too often it insensibly influences the conduct and thoughts of God's saints. Unseen and unsuspected, it breathes a noxious vapour, deadening the liberality, and checking each generous impulse; or, watching its opportunity, it comes forth and lords it for a time with all its former sway. How absolutely necessary, then, that there be a perpetual check to this universal tendency! —a perpetual reminder to man that he is not a sovereign, but a subject; that his goods are not his own, but God's; and this is found in that perpetual ordinance in force in patriarchal, and Jewish, and Christian times alike, whereby God has reserved for

* Ps. xii. 4.

his own especial glory and service a portion of that which in his bounty he has bestowed on man. This is the rent, which reminds the tenant that he is not owner in fee; this is the interest, which reminds the borrower that the principal belongs not to him; this is the tribute-money, which reminds a subject nation that it is not independent; this is God's share, to remind his creature that all belongs to him.

What that proportion may be is not the subject of the present chapter, but will be discussed in those that follow. All that is here insisted on is this, which every page almost of Old and New Testament asserts, that while to God belongs our all, and while at times he insists on this his claim, he *at all times* requires from us *a portion* of our goods, a tribute to his sovereignty, and a means of spreading his name and glory throughout the world.

CHAPTER IV.

"THE WAY OF MAN IS NOT IN HIMSELF."—*Jer.* x. 23.

I HAVE thus prepared the way for the consideration of the chief point of inquiry in our Essay,—What is the proportion of his means which the Christian should give to God? The Lord's right to a portion or to all, will not now be contested; nor will it be denied that he actually claims a part. It remains to be seen if we have any sufficient reason to decide what that part should be. Has God left the decision of this important matter to each man's conscience and judgment, or has he made known his own will thereon?

I do not think that any *à priori* reasoning can determine this point,—at least with such as are disposed to reduce God's claims to as small a compass as they can; but I certainly think that the weight of antecedent probability is in favour of his having done so. Let us remember at this stage of our inquiry, that the gift of *any portion*, no matter what, of our goods to the bestower of them does not appear by any means to be a natural suggestion of the mind, as some might suppose. To propitiate an offended Being with presents does, indeed, appear natural to man; but it was not with such a view at all that the men of enlightened religion, such as Abraham, offered their gifts to God. They regarded their Maker as their friend, and gave him a portion of their substance in thankful acknowledgment that it was he who had given it all. Now, if we reflect, we will see that this is by no means an obvious conclusion to come to. The recipient of bounty with ourselves does not feel himself called on to return a portion of that bounty to the giver. And far less would he feel the necessity of such a return when it was God who was the bestower, from the consideration that he, who had all things in his power, could not possibly want anything at his creatures' hands. If, then, it be but reasonable to suppose that it was God who first claimed from the creature a portion of his gifts, it seems equally reasonable to suppose that he mentioned what that portion was to be. This is the natural inference, unless we are to suppose that *anything*, no matter how mean, and trifling, and worthless, is sufficient *for God*. But few, I imagine, will suppose this, who reflect upon the goodness and greatness of God as seen in the creation; and most assuredly none will allow it, who will learn God's character from his own account of it in Scripture, where they find him rejecting with disdain the unsuitable acknowledgment of his mercies. If it be, then, a matter of importance what is the suitable proportion that man should give, does it not seem most likely that he, who could best determine this, and alone with authority determine it, should, indeed, have done so? Man were else left to a painful uncertainty. The scrupulous mind, anxious to please God, could never be certain of having done so, and would, in many instances, even when far exceeding the expected proportion, be yet subject to perplexity and uneasiness; while in the case of, we fear, the vast majority of mankind, the fact of this portion being left entirely to their discretion, would be made the pretext of their reducing it to so small a point, that the gift, so far from honouring God, would rather be an affront to his name.

For these, and other reasons, I think that the probability is, that God would himself decide this matter, and declare plainly what proportion of man's substance he expected as a suitable tribute to his sovereignty, a becoming token of our gratitude, and a sufficiency to uphold his worship in the world. But on this point I will not argue any further. To some it may appear of force, to others it may seem destitute of strength. All that I will require to be conceded is, that at any rate no antecedent improbability lies against my argument. The great and deciding arguments must be drawn from other sources; and, beyond all others, from the inquiry, "What hath God said?" Has he spoken to us in that Book which is the lamp to our feet and the lantern to our paths,* or has he been silent there? If he has spoken there, clearly then the controversy is decided with those to whom this essay is addressed,—namely, such as take the Bible for their one infallible guide; if he has not spoken, I should despair of deciding it by any other reasoning. But that he has done so,—not merely for one time, dispensation, or people, but for all times and dispensations,—that he has done so for us Christians, as he did for his ancient people, Israel, is the conclusion to which a careful examination of Scripture has led me, and which I will endeavour to prove in the following pages.

In pursuing my inquiry, I will first advert to the fact of a certain proportion being found among a great variety of nations as the measure of their gifts to God; I will then examine what the Old Testament has said upon this subject,—not confining myself to any one part of it, but examining its several notices upon the subject; satisfied that each throws light upon and confirms the rest, and that the whole taken together, with the evidence of the New Testament, leads to one incontrovertible conclusion. The conclusion is, that God requires from men in general a tenth part of that increase with which he blesses them, to be spent in his especial cause; while from some more peculiarly favoured he looks for more; the gift of the former portion being to be regarded as a positive duty, that of the latter as the free-will offering of loving and grateful hearts, left in its amount to each according as he is disposed to act according as circumstances

* Ps. cxix. 105.

seem to call for an extended liberality, or his own generous and grateful impulses, quickened by a sense of God's exceeding goodness, lead him to bestow it. Our review of the Old Testament will lead me to dwell chiefly on four points,—namely, the gift of a tenth by Abraham to Melchizedek, Jacob's vow of a tenth to God, God's requirement of a tenth from his people Israel, and that people's free-will offerings on extraordinary occasions over and above their tenth.

And may He, whose office it is to guide to truth, by enlightening the understanding and purifying the wills of his people, guide us in our inquiry on this important subject, enable us to perceive what is revealed to us, and to regulate our practice thereby.

CHAPTER V.

"Is he the God of the Jews only?"—*Rom.* iii. 29.

THAT God has in the case of his people Israel required the tenth of man's substance to be given for his service, and expended as the circumstances of that dispensation required, is not disputed. The first question, then, that meets us is, When did he first require it? Was this, *as a divine institution*, first imposed on a particular nation, and first ordained in the Mosaic law, or does it date from a much higher antiquity? Do we draw our first great argument with Christians, that it is their duty to devote a tenth to their Lord from the fact of their being the successors of Israel to whom it was a duty, or can we appeal to an earlier authority, before Moses gave the law from Sinai, or Abraham was separated from the Gentile world? It will be perceived, that I rest my great reliance in this question on the *divine institution* of this proportion of a tenth. I certainly do so. I am fully persuaded, that if it has not this foundation to rest on, other arguments, however forcible with individuals, will have no overpowering weight to silence the objections or overcome the natural selfishness of the mass of men, even of men professing godliness.

The mere fact that this or that person, however wise and pious, gave a tenth of his goods to God, and that God was pleased with his servant for thus honouring him with his substance, will not, I think, come home with such conclusive power to the Christian's conscience as will make him say that he is to do the same, as an act of duty expected from him by his God. Man's ingenuity, quickened by his selfishness, will, in such a case, straightway set to work to discover some differing circumstances between such individuals and himself, as will, in his opinion, fully excuse him from the necessity of imitation. He will say, suppose of Abraham and Jacob, "These were men who attained to far greater wealth than I am possessed of, nor had they in those simple ages the same pressing calls upon their means which daily meet me; I am, therefore, no more bound by their voluntary act to give a tenth, than I am bound to give a half because Zaccheus gave one,* or to give the whole of my substance, because the first Christians of Jerusalem did so."† And if he is reminded that Abraham and Jacob's acknowledgment to God were blessed by him, he can also reply that Zaccheus's conduct was approved by Christ, and that of the saints of Jerusalem mentioned by an inspired writer as indicating a love and a self-denial beyond all praise. Men will, in fact, find so many reasons, to them at least plausible and convincing, why they are not bound by such voluntary acts of individuals, that, while they are free to confess that God expects from them too *a portion* of their substance, they will wholly deny any necessity of that portion being a tenth. And so we shall be forced to leave the matter to each man's judgment and discretion; and while some few will not feel this to be any release, many more will seize upon it as a full excuse for the miserable share they give to God,—which, perhaps, they call "honouring him with their substance," but which is far more like dishonouring him with their niggardliness.

I, therefore, place my main reliance in this argument on the

* Luke, xix. 8. † Acts, ii. 45.

proportions of a tenth being of divine institution. Other arguments need not be discarded, but in their place may come in with such force as they possess. But it is on God's ordinance of the thing that I rely, and without it I should despair of establishing the matter. Now we have without any controversy his institution of this proportion in the Mosaic ritual, and even if we could trace the institution no higher—if we were forced to allow that here first was the payment of a tenth to God imposed as a duty upon each member of his church, even from this, as I trust will be seen in a succeeding chapter, can be shown that the same proportion is required from the members of the Christian community. But I apprehend that a far earlier origin may reasonably be concluded for the divine institution of a tenth—that it probably dates from the very first promulgation of fallen man's religion, that it certainly dates from times long anterior to that of the law of Moses.

The argument is one to which no claim of originality can be made, and is simply this: We find that, as well among the ancestors of the Jewish nation as among Gentile nations remote from and unconnected with each other, the payment of a tenth for purposes of religion was a recognised custom, pointing clearly to a common authoritative origin, which could be no other than the command of God. To give instances of this custom would far exceed the limits of the present essay; they may be found in detail in the learned writings of Spelman and Selden,* who have traced back the custom of dedicating tithes to religious purposes to a very remote antiquity. The statement of two of our ablest writers on this point are so forcible that I will quote it in preference to any language of my own. "Whatever custom," says Dr. Kennicott,† "has prevailed over the world, among nations the most opposite in polity and customs in general, nations not united by commerce or communication (when that custom has nothing in nature or the reason of things to give it birth, and establish to itself such a currency), must be derived from some revelation, which revelation may in certain

---

* Spelman and Selden on Tithes.
† Kennicott, Two Dissert., p. 161.

places have been forgotten, though the custom introduced by and founded on such revelation still continued; and, further, this revelation must have been made antecedent to the dispersion at Babel, when all mankind, being but one nation, and living together in the form of one large family, were of one language and governed by the same laws and customs." Collyer, in his "Sacred Interpreter,"* writes to the same effect: "From Pagan writers we learn," he says, "that several nations, very far distant from each other, in different parts of the world, and, as it seems, without the least acquaintance or commerce one with another, observed this custom. Now since this proportion of one in ten is certainly indifferent in itself, any more than one in seven or eight, it is reasonable to believe that this custom of paying tithe, like that of sacrificing, had some divine direction for it; and that it was derived from Adam to Noah, and from him to his posterity, till at length, at the dispersion of Babel, it spread over all the world." The conclusion of Kennicott and Collyer is surely the conclusion of unprejudiced reason. The wide-spread establishment of a custom, which does not certainly suggest itself naturally to the mind, and which requires of man the surrender of what he values most, can be accounted for in no other way. Even if men in different places might agree in giving a portion of their goods to God, they would not all hit upon the same proportion. Some would give more, others less, and probably no two would be agreed. It may, perhaps, somewhat serve to confirm this argument, to show its force in other cases. For instance, the divine origin of the institution of sacrifice is generally admitted among Christians. Now what is the proof on which men rely for it? We read indeed in Scripture of the offering of sacrifices from the very earliest times, but in no part are we told that God had first appointed that mode of worship. Its origin is not told us in the book of Genesis, nor does any subsequent Scripture refer to it. Its divine institution is received chiefly on these grounds, that while there appears no reason for supposing that the propriety of such a mode of worship would naturally suggest itself to the

* D. Collyer, "Sacred Interpreter," vol. i. p. 162.

minds of all men, there has yet never been a nation, however remote or ancient, amongst whom this practice has not prevailed. Hence we learn to refer it to one common authoritative origin,—to attribute it to the command of God to mankind, when mankind formed but a single family, which family in its subsequent increases, separations, and migrations, would carry into every land the original tradition, more or less impaired, or altered, or obscured by the various phases of the superstitious and cruel idolatries, which everywhere, alas! overspread and debased the primitive religion of mankind. I think, then, that we are justified in concluding that the origin of the giving of a tenth was God's express command,—a conclusion reasonable even at this stage of our argument, and which, as it appears to me, when taken in connexion with the succeeding proofs, will amount to an evidence convincing and entire. I will now direct our attention to the declarations of Scripture on this head, where we will find every notice of it, and every inference deducible from its notices, in full and perfect harmony with our argument.

CHAPTER VI.

"OF ALL THAT THOU SHALT GIVE ME, I WILL SURELY GIVE THE TENTH TO THEE."—*Gen*. xxviii. 22.

WE have reason to conclude from Scripture that every important part of human worship and obedience has had its origin, not from man, but directly from God himself. Man did not form his religion from the dictates of his own reason and conscience, but received it by revelation; and it has ever formed one grand distinction between false religions of every shade and the true, that the former have, in greater or less degree, sprung from what St. Paul calls "will-worship,"* while the latter has adhered to the declared will of God, neither daring to add to

* Col. ii. 23.

nor detract therefrom. True worship never sprang from the earth, and ascended with acceptance to heaven; but from heaven she came to earth, and thence went back, a welcome visitant to her original home, the bosom of God.

No worship of man's own choosing, *i. e.* no heresy, was ever acceptable to God; to all such he replies, "Who hath required this at your hands?"* So persuaded was Mr. Hallet of the force of this, that he does not hesitate to pronounce that God's acceptance of Abel's offering was "a demonstration"† of its being in obedience to the divine commandment, according to that obvious maxim of all true religion, "In vain do they worship me, teaching for doctrines the commandments of men." Even apparently minute and unimportant matters have not been thought by God unworthy of notice, or the deviation from them undeserving of condemnation. How minute, for example, are the directions of the Levitical law, and yet how sorely was their infraction punished, as witness the account of Korah and his company,‡ of Uzzah,§ and many others. And hence we have scriptural reason for supposing that the important matter of the proportion of man's acknowledgment to God was not left undetermined,—that believers, in the early days of the world, did not offer their tenth to God from their own spontaneous impulse, but in obedience to a known commandment. And if it be said that this argument might hold good for the direction of *a portion* of man's substance being given to God, but that God would, probably, leave the exact proportion to each believer's own discretion, we answer, that he has himself shown that the proportion of the gift is not beneath his notice, for in the Mosaic law he has ordained a tenth.

The institution of the Sabbath day affords a parallel case, and one bearing very forcibly, as it appears to me, on our present inquiry. In acknowledgment of the great fact of the creation, and of the sovereign power of the Creator over his creature, God would have man to dedicate a portion of his time to his service. Did he then leave this portion undefined? Had he done so,

* Isa. i. 12; Mark, vii. 7. † Hallet on Heb. xi. 4.
‡ Numb. xvi. § 2 Sam. vi.

humanly speaking, we would not have had a Sabbath day at all. Men, left to their own judgment, would have varied from each other in the portion set apart. Indolence and aversion to spiritual things would narrow and curtail that portion, till, at length, the very semblance of it would have vanished from among men. But he strictly defined its duration in the beginning, and, on the giving of the law to Israel, repeated that definition; and so we Christians have the Sabbath day, the sweet season of bodily rest and spiritual activity, whose observance is the great means of upholding religion in the world, and which ever points the hopes of the way-worn pilgrim of the Cross to his eternal rest. If, then, the proportion of man's time that was to be specially dedicated to God has been dictated by him, is it not in strict analogy that he should also have defined the proportion of man's substance? And if this, and the offering of sacrifices, and, in fact, every other portion of worship, were revealed from on high, this is surely a scriptural argument for concluding that this part alone was not left unrevealed, in what way and with what proportion of his goods man should honour the Creator and Giver of all!

Before we come to the consideration of the tenth prescribed in the Mosaic law, we have two extremely important references made to them in the Bible:* the first is Abram's gift of a tenth to Melchizedek, and the second Jacob's vow of the same proportion to God. To both of them particular attention is due.† The first of them, in all its circumstances, forms one of the most marvellous episodes in Scripture history. It brings forward, for a moment, upon the stage that man of mysterious origin and existence,—Melchizedek, to whom David makes one glorious allusion,‡ and of whom Paul speaks in language,§ which, while it heightens our veneration, increases our wonder, till, lost in amazement, we are ready to muse in our hearts, as the people did of John, "whether he were indeed the Christ or not."|| However this be, the transaction is an important one in our argument. It agrees most completely with our hypothesis of the divine origin of the tenth, and with no other; and the time

* Gen. xiv. 20; xxviii. 22.   † Gen. xiv. 20.   ‡ Ps. cx. 4
    § Heb. vi. and vii. || Luke, iii. 15.

when it occurred, and the persons concerned in it, make it of peculiar force.

Chedorlaomer and his confederate kings make war on the king of Sodom and his associates, and prevail in battle.* The victors seize upon the persons and goods of the vanquished, and with them of Lot and his goods, and proceed with them to their own country. Abram, hearing of his nephew's captivity, arms his dependants—probably few in number compared with those against whom they went—overtakes them on their return, defeats them, and recovers Lot and all the persons and goods that had been carried off. To God he owed his victory, and to God was due an acknowledgment of his aid. Accordingly, returning, he meets God's high-priest, and to him he pays a tenth of all the spoils.

Now, every part of this transaction has force. The goods, let it be remembered, had been all of them the property of those to whose rescue Abram had gone; none of them had belonged to the party of Chedorlaomer, and, consequently, Abram's only claim to them lay in his having recovered them in battle.† This did give him a claim, which the king of Sodom was willing to acknowledge, but which Abram wholly refused to profit by for himself. "I will not take," he said, "anything that is thine."‡ Now this, I think, places his gift to Melchizedek in a far stronger light than it would have been in had we viewed it as simply having been an acknowledgment to God for having restored to him his own property, or for having placed within his hands the property of the kings he had subdued. He had in the transaction gained nothing for himself; he will accept of nothing for himself; he disowns his own claim to any portion of the spoils. But he evidently knew that God had his claim to a part of them, in token of his right to all; and the only use he will make of a victory, which had placed all in his possession, is to pay to God his portion of a tenth: the rest he returns to the original owners. This fact is, I think, inconsistent with any other theory than that here advocated,—that the gift of a tenth was *at this time* of divine appointment. § Had the goods been his own it might have the

* Gen. xiv.   † Verse 21.   ‡ Verse 22.
§ See Poole, Annot. in Heb. vii. 2-4.

appearance of a voluntary act of gratitude ; but, since he refused any personal right in them for himself, it has all the appearance of being an act of known and recognised duty. If they had been his own, he might, doubtless, have given to God what proportion of his goods he pleased ; but, as they were not his own, he would scarcely have been generous with another's property. He surrendered his own claim, but he could not surrender God's. The tenth which he gave him he must have felt was not his to withhold,—that it was the peculiar property of him to whom all belonged.

With this agrees every other circumstance of the narrative. Thus the manner in which it is spoken of is just that in which a thing of usual and expected occurrence would be mentioned. Were it new or unusual, some notice of the novelty might be expected, as we are told in Scripture of the invention and introduction of other and far less important matters. But this is treated of as a matter of course. Again, Abram's gift is accepted by Melchizedek plainly as his right. As God's priest he blesses Abram, and as God's priest he receives tithes from Abram. The one appears just as much a part of his office as the other. Now, this gift of a tenth was certainly an act of religion. It was not required by Melchizedek from any poverty of circumstances, for he was a king, and probably a richer man than Abram. It was purely an act of religious homage, and so St. Paul reckons it in the seventh chapter of Hebrews.*

The same apostle's comparison of Melchizedek with the Levitical priesthood, and his assertion of the superiority of the former over the latter, absolutely requires us to believe that the payment of a tenth by Abram to him was not a voluntary act, which he might have withheld at pleasure, but was the discharge of positive obligation. If we consider his argument with a little attention we will not fail to see this. The Levitical priesthood, *by the command of God*, received tithes of their people. *Their command to do so* is noticed by the apostle in the fifth verse as their privilege,† and is certainly a most important part of it. But it follows as certainly that Melchizedek had *the same* claim

* Heb. vii.   † Heb. vii. 5.

to a tenth from Abram which they had from the Jews, *i. e.* a divine command. If you deny this, and say that Abram's gift of a tenth was purely voluntary—that Melchizedek had no positive right to this proportion—that it might have been withheld from him without any infringement on his just claims, you certainly place him in this respect on an inferior footing to the priesthood of Aaron, and take away one of those grounds on which St. Paul claims for him a superiority over Levi,—namely, his right to a tenth from Abram. This latter argument appears a conclusive one, and seems to follow from the apostle's comparison of the two orders of priesthood in the seventh chapter of Hebrews. For, surely, if a tenth were Levi's right by divine ordinance, while Melchizedek had no such right at all, he is in this respect inferior to Levi, and Paul's argument from his reception of a tenth from Abram an inconclusive one.

This case being then established, the time of the occurrence and the persons engaged in it render it of peculiar value. It took place before the covenant of circumcision was ordained; before the first step was taken towards the formation of that Jewish constitution which was developed under Moses; and, consequently, wholly free from the inference (a groundless one, as we shall afterwards see), that being a part of the Mosaic dispensation, it has been done away in Christ. Again, to whom was this tenth paid? To Melchizedek. I will not inquire here who Melchizedek was. It is beside our object, and perhaps beyond our power to determine. It is sufficient to say, that of all the personages of the Old Testament he is pre-eminently the type of Christ. Neither Moses, the great lawgiver of Israel; nor Aaron, their high-priest; nor Josuha, the renowned captain to lead them to their promised Canaan; nor David, triumphant over his people's enemies; nor Solomon, reigning in glory over a united and peaceful community, are to be compared as types of Christ with that great King of righteousness and peace, who was also, in a sense that none before or since, save the glorious Antitype, have been,—*the priest of God.*

It was then to a person who was the peculiar type of the Head of the Christian dispensation, and in times peculiarly pro phetical of the Christian era, as well as at a period distinguished by a plain mark of separation from all that might be distinctive of Judaism, we find this payment of a tenth to God in force by his own command. When we come to speak of the Christian's obligation in this respect to God we will draw our inference from this important transaction, and will now pass on to consider another of equal value in our argument—the celebrated vow of the patriarch Jacob.

With what deep delight does the believer's mind dwell on the vision of Bethel!* Sin had placed an infinite distance between heaven and earth, but here we find the communication of these two reopened and sweet communion established. The scene is, indeed, a bright spot amid a dark world,—a green, smiling region within a surrounding desert,—a transfiguration scene, which lights up the earth again with its former brightness, and points to the time when it shall be said of it with truth, " It is good to be here." It draws back the mind to that golden age when God walked with his newly-formed creature as with a friend ; and draws it on to the restoration of that age when the believer shall see heaven opened, and the angels of God ascending and descending upon the Son of Man.† But our argument confines us to a single feature in this transaction. Jacob, flying from his brother, lies down at the close of day to refresh himself in sleep. Alone he could not be, for he was the object of that care which never slumbers, and which selected the time when he seemed most friendless to display itself most fully. In his vision of the night he beholds the inhabitants of heaven, and heaven's great King, and hears from his lips the assuring promise of provision for " the life that now is, as well as for that which was to come." He awakes from sleep impressed with the certainty that this was, indeed, a "heaven-sent dream." The spirit of Jacob was the free spirit of all God's children. They bargain not to be admitted to his favour, but having "freely received they freely give ;" having been bought with a precious price, and loved with an endless love, they devote themselves and theirs to their redeeming God. Such was the spirit of Jacob. What he should

* Gen. xxviii. 22. † John, i. 51.

do for God in the heavenly rest to which he looked forward after his pilgrimage, he leaves for the arrival of that rest to determine: what he should do in the present time while his day lasted, like a wise man he determines. " The Lord shall be my God," is his resolution, " and this stone which I have set up for a pillar shall be God's house; and of all that thou shalt give me I will give the tenth part unto thee."

Our object confines us to noticing only the latter part of Jacob's vow, namely, the devoting a tenth of all his future increase to God. Having shown already, and particularly in the case of Abram, that the giving a tenth of our goods to God was in conformity with the divine command, we view Jacob's conduct in the same light. We regard him not as performing what he esteemed a mere voluntary act, but as discharging a sacred obligation; as making that return to God for his bounty which he knew to be expected from him. If we have consented to the reasoning in Abram's case, we can scarcely doubt that Jacob, his grandson, and of course acquainted with his conduct, acted on the same motives. He is a link connecting together evangelical and legal times,—the days of Melchizedek and those of Moses; exhibiting the harmonious action of believers in varying dispensations in obedience to an unchanged commandment. Regarded thus, it places our subject in, perhaps, a fuller and plainer light, more divested of circumstances not essentially connected with it, than any other similar transaction; and certainly supplies some matters of moment, which we could not with certainty have inferred from Abram's offering of a tenth.

And, first, Jacob's vow is a vow of all future blessing, and, therefore, to be continued through his lifetime. We might, perhaps, have supposed that Abram's offering this proportion was an isolated act on his part, called forth on a particular occasion. If such were our opinion, Jacob's vow corrects it. This proportion was God's due at *all periods* of the believer's earthly existence; whether at times when God more plainly and more remarkably opened his hand and filled him with abundance, or when in the ordinary course of his providence he " blessed his basket and his store." It was to be called forth, not merely on such occasions as the victory of a few over many, which restored to its owners what had seemed lost beyond recovery; but was also to be the return for those more unobtrusive, but equally eloquent proofs of the divine goodness, which nature in her revolving course presents,—that sun, which gives life to the creation, those dews, which refresh earth's parched surface,—those "rains from heaven, and fruitful seasons, which fill man's heart with food and gladness." Such is one lesson we learn from Jacob's vow, "Of all that thou shalt give me, I will surely give the tenth part to thee."

Again, Jacob's vow is to be regarded as of importance in this respect, that no part of it was for the use of a priesthood. Melchizedek had gone as he had come; the priesthood of Levi was not yet in being; the priest of Jacob's household was Jacob himself Yet now, as well as before or after, was this proportion of a tenth paid to God. Now, this fact is of value. It separates the matter wholly from man's jurisdiction, and places it in its simple original light, as an act of pure, unmixed homage to God. When there was no ministry to support, it was yet God's claim, and accorded to him. I do, therefore, value this fact highly. Had the tenth never been given save in connexion with a ministry, this might, with some minds, have obscured its great primary object. But here nothing stands between the offerer and the Being to whom he offers,—no class or caste may presume to say, "This is ours, it was ordained for us;" for here we see it to be God's, and God's only, ordained for his sole glory. Now, I am not arguing against the claim of God's ministry to a portion of this tenth, far from it. We will see, that in its distribution they are, in Christian as in Jewish times, to be considered as entitled to maintenance from it. I am simply laying down this fact, drawn from Jacob's case, that the institution of a tenth had this for its first, and, I may say, its sole object, the glorifying God in the offering to him a portion of that which all came from him, and which all, in fact, belonged to him. What God wills us to do with it, how to use it, and in what proportion, is another question altogether. But this we may be sure of, that it was for God it was ordained, that he might be glorified in that which was his.

The last consideration, that in Jacob's time no portion of the tenth was for the use of a priesthood, while it was yet paid to God, helps to make certain what we had previously shown to be at any rate probable, that this custom dates from the beginning: that when the Sabbath day was hallowed, and sacrifices ordained, then, too, a tenth was fixed on by God as the portion which man was to return to him. It might have been supposed, from the instances of Melchizedek and Levi, that this proportion was ordained for a priesthood, and therefore had its origin on the first formation of a separate ministry. Now, we do not reckon the heads of families to have been a separate order analogous to the Jewish priesthood or the Christian ministry. Melchizedek seems to have been the first to exercise by divine appointment a ministerial care over those not connected with him by the ties of family, and some might thence imagine that in his time the gift of a tenth was introduced. But the case of Jacob overturns this idea. Required in his time without any reference to a priesthood, there was the same reason at all previous times for its existence; and therefore we may infer, that it was the ordinance of God, not merely when Melchizedek walked upon the earth, or the sons of Aaron were sustained by it, but also when Adam lived by the sweat of his brow, and his children pursued their occupations of shepherds and husbandmen. I know not if this throws any light upon the much-vexed question of Cain and Abel's offering.* It was on the part of both an act of religious homage. Cain seems to have expected as his right that his offering would have been accepted, which he could scarcely have done if he had not known it to have been commanded. *Was not this his tenth*, which the reason even of the natural man allows to be due to God, and which therefore Cain offered, while he disdained *such an offering* as spoke of atonement? Abel in the firstlings of his flock paid his tenth, and also confessed his faith in a sinner's religion, which is the religion of atonement. Cain in the fruit of the ground paid his tenth too, but he would make no confession of sin, acknowledged no need of a Saviour,—a type of those later Pharisees, who would not so much as defraud God of the tithe of

* Gen. iv.

their garden herds, while they disdained the atonement of Christ and shed his innocent blood. To this the language of God to Cain seems fully to agree, "If thou doest well, shalt thou not be accepted?" *i. e.* "If thou art righteous, thou hast indeed made me the only offering I could require, an acknowledgment of my sovereignty, and a return for my bounty;" but "if thou doest not well," if thou be not righteous, "thy offering is not sufficient, thy sin still lies at thy door unremoved, and I can be pleased with no work of thine;" or, if we prefer Archbishop Magee's translation, who for "sin" reads "sin-offering," then God, in plain language, tells him that for the removal of his unrighteousness animal sacrifice was required, typical of the efficacious sacrifice of Christ.

CHAPTER VII.

"ALL THE TITHE OF THE LAND IS THE LORD'S."—*Lev.* xxvii. 30.

HAVING considered the cases of Abraham and Jacob, we come next to consider that of the Jewish tithe. Its institution by God is not disputed; the only inquiry here can be, Was this *his first* institution of it? If we have consented to the preceding argument, we shall have come to the conclusion that it was not. But here I would premise, that I do not rest the case solely upon the concession of this point. If it be allowed, then indeed my argument must be admitted, that a tenth is that proportion which a Christian should give to God. But if it be disallowed,—if it be supposed that the first divine appointment of a tenth dates no higher than the times of Moses, even on this lower ground I am of opinion that the matter may satisfactorily be established.

I do not, however, view the matter in this light at all. Agreeable to the whole tenor of our past reflections, I regard the Mosaic institution of a tenth as but the continuance of God's ancient claim, with a new application of it for the purposes of the Mosaic ritual. I regard it, not as a new ordinance, but the republication and assertion of an old one. For the proof of this I rely, of course, on what has been advanced in the previous chapters, and if the arguments there have been sound, the matter is placed beyond dispute. But I will, nevertheless, proceed to show, that every fair inference drawn from the mention of the subject in the law of Moses is in full conformity with the conclusion that has been already come to. In our inquiry I will not encumber the question by a reference to any of the Jewish offerings or sacrifices, except that tenth which was claimed by God as his portion, and by him appropriated to the maintenance of the Levites, and the service of the sanctuary.

And, first, I am glad to strengthen my position by the authority of a great reasoner, and one who has done good service in the defence of the vital doctrines of the Christian faith—I mean the late Archbishop Magee. In his great work on the Atonement,* he uses an argument in support of the divine origin of sacrifices, which applies in its full force, with merely a change of some of the names, to the establishment of the divine origin of a tenth; speaking of sacrifices, he says, "That the institution was of divine ordinance may, in the first instance, be reasonably inferred from the strong and sensible attestation of the divine acceptance in the case of Abel, again in that of Noah, afterwards withal of Abraham, and also by the systematic establishment of them by the same divine authority in the dispensation of Moses." For the names here mentioned, if we will use those of Abram and Jacob, Magee's argument stands in its entire force for our conclusion. That Abram's offering of a tenth was accepted by God, we know, from his having received the blessing of Melchizedek. That Jacob's vow of a tenth was equally so, we know from the abundant blessing which God bestowed upon him; to use his own simple, expressive words in his prayer to God before his meeting with Esau, "With his staff he passed over Jordan, and now he was become two bands."† While the appointment of a tenth stands on the same footing in the Mosaic law with that of sacrifice, viz., a divine command; if the argument holds good for sacrifice, it certainly holds good for tithes also.

* Magee on " Atonement," p. 52.   † Gen. xxxii. 10.

Again; it is much more consistent with the scriptural character of God to suppose that in this ordinance he continued a rule previously enjoined by himself, than that he adopted a scale which had first recommended itself to the uninspired judgment of man. The whole spirit of Scripture leads us to conclude that the true God borrows nothing from man. He is the Teacher, never the taught. The very minutest ceremonies of the law were dictated by him.* The most trivial portions of the Tabernacle were commanded to be made after his pattern.† The customs of the surrounding nations in their religious worship, however innocent some of these were in themselves, were forbidden to his people. Much less may we suppose that so important a part of the law as its tenth was borrowed by him from man. Nor will it answer here to say that those from whose example this may be supposed to have been taken were faithful men, unlike those idolatrous nations whom Israel was forbid to imitate. What is the wisdom of Abram or of Jacob in His sight "who chargeth his angels with folly?" It is, then, more reasonable to conclude from the scriptural character of God that his ordinance of a tenth in the Mosaic law was a continued assertion of his own commandment, than that it was copied from the example either of Jacob or of Abram.

Again; this is more consonant with the nature of the law itself, which, in all of it that is of a moral nature, and in much that is of a ceremonial, was but the republication of an older commandment. Imprinted at first on the unfallen mind, the moral law was never quite obliterated even from fallen nature, as St. Paul declares in the 2d chapter of Romans : ‡ it was revealed, in parts at least, from time to time, until the more full declaration of it by Moses, and has only had its full spiritual meaning brought out, and its deep obligation enforced, by the Christian dispensation. Now we claim for the giving of a tenth to God all the authority of moral obligation. It is from its nature wholly shut out from the domain of mere ceremonies and traditions, which may be of force in one dispensation, and abrogated in

---

* Exod. xxv.   † Deut. xii. 30; xvi. 21.
‡ Rom. ii. 14, 15, 26, 27.

another. The gift of *some* portion to him none can deny to have this force, always, in all places, at all times; and it only remains for God to name his proportion in order to give to that peculiar portion the force of a moral precept. We will again use the analogous instance of the Sabbath day to illustrate our argument. To devote a portion of our time to the special service of him to whom all our days are due is a moral obligation; but God having specified a seventh as the particular portion he claims, makes our observance of a seventh, rather than of any other portion, to be the point in which our obligation lies. The gift of a tenth, then, being morally obligatory, forming an important part of the moral law binding on the Jewish conscience, being no mean part of that worship due by them to Jehovah, and partaking in no degree of the nature of that code of ritual from which Christ has set us free, it is only agreeable with all we are told of the moral law to suppose that this, as every other part of it, came not first into force when it fell from the lips of Moses, but had its previous sanction of the divine commandment, and its previous claim to man's obedience.

Again; we have reason to conclude, that in the extent of moral obedience the Israelites were not subjected to a stricter law than the Church of God in preceding times. In one point we know that, from the hardness of their hearts, their departure from the purer and stricter law of earlier days was, we do not say approved of, but suffered to take place; we allude to the subject of divorce.* We may, then, reasonably conclude, that in other respects no stricter law of morals was imposed upon them, which would be the case if the Jewish proportion were a tenth, while believers of previous times could discharge their obligation by the gift of what portion they pleased,—a twentieth it might be, or less.

Once more; we rely on the manner in which tithes are spoken of in the law of Moses as establishing the fact that they were not then for the first time made the peculiar property of God. Particular attention is due to this. The 27th chapter of Leviticus and 30th verse is the first place in the law where a

* Matt. xix. 8.

tenth is spoken of. Let us mark the way in which it is spoken of: "All the tithe of the land, whether of the seed of the land or of the fruit of the tree, *is the Lord's: it is holy unto the Lord.*"* The use of the present tense forbids us to suppose that now first was a tenth made the property of God; it obliges us to allow that it *was already his*. Even if he had said of it, as in fact he does in verse 32, "*It shall be holy* to the Lord," this would not prove it to be then first ordained, for it might properly signify the continued appointment of a previous law, as we know to be the case with the ten commandments, which run in the future tense; but where he says of it, "*It is holy*" to him, this cannot signify any other thing than that what was spoken of was already established when the words were uttered. We need not fear relying on the plain grammatical sense of Scripture. It was written under the inspiration of that Spirit who would not allow error to be conveyed by its language. But if we turn our attention to the same expression in the case of other ordinances, we will be confirmed in our view of the sense we have taken of it when applied to a tenth. Another such expression precisely occurs in this chapter about the firstlings of beasts; and it is to be remarked that, with the exception of this and that of the tenth, every other ordinance in the chapter is in the future tense. The 26th verse reads thus, " Only the firstlings of the beasts, which should be the Lord's firstling, no man shall sanctify it: whether it be ox or sheep: *it is the Lord's.*"† Moses here speaks of a law already established on the departure of Israel from Egypt, and with this agrees the expression, "*It is the Lord's.*"‡ Poole's comment on this verse is short and striking. He says, that the Israelite "is forbid to vow his firstling because it is not his own, but the Lord's already, and therefore, to vow such a thing to God is a tacit derogation from, and a usurpation of, the Lord's right, and a mocking of God by pretending to give him what we cannot withhold from him."§ We should have expected to find him in his comment on verse 30 saying of the tenth what he has, when explaining verse 26, said

* Levit. xxvii. 30.   † Levit. xxvii. 26.
‡ Exod. xiii. 2-13.   § Poole's Annot. on Levit. xxvii. 26.

so well of the firstling; but we have no hesitation in asserting that the same expression is adopted in verse 30 of the tithe, because it was then no new ordinance, but God's old and long-established claim. Let us take another similar example in the case of the Sabbath day, ordained to be observed at the creation. The first mention of the Sabbath in the law is in Exodus, xvi. 23: "And he said unto them, This is that which the Lord hath said, *To-morrow is the rest of the holy Sabbath* unto the Lord."* Whatever Moses may refer to in his expression, "The Lord hath said," whether to his ordinance of the Sabbath in the 2d chapter of Genesis, or to a subsequent ordinance of that day, there is no doubt that the expression, "To-morrow is the rest of the Sabbath," means that it was an ordinance already established, not one now first introduced. Thus confirmed in the view taken of Leviticus, xxvii. 30, we need not hesitate in concluding that it supports all the preceding arguments on the subject of the tenth, establishing the fact, that it was not first introduced as a divine appointment in the Mosaic dispensation, but was continued in that dispensation from a preceding age.

We have thus far then proceeded in our argument, and will not, I apprehend, find much difficulty in the application of it to the Christian's obligations. We have seen that the ordinance of a tenth was originally the command of God to the world at large, and, as such, its traces have been met with in remote and unconnected lands. As in the late anxious searches for the gallant band lost amid Arctic snows, the discovery of somewhat that had belonged to them, or some other memorial, led the searchers to conclude, "Here Franklin passed, or here he spent, the weary polar winter;" so the traces of a tenth amid the superstitions and idolatries of many lands led us to acknowledge the existence of a divine law which traversed the world, and, piloted by heavenly skill, never wholly suffered shipwreck. We have seen even ungodly Cain recognising God's claim to a portion of his substance, though his gift was not accepted, being offered, not in faith, but in a self-righteous spirit; as in later times God disdained the offerings of those who rejected his only Son. We

* Exod. xvi. 23.

have seen Abram, the friend of God, paying to God's priest as his right the tenth of all his spoils, and Jacob vowing to the bountiful Giver of blessing the same portion of all his substance. And, finally, we have seen God himself, in the Mosaic dispensation, by his ordinance of a tenth marking by unmistakeable sign this law as having come from himself; acknowledging it there, not as the mere chance product of human gratitude seeking thus to express its deep obligations, but as his own command first issued to the world at large, to keep alive and perpetuate in the minds of those who would fain be independent his claim to universal sovereignty.

Before leaving this chapter there is one inference that I wish to draw. We saw, in the instance in Abram's life, that God's tenth was all of it given to Melchizedek; in Jacob's case we concluded, that none of it was devoted to the maintenance of a priesthood; while in the present chapter, we see that its principal object was for the support of the ministry of Levi, including the Jewish priesthood. What I would infer, then, is this, that while the tenth is at all times due and to be paid to God, the way in which he wishes it to be used is not always the same, but varies according to the dispensation and his appointment. It may all of it go to support a ministry, or none of it may be spent that way, or a portion of it may suffice. All depends on the expression of his will to whom it belongs.

We have hitherto strictly confined our attention to the subject of the tenth, and have prepared the way for the consideration of it as it affects us of the Christian dispensation. We cannot, however, come immediately to this point. Our scriptural inquiries will, I think, lead us to the conclusion, that while a tenth is God's general claim on man, on some he makes a further claim. From most, it may be, a tenth is all that he expects, but there would appear to be others from whom he looks for a far more bountiful gift. We propose, then, in reference to these latter, to consider the subject of the Jewish free-will offerings.

CHAPTER VIII.

"I HAVE SEEN WITH JOY THY PEOPLE TO OFFER WILLINGLY UNTO THEE."—1 *Chron.* xxix. 17.

A TITHE was the general law for Israel, but Jewish liberality was by no means confined within that limit. It was neither intended to be so by Him who, being himself all bountiful, loveth also a cheerful giver; nor was it so accepted by those to whom was given along with abundance the free spirit which loves to communicate. In God's ancient Church were those who disdained to set a limit to their bounty where the cause of Jehovah was concerned, but only thought themselves too highly honoured in bestowing their wealth on him. How delightful to look back upon those glorious pages of Jewish history, when this free spirit animated the nation as one man; when all, both high and low, from the prince and noble to the humblest Israelite, vied in pouring their gifts into the treasury of God!* The precious metals dug from the bowels of the earth, the costly stones gathered from the ocean and the mine, rich furs, fine linen, costly woods, and spices, all were offered willingly in the sacred cause Those who had none of these, but to whom God had given wisdom to devise or hands to execute, devoted freely the inventions of genius, the skill of art, and the strength of labour, in executing the work of God. No selfish thought seems to have come across their minds, no covetous reflections to have checked the free current of their bounty. They only reflected that it was for God they did it, and with that view no gift appeared too valuable or great. How sad the contrast with other periods when covetousness and selfishness took the place of bounty and of gratitude; when not merely free-will offerings were grudged, but the appointed tenth was withdrawn!† Not more striking was the contrast between the condition of Israel at these different times. In the one, the windows of heaven

* 1 Chron. xxix.; Exod. xxv. xxvi.; Ezra, ii. 68. † Mal. iii. 8.

were opened, and Plenty poured out from her free horn, while gladness dwelt within the heart, and joy beamed on the countenances, of a happy people; in the other, God in displeasure dried up the fountain whence the streams of refreshing had flowed in their various channels, and gloom overshadowed the face, and repining saddened the spirits, of the selfish nation; for it was true which Solomon said, "There is that scattereth and yet increaseth; and there is that withholdeth more than is meet, and it tendeth to poverty."*

The free-will offering differed from the tenth, not only in that it was not required from all the people, but that even where it was expected discretion seems to have been allowed as to how much or how little should be given. To give a tenth was the bounden duty of every Israelite, but the free-will offering depended on the ability and willingness of the offerer. The one was required of all the people; the reluctant and the grudging were scarcely invited to join in the other. "Speak unto the children of Israel," said God in one place to Moses, "that they bring me an offering: of every man that giveth it willingly with his heart, ye shall take *my offering.*"† Thus we see the discretion that was allowed in these offerings. That which man felt willing to give, God invited him to bestow; but where the willing spirit ceased, the offering was not pressed. It is still called, and really was as much God's, as was the tenth, and so we will see it a little farther on allowed to be by his servants, but yet it was ordinarily left optional with the Israelite. To him was said, as to his successor in this Christian dispensation, Let every man do as he is disposed in his heart, not grudgingly or of necessity. With this discretionary power were, however, added the restrictions, that whatever was offered should be perfect in its kind and without blemish,‡ and that what was once offered could not be withdrawn.§

The Jewish free-will offering was, in some instances at least, of a permanent nature. Ordinarily a gift, greater or less as occasional circumstances required, it was sometimes regular in

* Prov. xi. 24.
† Exod. xxv. 2.
‡ Levit. xxii. 21, 22.
§ Deut. xxiii. 23.

its payment and obligatory in its nature, because though at first voluntarily undertaken, yet when undertaken it could not be withdrawn, in conformity with the precept of Deut. xxiii. 23. Of this kind was that annual tribute which the Jews on their return from Babylon bound themselves to pay to God for the service of his house.* In the course of time it amounted to an immense treasure, contributed not only by those Jews inhabiting Palestine, but also by those scattered throughout Gentile cities, and exciting by its vastness the cupidity and rapacity of Mithridates, of Pompey, and of Crassus.† "Let no one wonder," says Josephus, "that there were so much wealth in our temple, since all the Jews throughout the habitable earth, and those that worshipped God (*i.e.* proselytes), nay, even those of Europe and Asia, sent their contributions to it, and this from very ancient times."‡

But, generally speaking, their free-will offerings were made on extraordinary occasions. The principal ones of these that we read of in Scripture were three in number, and all of them for the purpose of raising a house to God. The first of these was the erection of the Tabernacle in the wilderness;§ the second, the preparation for the building of the Temple in the reign of David, and its actual building by Solomon;|| the third was on the return of the captive tribes from Babylon, when they proceeded to re-erect on its former site the holy house, which had been laid waste for their sins.¶ On each of these occasions the enthusiasm of the people in offering was very great; and vast as was the amount of costly and valuable things required, all was supplied, and more than supplied, by the zealous liberality of the offerers. When the Tabernacle was being made and furnished, we are told that the people required not to be urged to give, but to be restrained from giving.** How extraordinary does it sound in these covetous times, the complaint of the overseers of the building, "The people bring

---

* Neh. x. 32. † Hooker's "Eccl. Pol." l. xiv. c. 7.
‡ Josephus, "Ant." l. xiv. c. 7. § Exod. xxv.
|| 1 Chron. xxix.; 2 Chron. iii.; iv.
¶ Ezra, ii. 68. ** Exod. xxxvi. 5, 6.

much more than enough for the service of the work, which the Lord commanded to make!" How strangely does it read, in these days of calculating selfishness, the command which Moses caused thereon to be proclaimed throughout the camp of Israel, " Let neither man nor woman make any more work for the offering of the sanctuary!" In the wealthy reigns of David and Solomon, the amount contributed almost exceeds calculation. While on the return of the captives, in poverty no doubt, .from Babylon, the language of the inspired historian is brief, but very significant, " They offered freely for the house of God," " They gave after their ability."

Such were the Jewish free-will offerings, when extraordinary occasions called for their liberality. In the times of their piety to God, his appeal was not made in vain. The treasures of the nation were expended in his cause with a zeal and a self-denial becoming the chosen people. Oh, had they been always thus, and in other respects as in this, then would Jerusalem have been, what she will one day be, " a praise upon earth."* Perhaps some are ready to say, " These were sad times in Judah, when the people thus alienated from themselves and their families their most valuable substance." So might covetousness say, but so saith not the bountiful heart. To such the joy of giving is greater, deeper, purer, and more lasting, than the joy of receiving. Let us turn to one of those occasions before referred to, when David assembles the congregation of Israel, and declares what he has offered, and receives from them their offerings for the Temple which Solomon was to build.† Among the many days of holy joy which rose upon the chosen people throughout their wounderful career, this was one of the brightest. It takes its place side by side with that glorious morning, when Israel, saved from the hands of the Egyptians, saw their enemies dead on the sea-shore; ‡ when Moses and the people sang their song of thanksgiving; when Miriam took the timbrel in her hand, and all the women went out after her with timbrels and with dances, and their glad hymn was, " Sing ye to the Lord, for he

---

* Isa. lxii. 7.   † 1 Chron. xxix.   ‡ Exod. xv.

hath triumphed gloriously, the horse and his rider hath he thrown into the sea."* It deserves to be remembered for its joy with that great Passover kept in the reign of Hezekiah,† after a long interval of neglect of that holy ordinance, when the pious king recalled to Israel's mind their ingratitude, and moved them to repentance; when, in their new-born zeal, they kept not only the seven days of the feast appointed by the law, but other seven also, "with exceeding gladness;" when there was great joy in Jerusalem, because since the days of Solomon there had been no such Passover; when the priests, the Levites, arose and blessed the people, and their voice was heard, and their prayer came up unto his holy dwelling place, even into heaven. It ranks with that day of rejoicing when the liberated captive took down the harp which he had hung upon the willows by the waters of Babylon—when, if he wept at the remembrance of Zion, it was with tears of joy at the prospect of soon again beholding her battlements and towers—when each said to the other, "Sing aloud unto God our strength, make a joyful noise unto the God of Jacob," and there was heard again in Judah "the voice of harpers harping with their harps." ‡ Even such a day was that when David and the people offered, with joyful willingness, the best of their substance for the Temple of their Lord.

Nor did they think in doing so that they were doing any such work of supererogation as made God their debtor. It remained for later times to set up this false and blasphemous claim of human merit. It remained for those, who assert for themselves exclusively the possession of the faith, but whom the Word of Truth describes as apostate from the faith, to put forward this arrogant pretension. In the seasons of deepest devotion to God, when all they had and all they were were laid at his feet, the feelings of the faithful Israelite, and his language, were ever the humblest. Then were their short-comings most keenly remembered, while their performances of duty were felt to be God's due, and at the best imperfect. The praise which

* Exod. xv. 21. † 2 Chron. xxx. ‡ Ezra, i.

was continually in their mouths was the praise of God; and when this praise was at its highest note, the deep bass which accompanied it, and gave it volume, was that of humiliation and self-abasement. As David prayed that the "free-will offerings of his mouth might be accepted of by the Lord,"* thereby confessing them unworthy of him whom they would celebrate, so he felt when offering his own and his people's offerings. He knew, after all, that the offerer was sinful, and his gift the property of God. "Who am I," he said, "and what is my people, that we shall be able to offer so willingly after this sort? for all things come of thee, and of thine own have we given thee."†

We reserve for a future chapter the discussion on the propriety on the part of some of free-will offerings over and above their tenth. With one single observation we will dismiss this present chapter. That which Solomon expended on the house of God brought a more pure and real joy to his heart, and more lasting honour to his name, than his subsequent vast expenditure on the splendour of his court and the magnificence of his harem.

CHAPTER IX.

"HONOUR THE LORD WITH THY SUBSTANCE."—*Prov.* iii. 9.

WE have now brought down our subject to that point when we are to apply it to ourselves. This is our serious inquiry, Have the foregoing arguments any reference to us or not? Are Christians under the same obligations to God in the expenditure of their substance, that we have seen his people to be under in the Jewish and preceding dispensations; or has Christianity, in relieving them from the burden of Jewish ceremonial, also left them at liberty to expend in the cause of God whatever portion of their substance they think fit themselves? Our position here is, that it has not; that God still expects from us the same proportion of our goods

* Ps. cxix. 108. † 1 Chron. xxix. 14–16.

to be used in his glory which he received from his Church in former ages. This is what we shall endeavour to establish in the present chapter. It is evident, that whatever reason there was for supposing that God would define plainly what portion of his substance he expected from man, exists as much for Christians as for those of previous dispensations. The same covetousness, alas! that has ever reigned in the natural heart, and exerted its influence even in the heart renewed by grace, is equally powerful now, as it has been. The same selfishness which led those of former times to grudge God his portion of their substance, and to expend their all on their own aggrandisement, or the advancement of their families, would also lead the Christian to contract his acknowledgments to God within the narrowest compass, and part with even his miserable mite with reluctance. Nay, it is of our dispensation in its latter periods that prophecy has given among its leading features, " Men shall be lovers of their own selves, covetous." *
If, then, we saw any probability that God would at any time define his claim, that probability still exists.

If a former part of our argument has been admitted,—namely, that the obligation of a tenth dates from times long anterior to Judaism, and was only continued, not commenced, in that system, —our conclusion that its obligation exists with Christians would very speedily be established. The argument was, that God imposed this obligation as a common and perpetual ordinance upon mankind. If in the days of Noah, or, as is much more probable, in those of Adam, the Almighty required of these heads of mankind that they should honour him, the Owner and Bestower of all, with a tenth of their substance; and if in consequence among various nations, and especially among those who in the earliest days worshipped God with acceptable worship, not self-devised but received from him, the distinct traces of this original command have been seen, it cannot be doubted in that case that the obligation to keep this precept still exists in all its force for us. The reason is a plain one. The commands of God to men continue in force until they have been repealed by him. Now this particular precept was never repealed by him. On the contrary,

* 2 Tim. iii. 2.

when a new dispensation (the Jewish), to answer peculiar circumstances, was instituted by him, he made this original command a part and parcel of its constitution; he gave it a leading position in it; down to the latest prophet* he insisted on it as most obligatory on his people, while not one of the prophets ever spoke of it as a temporary institution; by the mouth of his Son he continued still to assert his full claim to the observance of it; † and thus handed it over in all its force and all its freshness to the Christian dispensation. Not one link is wanting in the chain of evidence which brings this precept from the days of its primitive appointment down to our own. Not a shadow of pretence exists for asserting, that if it had once been imposed by God he had withdrawn its obligation, or suffered it to become obsolete from want of observance. In those days, when by Moses he published the original moral law of mankind,—wrote on tables of stone what had become defaced from the fleshly tables of the heart,— and in the permanent record of the Scriptures preserved it from being lost amid the ever-varying traditions of men, the obligation of the Israelite to pay a tenth to him was insisted on as plainly as any other obligation; while, being brought into the law from preceding ages, there could be no pretence for saying, that with the passing away of the peculiarities of Judaism this, too, had ceased to be of obligation. If, therefore, we admit that God ordained this practice before the days of Moses, and that in obedience to this ordinance Jacob vowed his tenth to God, and Abram paid his tithe to Melchizedek, we cannot deny that the same obligation continues with us, preserved unbroken through Jewish to Christian times.

In my own mind I am satisfied with the perfect validity of this argument, and would be content to close the matter here. But I am also persuaded, that even if the grounds of it should be disputed our conclusion may yet be proved in another way. Should any one think, notwithstanding what has been advanced, that the divine origin of a tenth cannot be established as of an elder date than the Mosaic law, even on this lower ground I am prepared to argue for its continued obligation in the Christian Church. Let it, then, for

* Mal. iii. 8. † Matt. xxiii. 23.

the sake of argument, be allowed, that in the Jewish dispensation we find its first distinct appointment by God. On this ground we will proceed in the remainder of the chapter to show its continued obligation upon us.

The Christian's estimation of the Old Testament Scriptures is not unfrequently very different from what it ought to be. It is too often supposed that they were only, or at least chiefly, intended for the Jewish dispensation, and that, when the Christian was introduced, they were, in great measure, to be laid aside, and the New Testament Scriptures were to take their place. They are imagined by some to be peculiar to the Jew, somewhat as the Koran is to the Mahommedans, and that the Christian finds his law of life in the writings of the evangelists and apostles. Now such an idea is wholly erroneous. The faith of the Old Testament and the New is essentially one. The moral duties inculcated by both are essentially the same. The New Testament is but the fulfilment and comment on the old, as the prophets enforce, illustrate, and expand the spiritual meaning of Moses' law. The difference between the two is but in development, not in sense. Now, this Old Testament is completely the book of the Jewish Church. Take away a portion of Genesis, and all the rest relates to Israel. Its call in Abraham, its bondage, its law, its Canaan, its sins, its punishment, its privileges, its promises,—these are the contents of the Old Testament Scriptures. And yet these latter, rightly understood, were a complete law of life and salvation to the faithful Israelite before Christ came,—to the faithful Christian after his coming. The pretence of Rome, that the Christian Church was for a considerable time left to oral tradition and teaching, is utterly false: she had in the Old Testament her perfect law. It was these that Christ commanded to be searched, as testifying of him.* These were Stephen's "lively oracles,"† handed down from Moses as a precious tradition to the Christian. It was after "the way" taught in them that Paul "worshipped the God of his fathers, believing all things that were written in the law and in the prophets."‡ These were the "Holy Scriptures," which Timothy had known "from a child;"§ which were

* John, v. 39.   † Acts, vii. 38.   ‡ Acts, xxiv. 14.   § 2 Tim. iii. 15.

"able to make wise unto salvation;" which were "profitable for doctrine, for reproof, for correction, for instruction in righteousness;" which could make the "man of God perfect, throughly furnished unto all good works." As the Scriptures of the Old and New Testament, then, are essentially the same, so the Churches ruled by both are essentially one. "They are not two Churches," says C. Leslie, "but two states of the same Church; for it is the same Christian Church from the first promise of Christ (Gen. iii. 15) to the end of the world; and therefore it is said (Heb. iv. 2), that the gospel was preached unto them as well as unto us."* And so Isaiah declares, that the change from Jewish to Christian times would be but God's "calling his servants by another name."† Our Lord declares, that it was not the setting up of another fold, but the calling of the wandering nations into the exisiting fold.‡ While Paul teaches the same important truth, when he declares that the baptism of the Gentiles into the faith of Christ was but their grafting upon the ancient stock of Israel. §

Now our conclusion from these undoubted facts is this, that the precepts of the Old Testament are still as binding as ever, except in such particulars as, having been fulfilled by Christ and performed their temporary office, have been done away, according to the declaration of our Lord, that "not one jot or tittle should pass from the law till all were fulfilled."|| We do not say that all that is in the Old Testament is binding still; we know that it had its peculiarities, and that these are abrogated; but we assert, that with the exception of these,—exceptions on which we can lay our hands and tell which they are,—those ancient Scriptures are as much our law as are the writings of the apostles of Christ. Now it is quite evident that if they are, as no doubt they are, our law, we must be able to separate between what is binding and what is not binding in them. If on this point we are doubtful, if we know not which is obligatory and which is not, their force as a law would be gone, for the "trumpet would give an uncertain sound." What is done away with we can only learn, either from

---

* Leslie's "Select Works," p. 348. † Isa. lxv. 15.
‡ John, x. 16.   § Rom. xi. 17. || Matt. v. 17-19.

those Scriptures themselves, or from those of the New Testament, or from both. Whatever cannot be proved from these sources to be abrogated must be considered still in force. We will show, then, not only that no such abrogation exists in the matter of the tenth, but that, on the contrary, we have every fair and sufficient reason for concluding that its obligation is continued in the Christian dispensation; and if we do this, and at the same time remove certain objections that might seem at first sight opposed to our conclusion, we consider that we will have gained our point.

When the preachers of the gospel addressed themselves to the Jewish mind, they never insisted on their reception of any truth, or their laying aside any practice, which they could not establish to them out of their own Scriptures. In their "witness, both to small and great, they said none other things than what Moses and the prophets did say should come."* The coming and circumstances of the Messiah,—the casting away of the Jews and calling in of the Gentiles,—the change of the priesthood,—the abrogation of sacrifices and of the ceremonial law in general,—all were reasoned with them out of the Old Testament; and it was only because they rejected Moses and the prophets that they rejected Christ. To mention particular parts of the New Testament where this can be seen may appear superfluous when traces of it are to be found throughout; but we may, before passing on, instance the 3d, 4th, 9th, 10th, and 11th chapters of Romans, the 3d, 4th, and 5th chapters of Galatians, and from the 5th to the 10th chapter inclusive of Hebrews, as remarkable examples. Now, neither in the New Testament—where, in all probability, every departure from Jewish practice has been noticed—nor in any part of the writings of the Old, has it ever been hinted, that in Christian times men were to cease to honour God with their substance as his servants of previous times had done. If such an intimation can be pointed out, we will at once confess ourselves mistaken; but since none such can be shown, it plainly follows that the obligation of Christians in this respect is continued in all its force.

* Acts, xxvi. 22.

Again, it is allowed that, while the civil and the ceremonial laws of Judaism do not bind Christians, its moral law is still as binding as ever. Now, the giving of a tenth was certainly a part of the Jewish moral law, and therefore it is of force with Christians. That the giving of a tenth was a moral duty to the Jews, is of easy proof. It had nothing typical or ceremonial about it. In all times, both previous and subsequent to Judaism, the giving of some portion of man's substance to God was esteemed a moral duty; and when God, in the Jewish dispensation, if not before, named a tenth as his expected portion, then the gift of a tenth to him became of moral obligation. Thenceforward it could not be altered, except by the same authority that imposed it. A parallel instance readily occurs to us in the observance of the Sabbath, or seventh day. In Eden, God ordained that the seventh portion of man's time should be dedicated to himself. If this specific portion had not been mentioned, its observance would have no stronger obligation than any other supposed proportion of our time. But no sooner had God fixed upon this proportion, than the observance of that, rather than of any other, became our moral duty, which no man might dare to alter—which no mere change of dispensation could set aside. The keeping of a seventh day has been a perpetual ordinance before the flood, in the patriarchal and Jewish age, and in the Christian Church. And so the gift of a tenth, made a moral duty to the Jew, continues a moral duty to his Christian successor, who has come in his place, and taken upon him his predecessor's privileges and obligations.

Every reason exists now, and exists even in greater force, for the giving of a tenth, which existed in Jewish times. God is still the sovereign Lord of all, and therefore to be honoured by his creatures in those gifts he has bestowed upon them. Man is still the recipient of blessings, and bound to show in some sensible manner his gratitude and love. The interests of religion are to be upheld in a world, which would quickly, if left to itself, turn aside from, and forget and oppose, the truth. The widow, the orphan, and the destitute, are still among us,—recommended to us by that same God who gave them in charge to his ancient people. In one most important respect the need of a tenth is more felt in the Christian than the Jewish Church. The latter was not missionary in its character,—its calling was merely to uphold the faith among the chosen people; while that of the Christian is to bear the name of Christ to every dark land of heathenism, and never to stay its labours till every child of the great common Father has been brought home "to the Shepherd and Bishop of his soul." It, surely, is not to be thought of for a moment, that the time of God's displaying most fully his love to man is to be seized on by the latter as the time for diminishing the expression of his gratitude; or that the acknowledgments of God's sovereignty are to be less manifest when he has made us and ours doubly his own. If in that elder and less privileged system men honoured God with the tenth of their substance, can it be imagined that we, so much more favoured, are to be behind them in our gratitude? For what the dim, cold light of breaking day, struggling with the mists of night, is to the glorious sun of noon, such is Judaism to Christianity. Bondage was the spirit of the former, adoption that of the latter dispensation. For in the one Christ was foreshadowed, in the other Christ was manifested; in the one men sought, in the other they found him.

As the grand reason—namely, the honouring God—still exists in all its force for the gift of a tenth, as well as the uses to which he would have it applied, so the New Testament everywhere requires of the believer a portion of his substance. This portion was to be greater or less, according as God had prospered each individual.* True, a tenth is not named in the New Testament; but that was not required, because that proportion was already fixed in the Old. This is quite a sufficient reason, as has been shown in the opening of this chapter.† Already laid down, there was no occasion for its repetition. From what we know of the liberality of the early Christians,—in some instances giving away their all,‡ in others, "out of a deep poverty abounding in liberality, to their power, yea, and beyond their power, being willing of themselves,"§—we should not expect that the

* 1 Cor. xvi. 2. † Chap ix. ‡ Acts, iv. 34. § 2 Cor. viii. 2, 3.

proportion of a tenth would be urged upon them as a duty, when, in all probability, few of them were satisfied with that portion, but gave much more. This same silence has been observed in the New Testament on another most important point. In the institution of the sacrament of baptism, it would be hard to show from its pages that infants were to be partakers of it. Its ordinance by Christ* has been quoted by the opponents of infant-baptism, just as freely as it has been advanced by its defenders, and not without some show of reason. While the cases which occur in the history of the New Testament Church— in the Acts of the Apostles and elsewhere—of whole families being baptized, are not conclusive on the subject, since it cannot be shown from any one of them that infants were among their number. The simple but satisfactory proof is to be found in the Old Testament. There God entered into covenant with the infant children of his people; and when he was establishing his new and better covenant with the Christian Church, he did not mention Children, because he had already declared his will that such should be brought into covenant with him. He changed the matter and the form of the accompanying rite, and, therefore, he plainly said, "Go, baptize in the name of the Father, and of the Son, and of the Holy Ghost;" but, intending no change in *the subjects* of the covenant, he speaks not particularly of them. Jewish fathers, the apostles and missionaries of the first Christian Churches, would have no hesitation on this point. They had circumcised, they would henceforth baptize, their children.

We will notice another instance which seems to establish the principle here laid down, that every portion of the Old Testament is binding, except that comparatively small portion which has been specially noticed as done away. By what do we Christians regulate the degrees within which marriage is permitted? By the laws of Moses contained in Leviticus? On all hands these are allowed to be in force. St. Paul, in one instance, refers plainly to their continued obligation, when, with horror, he mentions the sin committed by a member of the Corinthian Church in marrying his father's wife.† Now, this case, we contend, is

---

* Matt. xxviii. 19, 20. † 1 Cor. v. 1, 2.

far more difficult of proof than the obligation of the tenth. The prohibitions of marriage within certain degrees are found in the Levitical law, and in that alone. They partake more the character of a law enacted from motives of expediency than of a moral commandment. They certainly were not in force from the beginning, when marriages within the nearest degrees were permitted, and which seem to have been permitted down to times approaching the giving of the law, for we read of Abraham's marrying his sister by the father's side.* They oblige for one reason, and one only, but that is quite sufficient,—they are found in the law of Moses, and have not since been repealed. We need not say that the gift of a portion of our substance to God stands on a higher footing, for, whether it were a tenth or not, it has been in force from the beginning. Can it, then, be supposed, that the giving of our tenth to the Lord, which in its essence, if not in the mere circumstance of the exact proportion, was always a moral duty,—which has been commanded in the law, a command repeated throughout the whole series of the writers of the Old Testament to its latest prophet, without one hint of its being but of a temporary nature, should in the Christian Church have ceased to be obligatory? Let us select, for example, that proverb of Solomon, "Honour the Lord with thy substance, and with the first-fruits of all thine increase."† Surely this is obligatory on us. If it be not, it would be hard to show what part of Proverbs, or, for that matter, what part of the Old Testament, is obligatory. But if it does oblige us, in order to understand it correctly we must read it in the light of the Jewish law. What it meant in Solomon's days it means substantially in ours The inspiring Spirit had not, surely, two meanings for one set of words. Now, these words bring us of necessity to the Jewish tithe. They were spoken of that, and of nothing else. They had this definite meaning to the Jew; they have the same definite meaning to us. The "first-fruits," of which the wise man speaks, were not only the first, but also "the best of the wine, and the oil, and the wheat,"‡ and of the various products

---

* Gen. xx. 12.   † Prov. iii. 9.   ‡ Numb. xviii. 11-13.

of the land, which the Israelite offered to God,* and were identical with that tenth which was God's proportion of his people's substance. What was then their duty is ours also. We will not stop to notice such poor objections as that this precept cannot apply to us, since we cannot give the same natural productions as were supplied by the land of Canaan, or cannot pay in kind, having many of us no connexion with land, &c. The essence of the precept is all we contend for. The Jew in foreign lands was in the same condition with us, and, if too distant from Jerusalem, could convert his offering into money.†

But we have, besides, in the New Testament, express authority for concluding that this part of the ancient law, as well as that law in general, has still a binding power upon the Christian's conscience. If it be the case, that "whatever was written aforetime was written for our learning," and if it was written as a standing law for Israel, that they were to give to God a tenth of their substance, it is, we think, hard indeed for us to draw any other lesson from this precept than that we are to honour him in like manner. But the apostle Paul leaves us in no doubt that this particular part of the law is in force for Christians. In the ninth chapter of his First Epistle to the Corinthians ‡ he appeals to it as a living and authoritative law,—as binding in its spirit upon the Corinthians as it ever was upon the Church of Israel. He applies the offerings of the Jews and their application of them to enforce similar duties among Christians. He does not, indeed, advert to the very point of the example on which we are now insisting, for that was not his object. He takes the part that suited his own case. He wanted to establish the right of the Christian ministry to a maintenance by their people, and his proof was the case of the Jewish priesthood; "they which wait at the altar are partakers with the altar." But that the whole system under the law was meant to impart its lesson under the Gospel, he intimates from his general assertion in the eighth verse, "Saith not the law so also?" It was as much the teaching of the law that the people should offer to God a tenth, as

* 2 Chron. xxxi. 5–12.   † Deut.   25.   ‡ 1 Cor. ix.

that the priests should obtain a portion of their offerings. It is, therefore, as incumbent on Christians to give a tenth to God as to support their ministers. The same law which teaches the one, teaches the other also.

And here it may be as well to apply ourselves for a moment to the consideration of a point which the argument of the chapter has doubtless suggested ere this to the reader. If we argue from the institution of a tenth in the Mosaic law to the Christian's obligation to give the same proportion, must we not also insist that the Christian ministry has a divine right to this tenth, since that of Levi had? To some, this would be a consideration much in favour of our argument; to others, it would be a source of strong opposition to it. For ourselves, while we are clearly of opinion that its application by God to the support of the Levitical ministry establishes the full right of the Christian ministry to a maintenance in comfort and independence by their people out of their offerings to God, we do not see that it teaches the right of the latter *to the tenth*. Our reason is this. The Levites formed a twelfth part of the tribes of Israel; the Christian ministry has never amounted to anything like that proportion of their people. As the Jewish *priesthood* seem to have obtained but the tenth part of the tithe;* so all that seems taught us in regard of the gospel ministry is, that they should obtain an adequate provision for the maintenance in comfort and respectability of themselves and of their families.

We think that we have by this time established our object, which was to prove that God expects from us what he required from his people in other days,—a definite proportion of that increase with which he blesses them. But, before proceeding farther, it will be proper to notice one or two objections to the argument of this chapter, which might seem at first possessed of some force. The first of these is, that since the priesthood of Levi has been done away, that tithe which was used for their support has also been done away. Now, to this there are two distinct and sufficient answers. The first is, that the great object in the Jewish tithe was the honouring of God, and the

* Neh. x. 38; xii. 47.

great sin in refusing it was that in so doing God was defrauded.* The ministry of Levi has indeed passed away; but that God, whose service Levi waited on, still requires the same acknowledgment from his creatures in their substance. The second answer is, that while the Jewish ministry and the temple-worship have departed, their place has been taken in our dispensation by the Christian ministry and worship, requiring to be upheld in Christian lands, and to be propagated throughout the heathen world. Another objection might, perhaps, be made, from a hastily-considered view of certain passages in the New Testament, which may seem to speak as if the Christian's offerings to God were left wholly to his own discretion. It may be said that such passages as this, "Every man, as he purposeth in his heart, so let him give, not grudgingly, or of necessity,"† plainly signify a liberty permitted to the Christian in this respect, which is not consistent with the idea that a certain fixed portion of his means are expected from him by God. Now, if we have proved our point by other and sufficient reasons, such passages cannot have the least power to overthrow it. They are, in that case, in the New Testament, precisely parallel passages to others in the Old, which we have seen to appeal to the individual generosity of the Israelites, without their interfering in any measure with their obligation in the matter of the tenth. The passage above quoted can no more set aside the Christian's duty to give his tenth to God, than the following passage set aside the Jew's obligation to do so, "Speak unto the children of Israel that they bring me an offering; of every man that giveth it willingly with his heart ye shall take mine offering."‡ Both passages are, in fact, appeals to the free spirit of those who, having the means of being liberal above that measure of a tenth laid down for common observance, think they can expend their abundance no way so well as in the cause of God. Such texts as that from 2 Cor. ix. 7, are, in fact, passages which will come under our consideration in the next chapter, when we treat of the Christian's free-will offerings.

* Lev. xxvii. 30; Prov. iii. 9; Mal. iii. 8.
† 2 Cor. ix. 7.   ‡ Exod. xxv. 2.

We have now concluded our arguments on this important subject, and have, as we think, fully established that we are under the same obligations to God in the disposal of our means that his servants of old lay under. There must have been, we suppose, a peculiar propriety in the proportion of a tenth. Even if Abraham and Jacob gave it not in accordance with the divine command, which, however, we are quite satisfied they did, yet God in selecting their measure of liberality as that which was to regulate the liberality of Israel, stamped it with the impress of his approval as that which was from man a suitable acknowledgment of his sovereignty, a becoming expression of man's gratitude, and a somewhat adequate means of maintaining his worship in the world. Had we no other reason than that arising from this consideration, it would surely ill become fallible and erring man to attempt to set up any other standard for his liberality than that which Infinite Wisdom had set before him, doubtless for his imitation. It had been our part to follow in an humble spirit the guidance of the Most High, satisfied that it was the best.

In taking leave of this part of our subject, we do not feel ourselves bound, nor indeed would our space permit us, to enter upon the question as to whether there are not exceptions, and what they are, to this general obligation. That there may be such we do not deny, but neither do we suppose them to be more than may be supposed to have existed in the Jewish dispensation. The poor of the land doubtless were exempt; sudden and unexpected losses making it difficult, perhaps impossible, to meet our lawful engagements, in all probability excuse. But on this point we will not now enter any further. Man's excuses, let him ever remember, must be submitted to the scrutiny of Him whom they deprived of his required homage.

CHAPTER X.

"He which soweth bountifully shall reap also
bountifully."—2 *Cor.* ix. 6.

In the Jewish dispensation we have seen that there were those of whom God expected more than the general tenth, and who gladly responded to his call. We believe both that the same claim is made now, and that the Christian Church has afforded as bright examples of devotion to God as can be met with in former times. It would be strange, indeed, if it were otherwise: strange if, in the darker day and the less favoured Church, a greater return was either expected or made. It is not thus that God deals with man. The day of increased privilege is ever that of increased responsibility, and the season of bounty is also that of gratitude. As the rain and the sunshine are met by the earth's putting forth a fresher green, and arraying herself in fairer colours, so the dew of heavenly grace falls upon the believer's heart, and the quickening influence of the Spirit is imparted to him, that he may bring forth in his life the fruits of righteousness, and exhibit in his conversation the beauty of holiness. "Unto whomsoever much is given, of him shall be much required; and to whom men have committed much, of him they will ask the more."*

In considering the free-will offerings of Israel, we saw that in some cases they became of a permanent nature, while the more remarkable and important of them were called forth on the occasion of building and furnishing the house of God. It was well said by the pious Nehemiah, when asked to leave his work on the second temple, that he "could not come down, for he was doing a great work."† No doubt he was doing a great work in rebuilding, in the troubled times on which he fell, the house which Solomon had raised amid the quiet of a peaceful reign, and whose glory was to be greater than that of the former house

* Luke, xii. 48.   † Neh. vi. 3.

when sanctified by the footsteps of its Lord. But incomparably more majestic and dearer to God is that temple which is rearing now, and on which Christians are called upon to expend their free-will offerings. The Jewish historian mentions with his nation's pride the vast stones which constituted the beauty and strength of the temple on Mount Sion;* but each stone in the spiritual temple is an immortal soul, which nought but the blood of Christ could purchase, which is in itself a temple for the Holy Ghost. Josephus describes the Jewish building as covered with plates of gold, reflecting back at break of day the fiery splendour of the sun, or appearing at a distance like a mountain covered with snow.† To human eyes, indeed, in the spiritual temple is no such glory, but to the eye of God it is beautiful and glorious, "having neither spot, nor wrinkle, nor blemish;" but reflecting back the splendour of the incarnate Son, and clothed in the righteousness of Christ. The materials and workmen of Jerusalem's temple were brought together from various and distant places: ‡ the mountains of Judea afforded their quarries, Ophir its gold, Lebanon its cedars,§ Babylon its curtain veiling the holy place, Tyre its cunning worker in brass;|| but the materials and labourers of the Christian temple are collected from every clime. They come from lands bound by eternal frosts, or parched by a burning sun; the broad prairie, the deep valley amid Alpine mountains, the lonely isles of the Pacific, send their contributions; the huge cities of Europe, its dark mines unblessed by the light of day, its crowded factories and panting furnaces, supply their portion of the building; the rich plains of India, even unchanging China and suspicious Japan, are represented there. The Jew estimated the greatness of his temple by the length of time it took to perfect it;¶ but ours has been in progress of building since God laid its foundation-stone in the promise of Christ to our fallen parents. It is still unfinished after six thousand years; stone is being laid on stone, but the last is not yet placed. In the temple at Jerusalem David contemplated a house "ex-

---

* Josephus, "Ant." l. xv. c. 11. † Josephus, "War," l. v. c. 5.
‡ 1 Chron. xxix. 4. § Josephus, "War," l. v. c. 5.
|| 1 Kings, vii. 13. ¶ John, ii. 20.

ceeding magnifical, of fame and glory throughout all countries;"* and such a house *was* built whose fame attracted the attention, and, when they saw it, the wonder of those who had seen Nineveh and Babylon, Athens, and Alexandria, and Rome in their glory. But what was its fame compared with that of the temple of which we speak? When its first stone was laid, Satan saw it with dismay, and spoke of it in the councils of the fiends, while angels took up the song of praise. It has advanced amid the strife of tongues and the din of contention, the mean man and the great taking part either for or against, but none neutral here. To overthrow its walls and dig up its foundations, fiendish malice has plotted, and the brutal violence of man has toiled; while, to raise still higher those walls, and to crown them with battlements and turrets, zealous men have laboured, and enduring men have suffered, and angels have speeded on their errands; it is a "spectacle to the world, and to angels, and to men;"† it is spoken of beyond the confines of earth, wherever spirits go; its fame has spread even to the farthest stars. Such is the glorious spiritual temple which is ever in progress now; which calls on those who would be fellow-helpers to the truth for their free-will offerings with far more powerful voice than did the Jewish house, for even a heathen could say of God, "His pleasure lies not in the magnificence of temples made with hands, but in the piety and devotion of consecrated hearts."‡

If in the Christian dispensation there exists this great cause for the liberality of the affluent, do we not hear sounding in the believer's ear now the same divine voice which came to Israel in the wilderness? "Bring me an offering; of every man that giveth it willingly with his heart ye shall take mine offering."§ Yes, we are persuaded that it is thus that we are to take those passages of the New Testament which leave to the discretion and liberality of each believer the amount of his gifts to God. They clash not with that claim which God makes on us all alike for a portion of our substance, for surely in the New Testament it is not permitted to the believer, if he were so disposed, to close his purse

---

* 1 Chron. xxii. 5. † 1 Cor. iv. 9.
‡ Seneca, "Morals," p. 11. § Exod. xxv. 2.

against the claims of God's cause upon it, and to say, "My liberality is left absolutely to my own discretion; I will not surrender my liberty; I will give little, or nothing, if so I please." Against such ideas one text is decisive; "If any man provide not for his own, and specially for those of his own house, he hath denied the faith and is worse than an infidel."* We must then take such passages as 2 Cor. ix. 7, according to the analogy of Scripture; we must repudiate as wholly alien from their meaning that sense which selfishness and covetousness would put upon them, that the believer may, if he pleases, wholly refuse the aid of his means to further the cause of God, or may reduce his proportion to any amount, however small, that suits his narrow spirit. Such is altogether opposed to the spirit of the Christian dispensation, whose motto is, "Freely ye have received, freely give."† Such passages are appeals, not to the meanness of the covetous mind, but to the liberality of hearts which God hath touched with a sense of his own exceeding goodness and bounty, not merely in his gifts of temporal blessing, but more, infinitely more, in his spiritual blessings, the gift of eternal life in his dear Son our Lord, and the gift of the Holy Ghost to fit and prepare the Christian for his heavenly inheritance. It is to such that the exhortations of the New Testament are addressed, and they would never dream of taking advantage of the discretion left them, to narrow and curtail their bounty—to contract it within closer bounds than the minimum of Jewish acknowledgment, till it dwindled down to some mere trifle unworthy of them to offer or of God to accept. When salvation visited the house of Zaccheus, and this lost son of Abraham was found by, and had found Christ, straightway it was, "Behold, Lord, the half of my goods I give to the poor."‡ When the "free spirit" descended into the hearts, as well as dwelt upon the tongues, of the Christians at Jerusalem, in their love and joy "all that believed were together, and had all things common; and sold their possessions and goods, and parted them to all men as every man had need."§ It required but the announcement that famine was about to try

* 1 Tim. v. 8.   † Matt. x. 8.
‡ Luke, xix. 8, 9.   § Acts, ii. 44, 45.

those self-denying men, to determine the distant Christians of Antioch to send them relief, " each man according to his ability."* And when the same claim was laid before the Churches of Macedonia, he who had himself given up all for Christ, bore them the record, that " to their power, yea and beyond their power, they were willing of themselves,"† not requiring the golden tongue of eloquence to draw from them some half-grudged and insufficient tribute, but themselves supplicating the apostle " with much entreaty that he would receive the gift." It was to such men that discretionary appeals were made, " Let each give as he is disposed in his heart," and it is in the light of their abounding liberality that we must interpret such appeals. They are, in fact, the invitations of the New Testament to the Christian for his free-will offerings, even as we saw the same addressed in the Old Testament to those who in the wilderness gave with glad spirit their best and richest possessions, or, settled in Canaan, rejoiced to imitate the bounty of the princely hearts of David and Solomon.

Is any one, then, still disposed to rely on such texts as authorising him to give as little as he pleases in the cause of God? To him we would say, " It is not for you to interpret them differently from those to whom they were first addressed. Understand them as they did, and you will understand them aright; but in that case most assuredly you will take from them no encouragement for a niggardly offering, or a covetous refusal. Or, if you will insist on the letter of the text, while you deny its spirit, we must then only refer you to the apostle who wrote *for you*; he will tell you of what kind your faith is; he will describe it by one fearful word; he will tell you it is ' dead.'"‡

While the great majority of mankind hardly earn their " bread in the sweat of the brow;" while a smaller number are happily placed in that mean which the wise man describes as life's most desirable and safest condition,§ there are others, and they in every wealthy country no inconsiderable number, who abound in the possessions of this world. They are those whom

---

* Acts, xi. 28, 29. † 2 Cor. viii. 2, 3.
‡ James, ii. 17.   § Prov. xxx. 8, 9.

Scripture describes as "the rich;" whose besetting sins in some places it boldly denounces; whose deep responsibility it insists on in others; whose snares and temptations it delineates with the faithful and anxious tongue of love; whose great reward it delights to portray if they take heed to their trust. Such persons are in double danger, and Scripture does not disguise their danger. They do not often hear the truth from those who surround them. While their wealth places every gratification, sinful as well as innocent, within their power, and the craving of a corrupt heart urges them to gratify every wish, they seldom meet with those, who have sufficient love and boldness and purity of intention, to warn, exhort, and entreat them. Indifference carelessly sees them hastening to eternal ruin; or ensnaring fear ties the tongue that might otherwise have uttered the seasonable saving word,—or self-interest silences him who fears to make an enemy or alienate a patron by speaking the truth. Oh, that such would turn in their danger to that guide which neither fears nor flatters, nor betrays,—to that word of life written by the hands of men, but bearing in its every word the impress of God's wisdom and love. There they would see their peril, and there the way of safety.

It is to such that special appeals are made in Scripture for special liberality, as one of the obligations consequent on riches, and one great means of escaping their dangers. What is enough from others, is not enough from them. When comfort, elegance, even grandeur, have been secured, there is yet an overplus, with many a large one. Now after a certain sum little can be spent *lawfully on ourselves*. It is related of the late Louis Philippe of France, the richest man in Europe, that of all his vast private income, he expended on himself not more than four hundred pounds a-year; the remainder was spent on other things,—the encouragement of the fine arts, the advancement of science, the promotion of industry, the improvement of agriculture and commerce. Now there are with us numbers of individuals, not possessed, it is true, of equal wealth, but yet possessed of wealth over and beyond their own personal wants. On what is this overplus to be expended? We speak not of unlawful gratifications; on them the Christian may not expend, at the peril of his salvation, any the smallest portion of what belongs all of it to God. The lusts of the body, the covetous desires of the mind, cannot justify the expenditure of the least of God's goods; and fearful will be the account which he must render to his Judge, who shall be compelled to own that in his stewardship he expended his master's money in oppressing the poor, or defrauding his creditor of his right, in gluttony or drunkenness, at the gaming-table, or in the degrading pursuits of impurity and lewdness. We speak not at all of such a use of riches, nor do we pretend to condemn the application of them to the useful or the elegant arts and industries of life. We do not see why, according to his taste, the wealthy man may not have his gallery of paintings and sculpture, or his splendid conservatory, or his noble mansion, or his tasteful pleasure-grounds. These are all lawful in their way, and the expenditure upon them supports the industrious classes of the community. But what we do insist upon is this, that amid the plans and speculations of the wealthy, the honour and cause of Him who bestowed all this wealth should not be forgotten, or rather should surely occupy a prominent place. To what can wealth be so worthily devoted as to the glory of its great Owner? Nor can we see how in any other way the heart of the rich man can be preserved from the ensnaring power of Mammon than by spending it freely in the service of God. So thought one, who had wealth in his power, but gave it up for Christ. "Charge them who are rich in this world,"* he wrote to Timothy, as an essential part of his duty, "that they be not high-minded, nor trust in uncertain riches, but in the living God; that they do good, that they be rich in good works, ready to distribute, willing to communicate." Here was the apostle's safeguard against the snares of wealth,—a recollection of its uncertainty, and of God's eternal life, together with a free expenditure of it in every way that the cause of God requires. How many those ways are we will see in a succeeding chapter.

In the expenditure of the wealthy we claim a place—the

* 1 Tim. vi. 17.

leading place, for God. Amid the expense of equipage, and servants, and horses,—amid the decoration of houses, and the arrangement of landscape and garden,—amid the encouragement of those arts which embellish life, or expand a nation's industry and wealth,—oh, let that greatest of all causes be first in your mind—the cause of God and of eternal life. To relieve even the temporal wants of struggling industry; to cheer the home of the widow and the orphan; to remove the spiritual darkness of a benighted district; to be the humble but most honoured means of adding even one living stone to the glorious temple of the living God—these are more useful, greater, and more enduring works than to erect a Crystal Palace for the admiration of the world, to cast across an arm of the sea a great highway of communication, or to send beneath the broad ocean with the swiftness of thought the interchange of the messages of the nations. These works, no doubt, are wonderful,—suggestive of the greatness of man, who conceived and executed them,—suggestive of the infinite greatness of Him, whose creature man is. But they may disappoint the hopes which attended their formation, and are, after all, to perish; some, perhaps, like the dream of the night; all, however lasting, when "the earth and the works that are therein shall be burned up." The telegraph may oftener communicate the tidings of wrong and of disaster than of right and prosperity; may oftener convey the tones of anger or the message of defiance than those of peace and of good-will among men; and the glittering fabric, which in the bright anticipations of many was to usher in the brotherhood of nations, may only have been the harbinger of war and desolation. But the least work done for the love of Christ, and in the mind of a disciple, is never lost—it survives the wreck of nations and the ruin of the world: it follows the believer to his place of glory, it is never forgotten by Him who treasures up the actions of his saints.

And He does so precisely in the degree that they feel themselves undeserving of his goodness. With the bountiful Christian there is as little notion of merit in his works as we saw to exist in the mind of the bountiful Israelite. There is, in fact, no such word in his lips. He gladly turns from his merits, since God does not mention them; for what are they? Not the merit of eternal life—that he knows to be the gift of God in Christ; his merits are, separation from God, exclusion from heaven, the society of the lost. He knows of no other that belongs to him

CHAPTER XI

"THE FIELD IS THE WORLD."—*Matt*. xiii. 38.

WE have thus considered the main subject of our essay, What is the proportion of his means which the Christian should give to God? We will not, however, take our leave of it without some further reflections. The inquiry soon suggests itself to the mind in immediate connexion with our conclusion, If we are thus to give to God of our substance, in what manner does he expect us to bestow it? The answer opens a wide field, indeed, for reflection; but one over which we must now pass very swiftly. The briefest consideration of it will show us how many are the objects which call on us with loud voice for assistance, and attention to which redounds not only to the glory of God, but also to the best interests of man, even in this present life. In what manner the offerings of the ante-Mosaic times were expended we cannot certainly know, farther than that a portion of them at least were used in sacrifices to God, in hospitality to the stranger, and relief of the poor. Their use in Jewish times is pointed out by God himself in the law; while the New Testament, also, is explicit in informing us of the manner in which he requires his portion of the Christian's substance to be used. Various, indeed, are the objects which he lays before his people, and intrusts to their care and liberality. The Christian dispensation is intended for the world at large; the field of the Christian's sympathy and aid is co-extensive.

One brief reflection will not be out of place before we consider the subject of the present chapter. If we will but remember what is literally the fact, that in bestowing his assistance on its various objects, the Christian is only giving what belongs, not to himself, but to God, it will be apparent with how much greater authority he may be appealed to, and what far greater power such appeals will be likely to have. It is too frequently the case, that in the bestowal of his means in the service of God the notion of duty or obligation is often as little felt as it is in mere secular matters; and so it happens that what may be given to a cause eloquently pleaded is denied to the same cause when feebly put before us. Let the believer but reflect that in reality he has no right to withhold his assistance, that he is only allowed the discretion of selecting such objects as appear to him most to require aid, but that what he is asked for is not really his but God's, and he will see the propriety of altering his conduct, and to look less to the manner of advocacy, and more to the cause which is advocated.

In the expenditure of the Christian's offerings the support of the gospel ministry amongst ourselves occupies the leading place. They who are God's ambassadors to convey his message to man are his first objects in the distribution of the portion which he claims for himself. It is their right, which cannot be withheld from them without guilt. "They who preach the gospel should live of the gospel,"* by the same divine ordinance that gave to the Jewish priesthood a share of the altar sacrifices. They who have separated themselves from secular business to devote themselves to the service of their Redeemer, and the salvation of his wandering sheep, should not have their thoughts distracted from their calling by poverty and want at home. "Let it not be thought," says Mr James, speaking on this subject, "that what is given to a minister is a charitable donation; it is the payment of a just debt. It is what Christ claims for his faithful servants, and which cannot be withheld without robbery. I spurn for myself and my brethren the degrading apprehension that we are supported by charity. We are not clerical pensioners upon mere bounty. Our appeal is to justice, and if our claims are denied upon this ground, we refuse to plead before any other tribunal,

* 1 Cor. ix. 14.

and refer the matter to the great assize."* We know of no money so well spent as this, in whatever view regarded. It is the most direct homage to God, being given to his servants. It maintains the preaching of those grand truths, which are for the salvation of immortal souls. Even on the grounds of worldly expediency, it is more for the temporal interests of nations than any other expenditure. "Ye are the salt of the earth,"† said Christ to his apostles; and well and truly has Hooker called every ambassador of his "a pillar of that commonwealth wherein he faithfully serveth God."‡ Take away from a nation its gospel ministrations; silence the message of peace, and the word of exhortation, rebuke, and warning, and you will quickly reduce it to that utter degeneracy of mind and morals, which is the certain precursor of decay and ruin. It is righteousness which is the great exalter of one nation above another;§ and true religion, more, far more than any other thing, produces those principles of morality, of activity, of prudence and industry, of temperance and endurance, which make a people great at home, and respected and powerful abroad. What has preserved wealthy England from falling into that effeminacy of manners, that luxury and vicious indulgence, which extinguished the spirit of Greece and Rome, and paved the way for their downfall? Without hesitation we say, it is her possession,—too, partial, alas!—of true religion. What the Latin poet said to Imperial Rome may with much greater truth be said of Britain:—" Thou bearest rule, because thou submittest thy will to heaven."‖ To the possession of the truth and to its influence we refer, under God, the greatness of our country, and while she retains them we will not fear her overthrow.

The education of the young of our land, not merely in secular learning, but far more in instruction taken from God's holy word, is another leading object which God has placed before us. No wise man will esteem as of little importance the education of youth for their calling in this present world; but most assuredly,

* J. A. James, "Christian Times," pp. 68, 69.   † Matt. v. 13.
‡ Hooker, "Eccl. Pol." v. ii. p. 413.   § Prov. xiv. 34.
‖ Horace, lib. iii. od. 6.

too, there is no man of real wisdom who will not hold it of infinitely greater moment to train the soul for heaven. If it be the mark of a contracted and mistaken mind to despise and neglect man's education for his position in this life, it is the mark of a mind immeasurably more narrow and mistaken to neglect the moral training and the religious knowledge without which man cannot be fitted for his heavenly inheritance. And therefore it is that the infallible guide-book of the Christian is so explicit and so earnest, " Thou shalt teach them diligently unto thy children."* The scriptural school, then, in which the poor of our land and of our people may learn of their Saviour, and be taught to aspire from the midst of their poverty and lowliness to a place in his kingdom, is a fit object of our sympathy and assistance.

The propagation of the religion of the Saviour throughout the world by the circulation of Holy Scripture and missionary exertion is another grand object, which God has commended to our care. " Preach the Gospel to every creature,"† is the divine command : " be fellow-helpers " to those who " go forth for Christ's sake "‡ is the duty of all Christians, according to St. John. This subject naturally divides itself into efforts to evangelise the heathen, to turn the heart of Israel to that Lord and Messiah whom they have denied, and to reclaim from the superstitions and idolatries into which it has fallen a large portion of the professing Christian Church. We need not dwell on our duty of evangelising heathen lands. No Christian can for a moment doubt his duty on this head, or its urgent need to those who, " being without God, are also without hope in the world."§ Over how large a portion of mankind the shadow of heathen darkness still rests, it is fearful to contemplate. As little doubt can there be of our duty to proclaim in the Jewish ear the Gospel of our Saviour. It is true they have, and hold with wonderful tenacity, their ancient law, and that in that law the Gospel is preached. But, alas ! the veil is on their hearts when they read the law, and they do not see that Christ crucified, as well as glorious, is its

---

* Deut. vi. 7. † Matt. xxviii. 19.
‡ 3 John, 7, 8. § Eph. ii. 12.

hope and its fulfilment. They come, then, under the class of those who, having not the Gospel, require its proclamation; and sure we are that right dear in the sight of the Lord is their work who seek to bring to Jesus the people that once were, and will again be " the apple of his eye,"* Nor can it be doubted that it is the believer's duty to reclaim from error fallen Churches. Prominent among these is that gigantic Church of Papal Rome, which has extended her sway, and spread her corruption, over the earth. To her, as their proper object, point all those various marks which inspiration has given us, that we may know, guard against, and shun the grand apostasy from the faith. And though some sound and earnest upholders of the truth may doubt if Rome be indeed *the* predicted apostasy, none of them doubt that she has in many most vital points departed from the faith, and is " a blind leader of the blind." Now, departure from vital truth, and choice of falsehood instead, is laid down in the Scriptures as fatal to salvation. Heresies are classed with the other works of the flesh, as, when persevered in, excluding from eternal life. The warnings of Christ's faithful apostles, and of the great Shepherd himself, against unfaithful teachers within the fold, are more solemn, and their denunciations of the terrible guilt of such persons are even more severe, than against the infidelity of the avowed unbeliever. Nor is there in the whole Scripture a more encouraging promise held out than to those who are the honoured instruments of restoring such: " Brethren, if any of you err from the truth, and one convert him, let him know that he which converteth the sinner from the error of his ways shall save a soul from death, and shall hide a multitude of sins."†

The suffering poor of every communion and opinion, and more especially those " of the household of faith," are another object, which we cannot neglect to consider, in our distribution of what is God's. We do not speak in support of an indiscriminate system of almsgiving to every miserable-looking object that claims it, which is as much opposed to the teaching of Scripture as to the maxims of a sound political economy. Whatever tends to encou-

* Deut. xxxii. 10.   † James, v. 19.

rage a system of idleness, and to lead men to prefer a life of mendicancy to that of honest and laborious industry, certainly finds no countenance from that Book which has commanded us to labour on six days of the week,* and has ordained that "if any would not work, neither should he eat." Indiscriminate almsgiving, therefore, or the support in a lazy idleness of those who can but will not labour, is no part of a Christian's duty. But still there are always cases, even in countries where the fullest State provision is made for the relief of poverty, which call upon the merciful for their aid, and which the merciful God requires us not to disregard. They may be known by the judicious and inquiring; by those who will take a little trouble to discriminate between real and fictitious distress,— between the difficulties of struggling industry and sinful sloth. There are, in fact, few of that class who come under the title of the poor, who at some period or other of their lives are not in circumstances which justly entitle them to the sympathy of their more fortunate brethren. Want of employment or a season of sickness will sometimes deprive the most industrious and deserving of a sufficiency for their support. It is at such times particularly that the hand of kindness should be stretched out to their assistance. A generous and sympathising conduct on the part of the upper towards the lower orders, as it is in accordance with God's will, so it is the best preservative of society against the levelling doctrines of spoilation so prevalent in the present day. It is the gorgeous luxury and selfish carelessness of the poor by those above them, that far more than anything else produce that envy and hatred which pave the way for the introduction into their minds of anti-social principles, which in times of trial issue in the overthrow of government and order. A little love, and kindness, and sympathy, if generally displayed by the independent towards their humbler brethren, would be far more effectual for the preservation of property and society than stringent laws and armed millions.

Such are the objects which God has in his word placed before Christians for their support. On the upholding of these he expects

* Exod. xx. 9.

them to bestow that portion of their income which is especially claimed by him. And we thus perceive that the tenth, which belongs to God, is not too much for the purposes for which it is designed; that if it be on our part due to him as an acknowledgment of his bounty and sovereignty, so he has marked out an ample and most worthy field for its employment. And so long as any of these objects require our aid, so long can no Christian plead the smallest excuse for withholding from the Lord his right. Until struggling industry cease to advance its claim, and age and sickness supplicate not for relief; until ample instruction has been provided for the youth of our land, and each ministering servant and ambassador of Christ can say that he who supplies the spiritual wants of his flock has had his own temporal wants fully answered; until in casting our eyes over the wide world we can see no dark spot to which the glorious Gospel has not been sent: until this has been done, and done well, no Christian can pretend to say that he may withdraw his share from the treasury of God. Which of these great objects is properly or fully supported? The answer, alas! must be, "None." When has any one of them met its becoming assistance? We must reply, "Never." No man, therefore, can say with truth that he knows not on what to expend that portion which God claims for himself.

If such are the general calls on all Christians, we will also find abundant to require the free-will offerings of the wealthy. Who that is disposed in his heart out of an overflowing abundance to give abundantly, but will with little pains find some befitting object on which to God's glory he may expend a portion of his riches? He will fix his eyes but too readily on some neglected district of his own land, perhaps in his own immediate neighbourhood, which, though situate in a so-called Christian country, is almost as destitute of Gospel privileges as if it lay within a heathen land. What more suitable, then, for a wealthy individual, or a number of such united, than to devote their care to this benighted spot? At their cost let a house of God arise in the midst of it, elegant in structure, while devoid of meretricious ornament, whose spire may point to heaven, and whose open doors may invite to prayer and to praise. Let some faithful minister of Christ be chosen to conduct its ministrations; by a holy life and a pastoral care to attract the careless and the godless; to win to and keep for the great Bishop of souls his wandering sheep. Let an endowment provide, so far as man can provide for futurity, that the Gospel sound shall never be silent within those walls; that when its pious builders have mingled with the dust, and the lips that first within them testified of Christ are hushed in the grave, the same "faithful saying, worthy of all acceptation," may yet be heard, and "the people that come after" may learn to praise the Lord. It was no mean recommendation of the centurion to Christ the report of the Jews, "He hath built us a synagogue."* And, surely, the pious action of the Christian, who in honour of his Lord raises a house to his name, and provides for it a gospel ministration, is a most suitable object for his free-will offering, and will bring down in the goodness of God a blessing upon him and his.

Or with equal propriety may the man of wealth devote a portion of it to the erection of a school-house, and provision for the instruction of youth, where such has not been adequately provided. Second in importance to none is such a work. It is the just observation of the poet Wordsworth, "The child is father of the man," which is but another form of what Solomon said long before, "Train up a child in the way that he should go, and when he is old he will not depart from it."† For what we sow we must expect to reap. From an ignorant youth we must look for a population a prey to the vile purposes of the designing and the crafty; from such as have only received a secular learning we may expect a population armed with power for evil, and in the pride of unsanctified intellect inclined to infidelity. From those alone whose education has been based upon divine truth may we hope for a people the pride and strength of their country. Such, to an extent probably unequalled elsewhere, were, and we trust in a great measure still are, the youth and manhood of Scotland.

Many, besides, are the ways in which the substance of the rich may be expended to the glory of God. In the erection of an hospital for the sick, or an almshouse for the aged and infirm, who

---

* Luke, vii. 5. † Prov. xxii. 6.

have perhaps seen better days, and been reduced through no fault of theirs; in the provision for the orphan, whom death may have thrown helpless on the world: in such ways as these riches cease to be "the unrighteous mammon." Or wealth may cast a generous eye upon some man of genius, whose soaring intellect is cramped by that old complaint of mental power, the "*res angustæ domi*," domestic poverty. Brought out of want, this man may apply his mighty mind on labours which shall enrich unborn generations. To the liberality of Robert Boyle we principally owe the publication of "Saunderson's Book on Conscience," and "Burnet's History of the Reformation." To the discriminating kindness of Bishop Jewel we owe it that Richard Hooker was not a tradesman. To similar conduct we owe the bringing forward of many of our greatest men and their immortal works.

Such are some of those objects which indeed commend themselves to the attention of those to whom God has given riches. These are works worthy of men and of Christians. These are works which give glory to God, and procure an enduring fame. Oh, how far more worthy of man than the extravagant and idle freaks in which wealth sometimes indulges! In ancient times we read of one whose profuse luxury has handed down a name which would otherwise have been forgotten. Of the Roman Apicius we are told by Seneca that he expended on his table nearly a million sterling of our money; that he kept an academy of gourmands, and made the invaluable discovery that the tongue of the red-wing was a delicacy; that he sailed to the coast of Africa to eat crayfish, and not finding them so good as he expected, returned without deigning to land. It is but too true that Christian times could furnish many examples of an expenditure as foolish and far more wicked than this. Nobler, too, are those works which we have mentioned than the greatest undertakings, which have not the glory of God for their special object. The record of these is kept on earth, and is a fading one; the record of those is in heaven.

CHAPTER XII.

"IT IS MORE BLESSED TO GIVE THAN TO RECEIVE."—*Acts*, xx. 35.

In speaking in the preceding chapter of those objects which God has commended to his people's care, we adverted to some reasons which show our own great personal interest in them, and which should therefore make us the more willing to support them. We now propose, as briefly as possible, to place before our readers the various motives which should influence them in giving of their substance to the Lord.

Having throughout the Essay described the bestowing a portion of our increase in the direct cause of God as being a tribute to his sovereignty, a confession that he is the true owner of all things, and an act of obedience to his express commandment, we will not further dwell on these motives, the first and leading ones in the Christian's mind. The feeling that all things come from God, and still belong to him, is at the foundation of the creature's worship of his Creator; and the disposition to obey unreservedly and from the heart the will of God, whether in believing what he places before us as the objects of our faith, or performing what he requires us to practise, is after all the great distinction between those who really are his and those who know him not, by whatever name they may be called. The first motive, then, in the believer's mind in the gift of his substance is this, that God his Maker and Father in Christ Jesus requires it from him, in token that he and his are God's.

Another strong motive with the believer will be gratitude. "What shall I render to the Lord for all his benefits to me?"* is a question that often rises to his mind. Gratitude is indeed the very essence of the Christian's spirit, the unfailing sign of that soul which has been redeemed from death and brought to life eternal. How shall it attain its high aspirations, and find a field of exercise for its ardent longings? How shall the soul, which the "love of

* Psalm cxvi. 12.

Christ has constrained," show the love which it feels in return? It cannot exhibit it in self-chosen acts, in works of whatever kind, whether painful or otherwise, exceeding duty. It were too presumptuous for the creature to choose the worship it should pay to God,—to bind the approval of the All-wise to its self-elected acts. When the believer, then, reflects on all that God has done for him, from the first-work of creation to his wondrous love in redemption,—when he reflects truly, though, alas! most inadequately, on his infinite obligations—when he casts about him to discover what return he can make,—he finds the only acceptable return he can render is his cheerful and joyful acquiescence in the path of defined duty. "Ye are not your own," said Paul to the Corinthians, "for ye are bought with a price; therefore glorify God in your body and your spirit, *which are his*."* The grateful mind then seeks to know the will of God, that it may do it from the heart. In the gift of his substance, as in other things, he recognises God's expressed pleasure, and that which to the covetous is a reluctant act, gratitude makes delightful, and love makes easy, to the servant of the Lord.

Godliness is true wisdom, even in regard of man's present advantage. Indeed none but he who glorifies God is wise for himself. So it is in regard of that duty which we are now considering. The giving in God's cause of that which he requires from us is assuredly the best safeguard we can have for the safety of our substance, and the best guarantee for its increase. Who can lay his hands on wordly possessions, and stay them with him at his pleasure? They can elude the grasp of their most devoted lover in a thousand ways that are under his control whom all things obey. They have truly the fabled power of Proteus, and none but God has the art of securing them. He has himself made special promises to those who honour him with their substance and expend it to his glory: "Bring ye all the tithe into the storehouse, that there may be meat in my house. And prove me now herewith, saith the Lord of Hosts, if I will not open you the windows of heaven, and pour you out a blessing, that there shall not be room enough to receive it."† Such is the promise of God

* 1 Cor. vi. 20. † Mal. iii. 10.

on which the believer relies, but from which the unfaithful mind turns with distrust. Yet how foolishly! What hold have we or any one on his possessions? Are we rich and powerful? What warrant have we that before a year is passed, " our riches may not have made to themselves wings, and flown away;" our greatness only made our fall the more remarkable? Or are we dependent on our vigour of mind and strength of body for support? From whom comes this vigour of body and mind? From Him whom we are perhaps defrauding of his claim. Do we not then provoke him to withdraw his gifts, and in that case where are we? Wiser surely, even for this world, is the man who with the confiding spirit of a child walks in the path of duty, and leaves himself simply to the care of God. He has a power on his side which orders all things; a wisdom which provides for every want; a love more tender of his safety than the fondest parent's upon earth. "That which is presented to God," Hooker says, "is neither lost, nor unfruitfully bestowed, but sanctifies the whole mass; and he by receiving a little undertakes to bless all. In which consideration the Jews were accustomed to call their tithes the hedge of their riches."* It is the remark of the greatest philosopher of England in one of his Essays, that great lovers of themselves "are frequently unfortunate. And whereas they have all their life sacrificed to themselves, they become in the end themselves sacrifices to the inconstancy of fortune, whose wings they thought by their self-wisdom to have pinioned."† And in exact agreement with this, the writer has heard a friend of his, one who has seen much of the world, and observed it very closely, remark as the fruit of his observation, that in the trying times, which have passed and are passing over this country, he has seen those who have been accustomed to give freely of their substance in the cause of God surmounting their difficulties, and those who refused God's claim sinking beneath them. It is but the fulfilment of God's promise, and we need not wonder at it. The examples of Scripture present us with the same result. We will refer briefly but to one, that of Jacob. His vow at Bethel, doubtless, was performed, and what was the consequence? Listen to the words of the sons of

* Eccl. Pol. lib. vi. s. 79.   † Bacon's " Essays," No. 23.

selfish Laban: "Jacob hath taken away all that was our father's."* Hear his own confession of God's bounty: "With my staff I passed over this Jordan, and now I am become two bands."† Regard the wonderful history of Joseph's life, a life fore-ordered for this among other purposes, to supply to the faithful patriarch abundance in the days of dearth. And when the time for dying came, and Jacob from the conclusion of life reviewed in memory its eventful scenes, he included this in his most beautiful description of the character of Jehovah, "The God which fed me all my life long unto this day."‡

Again, the practice of this duty is the best remedy against the sins of covetousness on the one hand, and extravagance on the other. The exercise of any grace is the most effectual safeguard against the prevalence of its opposite vice. It is, indeed, the only effectual safeguard. "Break off thy sins by righteousness," said Daniel to Nebuchadnezzar, "and thy iniquities by showing mercy to the poor."§ The heart of man cannot be unoccupied; it must be the seat either of good or evil. Against that deadly sin of covetousness, then, the best resource is a glad compliance with God's precept in the bestowal of our substance. Nor is this to be thought a trifling reason to influence us to this duty. Most insidious, most fatal, and most common, is the sin of covetousness. "The disease," says Dr. Chalmers, "is as near to universal as it is virulent. Wealth is the goddess whom all the world worshippeth. There is many a city in our empire, of which, with an eye of apostolical discernment, it may be seen that it is almost wholly given over to idolatry."|| It begins, perhaps, with the specious plea of providing for the present and future wants of one's family, and passing through intermediate stages, ends not unfrequently in being idolised simply for itself, until we see the fearful picture of the miser, devoted to the acquisition of money without any reference to the gratifications it is capable of procuring, and who, delighted in the possession of imaginary riches, lives and dies amid the realities of the direst poverty. Nor is it to be thought

* Gen. xxxi. 1.   † Gen. xxxii. 10.   ‡ Gen. xlviii. 15.
§ Dan. iv. 27. || Chalmers' Works, vol. vi. p. 204.

an unimportant consideration, that the exercise of this grace tends very materially to check that thoughtless extravagance, which is as much opposed to the teaching of God's word as it is productive of misery in this present life. If the Christian is indeed to allocate a fixed and important portion of his income in the cause of God, this will almost of necessity compel him to look somewhat closely to his means and to his expenditure, lest by carelessness he be compelled to break in upon that portion which he now feels to belong to God.

Again, the practice of Christian liberality and kindness is most conducive to our own happiness. It was He who knew the human heart, and the deep joy of a bountiful spirit, who said, "It is more blessed to give than to receive."* It must be more blessed; for it is to be like God, the source and fountain of blessedness. He is the great Giver from whom all receive, and to whom none can give. His joy, as relates to all without himself, consists in bestowing. The creation and preservation and redemption of his creatures gives satisfaction to the infinite mind. It is so too with man, in so far as he has not lost, and in proportion as he has been restored to his original condition, as made "in the image of God." Behold the deep joy of a mother over her infant incapable as yet of making any return. The anguish of her travail is forgotten in the delight of having brought a child into the world; and, perhaps, no subsequent joy at its filial affection or its success in life is so heartfelt as that with which she affords it nourishment, or bends over the cradle of her child, who, whether waking or sleeping, is unconscious of her love and care. And so in other matters where the heart is right. We are sure that Howard, the philanthropist, was one of the happiest of men. We could never dream of comparing the happiness of him who dwells all his life long amid scenes of comfort and of elegance, and never sacrifices an iota of his personal convenience to the welfare of others, to his who, out of an ample fortune, spent little of it on himself, who left the lovely scenes of England's rural life, in which none took more sincere pleasure, to pass his life in visiting the gloomy prisons

* Acts, xx. 35.

and the noisome lazarettos of the world, to alleviate the sorrows of suffering humanity, regardless of the toil to which he was exposed, and of the danger to which at last he fell a victim. The Christian poet could enter into his feelings—could rest assured that he was no fit object for pity, but rather of envy, whose love for man led him

> " To quit the bliss his rural scenes bestow,
> To seek a nobler amid scenes of woe." *

Where selfishness and covetousness have not dried up and extinguished the benevolent affections, there is, indeed, a truer satisfaction in their exercise than in the pleasure we experience in receiving. It was such a feeling that impelled one, whose name deserved to be remembered, the Portuguese Andrada,† to continue in an African prison, and laden with fetters, that he might continue to console his fellow-prisoners. This he preferred to his own personal freedom. Of Bishop Burnet an anecdote is told which illustrates this truth.‡ One of his parishioners was distrained for debt, and came to him for some small assistance, when the bishop inquired of him how much would again set him up in his trade. The debtor named the sum, which a servant was immediately ordered to pay him. " Sir," said the domestic, " it is all we have in the house." " Well, well," replied Burnet, " pay it to this poor man ; you do not know the pleasure there is in making a man glad." We have seen already in Scripture the deep joy of Israel on those occasions when the nation was most forward in its offerings to God. As Shakspeare has beautifully described the bounty of Mark Anthony by the expression, "There was no winter in it," so in him to whom God has given the grace to be a " cheerful giver" there can be no winter of gloom and discontent, the bountiful spirit is a perpetual source of satisfaction, his good deeds to others, for Christ's sake, return into his bosom an hundredfold.

---

* Cowper's poem on Charity.   † Rose, " Biog. Dict."
‡ History of His Own Times, p. 4.

CHAPTER XIII.

"BEWARE OF COVETOUSNESS."—*Luke*, xii. 18.

HAVING brought our subject to its close, it only remains for us to say a very few words. The subject of which we have endeavoured to treat is beyond any doubt one of great importance, both as regards the honour of God and the state of our own souls before him. On the one hand, there is his cause to uphold and advance in a world which knows him not. Shall we refuse to uphold it? On the other hand, there is the fatal tendency of covetousness, a sin most insidious and most prevalent to guard against, if we would enter into life.

"Who is covetous?" is a question often asked, but to which very few indeed can be brought to reply, "I am the man." And yet covetousness is a sin spoken of in the Scriptures in numberless places, described as most common, and as possessing a deadly power over the soul, which has admitted it. It would then be a great advantage if we could by any means help ourselves in finding out whether we may be ourselves, without suspecting it, more or less under its dominion. To value riches is not to be covetous.* They are the gift of God, and, like every gift of his, good in themselves, and capable of a good use. They are among the other talents which have been bestowed by the Creator on his creature. To overvalue riches,—to put them into a position in our hearts which God did not design them to fill,— this is covetousness. The sin to which it is most allied, and with which it is indeed identical, is idolatry.† Now the essence of idolatry is the preference of the creature to the Creator, in whatever way this may appear. Idolatry causes man to abandon God for something else, either openly or at heart; and when man turns to God, he also leaves his idols.‡ We will accordingly find that that love of riches, which is branded in Scripture as covetousness, is such a love of them, and such a regard for them,

---

* Prov. x. 22. † Col. iii. 5. ‡ Ezek. xliv. 10; 1 Thess. i. 9.

as takes from man his trust in God, and transfers it to his possessions. Jeremiah, warning the covetous, says, "Let not the rich man glory in his riches, but let him that glorieth glory in this, that he understandeth and knoweth the Lord."* David describes the covetous man as he that "made not God his strength, but trusted in the abundance of his riches:"† and so our Lord described the covetous as those "that trust in riches."‡ But then the question comes—How is this trust in riches and distrust in God to be known? How is the covetousness of the heart to be distinguished? We know of no test more effectual than this, namely, are we willing, or do we refuse, to part with such of our substance as God requires at our hands? If we are willing to do so, not in any self-righteous spirit, as though by this means we made God our debtor, but as obedient children, preferring his will to ours, and taking him as our sufficient and unfailing portion, then we may reasonably conclude that wealth is not our idol. If we refuse to do so—if we cannot bear, at his command, to part with a portion, or with the whole of our substance, in reliance on his promise of provision, it is then but too plain that we have placed riches in God's room, and are idolators of them. The ruler that came to Jesus was a covetous man, because being commanded by his Lord to part with all he had, and refusing to do so, he showed that his heart was more set on them than on God, and his trust in them stronger. He saw more to confide in in his houses, and lands, and money, than in that which Christ would provide for him instead, implied in the words, "Come and follow me."§ The Israelite was covetous that refused to pay to God his tithe, because he so indicated his preference of present worldly substance to the care and promise of God; he thereby virtually said, "If I give up this, and confide in God, it will be worse for me."‖ Now if we have established the principal object of this Essay, and shown that our obligations to God are at least as great as those of Israel were, it will then be plain that we have for ourselves the same test of covetousness. If God requires of us a tenth for himself, and tells us, in lieu

* Jer. ix. 23, 24.   † Psalm lii. 7.   ‡ Mark, x. 24.
§ Luke, xviii. 22.   ‖ Mal. iii. 14.

thereof, to accept his care, protection, and love, as our ample provision, and we refuse his offer, and prefer our visible and tangible means to his promises, then we think that the sin of covetousness attaches itself to us.

Let us, then, well weigh what has been said upon this subject. There seems to be much in favour of the conclusion we have come to, and are ignorant that any serious objection can be raised against it; for, surely, when the cause of God requires it, and when that cause has been intrusted to us, we can give no good reason for bestowing less upon it than it was Israel's duty and Israel's privilege to give. We would, then, in conclusion, seriously and affectionately put it to the reader's conscience to ask himself, after fairly and dispassionately reviewing the reasons we have given, Is there force in them or not? If it be allowed that there is, we will then only ask, Is nothing to follow from this allowance? Is it to be on our part a nominal admission, of God's claim, but a practical independence of its authority, like the empty homage which a powerful vassal or province pays to a feeble superior? But God is not a weak king, and let us beware how we trifle with his claims. Let us rather, however, regard his love and kindness as our strongest motive to obedience, and to Him who made and preserved and redeemed us, let us gladly give of that which he has given us.

THE
Scripture Rule of Religious Contribution:

OR,

IN WHAT PROPORTION SHOULD A BELIEVER IN REVELATION
DEDICATE HIS PROPERTY TO THE CAUSE OF GOD?

BY THE

REV. JAMES MORGAN, D.D.

BELFAST.

"See that ye abound in this grace also."—2 *Cor.* viii. 7.

CONTENTS.

Chap. I. THE BIBLE.
II. ABRAHAM.
III. JACOB.
IV. MOSES.
   1. The first tithe.
   2. The second tithe.
   3. Tithe for the poor.
   4. The Levites' tithe.
   5. Stated services.
   6. Various sacrifices.
   7. Free-will offerings.
V. THE DAY OF PENTECOST.
VI. MACEDONIA AND CORINTH.
Chap. VII. THE FIRST DAY OF THE WEEK.
VIII. EXAMPLES.
   1. The Tabernacle.
   2. The Temple.
   3. The widow of Sarepta.
   4. The widow's mite.
IX. MISCELLANEOUS.
   1. Precepts.
   2. Warnings.
   3. Promises.
   4. Prophecies.
X. CONCLUSION.

CHAPTER I.

THE BIBLE.

" The law of the Lord is perfect, converting the soul: the testimony of the Lord is sure, making wise the simple."—Ps. xix. 7.

"To the law and to the testimony; if they speak not according to this word, it is because there is no light in them." It is in the spirit and under the solemn impression of this divine testimony the subject of contributing our property to the cause of God should be discussed and determined. To "Search the Scriptures" is a duty commanded by Christ, and comprehends not merely an investigation of what is taught respecting himself, but also of all the duty which we are required to render him. What may we learn *of* him? and, What shall we do *for* him? are both questions to be referred to the authority of Scripture, and to be decided by it. "What saith the Lord" on the duty of devoting our substance to him?—this is the inquiry now to be entered upon, and this is the manner in which it is to be pursued to a satisfactory conclusion.

At the outset of such an investigation it may be necessary to consider whether it has pleased God to lay down, in his Word, any specific rule of religious contribution. Is there any Scripture law upon the subject? Or has it been left to every one to determine the matter for himself, according to his circumstances, and agreeably to his own sense of duty? Most assuredly men have acted as if God had given no specific rule. So far as appears to the eye of an observer, there does not seem to pervade the Christian Church any anxious concern, any jealousy of spirit lest there should be a law of God in this matter which is not obeyed. Even the public teaching of the pulpit and the press has not given a uniform and "certain sound." A spirit of hesitation and doubtfulness has prevailed extensively. There have been noble exceptions, in both the principles inculcated and the practices pursued by many persons; yet as to the prevailing views and habits of the members of the Christian Church, it is notorious that they have not recognised the duty of entertaining any decided views or of pursuing any determined practice. Go into any of our most enlightened and best organised churches—meet its members as they come away with warm hearts and weeping eyes from the table of the Lord—propose to each of them the plain question, How much of your income do you believe it to be your duty to give to the Lord, and in what proportion is it your habit to employ it? and who does not know that generally no answer could be obtained? The majority, it is to be feared, have not considered, far less determed, the question, "How much owest thou to thy Lord?" And as to those who have sought and discovered and walked in the right path, alas! it may be said, "few there be that find it."

A few years ago a great impulse was given to the cause of Christian generosity by the publication of a volume under the title of "Mammon; or, Covetousness the Sin of the Christian Church. By the Rev. John Harris." In that volume the following sentences occur at pages 245-7 (19th thousand), "What *proportion* of our income ought we to devote to charitable uses? If Christian love be permitted to answer this question, and assign the amount, there is no reason to fear a too scanty allowance. On the other hand, if selfishness be suffered to decide, there is ground to fear that even an inspired reply, could such be obtained, would be heard only to be overruled. Besides which, the Gospel of Christ, in harmony with its great design of establishing a reign of love, leaves its followers to assess themselves. It puts into their hands, indeed, a claim upon their property, but leaves the question, *how much?* to be determined by themselves. In assisting them to fill the blank with the proper assessment, the only step which it takes is to point them to the cross of Christ; and, while there eye is fixed there in admiring love, to say, 'How much owest thou unto thy Lord?' 'Freely ye have received, freely give.'

"It is observable that Abraham and Jacob, on particular occasions, voluntarily devoted to God—what afterwards became a divine law for the Jewish nation—a *tenth* of their property. Without implying that their example has any obligation on us, we may venture to say that one *tenth* of our whole income is an approved proportion for charity for those who, with *so* doing, are able to support themselves and families. For the more opulent, and especially for those who have no families, a larger proportion would be equally easy. For some, one-half would be too little; while, for others, a twentieth, or even a fiftieth, would require the nicest frugality and care. Indeed, of many among the poor, it may be said, that if they give *anything* they give their *share*,— they *cast in more* than all their brethren." It is cheerfully and gratefully acknowledged, that the volume from which these sentences have been extracted proved to be seasonable and salutary in no inconsiderable degree. It is eloquent, earnest, and effective. On this special topic, however, to which the quoted passage refers—the proportion of contribution to income—a few strictures may be permitted and are required. Without at all entering on other exceptions which have been taken to the volume on the ground of a defective statement of Christian doctrine, its views of proportionate giving may be fairly disputed. It is worthy of observation, that in the whole book this is the only passage directly referring to that branch of the subject. So far therefore as it is concerned, that topic requires yet to be discussed. It is at least too important to be so slightly dismissed. There is, besides, a hesitation in the manner of setting forth what the law of the Scriptures is upon the subject which greatly weakens its force. It is not misrepresenting it to say, that it recognises no specific law of giving now binding on the conscience and practice of the Christian. It is taught, that "the Gospel of Christ leaves the question, *how much?* to be determined by Christians themselves,"—that while "we may venture to say, that *one tenth* of our whole income is an approved proportion of charity," this is to be understood only of "those who, with *so* doing, are able to support themselves and families,"—that there are some for whom to give " a twentieth or fiftieth would require the nicest frugality and care,"—and that " of many among the poor it may be said, if they give *anything* they give their share." Are these representations in accordance with the revealed will of God? We hold that they are inconsistent with it. It is our belief that a law for the regulation of giving is laid down in the Scriptures of the Old and New Testament. It is our conviction that no one, taking these for his guide, can devote less than a tenth of his available income to the cause of God. He may give more, as much more as he will or his circumstances warrant, but less he cannot possibly give and act consistently with the inspired standard of man's duty. The case of a pauper in a poor-house may be pleaded against this view; but what income has he? He has none, and where there is no income there is no obligation. Let that pauper, however, receive a shilling from the passing visitant, and he is bound to recognise the claim of God to at least the tenth. Yes! and he may devote it to him with as high a principle and as holy an affection as he who gives his thousands out of his great abundance. Or we may be told of others who are sunk in debt and under obligations which they are unable to discharge; but what comes to them is not their own, it is the just property of their creditors, and can only pass through their hands to them. Every man must be able to say with David, in his religious contributions, " I have of mine own proper good given to the house of my God." Let the subject be cleared of all extraneous matter—let the question stand in its simplicity. What proportion of his income should a believer in Revelation dedicate to the cause of God? And without hesitation it is affirmed, he cannot consistently give less than a tenth. It will be observed the phrase, *a believer in Revelation*, is used designedly, for our appeal is to the whole word of God. The Jewish and the Christian Scriptures are not to be paraded against each other as though they inculcated different or contrary doctrines. They are together the exposition of one system of religion. They contain the records of various dispensations of religion, but the religion is throughout one and the same. The same moral law pervades the Old and New Testament. Their principles are identical. These are taught in a peculiar manner under the ancient economy, and they are brought out differently under the present dispensation. Essentially and substantially they teach the same lessons. Our inquiry, therefore, will lead us to investigate the instructions of both on the subject of giving to the Lord. Beginning with the early intimations of the divine will, we shall be carried forward to the meridian light of the last and best economy. The subject is regarded to be so important as to have a prominent place in all parts of divine Revelation. Our object shall be to compare Scripture with Scripture, and so learn the will of God. Their scattered light will be viewed apart, and then, brought together, shall be made to converge their rays on the one subject. Thus in the light of the Lord we hope we shall see light.

In conclusion, if God has given a law, it ought to be known and obeyed. Great injury has arisen to the cause of Christ from the indistinct and undecided views which have prevailed respecting the duty of religious contribution. We may give, or we may withhold; we may give little or much, every man may do what is right in his own eyes—this is the doctrine which has guided the Church too long. On the contrary, we hold that "God hath spoken once, yea twice;" that he has plainly made known his will in his word; that he has given a law to regulate the conduct of Jews and Gentiles; that no believer in his word can consistently give less than the tenth of his income to the cause of God; that he ought to know this, and act upon it; and that he cannot neglect to do so without sin. For these statements, we "bring forth our strong reasons" from the divine record. While we do so, let us "tremble at the commandment of the Lord." Great evil and neglect have arisen from the members of the Church being hitherto "at ease in Zion" on this important question. May much good arise from the prevalence of another and a better spirit! Something needs to be done. There is indecision in the counsels of the Church, and feebleness in its efforts. Surely if its members saw their duty and the law that God has given to regulate it, they would be roused to more consistent and vigorous efforts. If any are offended with our plainness, we can only plead the word of the Lord. "We believe, therefore we have spoken." "We speak as unto wise men, judge ye what we say." The time demands new views of duty, and all we ask is that the members of the Church of Christ shall honestly inquire, "Lord, what wilt thou have me to do?" Let us adopt the Psalmist's prayer in reference to the duty into which we are about to inquire, "Show me thy ways, O Lord; teach me thy paths. Lead me in thy truth, and teach me; for thou art the God of my salvation; on thee do I wait all the day." If "whatever is not of faith is sin," we must either be guided by the law and authority of God's word in giving to Him of our substance, or our conduct in this respect must meet with the reproof, "Who hath required this at your hands?"

CHAPTER II.

ABRAHAM.

"He gave him tithes of all."—Gen. xiv. 20.

THE accomplished author of "Mammon," referring to the conduct of Abraham and Jacob in giving a tenth of their property to God, uses the phrase, "without implying that their example has any obligation on us." The meaning of this saying is by no means clear. It would be injustice to interpret it to signify that, in the writer's opinion, the example of Abraham and Jacob should have no influence upon us, although such a meaning might fairly be ascribed to the terms employed. It must be explained as conveying the sentiment that in this particular case we are not bound to imitate their example. Even so understood, however, its correctness may be questioned. We cannot but regard it as one of those unsound interpretations which prevail so generally on the subject of religious contribution. For in these views this distinguished author is far from being singular. In an admirable sermon preached before the London Missionary

Society, by the Rev. Dr. Brown of Edinburgh, so long ago as the year 1821, on the duty of "pecuniary contribution to religious purposes," the following sentiment is expressed : " From the circumstances of the *tenth* of the income of the Israelites being appropriated by express divine law to pious purposes, it is surely a fair conclusion, that among the middle and higher classes, in all ordinary cases, Christians should not devote a less proportion of their worldly substance to the service of God." Why is the rule confined to the middle and higher classes ? It is our conviction the Spirit of God did not so intend it. The rule is one of universal obligation. To make this apparent is a prominent design of these pages. And it is to enforce the necessity of proving and confirming such a view that reference is made at all to such eminent servants of the Lord as have been named. Their views are, in our judgment, defective, and not sufficiently explicit. We think they have not done full justice to the plainness and authority of the inspired rule and practice. We are deeply solicitous to place the subject in what seems to us to be the proper aspect, to lay the duty of giving to God on its right basis, and with this object the following remarks are submitted on the example of Abraham.

It is by no means a right principle to approve and imitate whatever is recorded to have been done by the eminent servants of God in other ages. Abraham did many things that were reprehensible, and they are narrated, with their consequences, for our warning. Still, it is written, " Be ye followers of them who through faith and patience inherit the promises," and Abraham is named as one of them. A careful consideration of each case must be entered into in order to ascertain whether it is designed to be an example for imitation or a beacon for warning. Its history will usually enable us to determine. As to the specific case before us, that of Abraham, there can be no hesitation how it is to be understood ; it is expressly recorded that we may go and do likewise. We are bound to imitate him. Of this position the evidence is full and clear.

An inspired writer in the New Testament expresses approval of Abraham's conduct : " Consider how great this man was, unto whom even the patriarch Abraham gave the tenth of the spoils." He speaks with high respect of his character, as a distinguished servant of the Most High, and in this particular instance applauds what he did. Although, therefore, the incident is introduced from the life of the patriarch for the illustration of another subject, yet the act which he performed is approved, and in similar circumstances we are called upon to act in the same manner.

There is something, indeed, very peculiar and impressive in the record of this part of Abraham's conduct. It is the first notice contained in the Scriptures of the dedication of any distinct proportion of property to God. This circumstance alone increases its interest and strengthens its obligation upon us. Its novelty has a charm that ought to please and captivate. In this instance, however, it is the singular case of novelty in combination with antiquity. While novelty pleases, antiquity commands our reverence. If we inquire after "the old paths," here they are, and it ought surely to recommend them to us that Abraham walked in them. The traveller in Palestine enjoys the scenery the more, as he thinks how the eyes of Abraham gazed upon it, or his feet trod upon its surface. Why are we to be less impressed by his higher mental exercises or moral engagements? As these are more exalted in their nature, their claim is greater upon our attention.

There is another feature in the manner of the record not to be overlooked. The fact is stated, as to the conduct of Abraham, as though there was nothing remarkable in the mere act. It is given as if he had only complied with a well-known usage. His dedication of the tenth of the spoils to the service of God must have been in accordance with the practice of the times or the known will of God to accept it. In either case we are entitled to infer a revelation had been given of the divine mind upon the subject. It must have been conveyed to Abraham, either by tradition from former ages or by an express communication from heaven. He must have been satisfied the law came from God, or he would not have practised it. We do not expect to find will-worship in the "father of the faithful" and "the friend of God." The fact that he gave the tenth is sufficient to prove that he knew it to be in accordance with the will of God, and this carries us to the conclusion that a divine revelation or law had been given upon the subject. It is customary to reason after this manner in other questions kindred to that in hand. The existence of sacrifice in the time of Adam is held to be a proof that its origin was divine. God appointed it, it is argued, or he would not have accepted it, nor would Adam have offered it. So also with the observance of the Sabbath on the first day of the week—our authority is the example of the apostles. We infer from their conduct that they had a divine warrant for it, although there is not the record of an express law. They would not have acted as they did, without knowing the will of their Master. And this is all we require in the conduct of Abraham. It is to be vindicated on the ground of a known law which regulated the practice. And if so, we are bound to conform to that law as well as Abraham. His example is recorded for our imitation.

What, then, is the amount of his example? What was it that Abraham did? We have no desire to press his example beyond its legitimate boundary. He gave to Melchizedek, the priest of God, the tenth of the spoils he had taken in battle as he returned from the slaughter of the kings. God had given him the victory, and he thus acknowledged the divine interposition and his own obligation. His example abundantly establishes, that in every deliverance we should honour God, and especially that we should declare our sense of his goodness when he preserves our property, by dedicating a portion of it to him. We may go farther. If God is pleased in his providence to increase our property, we should observe his hand in it, and give at least a tenth to him. Whether, therefore, our property is preserved or increased, the example of Abraham establishes a divine claim to at least the tenth. Here, then, we gain an undoubted rule of conduct applicable to given circumstances in our situation. Our property, like that of Abraham or Lot, for whom he contended, is continually exposed to destruction, and if God protects or preserves it, we should devote to him a tenth of whatever it is calculated to yield us. We are continually receiving new favours from the Lord, and whatever he confers we should in like manner acknowledge him. We will not at present press the inquiry how far such a rule would cover the entire income of every man. We are satisfied to confine it to such special cases as may legitimately fall under that of Abraham—to that portion of our property that has been preserved from danger or added to our former store. Other cases will arise to extend the rule. In the meantime there are certain claims upon our imitation of the conduct of Abraham which cannot be passed over without special notice. " Know ye therefore that they which are of faith, the same are the children of Abraham." " Now we, brethren, as Isaac was, are the children of promise." Abraham's faith was his peculiarity, and with every genuine Christian it is the same. The faith of Abraham wrought in his heart a moral renovation, and the same faith is always productive of the same result. Faith and regeneration are twin sisters, ever found associated, born together, and strengthening one another. Having therefore the mind and heart of Abraham, his views and feelings, we must act as he also acted. The same principles produce the same practices in all ages. As then " he that was born after the flesh persecuted him that was born after the Spirit, even so it is now." As then he that was taught by the Spirit and governed by the Spirit acted toward God, " even so it is now." Abraham gave to God the tenth of the spoils, and so will they act who inherit the faith of Abraham and are entitled to be called his children. The Christian soldier returning with the prize of victory will dedicate the tenth to God. The Christian merchant, having rescued his property from danger, will give the tenth of all it would have yielded. The Christian minister, or physician, or lawyer, whatever have been the gains of his profession, will in the same proportion lay his offering on the altar of the Lord. The Christian man, in the humblest or the highest circumstances of life, as the Lord has rendered to him, so will he return a corresponding measure for his service. All that are of the divine faith of Abraham will approve themselves his children, if they act consistently, by doing as he did, and giving as he gave.

Nor let us omit to notice the situation of Abraham, when he

acted thus liberally towards the cause of God. It was at an early period of his history in the promised land. As yet God had given him "none inheritence in it, no, not so much as to set his foot on." It was long afterwards he had to supplicate as a favour from the children of Heth a spot where he might bury his dead. He was "a pilgrim and stranger in the land." And although God had increased his flocks and herds, yet still his situation and property were apparently most insecure, and he might be considered a poor and very dependent man. But he gave the tenth of all. How readily might selfishness have found an excuse to withhold! He might have pleaded that he knew not how soon he might be in straits, and that it was his duty to provide against them. Or he might have argued, since God gave him such spoils, he might conclude it was the divine will he should possess them all. But no—thankful to God, and confiding in his providence, he gave to him the tenth of what he had gained. Where now shall we find an excuse for the many apologies which our selfishness is wont to plead? The example of Abraham silences them all. And the lesson is irresistible, that in all circumstances, whether poor or rich, we should acknowledge God in the preservation or increase of our worldly substance by dedicating at least a tenth to him.

There was also a nobility in the conduct of Abraham that cannot fail to command our highest admiration. We have seen his spirit toward God, let us look at his conduct on the same occasion to men. "The King of Sodom said unto Abram, Give me the persons, and take the goods to thyself. And Abram said, I have lift up mine hand unto the Lord, the Most High God, the possessor of heaven and earth, that I will not take from a thread even to a shoe-latchet, and that I will not take anything that is thine, lest thou shouldst say, I have made Abram rich; save only that which the young men have eaten, and the portion of the men which went with me, Aner, Eshcol, and Mamre; let them take their portion." Here is an example of noble-mindedness. Generosity, wisdom, and justice are united in his high-minded decision. The meanness of the world is overcome by the elevation of right principles. He who is right-minded toward God is generous and large-hearted to man. He who gives to the cause of God is the friend of every effort that breathes benevolence to men.

What a contrast to Abraham is Lot! He went to Sodom to gain the world, and he lost it there. He departed from God, and he fell into the hands of bloody men. His life and property were recovered, but he was indebted for both to the Lord's servant. He does not appear to have profited by the chastisement, and he was driven at last out of the wicked city, when he left his property in the flames. His last refuge was in a cave of the mountain, where he was abandoned to temptation, and fell into sin. How fearful must have been the accusations of his conscience, for he was "a righteous man!" He presents a fearful example of what even a godly man may suffer from worldliness. Let us be warned by his example, and let it operate to present more clearly to our minds, and enforce more powerfully on our hearts, that of Abraham, who dedicated to God, gratefully and joyfully, a "tenth of all."

CHAPTER III.

JACOB.

"*Of all that thou shalt give me, I will surely give the tenth unto thee.*"—Gen. xxviii. 22.

WHAT creation is to the philosopher, such are the Scriptures to the Christian. Each has his own book, although either should, and often does, study them both. The botanist goes into the fields and gardens, examines their plants and flowers, classifies them according to their properties, observes their habits and influences, and from the whole deduces the laws and principles by which they are governed, and lays down the rules by which his conduct toward them should be guided. So does the astronomer proceed in his observations upon the heavens, the mineralogist with his rocks and stones, and the metaphysician in his study of the human mind. In like manner the student of the Scriptures is occupied, whatever be the department of their varied contents to which his attention is directed, their doctrines, or precepts, or examples, or promises. It has become fashionable to decry a systematic study of the sacred volume, but it may be confidently asserted that he who does not so study it will never properly understand it, nor will he who does not so teach ever prove successful in imparting instruction. It is on this principle we are desirous of proceeding in our present inquiry. We are collecting facts out of the Scriptures that we may deduce principles and found rules of conduct upon them. Our investigation is confined to one species, as the botanist's to plants in the field of nature. We wish to ascertain what was done and approved in the matter of contribution to the cause of God, that we may learn our duty. We have seen how it was in the case of Abraham, and we now direct our attention to that of his most distinguished descendant, the patriarch Jacob.

It is worthy of notice that they both acted on the same rule, that of devoting a tenth to the Lord. It is therefore plain this was an early and well-known rule of conduct. They no doubt derived it from a common source, and that, in all likelihood, was an express divine command handed down from the beginning to generation after generation. There were many features common to the two patriarchs, and their use of their worldly property. We have already remarked on those which characterised the liberality of Abraham, and, omitting the same traits, so far as they are found in Jacob, we shall confine our attention to what was peculiar in him.

The first appearance of a generous spirit in Jacob was on the occasion of his departure from his father's house, to escape the fury of his provoked and injured brother Esau, and when he had gone so far upon his journey as Bethel. Previously to this time there is reason to believe he was under the dominion of a worldly and grasping spirit, so much so as not to stop at plans of deceitfulness and acts of injustice. In concert with his mother, Rebekah, he devised a scheme to deceive his father, and possess himself of the portion of his elder brother. It is no excuse for his conduct that Providence had revealed to his mother how the elder should be subjected to the younger; it was rather an aggravation of his sin, for he and his accomplice should have confided in that Providence to fulfil the divine promise in his own lawful time and manner. Jacob, therefore, is presented to us, in the truthfulness of the Scriptures, as in the outset of life characterised by selfishness and cunning. This constitutional temperament indeed appears again and again throughout his entire history. Though it was overcome by grace, still nature often asserted its power. And many were the troubles into which the patriarch was brought by the remainder of this indwelling sin. He had a sore struggle all his days, and did not always come off victorious. It is most interesting and instructive to observe the providence and power of God breaking this natural propensity of Jacob's corrupt heart.

What first strikes us with surprise is that his very sin was overruled to be the occasion of its own overthrow. His love of the world led him into sin, and that sin drove him from his father's house. He sought all his father's property, and he was driven from it all. So soon did a retributive Providence overtake him, but it was guided by mercy. "Where sin abounded grace did much more abound." When the outcast son reached the end of his first day's journey, he sank down exhausted in body and sad in heart. He felt his solitary and desolate situation. We may assume that he looked to God that night as he had never done before. He laid himself down to sleep in a frame of mind such as he had never previously experienced, feeling that God was his only refuge, and resolved to seek him for his portion. The God of his fathers was not unmindful of their penitent son. He was not forsaken in his solitude and sorrow. The Holy Spirit visited him with his converting grace. "He dreamed, and behold, a ladder set upon the earth, and the top of it reached to heaven; and behold, the angels of God ascending and descending upon it. And behold, the Lord stood above it, and said, I am the Lord God of Abraham thy father, and the God of Isaac." The promises made to them were then renewed to him, and more were added. The mind of Jacob was enlightened by this revelation of God, and his heart was touched. From that day he showed himself a child of God. A new nature was given to him, and he entered upon a new course of life. One marked change was from selfishness to generosity. "Jacob vowed a vow, saying, If God will be with me, and will keep me in this way that I go and will give me bread to eat and raiment to put on, so that I come again to my father's house in peace; then shall the Lord be my God, and this stone which I have set for a pillar shall be God's house, and of all that thou shalt give me I will surely give the tenth unto thee." What a gracious change! Before, all was for the world, and all the world would hardly satisfy him; now, he asks only what is necessary for a sustenance. Before, all was for self, and nothing for God; now, all is for God, and self is overlooked. The connexion between the conversion of the soul and liberality to the cause of God is very marked. No sooner is that blessed change produced than this effect follows from it. The apostle Paul expresses the same sentiment when he says, "They first gave their own selves to the Lord, and then unto us by the will of God." Jacob gave himself to God in his conversion, and then his property. There is no doubt in some a natural generosity when compared with others, but there is no enlightened, enlarged, and consistent generosity but such as proceeds from a new heart under the dominion of grace. And wherever the new heart is found, it is impregnated with zeal for the glory of God and a deep interest in the extension of his cause, with a corresponding effort of labour and generosity of contribution. This generosity will be no doubt much affected by the circumstances of the convert, although it be in all radically the same grace. It will be interesting to trace some of its outgoings in Jacob.

Like Abraham he fixed on the tenth. This is noticed again only to impress it on the attention. That was the acknowledged standard, and wherever grace renewed the heart, its subject embraced the law of God as its guide.

Unlike Abraham, Jacob's dedication was not confined to one occasion or one possession. It comprehended his whole life and his whole property. As long as he lived he would dedicate this portion of his substance to God, and whatever he possessed, the tenth of it should be the Lord's.

Bringing these two cases of Abraham and Jacob together, what a rule do we discover for the guidance of all who would be governed by the law of Revelation! On all special occasions of the preservation or increase of property there is to be a special dedication of a tenth. Of all ordinary and stated income there is to be the dedication of a tenth. Can it for a moment be supposed it was by a mere accident the two patriarchs fell upon the same amount of contribution? Or is it to be supposed that either fixed the sum of his own mere will and pleasure? The tone of approval with which the conduct of both is narrated shows how agreeable it was to God, and we are shut up to the conclusion that they both adopted for a guide the law which their God had given, and that it is morally binding now as much as it was then.

This is not a little confirmed by what afterwards occurred in the life of Jacob. It appears that he forgot his vow, solemnly as he had made it. God granted him more than he sought. He returned to his father's house in peace, and greatly enriched. Yet the stone which was to be God's house, and to which his property was to be dedicated, was forgotten. He was therefore reproved and summoned to the promised duty. "God said to Jacob, Arise, go up to Bethel and dwell there, and make there an altar unto God, that appeared unto thee when thou fleddest from the face of Esau thy brother." The patriarch discovered a gracious disposition in an immediate and ready obedience. He made it a season of a thorough reformation and revival in his household. It is particularly to be observed that he called to mind the circumstances of his first dedication of himself to God, obtained fresh promises from God, and engaged with enlarged liberality in the service of God. "He set up a pillar in the place where God talked with him, even a pillar of stone, and he poured a drink-offering thereon, and he poured oil thereon." The promised dedication was demanded by God when it was forgotten by his servant, and when it was presented it was accepted and approved.

What is the legitimate inference from the conduct of Jacob?

When his heart was brought under the power of true religion, he gave the tenth of his income to God. Will not every truly converted soul feel the power of his example? This patriarch is continually presented to us in the Scriptures as a most approved servant of God. His faults are not concealed, but recorded for our warning. Still his gracious excellence is much commended, and his example is to be imitated. Shall there be an exception to that part of it which binds him to devote his property to God? The Christian who acknowledges the obligation of conformity to the patriarch in other graces, but overlooks this one, will require to assign a reason for the exception. It is to be feared many fail to imitate him in this respect who have not considered how they are to be justified in so doing. Let them think of the patriarch's example, and they will see good cause to follow it. They are as much bound to conform to him in this respect as in his agonising prayer at Peniel. Both are recorded for our benefit, and that benefit is gained only when we do as he did. It is a Christian purpose to say, " Of all that thou shalt give me I will surely give the tenth unto thee."

CHAPTER IV.

MOSES.

" *The law was given by Moses.*"—John, i. 17.

WE come now to a still clearer light and to a firmer footing. Abraham gave a tenth of all the spoils, and there is reason to believe he did so in compliance with an early and well-known law of divine authority. Jacob vowed he would give the tenth of all he possessed, and he came to this resolution whenever his mind was brought under the power of truth and was made the subject of a gracious change. It is a serious thing to depart from the practice of these men of God. If we have the faith of Abraham and the piety of Jacob, we shall assuredly do as they did, and at least give the tenth of all we have to God. We are willing to rest the question here, and ask, whether it is conceivable that any one having the character of these patriarchs could withhold this portion of his substance from the service of him who gave it all, especially when he knows that this was their practice? We are not left, however, to infer what our conduct ought to be from that of others. God has given a law, and we do well to consider it. There is express statute, associated no doubt with many temporary ceremonies, yet *substantially* unchangeable and binding universally and for ever. Let it not be said that since God publicly proclaimed this law for the first time to the Jews we are to infer it had never been law before. Is it likely that God adopted for a law what had previously become a prevailing practice? How much more probable it is that the prevailing practice had originated in an ancient law, given by God, yet of the first publication of which we are not informed? We find that the law of the Sabbath was published to the Jews in the ten commandments upon Sinai; yet that same law had been given at the beginning, and we find it in the earliest records of the creation. The original law, there is reason to fear, had fallen into disuse, and therefore it is solemnly renewed and sanctioned. Even this reason, however, was not necessary to justify its re-publication. The same laws are again and again proclaimed and enforced by their divine Author. This remark is applicable to all the ten commandments. They were all laws of God before they were published to the Jews. From the beginning they had been the rule of human conduct; yet where can it be shown that each of them is, in so many words, to be found? They were authoritative from the first—they were known to the servants of God— they were, more or less, obeyed by them. And yet we find them embodied in a special law for the guidance of Israel. We believe it to have been the same with the law of giving to the Lord—it had been enjoined from the beginning, and it was proclaimed afresh and placed in new connexions when God revealed his will to Moses and Aaron. The re-enactment of this law is a subject of deep interest, and its associations are full of instruction. We shall therefore inquire with some minuteness into the arrangements which God was pleased to prescribe, and for this purpose shall place them separately as we find them in the ancient code of Israel's laws.

I.—THE FIRST TITHE.

"All the tithe of the land, whether of the seed of the land, or of the fruit of the tree, is the Lord's; it is holy unto the Lord."* "Behold, I have given the children of Levi all the tenth in Israel for an inheritance, for their service, which they serve, even the service of the tabernacle of the congregation."† The statute is explicit, and its special requirements are worthy of careful observation, for they cast much light on the general question under consideration. The lowest proportion which the law could accept was a tenth, conveying the sentiment that less had never previously been given, nor could less suffice now. The law of Moses was not designed to reduce the claims of God on the gratitude and offerings of his people. This tenth was also exacted on all property, "the seed of the land and the fruit of the tree" alike. All came from God, and in all God is to be acknowledged. "Of thine own have we given thee," said David, and the same is in all ages the language of piety. And for what was this tenth demanded? For the children of Levi, a reward for their service in the tabernacle of the congregation. It was for them as the ministers of God. The end of the law was the glory of Jehovah, that the knowledge and worship of his name might be propagated and extended. Its essence lies in this, that God by an express statute demands the tenth of our property for the promotion of his cause. The *principle* of the law is as binding now as it was on Israel.

II.—THE SECOND TITHE.

"Thou shalt truly tithe all the increase of thy seed, that the field bringeth forth year by year. And thou shalt eat before the Lord thy God, in the place which he shall chose to place his name there, the tithe of thy corn, of thy vine, and of thine oil, and the firstlings of thy herds and of thy flocks; that thou

* Levit. xxvii. 30. † Numb. xviii. 21.

mayest learn to fear the Lord thy God always."* This was clearly a different tithe from the former. That was given for the support of the Levite, this for the maintenance of the various feasts and sacrifices. Behold, then, the increased demand on Israel: first a tenth for one purpose—then a second tenth for another—so that by a permanent statute every Israelite was required to give at least a fifth of his yearly income to the Lord. Under former dispensations we read only of a tenth. As the world grows older the claims of God are not lessened. Privileges are increased and responsibilities are increased with them; "To whom much is given, of them shall much be required." The Jew might say, "What advantage then hath the Jew? or what profit is there of circumcision? Much every way; chiefly because that unto them were committed the oracles of God." But as he thus reasoned he was summing up arguments to enforce the claim of God on himself and his property. Let this principle also be distinctly apprehended, for it will come with mighty force when it is applied to the privileges and responsibilities of the best, the brightest, and the last dispensation.

III.—THE TITHE FOR THE POOR.

"At the end of three years thou shalt bring forth all the tithe of thine increase the same year, and shalt lay it up within thy gate. And the Levite (because he hath no part nor inheritance with thee), and the stranger, and the fatherless, and the widow, which are within thy gates, shall come, and shall eat and be satisfied; that the Lord thy God may bless thee in all the work of thine hand which thou doest." † It is doubtful whether this third tithe be entirely distinct from the other two already noticed, and therefore whether it were an additional claim on Israel. It may have been so, but the evidence is not fully satisfactory. We found no argument therefore on that consideration, but we cannot overlook this new appropriation of property, this additional object of generosity proposed to Israel. "The poor shall never cease out of the land;" and one design of this providence is to teach us gratitude for our own mercies and kindness

---

* Deut. xiv. 22, 23. † Deut. xiv. 28, 29.

to the necessitous. Generosity to the cause of God is here linked with benevolence to man. It is the same condition of mind that produces the double fruit. "Thou shalt love the Lord thy God with all thy heart, and soul, and mind, and strength, and thou shalt love thy neighbour as thyself." The love of man springs out of the love of God. If we love the Creator we shall love the creature whom he hath made. The love of the father ensures the love of his child. Let none fear that because much is demanded and done for the cause of God, the interests of man will be therefore likely to be neglected. The reverse may be expected. And let none excuse themselves by alleging they have so much to do for man they can do nothing for the cause of God. It is a mere pretence. Jesus could say to God, "The zeal of thine house hath eaten me up," and at the same time he healed the bodies and saved the souls of men. He hath left us an example that we should follow his steps.

IV.—THE LEVITES' TITHE.

"Speak unto the Levites, and say unto them, When ye take of the children of Israel the tithes which I have given you from them for your inheritance, then ye shall offer up an heave-offering of it for the Lord, even a tenth part of the tithe."*

The Levite's concern with the tithes was not merely to receive and enjoy them. He had his own tenth to pay to Aaron and his sons. None were exempt in Israel. All were recipients, and all must acknowledge the bounty of God. The ministers of religion are not merely entitled to live by the altar, which they serve, they are bound to devote of that which they receive to the cause of God. The apostle Paul applies the former part of this statement to the ministers of Christ, even adducing the Jewish illustration, "Thou shalt not muzzle the ox that treadeth out the corn;" and it will not be questioned that the latter part of it is equally applicable under the Christian economy. The lesson is clearly taught that all should devote to the Lord of that which they receive. No rank or station can plead immunity. The

* Numb. xviii. 26.

higher the position the stronger the claim. Ministers of the gospel especially should feel the powerful claims that the cause of God has upon them. They are exalted to great honour as ambassadors for Christ. They should manifest the generous spirit of the religion which they teach. They should be an example to the Church in all things. But if they shall be so, the people to whom they minister must consider their liabilities. They cannot give of that which they possess not. It is the duty of the churches to put it in the power of their ministers to be examples of liberality. In doing so they consult their own interests. In that respect they will find the saying eminently true, that "it is more blessed to give than to receive." They are just filling up the reservoir which shall pour out fresh streams of pure water to refresh and fertilise themselves.

V.—STATED SERVICES.

"Speak unto the children of Israel, and say unto them, Concerning the feasts of the Lord, which ye shall proclaim, even these are my feasts."*

They were to be observed at all times—daily—weekly—monthly—yearly—every seventh year—every fiftieth year. Each of these had its own peculiar claims and responsibilities. One feature, however, marked them all—the expensive character of the service. The Israelite might indeed say, "I will not render to the Lord of that which cost me nought." He could not do so. The prescribed service was in itself a serious claim. It is true there were services adapted to the poor; but let it be remembered there was no exception for the poor; the poorest must give. It is said in "Mammon," for some to give "a twentieth, or even a fiftieth, would require the nicest frugality and care." This was not the spirit of the ancient law of Israel. Every man received something, and every man must give something. Where is the exception releasing the poorest from the tenth? This law is as wise as it is stringent. The poor man is benefited by the exercise of the "nicest frugality and care." It is the most salu-

* Lev. xxiii. 2.

tary discipline for himself and his household. It is the very habit which the poor most need to form and cherish; it elevates the mind to save something for the cause of God. He knew human nature well who has imposed this duty upon it. "He needed not that any should testify of man, for he knew what was in man." It is a mistake to lead the poor to think they have nothing to do or to give to God. This is a lesson never more required to be taught than in our day. The rich are to give abundantly out of their abundance, and the poor are to give out of their poverty. God designedly made his service heavy in the ancient economy. His demands never ceased, and none were exempted.

VI.—VARIOUS SACRIFICES.

"This is the law of the burnt-offering, of the meat-offering, and of the sin-offering, and of the trespass-offering, and of the peace-offerings."*

No doubt these various services had mainly a typical meaning; and very gracious the instructions were which they were designed and calculated to convey. In the burnt-offering we behold the sacrifice of the Son of God; in the meat-offering, the devoted gratitude of the believer presenting himself, all he is and has, as an offering to the Lord; in the sin-offering and trespass-offering, that life of faith upon the Son of God, and that constant effort after purity of life which a sense of sin and the love of holiness inspire; and in the peace-offering, the fellowship with God, without which the renewed soul cannot rest, with the manner in which it is to be maintained, even through the peace-speaking blood of Christ. All this is true, and it is important. Yet there is, besides, a moral aim in all these institutes not to be overlooked. Observe the state of mind which they are calculated to produce and foster. They require intelligence, consideration, discrimination, frugality, and carefulness. They teach how much God demands and how much we must do in order to render it. They enlighten, enlarge, and exercise the mind. They train the soul to lofty conceptions, to large services, and to make sacrifices for

* Lev. vii. 37.

God. They teach us to make religion our business, and they give us to understand that the requirements of the Lord at our hands are neither few nor small.

VII.—FREE-WILL OFFERINGS.

"These things shall ye do unto the Lord in your set feasts, beside your vows, and your free-will offerings."*

Over and above all that has been described, the Israelite might dedicate whatever beside he desired unto the Lord. There was a limit on the one side, and the law made its demands, but there was no limit on the other, and the devout soul might devote as it would. In all who had a right frame of mind this would not be a dead letter. Much would be added to the requirements of the law. As fresh occasions arose for gratitude to God, in the preservation of health, recovery from sickness, the increase of property, or the prosperity of friends, God would be acknowledged in all. This, therefore, is to be added to what was noticed before as the requirement of law and statute. A fifth proportion of all was certainly demanded. It may have been more, if the tithe for the poor is considered to be distinct from that for the Levite and that for the feasts. It is not too much, on that interpretation, to assume there was a fourth required. And when to all these are added the vows and free-will offerings, may it not be alleged that the devout and consistent Israelite felt the claim of God to be annually upon him for not less than a third of the income which was graciously confided to him?

This is the conclusion to which the review of the ancient law of Israel has conducted us. We appeal to the impartial inquirer whether we have not arrived at this issue by an unvarnished statement of clear statutes and undoubted facts. And now, what is the moral to be drawn from all? God has shown us that he considered it good for Israel to press his demands upon them at all times and seasons, for all pious and benevolent purposes, and in all measures adapted to the rich and the poor, and obligatory upon all. This was the education he gave his own children

* Numb. xxix. 39.

whom he adopted to train for himself. Was it not manifestly designed to counteract the selfishness of the human heart, and open within it a fountain of generosity and benevolence? As the water drawn from the living well is renewed again with quickened and enlarged supplies, so as the heart is accustomed to give out of its fulness, the streams of grace and providence supply it afresh. The vapours that arise from the earth gather into clouds, and thence distil again, to water and fertilise the ground whence they first proceeded, and so he that giveth getteth, he that does good receives good, and as we yield ourselves and our property to God we are filled with the fulness of God. Truly is charity said to be twice blessed—blessed in him that gives no less than in him that receives. With these facts and views before us, it is confidently asked, What proportion of his substance will the believer in Revelation dedicate to the service of God? Can he give less than a tenth? Is he consistent? And can he satisfy his own conscience if he does so? What is the law of the Bible, and of God its Author? Is it optional with every man to give or withhold as he pleases? to give in what measure and proportion he thinks proper? We are confirmed in the conviction that no enlightened and consistent believer can devote less than the tenth to the Lord of the annual income which providence has placed at his disposal for the maintenance of himself and those who are dependent upon him. "Let God be true, but every man a liar." We think we have spoken the truth of God, and stand on the sure ground of his testimony; let all beware how they depart from it by a false or unsound interpretation, involving a great practical question bearing mightily on the cause of God in the earth.

CHAPTER V.

THE DAY OF PENTECOST.

"*All that believed were together, and had all things common.*"
—Acts, ii. 44.

HEAR what the law saith! What saith it? It saith that Abraham gave the tenth of the spoils — that Jacob gave the tenth of all he possessed — that Israel was required to give a tenth to the Levite, a tenth to the feasts, a tenth every third year to the poor, to give constantly, to give for all pious and charitable purposes, and over and above all that the statute prescribed to give the free-will offerings which gratitude and love might prompt. This is what the law saith. We leave it to produce its effect on all who regard it; and we proceed now to inquire, What saith the Gospel? For this purpose we direct attention to its opening scene. That scene was no doubt intended to give a faithful representation, and convey a just impression of the new economy—what it was to be, what it was to do, and what was to be expected from it. On a full consideration it will be found every way worthy of the gracious and glorious dispensation which it was designed to usher into the world.

At the outset let us inquire what we are to expect from Christianity on the subject of religious contribution. We are to remember it is the consummation of a religion which had been taught from the beginning. It is somehow assumed by many that it set aside all that had gone before, and was altogether a new religion. This is a most unsound and dangerous principle. What was merely ceremonial and had served its purpose was certainly withdrawn, but the great principles inculcated from the first remained as they were, and Christianity is simply Judaism perfected. We are, therefore, not to expect that on every subject treated under the first dispensation we shall have new and distinct instructions laid down in the second. The lessons of Moses passed into the hands of the disciples in the school of Christ, and the New Testament did not supplant, although it more fully explained and powerfully enforced, the instructions of the Old Testament. These remarks have an important bearing on the subject before us. The views of giving to the Lord, held and taught and practised by Abraham, Jacob, and Moses, are not disallowed by Christ. They were not merely ceremonial, and have not ceased to be binding. So far as they were founded on the principle of human nature and the relations of man to God, they are the same yesterday, and to-day, and for ever. They arise out of the nature and necessity of our position toward both God and man, and cannot cease to be obligatory. We are therefore to study the teaching and example of ancient patriarchs and lawgivers on this subject, as much as those who lived in their times, and served God under their dispensations. Nor are we to be surprised if we do not find any new and explicit directions in the New Testament. It may be assumed these were given sufficiently before. There are various subjects of great moment in which this was manifestly the course pursued by the early Christian Church. We may instance the admission of the children of believers to the membership of the Church by the initiatory ordinance of baptism. It has often been remarked there is no express appointment of that observance of the ordinance in the New Testament. But it has been very properly replied, it was not necessary there should be any such fresh appointment. It had ever been the law of the Church of God to receive the children of its members into fellowship. Abraham and Moses alike practised it in their day. Christianity assumed its existence. It did not abrogate it, and unless it could be shown that it did abrogate it, the observance must be regarded as continuing in all its force. Similar remarks might be applied to the perpetuation of the Sabbath. There is no fresh and express appointment of it under Christianity, yet the judgment of the Christian Church has in all ages been almost unanimous on the subject of its perpetuity. Let the same view be taken of religious contribution, and it will show that the instructions drawn from Abraham, Jacob, and Moses, remain in all their authority, although a word had not been added respecting it in the New Testament.

We make these remarks, however, not because we fear to canvass the subject in the light of the New Testament. Our object is to maintain the place we have already gained in this argument, not to lose the weight of any consideration hitherto advanced, and to stand by the assertion of right principles in the interpretation of the word of God. With this understanding, we now proceed to inquire what may be expected under Christianity, and what development of its views in the grand opening scene of that economy? At once, then, it must be felt by all that we are not to expect any retrograde movement here. We are not prepared to find that the gospel of Christ will ask less than the law of Moses in the matter of contribution to the cause of God. Rather would we expect to hear in relation to it what is said of another duty,—" A new commandment give I unto you, that ye love one another." Love had always been a duty, and always was taught and required. Yet it is denominated a new commandment. It is new, in one sense, although not in another. It is new in the reasons by which it is enforced in the gospel, and in the measure in which it ought to be exercised. But it is not new as though it became a duty now, while it had not been such before. Just so with the subject in hand. It might be said of it in the same sense, " A new commandment give I unto you." Moses taught the duty of giving, but Jesus Christ taught it more fully still. There are reasons for it now which never existed before, and it ought to be exercised in a degree far exceeding the measure of former times. The light which Christianity pours into the mind on the great questions of time and eternity, requires that we should put forth efforts and make sacrifices to render time subservient to the interests of eternity, such as never were made before. The views which the Gospel gives of the comparative value of the body and the soul should inspire an earnestness and self-denial in the salvation of souls, which could not have been expected under darker dispensations. The obligations under which Christians have been laid to Jesus, the Author and Finisher of their faith, should rouse to doing and suffering in his cause altogether new in the earth. His life and death are an argument which should tell on the heart as none ever told before. His honour should be an object for the promotion of which all his followers should feel they could never do enough. His command should come upon them with a power which they would feel it to be impossible to withstand. He died for us, and we should live to him. He gave himself for us, and what shall we withhold from him? What shall we render to the Lord for all his benefits? This is Christianity. What saith it on the giving of our substance to the Lord? Shall its claims be supposed less than those of the law? If Abraham gave a tenth, and Jacob a tenth, and Moses required a tenth, or a fifth, or a third, what saith the Gospel of Jesus? The very manner of its claim should give it an increased power over us. It does not say, in so many words, a tenth, or a fifth, or a third, or any prescribed proportion; it does assume that its early lessons on these subjects, delivered under former dispensations, are in the hands of all who now profess its higher and clearer revelations; but this assumed, it leaves it to the Christian heart to decide the proportion of its contribution. It is not indifferent whether this shall be greater or less than it was of old. It is jealous of its own honour. If there be a falling back, even to the calculations of the law, the Gospel is treated injuriously. If there be satisfaction of mind with the old truth, and if it is felt when this is given we have come up to the mark of duty, and need go no farther, Christ holds himself dishonoured. But suppose even this to be withheld, suppose an argument constructed out of the very generosity of Christianity, that we need not give anything, or that we may give less now than they did in the old times, how must such a spirit be regarded by our divine Redeemer? Are we to wonder if he shall address to such the withering words, "Thou wicked and slothful servant?" Christ has not reduced his claims, although he makes no bargain with his followers. He expects that we shall say, "The love of Christ constraineth us." And he says by his apostle, "Every man, as he purposeth in his heart, so let him give, not grudgingly nor of necessity, for God loveth a cheerful giver."

With these general principles in view, let us look at the

transactions of the day of Pentecost, as illustrative of the generous spirit which the Gospel inspires. It was a day of great expectation. "When the day of Pentecost was fully come, they were all with one accord in one place." They had been encouraged to expect singular blessings, they had waited earnestly in prayer on God, that these might be dispensed, and now they were met to receive them. It was a day of the Spirit's power. This is what was promised and what they obtained. "Suddenly there same a sound from heaven, as of a rushing mighty wind, and it filled all the house where they were sitting. And there appeared unto them cloven tongues like as of fire, and it sat upon each of them. And they were all filled with the Holy Ghost, and began to speak with other tongues, as the Spirit gave them utterance." These emblems of the Spirit were fitted to give the apostles just ideas of his power. Who can withstand the rushing mighty wind or the devouring flame? So under their ministry sinners would not be able to withstand the Spirit by which they should speak. It was therefore a day of powerful impressions. As the apostles preached Christ, told of his life and death and resurrection, the hearts of the audience were smitten. Deeply convinced of sin, they cried out, "Men and brethren, what shall we do?" But they were enlightened by the same power that convicted them. They saw and owned themselves the murderers of the innocent Jesus, but in his blood which they had shed they saw a fountain opened that cleanseth from all sin. Into that fountain they went by faith, and were made clean. Nobly they avowed their convictions. "They that gladly received his word were baptized, and the same day there were added unto them about three thousand souls." And now look at this redeemed company. What distinguished them? "They continued steadfastly in the apostles' doctrine and fellowship, and in breaking of bread, and in prayers." It was no mere momentary excitement. It was a thorough, a sound, and proved to be a permanent work of the Spirit. But there was one feature of their case and character, which here deserves our particular attention, as directly bearing on our great subject. "All that believed were together and had all things common, and sold their possessions and goods, and parted them to all men, as every man had need." An extravagant and foolish impression has been taken up with regard to this transaction. It has been assumed that all the property which the disciples possessed they sold, and cast the produce into a common purse, that individual property ceased to be held, and that in the widest sense there was a community of goods. No such views are given in the passage. The meaning is that the disciples did what the urgency of the occasion required. Those who possessed property sold what was necessary to meet the emergency of their circumstances. There was no force on any believer to do so, each did as his generosity stimulated him. This is plain from the words of Peter, subsequently addressed to Ananias, "Whiles it remained, was it not thine own? and after it was sold, was it not in thine own power?" It was a proceeding every way worthy of the first disciples, decided, vigorous, self-denying, yet calm and full of purpose. Thus viewed it presents the duty of religious contribution, as connected with the Gospel of Christ, in a most instructive and impressive aspect. It represents it as the fruit of the Spirit. Wherever the Holy Ghost takes possession of the mind, he enlightens and enlarges it. He gives just apprehension of duty and stimulates the mind to a proper frame for the discharge of it. Especially does this transaction show us what was to be expected under the new dispensation. Thus it opened, and thus it was to progress. Oh! why have not scenes like these been frequent or constant? The Spirit has been grieved. The body of a cold profession has been left, but the warm Spirit of the Gospel has been driven away. The kingdom of God is among us in word but not in power. How cheering to contemplate this scene, with which the gospel economy opened! The selfishness of the human heart was overborne. Love took possession of the minds of the disciples. Zeal for their Master's cause and honour inflamed them. Theirs was a spirit equal to the occasion to which God had called them. And it was to themselves a blessed season. " Continuing daily with one accord in the temple, and breaking bread from house to house, they did eat their meat with gladness and singleness of heart, praising God, and having favour with all the people. And the Lord added to the Church daily such as should be saved." When we do our duty and act faithfully, we have our reward. These disciples enjoyed it in their own bosom richly, and in the prosperity that attended the cause that was dearer to them than life. Nor let us omit to notice the fearful confirmation which very soon after was given to these views of this blessed day. "A certain man named Ananias, with Sapphira his wife, sold a possession, and kept back part of the price, his wife also being privy to it, and brought a certain part, and laid it at the apostles' feet. But Peter said, Ananias, why hath Satan filled thine heart to lie to the Holy Ghost, and to keep back part of the price? Why hast thou conceived this thing in thine heart? Thou hast not lied unto men, but unto God." The sequel is well known. The judgment of the Lord fell upon them, and the deceitful husband and the consenting wife were speedily laid in one dishonoured grave. Their sin was deception and falsehood, proceeding from pride and worldliness. They need not have sold their property. Probably no one had asked them. But they wished to have the glory, and yet indulge their selfishness. It is a fearful reproof of a parsimonious spirit in the things of God and religion. It was a faithful warning of what might be expected from sinful men, yet no less a distinct intimation of what the Gospel deserved and demanded.

Thus Christianity opened, and now we apply the argument. What are we to expect from those who yield themselves up to the dominion of Christ? In the light and under the impression of the day of Pentecost let the answer be given. Has Christianity reduced its demands on the generosity of its disciples? Are they expected to give more or less to the cause of God than did Abraham, Jacob, and Moses? If a tenth was the least under former economies, shall that suffice now? Shame would not permit us to say it ought. "Ye are not your own, ye are bought with a price; therefore glorify God in your body and spirit, which are his." And if this is the demand upon us, what of our property? Let the parable of the Talents, spoken by Jesus himself, answer the question. He who received five talents made them ten for his master, he who had two by trading made them four, and he who had one hid it, and neither wasted nor employed it,—he returned it as he had received it. The first two were approved and rewarded, but to the third it was said, "Thou wicked and slothful servant, thou oughtest to have put my money to the exchangers, and then at my coming I should have received mine own with usury." And this was the sentence passed upon him: "Take therefore the talent from him, and give it unto him which hath ten talents. For unto every one that hath shall be given, and he shall have abundance; but from him that hath not shall be taken away even that which he hath. And cast ye the unprofitable servant into outer darkness; there shall be weeping and gnashing of teeth." Let it be observed, this man is called "wicked and slothful," and yet the amount of sin charged upon him is simply neglect to be diligent in the cause of God. How, then, in the judgment of Christ, must it be with the man who neglects to give to the promotion of his cause? The answer may easily be given. Nor is it easier than it is to determine what are the relative claims of the law and of the gospel. If the law, by express statute, demanded a tenth, what does Christianity, without a statute, demand? It has certainly not abrogated the law of the ancient economy, but it has powerfully inspirited it. It were a slander on the Gospel to suppose it lowers the claims of Christ and his cause. No, no, it elevates and enlarges them, and like itself it raises all who truly receive and consistently obey it to a high, holy, and honourable standing before God and men, where, with the cross full in view, they ask, What shall I render to the Lord for all his benefits?

CHAPTER VI.

MACEDONIA AND CORINTH.

" The grace of God bestowed on the churches of Macedonia."—
2 Cor. viii. 1.
" Thanks be unto God for his unspeakable gift."—2 Cor. ix. 15.

THUS begins and ends a statement of principles, and an argument founded upon them, illustrating and enforcing the duty of giving to the Lord, which, if accepted and acted upon by the Church of Jesus Christ, would issue speedily in filling the earth with the fruits of righteousness. It may be said, when we set forth the transactions of the day of Pentecost, that was a peculiar season, a time of excitement and powerful impulse, but it did not continue and could not be expected to continue, and does not apply to ordinary times and persons. Without at all admitting that this is a proper statement, we do not stop to dispute it, but we proceed at once to a case neither extraordinary nor exciting. We claim attention to the apostle Paul, sitting calmly to dictate what the Spirit desired him to write, coolly narrating what was done by one church, and drawing reasons from it to regulate the conduct of another. We will also present his account of the matter in a way the most remote possible from that which is fitted to produce any excitement. We will apply ourselves to a plain and simple exposition of what he said, doing little more than fixing attention on verse after verse, allowing it to speak for itself, and offering a few explanations which none can dispute. Only let it be remembered, as we do so, that we are using the language, and employing the arguments, of the Holy Spirit of God, and which he intended to form the faith and regulate the conduct of Christian Churches, till the final consummation of all things.

MACEDONIA—2 CORINTHIANS, viii. 1-5.

V. 1. "Moreover, brethren, we do you to wit (we call on you to witness while we inform you of) the grace of God bestowed on the Churches of Macedonia."

He invites them to admire what had taken place in them. He ascribes it entirely to the gracious operation of the Spirit of God. They would themselves have been the first to exclaim, "Not unto us, O God, not unto us, but unto thy name give glory." Still it is not to be overlooked that the Divine Spirit does make his servants objects of admiration. He beautifies them with his salvation. He puts his own image upon them, and he makes them beautiful through his comeliness. Nor is it wrong, it would seem, to notice and express our admiration of the Christian loveliness. Great care, it is true, should be taken in speaking of it to themselves, lest it should become a temptation to pride. Circumstances, however, may arise when it is both lawful and proper, for the sake of encouragement, to do even that. But, whether or not, we may speak of it to others, for there is here the example of an apostle, and that too in the most public manner, not merely spoken but published and handed down from generation to generation, so that, as in the case of Mary, it may be said, "Wherever the gospel of the kingdom is preached, there it is told for a memorial of them."

V. 2. "How that in a great trial of affliction the abundance of their joy and their deep poverty abounded unto the riches of their liberality."

This is the special grace which was so estimable in the judgment of the apostle and of the Spirit by which he spake, and which he calls upon the Corinthians, and all others, to admire. The grace itself is beautiful, liberality in the service of the Lord. It is a fruit of the Spirit. It is a triumph over the selfishness of the human heart. It spreads happiness as far as it goes. It assimilates its subject to God, who delights in doing good. And it is a noble testimony to the power and grace of the gospel. In the circumstances of those who exercised it, however, it was greatly enhanced. It was in the midst of deep poverty and affliction, yet it abounded, and that joyfully. Their own affliction might have swallowed up their sympathies, their poverty might have been a ready excuse for neglect; but no, in spite of all obstacles, the gracious affection of love for others burst out. It urged its way through every obstruction, overcame all difficulties, and triumphed in alleviating distress and promoting happiness. The grace was every way worthy of admiration.

V. 3. "For to their power I bear record, yea, and beyond their power they were willing of themselves."

Their charity was spontaneous, vigorous, and efficient; like the living well, the waters came of their own accord. It reminds us of the words of Jesus, "The water that I shall give shall be in him a well of water springing up into everlasting life." Grace is exhaustless, because it is supplied by the infinite Spirit. The disposition is strengthened by exercise. And like the source, so are the streams that flow from it. They go gushing out in strong and rapid movement. They are not as those who say, "Be ye warmed and filled, nevertheless they give them not those things which are needful to the body." The warm heart puts forth the ready hand, and the generous spirit opens it wide to dispense its gifts. It knows the luxury of doing good, and only follows the propensity of its renewed nature.

V. 4. "Praying us with much entreaty that we would receive the gift, and take upon us the fellowship of the ministry to the saints."

What a scene! The giving and receiving of the rich and poor a means of Christian fellowship, and an inspired apostle the medium of maintaining it! All the entreaty is on the side of the rich, that they may be permitted to give; and they ask the good offices of the apostle, that they may be indulged in charity. Compare that scene of apostolic times with the poor-laws and the distributions and the distributors of our day. Where is our religion? or is the real spirit of it, as manifested of old, to be found on earth? We speak of apostolic churches and apostolic practices? Here they are. Are our churches and practices like these? So far as they are, they are apostolic; so far as they are not, they are not apostolic.

V. 5. "And this they did, not as we hoped, but first gave their own selves to the Lord, and unto us by the will of God."

They far exceeded all the expectations and hopes which the apostle had formed and cherished. But he reveals the secret of all. They had given themselves to God, and what then would they withhold from him or his people? And this, alas! reveals another secret. It makes an awful disclosure, which it may be unpleasant to divulge. It teaches the reason of the want of liberality to the cause of God, even the want of religion. It traces the closed hand to the shut heart. It brings us to the foundation of things. And as we cannot expect to raise a superstructure where there has been no foundation, so we need not look for doings of liberality where there is not a renewed heart. "Who can bring a clean thing out of an unclean? Not one." "Can the fig-tree bear olive berries, either a vine figs?"

Such, as described by the pen of inspiration, were the churches of Macedonia. They were the first churches in Europe. The apostle was called there in a vision by the cry, "Come over and help us." He found, when he went, that the Lord had work for him to do. There he saw the Gospel entering the heart of Lydia, like the sun rising gently and gradually and pouring its light into a darkened world. And there he saw its conflict with the hard-hearted jailer of Philippi, and forced from him the cry, "What must I do to be saved?" The church in other times was worthy of its origin. It maintained its high character years after, when the apostle wrote of it, and held it up as an example to others. How many churches in Europe are like it now? How is the gold become dim, and the fine gold changed? Yet the obligation to imitate it still remains, as we shall now see, by considering the apostle's exhortation, founded on what he had said to the Church of Christ at Corinth.

CORINTH.—2 CORINTHIANS, viii. 6-9; ix. 6-8, 12-15.

V. 6. "Insomuch that we desired Titus, that as he had begun so he would also finish in you the same grace also."

What he had seen at Macedonia he desired to see at Corinth.

God, he knew, had all hearts in his hand, and could and would do again and elsewhere as he had done before. Nothing but the advancing power of the Gospel will satisfy a mind rightly disposed toward God. The subjection of the earth to Jesus is the object at which he aims. But means must be used to gain the end. On this occasion the ministry of Titus was employed. It is a legitimate work to occupy the attention and labours of a minister of Christ, when he sets himself to produce and cherish in the people of his charge an enlarged liberality in the service of God. And when any success is obtained, that should be accounted an encouragement to persevere. Where we have begun to do good we should not rest till we finish the work.

V. 7. "Therefore, as ye abound in everything, in faith, and utterance, and knowledge, and in all diligence, and in your love to us, see that ye abound in this grace also."

The possession of some graces should never be esteemed an apology for the want of others. Rather should the deficiency be regarded as more inexcusable and inconsistent for that reason. Particularly it is most carefully to be avoided, that while some other graces are apparent that of liberality should be wanting. If a man be very zealous and stringent for holding the faith of the Gospel in purity, if he be eloquent in its advocacy and defence, if he be possessed of clear and enlarged views, if he be active in many external duties, if he show a great interest in the ministers of religion, and yet, after all, be deficient in liberality, it is a sad spectacle. The world see it and understand it. It brings the Gospel into disrepute; it causes the way of truth to be evil spoken of; it is the very circumstance which will be most readily seized upon to disparage true religion. And, therefore, while we do not fail to possess and cultivate other graces, we should be specially careful to exercise that of generosity in the cause of God.

V. 8. "I speak not by commandment, but by occasion of the forwardness of others, and to prove the sincerity of your love."

After all, let it not be supposed the apostle was dictatorial. What he said was in love and zeal, and he could not help it. "Out of the abundance of the heart the mouth speaketh." It was in his mind, and it would have been as a fire in his bones if he had not given vent to it. And there was some excuse for him. Others urged him, both by their example and their words. He wished also to have the same regard for the Corinthians as for others, such as the Macedonians, and the same reasons for it. He longed to see the sincerity of their love tested and proved. And when he did see it, it would contribute alike to their credit and his gratification.

V. 9. "For ye know the grace of our Lord Jesus Christ, that, though he was rich, yet for your sakes he became poor, that ye through his poverty might be rich.

Ah yes! This motive would justify all his earnestness, and might stimulate all their love. Who could resist it? or how? They were not ignorant of it. They knew it theoretically, and had in some measure felt it experimentally. What was it? They knew that Jesus had been rich—that he had dwelt in the glory of the Father in the highest heavens. They knew that he had become poor—so much so as not to have where to lay his head and to suffer as a common malefactor on the cross. They knew that to all this he submitted on their account,—that they might be rich, in the pardon of sin, the gifts of righteousness, the blessedness of true religion here and its everlasting joys hereafter. And if they knew and confessed all this, what might be expected of them? What would they do in the cause of this divine Master? What would they give for its advancement? What would they withhold? Surely such an appeal was irresistible.

Having made it, he explained to them at length some arrangements he had made for carrying forward the particular exercise of liberality then required of them to maturity And having done so sufficiently for his purpose, he proceeded to urge certain motives upon them, which it is important to notice as a specimen of apostolic dealing with a question of contribution to the cause of God.

Chap. ix. 6. "But this I say, He which soweth sparingly shall reap also sparingly, and he which soweth bountifully shall reap also bountifully."

This is reasonable. As it is in nature so also may we expect to find it in grace. He who does little good may expect to receive little. And this is applicable as well to time as to eternity. God has so ordered it, that in the very exercise of serving others we best serve ourselves. There is a providence, too, which goes by the rule, "With what measure ye mete it shall be measured to you again." And it is the plain testimony of the divine word that men shall be judged, if not by, yet "according to, their works." It must in the nature of the case be so, for just as by exercise the capacity for happiness is enlarged, so shall the measure of final enjoyment be.

V. 7. "Every man, according as he purposeth in his heart, so let him give, not grudgingly or of necessity, for God loveth a cheerful giver."

We should be at pains with the state of our hearts. We should not be satisfied merely with the doing of the generous act,—we should see that it is done in the right spirit. And this may be obtained by induiging such considerations as the apostle had suggested. Let them keep "looking unto Jesus," and the fire will burn within them. Besides, the doing of the acts of generosity has a tendency to improve the heart. Christ said, "If any man will do my will he shall know of the doctrine whether it be of God." Right performances would clear the intellect and promote knowledge. It would teach experimentally. And so here also the right occupation of the hands would extend its influence to the heart, and deeds of charity would promote a spirit of love.

V 8. "And God is able to make all grace abound toward you ; so that ye, having all sufficiency in all things, may abound to every good work."

It was not merely the natural effect of such a course as he had recommended they were to consider. There was, besides this, the promised and direct influence of the divine blessing What could not God do with their hearts ? What would he not do? What had he not done with many? He was able and willing, and they had only to ask and receive a right hearty and generous spirit from him. O how little this is remembered ! How few remember to ask God for liberality of soul, and how feebly! Yet be it not forgotten, the want of it is a sore calamity, the possession of it is an unspeakable blessing, and from God only can it come, and out of his fulness it may constantly be received.

V. 11-14. "Which causeth through us thanksgiving to God, they glorify God for your liberal distribution, and long after you for the exceeding grace of God in you."

They benefited not merely themselves and their fellow-creatures, but they brought glory to God in the highest. They acted on the exhortation, " Let your light so shine before men, that they may see your good works, and glorify your Father which is in heaven." And what effect ought such a thought to have on a generous heart? To be permitted to honour God!—what an honour! The very act of liberality itself honours him. It honours his grace which prompted it, and thus its effects increase his glory. They who participate in the kindness expressed are benefited, not only in the improvement of their outward circumstances, but in the state of their minds towards God and toward man. There is thus no limit to the widening circle of a generous liberality. As the pebble dropped into the lake puts its waters into motion, and circle rises after circle, till all is stirred, and the whole borders around are bathed by the waters, so a Christian deed may prove the means of an excitement which shall grow and increase from person to person, and from place to place, and from age to age, until it shall reach eternity itself, and encircle the throne of God with a halo of glory.

V. 15. "Thanks be unto God for his unspeakable gift."

No wonder the apostle should thus close his exhortation. He calls the grace of liberality an " unspeakable gift," for which he gives God thanks. And so it is, and so he ought to do. It is unspeakably good in its nature and effects. It is lamentable that it is so little contemplated under this aspect. How many quote the apostle's words, and yet do not apply them to his subject! Their modes of thinking are not like his; they have not the elevated views of gracious affections which he had. He calls charity an unspeakable gift, and until the same views prevail more generally the Christian Church can never be expected to do its duty in the devotion of its property to God. Oh! that men might so see this grace, as to be impelled to cry out, both on account of its own lovely character, and the extent to which they behold it exercised,—"Thanks be unto God for his unspeakable gift!"

Well, then, if these be the principles which the apostle Paul inculcated on the subject of religious contribution, what say we to the special question which they were introduced to illustrate? What testimony do Macedonia and Corinth bear to the proportion in which Christians should contribute to the cause of God? Would they say a tenth? Did this suffice for them or the apostle their teacher? They were all familiar with the laws and customs of ancient times. Although none of these persons had been Jews, and the members of both Macedonia and Corinth were either generally or exclusively Gentiles, and even Lydia seems to have been a proselyte, yet they would have learned from the Jewish Scriptures, and the Jews scattered among them, what had been the habits and practices of the ancient people of God. They knew well what God had required in the Jewish Scriptures. And now, when they came to interpret these passages by the principles which Paul had inculcated upon them, at what conclusion would they arrive? If we were told some gave a tenth, others less, others nothing, what opinion would we form or express of those churches? We would be ashamed of them. We would say they were utterly unworthy of their high privileges and honoured teachers. We could not help pronouncing upon them the severest censure. Then let us beware lest it be said to us, "Thou art the man;" "Physician, heal thyself;" "Thou that teachest a man should not steal, dost thou steal?" "Thou that sayest a man should not commit adultery, dost thou commit adultery?" "Thou that abhorrest idols, dost thou commit sacrilege?" Let us not expose ourselves to a retort so fearful. We see what are the great principles of the apostle, and by what motives he urged them on the early Church. Let us remember, in speaking to them, he being dead yet speaketh to us. Let us adopt his principles and act upon them; let us become distinguished by liberality in the cause of God as we have hitherto been by the want of it. Let it no more be said, "All seek their own, not the things which are Jesus Christ's." Let his cause be ours, and under a deep and growing sense of what he did for us let us uphold his cause till "all nations shall be blessed in him, and all nations shall call him blessed."

CHAPTER VII.

THE FIRST DAY OF THE WEEK.

"*Upon the first day of the week, let every one of you lay by him in store, as God hath prospered him.*"—1 Cor. xvi. 2.

"A WORD fitly spoken is like apples of gold in pictures of silver." It is in the Holy Scriptures these fitting words are found in perfection. Very frequently the weightiest sentiments are conveyed there in the fewest and simplest words possible. Great good is gained by this peculiarity of style. The truth so expressed is easily apprehended, easily remembered, and easily applied to practical uses. It is like the concentrated essence of the best food or medicine, in the composition of which the greatest nutrition is secured by the smallest quantity. Examples of all kinds abound. Do the Scriptures describe God? It is thus: "God is a spirit;" "God is light;" "God is love." What a fund of thought and truth is here, which the most profound philosopher cannot fathom, and which yet the simplest child can in some degree apprehend and remember perfectly! Or do they set forth the way of a sinner's salvation by God? It is thus: "God so loved the world that he gave his only-begotten Son, that whosoever believeth in him should not perish, but have everlasting life;" "This is a faithful saying and worthy of all acceptation, that Christ Jesus came into the world to save sinners, of whom I am chief;" "By grace are ye saved through faith, and that not of yourselves; it is the gift of God." In these brief sayings the leading features of the way of salvation are fully and clearly intimated. It is the same with practical duties.

Every class will be found expressed in some comprehensive and short sentence. To confine ourselves to the one before us, the duty of religious contribution, the whole subject may be said to be laid down in the few terms prefixed to this chapter: "Upon the first day of the week, let every one of you lay by him in store, as God hath prospered him." A full development of the great principles of the duty has already been considered in the apostle's argument addressed to the Corinthians. On every one of them we might have dwelt at length, but their number and weight permitted only a cursory glance at them. Enough, however, was said to show their extent and depth. Oh! that the members of the Christian Church would ponder them deeply, drink into their spirit, feel their power, and obey their requirements. But we must now turn from them, and claim attention to the brief rule which has just been intimated, and which will yet be found to have the most extensive application.

1. The time of religious contribution is marked,—"the first day of the week,"—the Christian Sabbath. There is much significance in the fact that a time is thus divinely fixed. It assumes that the duty as a matter of obligation must be discharged at some time, and that it is well to have an appointed time for it, lest it should by any possibility, through neglect, be omitted altogether. It is too often found, that what we think may be done at any time is never done. Nor is it merely that the time is fixed; the frequency of its recurrence is important to be observed. It arrives weekly. The duty is to be habitually performed. It is not a mere momentary excitement, to be spent in a strong impulse, from which we may fall back into apathy or neglect. It is a duty to be kept constantly before our attention, that as its obligations never cease, so neither shall our exertions. The tone of the prescribed rule implies that there is the utmost concern and consideration that the duty may be done perseveringly and effectually. Above all, it should be carefully noted under what powerful impressions and motives the apostle would have our minds when we would thus habitually devote our property to God. "On the first day of the week!" What associations are connected with that day! It reminds us of Jesus, it is

sacred to his memory, it is the Lord's day, it brings us into fellowship with him, and it irresistibly urges upon us, "Whatsoever ye do, do it heartily, as unto the Lord, and not unto men." It reminds us especially of his triumph. We may say, "This is the day the Lord hath made, we will rejoice and be glad in it." "I will triumph in the work of thy hands." On this day our divine Redeemer rose from the grave, "spoiling principalities and powers, and making a show of them openly." We have, therefore, vividly presented to us all the blessings which we enjoy by means of the death and resurrection of the Son of God. An appeal is made to the heart by their value and number. As we contemplate what he has done for us, we are asked, what we are ready to do for him? By the Sabbath we are further reminded of the outpouring of the Spirit of Christ. As on this day he arose and ascended, so also on it he sent the Holy Ghost. And the effusion of the day of Pentecost was only an emblem and earnest of what might be expected in future years. Long after, John could say, in the lonely isle of Patmos, "I was in the Spirit on the Lord's day." So should every believer have the same experience. He needs the weekly return of the holy day, and it is expressly provided for him. His prayer should be, "Visit me with thy salvation;" and nothing less than the enjoyment of its answer should satisfy him. What, then, is to be its effect in the enlightenment and enlargement of his mind, discovering to him the duty of yielding himself and all he has to God, and engaging him heartily and earnestly to make the surrender? But it is in the ordinances of grace the Spirit is to be expected on that day, and hence arises another powerful influence under which the believer is to be prompted to act. These are wondrously adapted to both his mental and bodily constitution—the singing of God's praise, pouring out the heart in prayer, the Word read and preached, the fellowship of the body and blood of Jesus, and the pronouncing of the benediction in his name. How calculated are these services powerfully to impress and excite the soul to duty! They may well be anticipated, as was done by David, saying, "I shall be anointed with fresh oil." Fresh supplies of the grace of the Spirit are needed and expected in the ordinances of God's house. And, to sum up all, the rest of the Sabbath is the emblem of heaven itself. Heaven is only an unbroken Sabbath—unbroken by worldly cares or sins, unbroken by any limitation of times or seasons. We are reminded how short our time on earth is, and how long the eternity on which we are about to enter. In the same measure we learn the necessity of redeeming the time now, and doing something that will tell upon eternity for the well-being of ourselves and others. This is the time which the apostle has fixed for religious contribution. And is it not manifest he did so with good reason? He has chosen the time when the mind is under the best and most powerful influences, the period at which the duty bids fairest to be best discharged, when if ever it shall not be neglected, and when every temptation to neglect is most likely to be resisted and overcome.

Attention is specially requested to this view of the subject. In almost no instance is the apostolic rule, in this matter, obeyed. In a large proportion of the churches of these lands no religious contribution is made on the first day of the week. In many, a halfpenny or penny may statedly be given. But as to meeting the spirit or the letter of the apostolic rule, where shall we find it? Personal enjoyment and profit seem to be the grand absorbing objects of attendance upon public worship. We go to receive good, and forget the apostle has also taught us we should no less go to do good. "To do good and to communicate forget not, for with such sacrifices God is well pleased." It is to be feared we are in no readiness to act upon this apostolic rule. The church that would earnestly call upon its members to do so would be apt to endanger its peace or outward prosperity. Its habitual calls to generosity would be felt to be irksome, and there would be rebellion against them. Let us alone, and let us have the undisturbed enjoyment of the word and ordinances, would, it is feared, be the saying of many. Yet this is a great mistake. Never do we find a Scripture rule either unwise or unsuited to our highest benefit. It is in doing good we obtain good. If the churches of Christ would only consent to act on the apostolic rule, they would speedily experience the advantages in their own edification. Only suppose that their members did, as the apostle recommends, exercise frugality and care thoughout the week, that they might be prepared to present their offerings to the Lord and his cause on every first day of the week, and what rich enjoyment would they soon experience in their own souls? God would meet them, and shower his blessings upon them. They would soon have the aspect of a garden which the Lord himself had watered. And they would be constrained often to cry out, "God is in this place; this is none other than the house of God, and this is the gate of heaven." There is one practice, in particular, to which we cannot but advert for a moment, in connexion with this view of the subject. It is the custom of most churches to sustain their Christian efforts by occasional addresses and collections on days specially appointed for the purpose. For these all preparation is made. Notices are previously given of the intended appeal, and the object of it. Information is circulated to arrest attention, and stimulate zeal. When the set day arrives, the preacher puts forth his utmost power to rouse the assembled church to a sense and performance of its duty. And on the success of this attempt the cause in question is dependent for a year to come. It is cause of thankfulness that even this much is gained. Not long ago nothing of the kind existed. Churches met and parted, and thought not of any duty they were called on to discharge for the benefit of others. It is hoped there will be a growing spirit of earnest zeal, and that nothing shall be left undone which wise and prudent measures can obtain for the upholding of the cause of Christ on earth. As matters are, ministers must thus statedly preach, they must go forth from time to time, and place to place; they must circulate information, and try to call forth zeal; they must devise expedients, and use all their sanctified ingenuity to raise the funds that are required for carrying the truth of Christ and its messengers though the whole earth. All this, it is admitted, must, in the present state of the Church, be done. None, we trust, will misunderstand our remarks, nor turn them into an excuse for the neglect of present duty. After all, however, may we not say, "I show unto you a more excellent way?" And what is it? many will say. They feel the present plan is inefficient, and does not reach the necessities of the case. Our most important plans for the evangelisation of the world are languishing for the want of support. Can you point out a way to fill the exhausted treasury? Yes, and a simple one too—a way simpler and easier far than that which is at present pursued, and as much more efficient as it is easier and simpler. It is just to return to the apostolic counsel, "On the first day of the week" give your substance to the cause of God. It is obvious he means, not as we seem to have understood it, a special day selected now and again, but every "first day of the week." Wherever the Church of Christ assembles on that day, let its members give what their painstaking has enabled them to provide for the cause of God. Observe how an operation so simple would tell advantageously on the finances of the Church. It would set us free from the disaster which a day of stormy rain and tempest must inflict upon the cause which had its advocacy confined to that special season. With what dismay have the managers of many a noble cause looked out on such a day, as they felt the responsibility that rested upon them to meet the necessities of those who bore its toils and conducted its labours. It has been stated that the character of the appointed day determined in some instances whether the effort made over the churches of a certain district would raise the cause to a position of safety and prosperity for the coming year, or leave it to struggle as best it might with the difficulties of poverty until Providence might be pleased to favour it, in some future day, with a season of calm and sunshine. Is it a wise or proper arrangement that leaves an important cause dependent upon such a circumstance? The apostolic rule would remove the difficulty, and it would do more and better still. It would bring the claims of God's cause before all the members of the Church. On those special occasions which we have fixed many may not be present. Either they must have zeal to remedy the loss of their presence by a voluntary donation of their generosity, or their help must be lost until another distant opportunity shall be granted. And then the same disappointment may arise again. The stated and habitual offering at once remedies this evil. At the same time its amount of contribution would be a mighty increase on the present forced collection. A penny every week would seem a trifle to many who would scruple to present the shillings to which it would rise at the termination of the year. A shilling would be an easy weekly offering to some, who would be alarmed by the idea of laying fifty-two together on the plate of solicitation after the financial year had come to a close. Even the more extended offering of the pound, or more, would not seem extravagant to some, who would feel a strong temptation to curtail the donation of not a few when they were to be presented in a single offering. The finance of the Scriptures will be found as wise and efficient as it is simple. It is the best by far to meet the temptations to which human nature, in the frailty of its best estate, is liable, and by the easiest means to secure the best results. And is it nothing to substitute the calm doings of principle for the stimulus of occasional excitement? We should look well to our motives. God searcheth the hearts, and trieth the reins of the children of men. Pride and vain-glory are besetting sins of men. They are in all circumstances evil, chiefly so when allowed to influence in the cause of God. We should be careful not only to do what is right in itself, but to do it in the right spirit and manner. And that the change of measures suggested would be calculated to have a favourable influence in this respect who can doubt? It may be added, that the very habit of looking to our affairs habitually throughout the week, that we may have to give to the cause of God on the approaching Sabbath, and that we may know what we ought to give consistently with other claims, would greatly minister to a proper frame of mind. It would be a most valuable and habitual discipline of the soul. It would bring God into the most ordinary concerns of life, and elevate the lowest engagements to the dignity of the highest principles. Let it not be said, Such a habit would lay upon us a yoke of intolerable bondage. Recollect it is God who has laid it on. The rule we are recommending is divine. It is also both wise and mercifully adapted to its purposes, and not less so to the happiness and prosperity of him who acts upon it. Alas that the churches of Christ should be so little in a condition to adopt such a rule! We are far from violently forcing it on any. We fear great changes must come before it will be generally adopted. But one day, no doubt, it will be the rule and the practice of the Lord's people. Let those who can, begin to act upon it now. Let those who cannot overcome the difficulties in their way, pray and wait till God shall make the path plain before them. But in this as in all things let us feel assured it is well to say, " O that my ways were directed to keep thy statutes! Then shall I not be ashamed, when I have respect unto all thy commandments."

2. Not merely, however, does the apostolic rule determine the time of contributing, it fixes attention also upon those whose duty it is to contribute—" Every one of you." Who are meant? In some sense it may no doubt be said, all men are comprehended in the description. Whoever they are for whom the blessings of the gospel are intended, they certainly should acknowledge the obligation here laid upon them. We do not enter into any inquiry respecting the extent of the atonement. It would be manifestly out of place. We proceed merely on the general ground, which none will dispute, that the gospel is to be preached to all men, and that all are invited to participate in its benefits. None will be so infatuated as to exclude themselves from the number of those invited and entreated to believe on Jesus Christ, and obtain eternal life in him. Then must all such own that they are included in the " every one" of the rule. For if the gospel is preached to them and they may enjoy its benefits, surely it becomes their duty to give of their substance that these same privileges may be extended to others. Let it not be said, there can be no obligation on any to extend the gospel until they themselves become recipients of the gospel and its salvation. This involves a most fatal principle in morals. A man's unfitness for a duty, or his indisposedness for it, does not release him from the obligation of it. So, because a man does not receive the gospel, it does not follow that it is not his duty to receive it. He is bound to receive it, and to discharge every duty which it requires. Until he does so, he is living in sin, and nothing can free him from the demand which his great Creator has laid upon him. These remarks apply directly to the special duty which we are enforcing. It is the duty of " every one" to receive the gospel himself, and to send it

to others, and to do whatever he can to advance this object. We have no hesitation in saying this is the duty of a deist, or even of an atheist, if such is to be found. "Unto you, O men, I call, and my voice is to the sons of men,"—this is the address of Christ in his word. And whether men will hear, or whether they will forbear, here are their privileges, and duties, and responsibilities. Literally and universally, therefore, it is the duty of "every one" to consider and contrive that he may have to give of his substance "on the first day of the week." Nor let it be overlooked, that whoever fails in this duty is so far hardening his own heart, and shutting it up more and more against the reception of Christ and his truth into it. It is with this sin as with every sin. All sin is not only evil in itself, but is exerting an influence for greater evil over every mind that is subjected to it. And this is a fearful consideration. The ungodly are "treasuring up wrath against the day of wrath and revelation of the righteous judgment of God." On this principle we deem it an object worthy of all zeal and effort to hinder an ungodly man from contracting more sin. Even though he become not a subject of God's converting grace, it is of high moment to keep him back from any sin, or to engage him in the performance of any duty. Often the very performance of a duty is the beginning of a state of mind that leads to the most gracious and blessed results. One thing is clear, it was a marked feature in our Lord's ministry to engage "every one" in well-doing. His sermon on the mount is a noble illustration of it. "Then came publicans also to be baptized, and said unto him, Master, what shall we do? And he said unto them, Exact no more than that which is appointed you. And the soldiers likewise demanded of him, saying, And what shall we do? And he said unto them, Do violence to no man, neither accuse any falsely, and be content with your wages." Proceeding on this high authority, we call upon "every one" to give unto the Lord. Oh! that we could engage even an ungodly and careless community in this duty. It would soon produce a wondrous change on their spirit, and habits, and practices. Caring for others, they would begin to care for themselves. This would bring them to God, and, sensible of their own necessities, they would learn to cry mightily to him, that they might be healed of their sins God would bless them, too. Not only in the nature and necessity of their new engagements would there arise a cessation from much that was evil, and an engagement in that which was in itself good, but the Lord would look favourably upon them; not, certainly, because they thus entered upon a course of reformation, yet in the way of entering on such a course. We are urgent in the assertion of these principles, because we think they have been sadly perverted, and a secret feeling seems to have spread too generally in the minds of men, that because they do not profess religion, its duties cannot be expected nor are they required of them. It is a fearful delusion, by which Satan has slain his thousands and tens of thousands. We have done what we could to detect and expose his design, and we now proceed to contemplate the phrase before us in its more restricted acceptation. This was no doubt in the apostle's mind when he said, " Every one *of you*." He spoke to the members of that church which he had described as " sanctified in Christ Jesus, called to be saints." "Ye are washed, ye are justified, ye are sanctified, in the name of the Lord Jesus, and by the Spirit of our God." They were called upon, therefore, by a regard to their own consistency and profession, to be liberal in the cause of God. They had declared by their conduct that they acquiesced in the sentiment of Christ, " What is a man profited if he shall gain the whole world and lose his own soul? or what shall a man give in exchange for his soul? " They must, therefore, do what in them lay to show their value for the souls of men, and make every sacrifice to save them. Even although the special duty required of them was to contribute to the temporal relief of the saints at Jerusalem, yet there was much that was spiritual in the duty. Their temporal state powerfully affected their mental exercises. It was as the saints of God, having claims upon them as part of the Christian brotherhood, they were required to provide for them. And they were under the necessity of doing it out of regard to Jesus Christ, their Master, and that of the objects of their sympathy too — regard to his example, authority, and the solemn anticipations of the final judgment, which he had so minutely described in his ministry on the earth, and in which description he gave so much prominence to what was done for his disciples in his name: "Inasmuch as ye have done it unto one of the least of these my brethren, ye have done it unto me." The duty, therefore, was to all intents and purposes one highly spiritual in its character, as much so as if its direct object had been the saving of the souls of them for whom they were concerned. Then, again, they had by their conduct acknowledged the fulness and sufficiency of Christ for the salvation of their own souls. They had committed themselves into his hands, and this was the highest testimony they could give to others how highly they prized him. If they were sincere herein, what would they do to lead others to do as they had done themselves? How paltry would any earthly sacrifice seem in comparison with the high and holy object which they sought to gain! Not only had they made their confession by the act of embracing the Saviour for themselves in faith, but they were accustomed to avow that faith in the most public and emphatic manner. Their Sabbath assemblies and their holy communion in bread and wine at the table of the Lord were known and read of all men. In all consistency, then, what service might be demanded at their hands? Surely "every one" of them would own and act on his obligation to give to the utmost for the temporal, spiritual, and eternal well-being of others. These remarks are as applicable to the members of the Christian Church now as they ever were to those whom the apostle immediately addressed. Christians make the same professions now as ever were made in apostolic times. It is the profession of a "common salvation." They have their assemblies now, as of old—the same solemnities—the same table of the Lord. The same obligations, therefore, rest upon them. On "every one" who professes Christ is laid the obligation to do what he can for the spread of his truth. And is there any "one" who could not do something? Is there "one" who could not give something? God knoweth, and it were presumption in us to speak peremptorily, but if there be "one" who could not give something for Jesus, who gave himself for him, his circumstances must be very peculiar. Yet how many there are who act as if such were their case! They give nothing.

It is idle to inquire into the various reasons which would be alleged for the neglect, but the fact cannot be questioned. Many, very many, do not give at all. The majority do not give. The smallness of contribution in the earth to the cause of Christ is a proof that few give. It may be presumed many have not been told of their obligation to do so. To others it has not occurred. It is a prevailing idea with many that all they could give is so little, it would be neither worth their offering nor the Church accepting. This is a sore evil. As well might the drops not fall because they are not each a whole shower of rain. As well might the stream let from the mountain stay its course because it is not the broad river on which go the gallant ships. This is a matter of deep concern to the interests of religion. Personal responsibility is the great duty needed to be known and felt. If the members of the Church were brought to understand it, all would be well yet. If each would do what he could, there would be enough. It is not easy to learn what might be the number of professing Protestants, who sit down at the table of the Lord. There are no data within reach on which we can arrive at an average number. So far as we know the state of Protestantism in this land we would be disposed to say, that in the most favourable circumstances there are about a tenth who confess publicly their faith in Christ at the table of the Lord. Suppose that even this tenth did "every one" something, gave "every one" something, the result would be blessed. In one section of the Church with which we are acquainted, where the number of communicants is probably about one hundred thousand, and where a considerable missionary spirit prevails, in which there have been some noble and zealous efforts, and over which considerable pains have been taken to improve the spirit and form a habit of giving to the Lord, the average annual contribution has not exceeded 10,000*l*. Only let the apostolic rule be unanimously adopted and acted on by the Church, and let each of its communicants give but a penny in the week, and its annual contribution would be 20,000*l*. Thus at once would the funds for the treasury of Christ from that single source be more than doubled. Yet who would assign a rate so small as this? A penny in the week! This specimen is only given that it might be seen what a little calculation and a little effort might do. How wise is the Spirit of God! How apparent is that wisdom in the rule of contribution which we have been considering! If it were obeyed, and "every one" would give, it would change the whole aspect of the Church and the world. The discovery of the law of gravity did not produce a greater change in the philosophy of the world than the obedience of this simple rule would produce in the moral condition of the world. The discovery of steam, with all its wondrous powers and extraordinary effects and unexpected changes, would not match the results of this one simple principle, were it only carried out into the conduct of professing Christians. We submit it to their consideration, and call upon "every one" to say whether he will accept it for his rule, or plainly and confessedly reject it from his creed. Only let "every" one know that whosoever rejects it rejects the apostle and Him also who sent him, the Lord Jesus Christ.

3. Lengthened, however, as our remarks have been on this apostolic rule, we have not yet done. It is, as we have said again and again, remarkable for its simplicity, and it should have required nothing to be said in either the illustration or enforcement of it. But its neglect, its almost entire oversight, has rendered it necessary that all should be said which has been now advanced, and more too. The longer a noble building has lain in ruins the more it is covered over with accumulated matter, and it needs the greater labour to remove the rubbish, and more excavation to bring the buried columns to the light of day, and replace them on their ancient foundations, until the once perfect building is restored again to its former symmetry, and beauty, and strength. So with this principle on which we have been dwelling. It appears to have been concealed from the view of the Church. Amid the dilapidations of the truth and of the Church upon the earth, the rubbish of long-established usages, and mistaken principles, and erroneous views, has covered it over so as to have put it out of sight. Much labour, therefore, is necessary to bring it out again, and let men see it in its beautiful proportion and mighty strength. We have already presented some portions of it to their notice and

admiration, and now we proceed to exhibit one other feature which will complete the description. It is the measure or proportion in which "every one" is required to give—even "as the Lord hath prospered him."

At first sight the meaning would seem to be sufficiently clear. Indeed, it would appear as if it were hardly possible to mistake it, —that as God gives us means from week to week, so we should give in the same proportion to his cause. But there are none so blind as those who will not see. Where no obscurity exists, there are those who take pleasure in creating it. The more simple anything is they make it the more difficult to understand. And even on this unmistakable rule questions are asked which no casuist is able to answer, and prolixities are woven out of it which it is impossible to unravel. What is meant, says one, by giving as the Lord hath prospered? Does it mean our annual income? or our whole estate? Supposing the tenth to be the proportion of giving, am I called on to give that measure of all I have or of what God has given me during the year? The principle of explanation is manifestly contained in the rule itself. It is a proportion to be given according to the increase of the time mentioned, and in the present instance it is a week. This may be extended to other periods of time, a month or a year. Thus the text itself fixes its meaning to refer to income, and not to the amount of property possessed. It need not be said this property will affect the income, but it is by the increase of what it yields that the proportion to be given shall be measured. In this arrangement the wisdom of the Scriptures is great. They promise to the believer worldly prosperity among other blessings. "Godliness is profitable unto all things, having promise of the life that now is, and of that which is to come." Wealth is an unspeakable blessing in the hands of the godly. Constituted as the world is, we do not see how the cause of God is to be carried forward without the help of the rich. True, the offerings of the poor are to be highly prized, Perhaps, too, they will ever be, as they have ever been, the chief source of support to the Church of Christ. Still there are noble examples of great good effected by princely offerings from the rich. Great and gracious promises, too, are held out to this effect in the

Scriptures. We rejoice, therefore, when God in his providence is pleased to prosper his people. It is good to see them growing in wealth and influence. The world shall be the better for it all. Let it not, therefore, be supposed we frown upon the wealthy or make little of their wealth. On the contrary, we praise God on their account; and we admire the rule which is now before us, because, while it provides for the necessities of the Church, it does not interfere even with their worldly prosperity. Understanding it thus, then, its directions are plain, and we hold them to be universally applicable. Fixing attention, for the sake of illustration, on what we have shown to be the lowest proportion of giving ever sanctioned by the Scriptures,—a tenth,—observe the practical application. And we specify it, not because any can fail to apply the rule to themselves, but because, even where duty is clear, we need "line upon line and precept upon precept." The income of one is ten pounds in the year; then the claim of God is one pound. That of another is double, and the claim upon him is double. A third has received one hundred pounds, and ten pounds is his proportion. If it be a thousand pounds, a hundred can readily be spared. If it be many thousands, there may be as many hundreds. Plain and specific, however, as we desire to be, there are those who cannot understand the matter. How, they ask, can a man who has a large family, and only one hundred pounds a-year to provide for all their wants, devote a tenth to the cause of God? Then, I ask, is a man having only the half of it, or less, to give none at all? Nay, I ask, How are many families supported on the fourth of it? And on less by far? But, you say, we have a station to support which they have not. Will you plead that argument with God? The conscience that could do so must be seared as with a hot iron If God has placed you in those circumstances, it is an intimation of his will that he would have you to live according to them. He has not relaxed his law that you might live after certain conventional rules which men have made, but which he has never sanctioned. After all, are you not satisfied with our explanations? Then we are sorry for it, but cannot help it. Only you must allow us to ask, Where lies the fault?

In us, or in you? To bring this question to a test, let us entreat that you will give us your interpretation of the apostolic rule. You do not approve of ours; what, then, is your own? There are those who can reject all that others propose, but have no proposal of their own to make. Are you of that number? There is a mighty power in some to pull down, but they will never give a hand to help to build up. We must leave you, if you be such, to Him who shall judge both you and us. And we turn away to indulge the sad reflections which are forced upon us while we look at the rule which the apostle has prescribed, and compare it with the conduct which many evince. How few, alas! there are who are giving even according to the lowest proportion of a tenth! But, not to dwell upon this, we mourn especially, how little the claim is considered that each shall give "as the Lord hath prospered him." Last year the income was increased, but the subscription is the same. The income of one is double that of another, but their donations to the cause of God are equal. In some instances the income has been growing, and the proportion of contribution has been decreasing. Years have been accumulating, and wealth has kept pace with them, but the heart has become more and more contracted, and the duty of giving less and less felt. It is a fearful proof of the depravity of human nature to find that the besetting sin of old age is covetousness. Just the opposite of what might have been expected is found to be the reality. As the world becomes less capable of affording enjoyment, it is held with greater tenacity. When men are about to leave it they cling closer to it. Be watchful. Nothing grows faster, or is harder to be dislodged from the heart, than worldliness. There may be some who feel difficulties, however, which are peculiar to their circumstances in carrying the apostolic rule into effect. The apostle seems to write to those who were in circumstances to know what their weekly lodgment for the cause of God should be. Some such there are still, it may be many. But there are some with whom it is not so. They are unable to tell what a week, or a month, or even a year, may enable them to make a just proportion. It is to be regretted that the state of commerce does in some instances create such difficulties. When the servant of the Lord finds himself in them, he must meet them as best he can. Stretching the time over more years than one, he must strike the proportion accordingly. He knows how to do so in other transactions, and his ingenuity will not fail him here. We may safely leave him to its exercise. Only let him not forget, the rule we have been expounding does not change with the changes of this earth's occupations. It is like him who gave it, eternal and immutable. Abraham acted on it in his day, so did Jacob. Moses enforced it by many sanctions, and Jesus Christ in his own ministry and by that of his apostles inculcated it again and again. However, therefore, it is to be obeyed—conformity to it is essential. If any find fault with our exposition of it, in understanding it of income, let them extend it according to their convictions of duty. If they think it embraces all property, let them so act upon it. We shall not complain of them. Perhaps, after all, they may reap their reward in so doing. It is a blessed thing to get above the earthliness of the present world. We are in great danger of being swayed by its vain calculations. Truly we need to cry, "O Lord, open thou mine eyes to behold wondrous things out of thy law." In no department is this more necessary than in those practical questions that are apt to come into contact with our selfishness and worldly prejudices. Blessed be God, however, the rule in this instance is plain. The wayfaring man, though a fool, need not err respecting it. He who runs may read. And we end with its repetition as we began, leaving it on the conscience of every man to act according to his view of what it requires. "On the first day of the week, let every one of you lay by him in store, as God hath prospered him." Noble principle this! And noble exercise where it is obeyed! The Christian keeping it ever in his eye! looking at his daily accounts in the light of it! regarding God as a claimant in all his transactions! and while just in his dealings with all men, resolved he will not "rob God."

CHAPTER VIII.

EXAMPLES.

"*Whatsoever things were written aforetime, were written for our learning.*"—Rom. xv. 4.

"As a man thinketh in his heart, so is he." As is our faith, so will be our conduct. Hence we infer, on the other hand, that as a man's life is, so we may judge of his sentiments. "By their fruits ye shall know them." Proceeding on this principle we may gain further information respecting the views taught in the Scriptures on the subject of religious contribution. We have only to inquire what was the conduct of those who believed them in order to ascertain what were their sentiments. Their actions are a comment on their principles. We have endeavoured to make manifest that the lowest proportion of income ever given by the people of God, and sanctioned by his authority, is a tenth; and now, in confirmation and illustration of that view, we appeal to this practice. Let this be contemplated in all relations, public and private, and under all dispensations, Mosaic and Christian, and the conclusion will be the same. It is worthy of observation, that the Spirit of God has seen good to record the doings of the Lord's people in this respect; and out of many examples we shall select a few that may be looked upon as a specimen of the rest, and very illustrative of their guiding principles. The first which we shall notice relates to the

ERECTION OF THE TABERNACLE.

The record of this event is contained in Exodus xxxv.—xxxvi. It has seemed good to the Holy Ghost to give us very minute details, and particularly to describe how means were obtained for the completion of such an undertaking. We shall endeavour to sketch the leading features of the interesting and instructive proceeding. The first thing that arrests attention is the proposal of

Moses: "Moses gathered all the congregation of the children of Israel together, and said unto them, These are the words which the Lord hath commanded, that ye should do them; take ye from among you an offering unto the Lord." He deals reasonably and candidly with them. He assumes no authority over them, but bears to them a message from the Lord. He explains to them the will of the Lord clearly before he proceeds to ask their concurrence and co-operation. Let this be noticed at the outset. We must never attempt to carry our measures for the cause of God by mere authority. We must be ready and careful to give a reason for our proposals. We must take care that both we and our measures are understood, and not till then are we in a condition to propose their adoption. This done, Moses at once gave them to understand the work was to be entirely voluntary; "Whosoever is of a willing heart, let him bring it, an offering of the Lord." There was to be no constraint; if any chose to avoid the work, they were at liberty to do so; if any took part in it, it must be heartily. Even though they helped by their contribution, if this were not done with sincerity and cheerfulness, the service would not be accepted by him who looketh not so much on the outward appearance as upon the heart. Then as to what each should bring to the work, the proposal of Moses was that every one should give according to what he possessed: "Gold, silver, brass, blue, purple, scarlet, fine linen, goats' hair, rams' skins, badgers' skins, shittim wood, oils, spices, and onyx stones." Anything offered in the right spirit would be acceptable. Every one could give something, although no one could give everything. None would be excluded from having some part in the delightful service; God would deprive no one of such an opportunity. His providence has put something in the hands of every one which may be employed for him. Such were the proposals of Moses, and now we are to look at their reception by the people. This was not immediate. They took time for consideration: "All the congregation of the children of Israel departed from the presence of Moses." How did they employ themselves? We follow them to their tents. Here is a company engaged in earnest conversation, by the way, on what they had heard, and every one gives his opinion freely, all approving the plan. There is a family group in affectionate fellowship, consulting what they can do to help the work forward. And yonder is an aged patriarch, alone, in prayer to God, wrestling with him, that he may give counsel to Israel in so great a work, and engage the hearts of all in it. All this augurs well. Soon, therefore, the people come to a decision, and return to Moses: "They came, every one whose heart stirred him up, and every one whose spirit made him willing, and they brought the Lord's offering to the work of the tabernacle of the congregation." It is most engaging to notice who came, and what they brought, and how they acted. Who? "Men and women," both the sexes alike. All are concerned in the work of the Lord, and none should abstain from it. There is work for man and work for woman. Both are under deep obligations, and both should acknowledge them. The one can do what the other cannot—together the agency is complete. What did they bring? The women brought "bracelets and earrings, and rings, and tablets, all jewels of gold." These would be better employed in aiding the work of the Lord than in adorning their persons. The men brought "blue and purple, and skins and wood," whatever any one possessed. How did they act? "The women did spin with their hands, and brought that which they had spun." "The rulers brought onyx stones, and spice, and oil." "The children of Israel brought a willing offering unto the Lord, every man and woman, whose heart made them willing to bring for all manner of work, which the Lord had commanded to be made by the hand of Moses." No sooner did this heartiness in the Lord's service appear, than the favour of Jehovah was manifested. He raised up fitting agents to do the work. "Moses said, See, the Lord hath called by name Bezaleel, the son of Uri, and he hath filled him with the Spirit of God, in wisdom, in understanding, and in all knowledge, and in all manner of workmanship." "And he hath put in his heart that he may teach, both he and Aholiab: them hath he filled with wisdom of heart, to work all manner of work, of the engraver, and of the cunning workman, and of the embroiderer, in blue, and in purple, in scarlet, and in fine linen, and of the weaver, even of them that do any work, and of those that devise cunning work." Let us address ourselves to God's work in good earnest, and he will further our endeavours. "Acknowledge God in all thy ways, and he will direct thy steps." Nor was this a momentary excitement. The work went on, and the interest of the people in it continued. "They brought free offerings every morning." Having begun a good work we must persevere. So they did, and a glorious issue they obtained. "The wise men that wrought all the work came unto Moses and said, The people bring much more than enough. And Moses gave commandment, and they caused it to be proclaimed throughout the camp, saying, Let neither man nor woman make any more work for the offering of the sanctuary. So the people were restrained from bringing." It should not be overlooked in what circumstances this noble outburst of sanctified generosity took place. It was in the wilderness. The people were assembled there amid its wild and rugged scenery. They were dependent every day on the providence of God to supply their returning wants. They had no resources either from agriculture or commerce. No people could be under stronger temptations to keep what they had against an evil day. Yet their zeal for God overcame all their fears. Their love for his service opened their hearts, and made them willing to give whatever they possessed. And a blessed work it proved to be. That Tabernacle became the dwelling place of Jehovah throughout many generations. There he met his people, and communed with them. It was like the building of a mighty reservoir of pure water, whence streams of blessing flowed after them while they sojourned in the desert, and long also after they entered into the promised land. The transactions of that glorious day, we may be assured, were never forgotten in Israel. An impetus was then given to the cause of God that did not spend its force for many generations. They are left on record to teach us to act in the same manner. We, as they, are invited to bear our part in the work of the Lord. We should, like them, entertain the proposal seriously and prayerfully We ought, after their example, to acquiesce in it. We should all do so, men and women. Every one should do what he can, and give what he can. God will bless us as we do so. He will provide agents to carry forward the holy enterprise on which we set our hearts; he will bring it to a successful issue. We shall find that we have been raising a memorial the most honourable to ourselves and beneficial to men; it will endure when we have mouldered into dust. In it we shall find we were blessed, and, after us, many shall find it to be a blessing. Is not such a work worthy of a generous offering? What shall it be? A tenth of our income? Read the doings of Israel and determine. They knew the law, but did they limit themselves to it on this occasion? Their conduct is the best exemplification of their principles. What think we of any Israelite who might be detected on that day keeping back from the work of the Lord? How we despise him! An Achan in the camp, he could only bring a curse on Israel. Then let us be both admonished and encouraged liberally to give to the work of the Lord, until his Tabernacle is built in the wilderness of the world, where he shall dwell, in manifest tokens of his presence, until his people are brought up into the land of rest and promise.

THE TEMPLE.

The Tabernacle had now stood for a period of about five hundred years. It was the will of God that it should at length give place to a more permanent structure. The circumstances in which the Temple that succeeded it was erected are fully detailed. And it is worthy of note that here again, as in the case of the Tabernacle, we are presented with a noble exhibition of generosity in the cause of God. This cannot be accidental. It is the will of God we should know, that under every economy, and in every change of administration, liberality in his cause marked his people. Israel at the building of the Temple presents a happy resemblance of the same Israel at the erection of the Tabernacle, and we shall now contemplate the prominent features of their conduct as narrated in the 28th and 29th chapters of 1 Chronicles. As might be expected, there is much in common with what happened at the building of the Tabernacle, but we shall endeavour to bring out mainly what is new in this example of generosity.

The objects were in some respects similar, but in others different. One great end was to be served by both, the maintenance of the worship of God among his people, a testimony to himself and his truth. But the Tabernacle was a frail and moveable erection, while the Temple was a permanent and stable structure. The one was adapted to an unsettled people on a toilsome journey, the other to a state of tranquillity and national prosperity. The narrative in both cases shows that a generous spirit can live under any circumstances, in poverty and in wealth, in journeying or abiding, at home or abroad. The principle is independent of changing circumstances. At all times and in all conditions the people of the Lord are expected to be generous in his service.

As the offerings for the Tabernacle were adapted to the wilderness state of Israel and to their condition of poverty, so their services for the Temple were worthy of their advancement in civilisation and prosperity. Their contributions were magnificent. They are thus described in the discourse of Dr. Brown, formerly referred to,—" The donations of David and his people astonish us by their magnitude. In addition to the immense sums which he had amassed during his reign for the building of the Temple, he, on the occasion referred to, devoted to this pious purpose what is equivalent to about *eighteen millions* of our money; and his people's joint contributions considerably exceeded *thirty millions.*" It is easy to pronounce these sums, but there are few who have any just apprehension of their value as they thoughtlessly read of them. They discover an amount of wealth and a largeness of heart to which in these days there is nothing to compare in the efforts of Christian benevolence. All the contributions of all the Christian churches on the face of the earth, for all missionay purposes, fall immeasurably short of this single offering on the part of ancient Israel and their king.

It is partly to be explained by observing who they were that gave on this occasion, and in what manner they did so. Here is the narrative. " David assembled all the princes of Israel, the princes of the tribes, and the captains of the companies that ministered to the king by course, and the captains over the thousands, and captains over the hundreds, and the stewards over all the substance and possession of the king, and of his sons, with the officers, and with the mighty men, and with all the valiant men, unto Jerusalem." " Then the chief of the fathers and princes of the tribes of Israel, and the captains of thousands and of hundreds, with the rulers of the king's work, offered willingly." And "the people rejoiced for that they offered willingly to the Lord, and David the king also rejoiced with great joy." The conduct of the parties was as noble as their station. Had such not borne their part in some measure commensurate to their position in society, the work could not have been accomplished. When shall such a scene be witnessed in Britain? Its nobles have yet to learn a lesson from the nobility of ancient Israel. If our beloved Queen and her royal consort, with all their great worth, and in many respects most praiseworthy example, were to go down to their Houses of Parliament, or summon their members to the royal palace, and make a proposal to them similar to that which David made to the nobles of Israel, how would it be entertained? The very suggestion seems to be ridiculous. It could not be done. And what says this for the state of our country? What a view does it give us of our superior Christianity in comparison with the defective system of Judaism? The fact that nothing of the kind could even be entertained, arise from what cause it may, is full of meaning, and deserves our serious consideration. But if no such matter could be entertained publicly, there is nothing to hinder that each shall do his part privately, within the little inclosure of his own church, and in accordance with all his peculiarities of taste and opinion. How is it, then? What aid are the rulers and nobles of the land giving to the spread of Christianity? Are their contributions commensurate with their position, and responsibility, and wealth? We are none of those who look with a jealous eye on the aristocracy of Britain. We would detract nothing from their greatness or their glory. But we are jealous of their consistency, and we must remind them of their accountability. Let us be borne with while we ask, What are even our ecclesiastical rulers doing to help forward the work of the Lord by their contributions? We have heard reports of their princely revenues; to what are these devoted? Are their names and subscriptions prominent in the lists of those who are trying to build up and enlarge Zion? We bring no railing accusation, but we cannot help saying there is cause for solemn inquiry. It cannot be that the cause of God shall be neglected by the great and noble without incurring much guilt. Oh, that Britain were as it was with Israel in the days of king David, when the king, and the princes, and the nobles, led the way in the work of the Lord! Were it so, we should enjoy a measure of peace and prosperity not at present known amongst us. "Then should the earth yield her increase, and God, even our own God, would bless us."

Yet there was no extravagant excitement in the conduct of David and his nobles. The whole proceeding was marked by a spirit the most calm and considerate. It was indeed a determined one, and in such a cause it ought to be so. "I have prepared with all my might for the cause of my God," said David. He weighed the matter well, and acted with a clear and steady purpose. Yet his uprightness is most prominent. "Because I have set my affection to the house of my God, I have of mine own proper good given to the house of my God." His affection for the work is assigned as a reason why he acted both generously and honestly. It opened his heart to give, but it taught him also that he must take care to give only that which was his own, knowing that no cause could have the Lord's blessing which was not sustained in accordance with his will and law. David and his nobles were as careful to give honestly as they were to give at all. This is a blessed example to the community. The great are not only to contribute, but to do so in a way that will command respect and approbation. It is when this is the state of a people, the rich and the poor will feel aright toward one another, and dwell in concord and common prosperity.

A beautiful example is presented on this occasion of the effect of the conduct of the great on that of the public at large.

"All the congregation blessed the Lord God of their fathers." "The people rejoiced." The poorest had their part as well as the richest. They never imagined they were exempted from the duty or excluded from the privilege of giving. And this is never to be forgotten. The work is to be done in common. All are to labour at it. Every one should resolve, I will have at least a stone in the building of the Lord. I cannot do what I would, but I will do what I can.

This work ended in a way worthy of its commencement. "David blessed the Lord before all the congregation, and said, Blessed be thou, Lord God of Israel, our Father, for ever and ever. Thine, O Lord, is the greatness, and the power, and the glory, and the victory, and the majesty; for all that is in the heaven and in the earth is thine; both riches and honour come of thee; and in thine hand it is to make great and to give strength unto all. But who am I, or what is my people, that we should be able to offer so willingly, after this sort? for all things come of thee, and of thine own have we given thee." It is where this spirit of piety and prayerful dependence prevails we may expect such results as these. When are we to witness or exemplify them?

With this example before us, let us judge what we are to give to the Lord and to do for his cause. What do we think of the tenth in the light of such a transaction? Not in vain had the law of God educated this people in an enlarged liberality. There must have been long training to call forth and exercise such a spirit. It was not the product of a day. Deep principles must have got hold of the hearts of the people, great and small. They show us what they were and what they thought. And their example of generosity ought not to be lost on the present generation. It is much needed. The Lord grant that through his blessing it may be effectual.

THE WIDOW OF SAREPTA.

It is not in one form only the examples of Scripture are presented to us. They are national and individual, public and private. We have seen what was done unitedly, let us also see what was done singly. There is some danger of being so dazzled with great and striking exhibitions of generosity on a broad scale as to cause us to forget our individual responsibility. We therefore select a special case, and that presenting as strong a contrast to what we have been considering as can well be imagined. The history to which we refer is recorded in 1 Kings, xvii. 8–24. All the features of it seem to be ordered so as to teach, there are none who may not and ought not to exercise generosity in the service of God. It was that of a woman. Often the Scriptures tell of such, that it may not be supposed they are exempted from taking part in the work of the Lord. She was a widow. The name is the strongest association we have in our language with helplessness and dependence. What can such a one do? She was poor. "I have not a cake, but an handful of meal in a barrel and a little oil in a cruse." She was in the extremity of a famine. "I am gathering two sticks, that I may go in and dress it for me and my son, that we may eat it and die." Yet to her the prophet Elijah is sent in his strait that she may feed him. This circumstance is specially noticed by Christ in the New Testament: "Many widows were in Israel in the days of Elias, when the heavens were shut up three years and six months, when great famine was throughout the land; but unto none of them was Elias sent save unto Sarepta, a city of Sidon, to a woman that was a widow." It is mentioned as a distinguishing favour conferred upon her, a proof of the sovereignty of divine grace. Difficult and distressing as her circumstances were, she fell in with the proposal of the prophet to relieve his hunger. At first she hesitated, and did not see either her duty or the possibility of compliance. But a word of encouragement and explanation satisfied her, and she was resolved to try what she could do for the Lord and his servant. "She went and did according to the saying of Elijah." And she had no cause to regret it. The Lord's blessing rested on her and rewarded her. "The barrel of meal wasted not, neither did the cruse of oil fail, according to the word of the Lord which he spoke by Elijah." Now, why is all this recorded? What is the purpose of this simple narrative of a lonely and destitute widow? Surely to teach us there is no one who may not do good. Surely to teach us a generous heart may dwell under a garb of the greatest poverty. Surely to teach us we should never decline a proposal to do good and relieve distress when it is in the power of our hand to do it. Surely to teach us we shall never serve the Lord nor his cause in vain. Many a widow's heart has this record cheered. Very good it is in God that he gave it a place in his word. It may be as the hidden flower in the luxuriant garden. It does not at first attract us. But when we take it up and examine it, how lovely! worthy of its Author! He is infinite in wisdom and love. Let none decline some part in the Lord's work. However humble, there is a place he is to occupy, and a work he is to do. The generous heart will move the hand to activity. Remember the widow of Sarepta.

THE WIDOW'S MITE.

One other example let us just notice before concluding this part of the subject. It is recommended to us as having occurred in the ministry of Christ, having called forth his most emphatic approval, and so being distinctly illustrative of the spirit of his Gospel. It is thus recorded: "Jesus sat over against the treasury, and beheld how the people cast money into the treasury; and many that were rich cast in much. And there came a certain poor widow, and she threw in two mites, which make a farthing. And he called unto him his disciples, and said unto them, Verily I say unto you, that this poor widow hath cast more in than all they which have cast into the treasury; for all they did cast in of their abundance; but she of her want did cast in all that she had, even all her living."* What a scene is here! Jesus was looking on. How little the crowds thought of this! And it is so still. His eye is upon all men, he is taking cognizance of their doings, and yet they perceive it not, think not of it, and are not influenced by it. What did he see, and what did he think and say of it? He saw the people casting their money into the treasury according to the law, and in particular he observed that many rich persons cast in much.

* Mark, xii. 41-44.

With this he does not find fault. The act was a proper one in itself, and whether it was acceptable or not depended on what he saw to be the spirit by which it was prompted. If it was pride or self-righteousness, it was hateful in his sight; if it was in compliance with the law, and out of regard to the authority of God and the good of men, it was accepted and approved. We are not told, however, what he thought of these rich men and their offerings. There is another person and another offering that attract and absorb his attention. And he calls the special attention of his disciples to what he observed and desired to say of it. The person was "a certain poor widow"—somebody whose name was not known there, suffering under the privations of poverty, yet casting in a farthing. And what of this? Who minds it? The poor woman and her miserable offering were perhaps in the way while some portly magnate strutted forward to deposit his princely gift. But hear the judgment of Him, who shall at last judge the world. He that made the worlds, of whom it is written, "The earth is the Lord's and the fulness thereof," remarks with emphasis, "This poor widow hath cast in more than they all,"—more in the account of God, more in the way of securing his acceptance and blessing, more for the furtherance of the great end for which that treasury had been appointed. But Christ gives the explanation himself; "They all did cast in of their abundance, but she of her want did cast in all that she had, even all her living." What they gave they could easily spare, and feel no inconvenience; what she gave left her, in all human calculation, to want the necessaries of life. Is our Lord's judgment of this case the opinion that would be entertained or expressed of it by thousands in our day? They would count such conduct the height of folly and absurdity, while He who had the treasures of wisdom and knowledge declared his admiration of it. What! God gives a poor widow a farthing, she needs it to buy bread, and yet she goes and casts it into a contribution for the spread of religion! Has the poor woman not lost her understanding? Many would think so. Well, be it remembered, Jesus thought the reverse. There is, perhaps, no passage in the word of God that has been more perverted and abused than this simple and beautiful incident. A rich man or woman proceeds to deposit an offering to the cause of God, and remarks, with an air of extreme humility, "I have been giving my mite to the cause." Indeed! Have you? Just inquire what is meant by a mite. We do not say that the term *mite* is synonymous with *moiety*, yet they so resemble one another as to suggest the idea of some affinity in their meaning. Moiety signifies the one-half of anything. If, then, mite be derived from it, it denotes a large share, even a half, of that which is in question. Have you, then, given the one-half of what you possess or of what you ought to give? But this poor widow is not said to have cast in her mite, but two mites, two moieties, two halves; that is, the whole sum which she possessed. And so our Lord explains it, "She did cast in all that she had." Let this language be laid aside, as it is commonly used. All allusion to such an incident as this is most unbecoming in those most given to the use of it. Their conduct is the very reverse of this poor widow's. They are to be classed with the rich on whom Christ looked, it is not said whether with approval or displeasure, and not with the poor widow, with whom they are not worthy to be associated. Yet this incident is a beautiful exponent of the spirit of the Gospel. It shows what Christ expects in his followers. No doubt, too, it has mightily tended to form and cherish a generous spirit in many of them. It is known to all, and many have caught his spirit expressed in it, and acted according to it. For, much as there is reason to lament and to complain of the sad prevailing want of liberality in the Church of Christ, there are yet those to whom there has been given a large and noble generosity. Such there ever have been, and their number, it is hoped, is not decreasing. They have been found among rich and poor, among the laity and ecclesiastics, among the judges of the land and rulers of the people. The Honourable Sir Robert Boyle with his high intellectual attainments, Sir Matthew Hale gracing the bench of justice, Richard Baxter, Dr. Doddridge, and John Wesley, all held high views of the duty of religious contribution, and they acted upon them. Every one of these great men held the opinion that no believer in Revelation could consistently give less than a tenth of his income to the service of the Lord, and some of them went much further in both their principles and practices. Some indications have appeared of an advancing attainment in this respect in the Church of our time. All churches are owning the obligations and making some feeble attempt to give and to get for the spread of the Gospel. Examples have appeared of large-heartedness that are a good earnest of a better state of things. It could hardly be otherwise than it is in the low views entertained by many. They have not been informed nor roused upon the subject. But the day of apathy, we trust, is gone. Many are asking for the "old paths," and soon, we hope, will be found walking in them. The spirit of Abraham, and Jacob, and Moses, and Christ, and of his early churches, will revive, and men will encourage one another, saying, " Who is willing to consecrate his service this day unto the Lord?" The Lord hasten it in his time!

CHAPTER IX.

MISCELLANEOUS.

"*Precept must be upon precept, precept upon precept; line upon line, line upon line; here a little, and there a little.*"—Isaiah xxviii. 10.

" GIVE a portion to seven, and also to eight; if the clouds be full of rain they empty themselves upon the earth." Although a curse be upon creation, by reason of man's sin, yet it is manifestly under a law of beneficence, and it is thus proposed as a model for our imitation. Everything is contributing to the good of man. The heavenly bodies give him light; the clouds pour out their rain; the earth yields its increase, and all that is upon it; the waters teem with living creatures for his food; all things are made for his benefit. Man himself is not an exception to the rule. He has been made not merely to receive, but to do good.

Fallen as he is, still this claim lies upon him. The Scriptures enforce it continually, in all places, at all times, and in all ways. Every argument that can avail with a reasonable mind is everywhere employed throughout their various revelations. We have precepts and promises, warnings and encouragements, facts and prophecies. To consider all these with any measure of minuteness is impossible; yet it may be well to glance at them, that we may see the fulness of Scripture in the enforcement of well-doing, and from its tone and spirit learn what must be our duty, especially in the way of religious contribution.

PRECEPTS.

These pervade the whole volume. It is not easier to gather flowers in the open fields of Nature than it is to find such precepts in the word of God. " Honour the Lord with thy substance, and with the first-fruits of all thine increase." " Cast thy bread upon the waters, for thou shalt find it after many days." " In the morning sow thy seed, and in the evening withhold not thine hand; for thou knowest not whether shall prosper, either this or that, or whether they shall be alike good." " A good man showeth favour and lendeth." " Give to him that asketh of thee, and from him that would borrow of thee turn not thou away." " Withhold not good from them to whom it is due, when it is in the power of thine hand to do it. Say not to thy neighbour, Go, and come again, and to-morrow I will give, when thou hast it by thee." " To do good and to communicate, forget not, for with such sacrifices God is well pleased." If thine enemy hunger, feed him; if he thirst, give him drink: for in so doing thou shalt heap coals of fire on his head. Be not overcome of evil, but overcome evil with good." This is the tone of Scripture precept. What is expected of all who truly receive it? A few remarks on these passages, taken almost at random out of thousands, may be helpful to illustrate and enforce the pure and delicate principles involved in them. They assume that God is to be acknowledged in all we possess. He must be honoured in such a use of it as shall show we feel it to be a gift from him, and that it is to be used for him. There is a peculiar force in the phrase, "all thine increase." Whatever is added to our income, the "first-fruits" belong to God. It is intended to keep us continually in contact with God, through the bounties of his providence. It is as if the commands were ever sounding in our ears, "Occupy till I come"—"Give an account of thy stewardship." The way in which we shall thus honour the Lord is also pointed out; it is by doing good to his creatures, expending our substance in a way that will be profitable to them. A parent feels himself obliged by all the kindness that is shown to his children, and God is pleased to assure us he is so pleased to regard whatever is done to his creatures. Especially does a parent estimate the kindness that is shown to his child out of regard to him, and this is a principle continually recognised in the Scriptures. "Inasmuch as ye have done it unto one of the least of these my brethren, ye have done it unto me." Not only so, if the kindness be not shown he resents it as an injury to himself: "Inasmuch as ye did it not to one of the least of these my brethren, ye did it not to me." And it is well known of what he speaks: "I was an hungered, and ye gave me meat; I was thirsty, and ye gave me drink; I was naked, and ye clothed me; I was a stranger, and ye took me in; I was sick and in prison, and ye visited me." Or the reverse, "I was an hungered, and ye gave me no meat; I was thirsty, and ye gave me no drink; I was naked, and ye clothed me not; I was a stranger, and ye took me not in; I was sick and in prison, and ye visited me not." It carries these solemn sayings to the highest pitch of interest and importance, when it is remembered that they are given as the proceedings of Christ in the final judgment of the world, and are to be followed by the sentence, "Come, ye blessed of my Father;" or "Depart, ye cursed;" and in accordance therewith, "These shall go away into everlasting punishment, and the righteous to life eternal." There is in some of these precepts quoted a tenderness and delicacy of feeling inculcated that greatly endear and recommend them. In the matter of lending we are enjoined to be frank, candid, and gracious—not constraining the applicant to feel that we are conferring a great favour upon him, but making him to perceive that what we do is done freely, and with a sincere desire to serve him. In showing a favour to another, it is not to be done in a way that may be irksome, as if we would have it to be felt we were making a great sacrifice; it must be done cheerfully, and at once. In aiding others who may be seeking our co-operation in helping them forward in a good cause, we must give no unnecessary trouble. We are not to say to this neighbour, " Go, and come again, when we have it by us." We must respect his feelings, and time, and convenience. And while there is this spirit of considerateness and delicacy in these Scripture precepts, some of them rise to the loftiest height of the noblest principles. No unkindness, or injustice, or cruelty, or sinfulness, or ingratitude in others, is to hinder us from doing them good. If our bitterest enemy hunger, we are to feed him. The harder the metal, the greater the heat that must be applied to fuse it. The greater the wickedness, the more the kindness that must be used to overcome it. Heap up coals of fire on his head, and melt down the hard heart of our enemy. This, assuredly, was the way of Christ. He acted on that principle. It is the very basis of his gospel. " Where sin abounded, grace did much more abound." It is the most open avenue to the heart of man. If it cannot be entered thus it cannot be entered at all. Would that it were more frequently tried! And of all forms of kindness none is more felt than the employment of our pecuniary means for the good of others. Men value money, and when they see that others use it for their benefit, it is an argument which they at once understand and powerfully feel. It strikes a chord of sympathy which vibrates through the heart, and takes the man captive in its bonds. Let it not be said, It is needless to dwell on counsels which all admit to be scriptural and binding. All admit them, and few act on them. We are persuaded there is much to be learned, not only in the duty of doing good, but the spirit in which it should be done; not only in the matter of giving, but the manner of it—cultivating that tenderness and delicacy of feeling which the Scriptures alone have ever fully apprehended, and rising to that loftiness of principle which they only who act upon them can attain.

WARNINGS.

Nor let it be supposed it is left optional with us whether we shall obey these precepts or not. We may disregard them; but if so, we are warned that we shall abide the consequences. These consequences are distinctly set before us, and if we expose ourselves to them we cannot plead the want of plain speaking in the word of God. Confining our attention to the single form of benevolence in pecuniary contribution, it will be well to listen to the voice of warning which the Scriptures raise in the ears of all who are not careful to practise it. The danger of covetousness is set forth with a strength of sentiment and a force of language seldom employed on other subjects. The tone in which it is spoken of betrays a sense of its evil which, it is to be feared, few estimate; and this renders it all the more necessary that we attend to the warnings of God's word, as though we heard the voice of Jesus saying, "He that hath ears to hear let him hear." Solomon saith, "There is that scattereth, and yet increaseth; and there is that withholdeth more than is meet, and it tendeth to poverty." This witness is true. A narrow-minded man does not usually prosper. He has not himself a heart to use the means that are necessary to success. Others take pleasure in thwarting his purposes; and the blessing of God does not rest on his basket and store. What a miserable object! The expenditure of a shilling might gain him a pound, but he cannot force himself to employ it. Proverbs usually have their foundation in truth and correct observation; and here we have an example of it. This man is known by the appellation of a miser, and the very term signifies misery. A greater than Solomon has spoken on the same subject. It was a frequent topic in the ministry of Christ. He has given a most emphatic testimony to his own estimate of wealth in the lowly position which he chose to occupy on the earth, in the companions with whom he thought proper to associate, and in the condition in which he has been pleased to place many of his people. His own mother he left a dependant on the kindness of a disciple; and this single fact is full of meaning. But his speech was often directed to this theme; and what said

M

he? In one place he warns—" Take heed, and beware of covetousness; for a man's life consisteth not in the abundance of the things which he possesseth." It is difficult to say which is more impressive, the counsel given here, or the argument by which it is enforced. " Take heed, and beware." A double warning is given. We require to take heed, giving our utmost attention to the subject; and when we have done so, we shall find that we must stand upon our guard in the attitude of self-defence. For why? There is nothing so insidious as the love of the world and its wealth. It creeps in unperceived and unsuspected; and when once it has got a footing it is hard to be dislodged, and it assumes a mastery over the mind which appears most unaccountable and unreasonable. Hence many who, in the time of their comparative poverty, were generous, have become, in the possession of wealth, narrow and illiberal. They say, and we fear they believe, they cannot contribute to the cause for which they are solicited. Covetousness thus seems to destroy reason as well as religion. It is no wonder, therefore, that Christ so loudly lifted up his warning voice against it. Then the reason which he assigns is in keeping with his counsel—" A man's life does not consist in the abundance which he possesseth." He may have " the abundance," but not the end for which life is given; that is, happiness. This is in strict accordance with the facts that lie all around us. Rich men are not more happy than poor men. The poor are apt to think they are, but it is a mistake, and it is often found that as a man increaseth wealth he increases sorrow. He will be delivered from this evil, certainly, if he attend to one thing; that is, if he rightly use the wealth which God has given him; but if he do not so, he will find, from bitter experience, that vain is the endeavour to extract sweetness out of gold. Our Lord does not hesitate, however, to use even stronger representations than we have been considering. To illustrate and enforce his saying he employs a parable. He describes a rich man in the height of his luxury and enjoyment, till he says, " Soul, thou hast much goods laid up for many years; eat, drink, and be merry." But, then, reversing the scene, he introduces God saying to him, "Thou fool, this night thy soul shall be required of thee; then whose shall those things be which thou hast provided?" and he draws this inference, "So is he that layeth treasure up for himself, and is not rich toward God." No wonder that he who thus viewed the subject of ill-used wealth should say, "It is easier for a camel to go through the eye of a needle than for a rich man to enter into the kingdom of God." He meant that a rich man, yielding to the temptation of trusting in riches, of which there is imminent danger, could no more, in that state of mind, become a subject of true religion here, or attain to its joys hereafter, than a camel, according to the Jewish proverb, could pass through the eye of a needle. The one is literally, and the other morally impossible. We cannot help adding to the testimony of Christ the words of his illustrious Apostle to the Gentiles. Paul says, "They that will be rich fall into temptations and a snare, and into many foolish and hurtful lusts, which drown men in destruction and perdition. For the love of money is the root of all evil, which while some coveted after, they have erred from the faith and pierced themselves through with many sorrows." Fearful warning! Let us not fail to understand it. It has in view the man that "*will* be rich." On this he is determined. To that he is resolved everything shall yield. He does not speak of the man whom God enriches, of him who in his providence prospers in his worldly calling, but of the man who at all hazards of character and principle is resolved to be rich if he can. Such a man he distinctly forewarns, that he will encompass himself with temptations which shall prove a snare to him, that these temptations shall provoke evil dispositions in him that will prove to be most foolish and hurtful, that they will end in utter destruction, in all kinds of evil, cause him to abandon the true faith of the gospel, and plunge him into sorrows which shall pierce him through at last as so many poisoned and fatal darts. So speaketh the Spirit of God of the "love of money." Let men be warned. Money is good, it is cause of thankfulness when God bestows it, it is a blessed talent to employ for the good of men and the glory of God, but if it be misused it is evil in proportion to the good that it might have achieved. The best food is the most injurious to the diseased body, it is not in a capacity to profit by it; and it is the same with riches—a blessing unspeakable to those who will use them as God commands, a curse terrible to those who misapply them. Faithful are the wounds of a friend, and so are the warnings of Scripture.

PROMISES.

We would like to see a complete collection of these brought together, and presented to our notice at a glance. The botanist takes great satisfaction in bringing together all the different species he can find of one admired plant, that he may look at their common features in connexion with their minute and beautiful varieties. So also the naturalist in every department of his study. All the works of God resemble each other. As it is in his creation, so it is in his word. Sameness and variety pervade the whole. At present we shall indulge our admiration of his word in the matter of his promises, confining our attention to one class, however,—those which relate to the right use of money, and so set forth vividly the advantages of liberality. Referring to a passage quoted among the precepts, Solomon having said, "Honour the Lord with thy substance, and the first-fruits of all thine increase," adds, "So shall thy barns be filled with plenty, and thy presses shall burst out with new wine." The wine and the barns express the enjoyments and necessaries of life. Both are guaranteed to every one who acts as is commanded. And why should we doubt the truth of the promises? How easy it is in God to make them good! He can touch a spring in providence that either opens or shuts the door of our prosperity. If we are dependent on the field, his elements can either mature or destroy our property at his bidding. If commerce is our pursuit, he can restrain or stimulate our minds or those of the men with whom we have had to do, so as to issue in our loss or gain. It is greatly to be deplored that this is not sufficiently considered. Even the Lord's people do not enough lay upon themselves the duty of remembering God and his providence in every transaction. If they did so, they would find it vastly to contribute to both their peace and their prosperity. In another place Solomon says, "He that hath pity on the poor lendeth to the Lord, and that which he hath given will he pay him again." The statement cannot be made plainer, and if any man doubt the truth of it we have no authority to plead higher than the word in which it is contained. God hath said it. David says of the righteous man, "Wealth and riches shall be in his house;" and then he proceeds to explain the graces, in the exercise of which he will be sure to meet with the promised reward, saying, "A good man showeth favour and lendeth; he will guide his affairs with discretion." The promise is not to every good man, act as he may, wisely or foolishly, but to the good man acting generously, and at the same time as discreetly as generously. The prophet Isaiah takes up the same subject, and says, "The liberal deviseth liberal things, and by liberal things shall he stand." God will so order it, that in serving others he will lay the foundation of his own prosperity. As the clouds pour out their water on the earth, and the very abundance with which it is given causes the vapour to ascend again and fill the clouds afresh, so "the liberal man," in doing liberal things, is creating, though without his own design, an influence that will return back again sevenfold into his own bosom. Jesus, too, has spoken on the same subject. "Seek first," he says, "the kingdom of God and his righteousness, and all these things shall be added unto you." "Give, and it shall be given unto you; good measure, pressed down, and shaken together, and running over, shall men give into your bosom. For with the same measure that ye mete withal, it shall be measured to you again." This is the faithful and true witness. And in corroboration of his testimony, let us for a moment look at the principles inculcated upon Israel, at the period of the return from Babylon, and the second building of the Temple, and the measures founded upon them. Haggai is commissioned to say, "Go up to the mountain, and bring wood and build the house, and I will take pleasure in it, and I will be glorified, saith the Lord. Ye looked for much, and lo, it came to little; and when ye brought it home, I did blow upon it. Why? saith the Lord of Hosts. Because of mine house that is waste, and ye run every man unto his own house." These words told upon the people, "they came and did work in the house of the Lord of Hosts." And the prophet was then commissioned to proclaim, "From this day I will bless you." Zechariah spake in like manner, "Bring ye all the tithes into the storehouse, and prove me now herewith, if I will not open you the windows of heaven and pour you out a blessing, that there shall not be room enough to receive it. And I will rebuke the devourer for your sakes, and he shall not destroy the fruit of your ground, neither shall your vine cast her fruit before the time in the field, saith the Lord of Hosts. And all nations shall call you blessed, for ye shall be a delightsome land, saith the Lord of Hosts." These are words of truth and soberness. They declare the unchangeable and eternal principles of the divine government. They were exemplified in the prosperity of Israel, while they acted in accordance with them. "All the promises of God are in Christ Jesus, yea, and in him, Amen, unto the glory of God." The glory of God is bound up in the fulfilment of the promises. And of these promises, as of all others, it may be said, "Hath he spoken, and shall he not do it? He is not a man that he should lie, nor the son of man that he should repent."

PROPHECIES.

Without a glance at these, the subject would be incomplete. We cannot repress the desire to know how it shall be with the Church in future times, and God hath graciously told us. Much darkness hangs in many respects over its coming history, yet in the matter of the enlarged and generous spirit which is destined one day to prevail, the Spirit hath spoken expressly. There are passages in his word, not a few, devoted to the delineation of the latter-day glory. They seem as if they were intended to sustain the drooping spirit of God's saints under their many difficulties and depressions. They cry, "Who hath believed our report, and to whom hath the arm of the Lord been revealed?" And he "puts a new song into their mouth, even praise unto our God." The book of Revelation, in particular, dark as some of its intimations are, is yet clear in the representation of the ultimate issue of all things in the universal spread and triumph of the gospel. However we may fail to trace the steps by which Jesus shall go forth conquering and to conquer, yet of this there can be no doubt, that he will continue his conquests until the cry is raised, "The kingdoms of this world are the kingdoms of our God and his Christ." Now in these sublime and encouraging predictions, one feature frequently marked is the generosity by which the Lord's people shall be distinguished in the day of coming glory. And to a few of these passages it will be suitable to recur. Isaiah, treating of this very subject, largely and expressly, says, "The vile person shall no more be called liberal, nor the churl said to be bountiful." He intimates that it may be so now, but that it shall not always be so. A complete change will pass over the views and judgments of men. Many are esteemed liberal men who would then be regarded as the personification of covetousness. See what men can give now for personal and family luxuries, and compare it with what they devote to the cause of God, and the proportion is miserable; not a tenth it may be, perhaps much less. Yet because they give at all, or betimes give beyond what is common, or what was expected of them, their character is elevated to the idea of liberality, and men speak of them as if they were indeed generous. It shall not be so in the day to which we look forward. Men will then judge righteous judgment. A narrow inquiry will be made into means and expenditure. A faithful rule of proportion will be applied to the contribution. And character and conduct will be estimated, not by the false and deceitful rules of a covetous generation, but by the broad and eternal principles of man's relation to God, and his obligations to Christ and his cause. Another prophet opens our view still further, and tells us what men will do in those days. To David this is a frequent and delightful theme, and in one of his psalms, expressly set to the music of the conquering Messiah's triumphs, he says, "The daughter of Tyre shall be there with a gift, even the rich among the people shall entreat thy favour." Tyre was the great mart of ancient commerce. This, therefore, is a prophecy that commerce shall be laid tributary at the feet of Jesus—its wealth, its enterprise, its discoveries, and its labours. Every one who looks at what is taking place in the earth must see that the destiny of the world is likely soon to be in the hands of its merchants. This is a consummation to be devoutly desired. There is no class whose influence is so great, and from whom so much may be expected. Commerce enlarges the mind beyond any other earthly employment. While riches increase by its energetic pursuit, they do not seem to take so fast a hold of the mind as when otherwise obtained. There is a readiness to give which is not found in other professions. The giving as well as the getting of money may become a habit. And there are thus even natural principles on which the greater liberality of this class of men may be explained. But above all, their enterprise, how it surprises and delights us! Whose are the railways that are now connecting kingdom with kingdom as hamlet used to be with hamlet? They have been devised and paid for by those merchants, who, we say, happily are become as princes in the earth. They are bridging over the nations that before were far apart, and making a highway for the redeemed of the Lord to pass over. They are constructing a pathway for the missionary to all people of the earth. They may not, some of them, or even many of them, intend it, yet God is doing it by them. We cannot help applying, almost literally, to this astonishing change in the state of things, the words of the prophet: "Every valley shall be exalted, and every mountain and hill shall be made low, and the crooked shall be made straight, and the rough places plain, and the glory of the Lord shall be revealed, and all flesh shall see it together, for the mouth of the Lord hath spoken it." Commerce has thus become the John the Baptist of the present day. It is the voice crying, " Prepare the way of the Lord, make his paths straight." Rather we should say, God is thus speaking by it. In his providence he is opening these facilities for the spread of his truth. Let us feel the obligations that are thus laid upon us, and all the more that the facilities for the spread of error and sin keep pace with those for truth and godliness. Only we have confidence in right principles. Great is the truth, and it will prevail. Better still, God has said, "The knowledge of the Lord shall cover the earth as the waters do the sea." All shall be directed and over-ruled to that end. So saith another prophet: "In that day shall there be upon the bells (or bridles) of the horses, HOLINESS UNTO THE LORD, and the pots in the Lord's house shall be like the bowls before the altar. Yea, every pot in Jerusalem and in Judah shall be holiness unto the Lord of Hosts; and in that day there shall be no more the Canaanite in the house of the Lord of Hosts." This is the purpose which the God of the whole earth hath purposed. Blessed be his name, none can hinder or frustrate it. On everything in the Church—on everything in the world, the inscription will be written, "Holiness unto the Lord." It is his, and it is hereby dedicated to him. Our souls are his, and we write upon them, "Holiness to the Lord." Our bodies are his, and we write upon them, "Holiness to the Lord." Our children and families are his, and we write upon them, "Holiness to the Lord." Our churches and their ordinances are his, and we write upon them, "Holiness to the Lord." Our labours are his, and we write upon them, "Holiness to the Lord." Our wealth is his, and we write upon it, in lines of deep and durable inscription, because it was so long withholden from him, but now wholly, freely, and for ever rendered up to him, to his service, and cause, and glory—

HOLINESS UNTO THE LORD.

CHAPTER X.

CONCLUSION.

"*Let us hear the conclusion of the whole matter.*"—Eccles. xii. 13.

WHAT proportion of his income should a believer in revelation dedicate to the cause of God? "Holy men of old spake as they were moved by the Holy Ghost,"—and they have answered the question. We have cited them as our only witnesses, and we have examined their testimony in detail. Desirous to know what the mind of God on the question is, and believing they were commissioned to declare it, we have consulted them one by one, and heard what each had to say. Before dismissing the subject, it may be well to cite them forward once more, and hear their united testimony. Let us consider ourselves a jury, solemnly empannelled in the presence of God, the Judge, adjured to give an honest verdict on the evidence to be laid before us, and to find whether any believer in the revelation they carry to us can consistently devote less than a tenth of his income to the cause of God.

ABRAHAM first claims attention, and gives his testimony. He deposes as follows:—God found me in Ur of the Chaldees, rapidly sinking with my fathers into idolatry. He called me in his sovereignty, and sanctified me by his grace. He honoured me with the appellation of "the friend of God." Deeply did I feel my obligation to him, but especially on some peculiar occasions when he interposed remarkably on my behalf, and not only preserved me and mine, but enriched me with increased substance. At such times, in token of my gratitude, I devoted the tenth of what he had given me to his immediate service. I did so because my heart prompted me to honour my benefactor; because it was right in itself; and because I knew, either from express revelation or the practice of God's people in those days, that such an offering was required, and would be accepted, by the Lord. This is the amount of my testimony, and for further information on the subject I refer you to my distinguished grandson Jacob, the younger son of my beloved Isaac.

JACOB bore willing testimony, and said—I have hearkened to the speech of my venerated forefather, and heartily acquiesce in all he has said. It is manifest from the light of nature, as well as from the law of God, and the practice of his people, that our obligation should be acknowledged to God by the dedication of some part of our property to him. My grandfather has told you what his practice was—that on every special occasion of increase to his property he gave a tenth to God. I have done the same, but I have also gone farther. Early in life I was favoured with a gracious revelation of the Lord, and was much moved by it. Under the impression which it made upon my mind I engaged, that of all the Lord should ever give me, I would give the tenth to him. Sometimes in the occupations of this life, I forgot my vow; but God in his providence reminded me of my duty, and roused me to the performance of it. Thus I had the express approval of the Lord to my practice, and so I continued to pursue it as long as I lived. You may judge from my practice, what I hold to be the principles of the divine Word. Look into the law of Moses, and you will find that he bears similar testimony, and carries the claims of God farther than I have done.

MOSES appeared, and presented himself with the law of God, written by his express command. He stated—Abraham and Jacob have both correctly stated how it hath been from the beginning. A tenth is the proportion in which it has been customary to serve the Lord. But the world is grown older than it was in the days of my fathers, and its obligations to the Most High are increased. He has now given his written oracles, and in them he has embodied, in the form of law, and under the sanction of express statute, what it is his will that his people should do. A tenth is the well-known proportion that has been offered from the beginning, and therefore it is recognised in the law—but it is not merely a single tenth. There is a tenth for the support of the ministry, a tenth for the feasts and sacrifices, a tenth every third year for the poor, a tenth from every Levite for the priesthood; and, as if to render these offerings essential, the services for which they are required are perpetual; they are the most various, as well as constant; and beyond all that are prescribed by law, free-will offerings are expected from every devout Israelite. The whole economy is so planned as to train the Lord's people to habits of generosity, and overcome the natural selfishness of the human mind. The testimony which I bear, therefore, is that a tenth is the lowest proportion ever recognised; that the law goes far beyond it, even to a fifth or a third, and that He who knew what was in man laid it as an indispensable obligation on the conscience of every man thus to honour God with his substance.

The APOSTLES followed Moses, and told how it was in their day.—We were present, say they, when Christianity was ushered into the world, amid the glories of the day of Pentecost and the effusion of the Holy Ghost. We did not forget that we were Jews, and amenable to the law of Moses. We were taught that its mere ceremonies, having served their purpose, were to cease. The stars disappeared when the sun arose in the heavens. Still the eternal principles of the ancient law continued. In particular, the duty of giving to the Lord remained in full force. As our privileges were increased, the demands were advanced; and so powerfully was this felt, that in the emergency to which the cause of Christ was then brought, the disciples felt the obligation of disposing of their worldly properties to contribute to the cause of Jesus and the maintenance of his truth. Wherefore our testimony is, that while none can give less than a tenth to God, as ancient law and practice had it, there is yet to be no express limit put to the generosity of the Christian heart.

THE GREAT APOSTLE OF THE GENTILES rose to confirm this testimony.—I was not present, said Paul, on the day of Pentecost. I was then the bitter enemy of Jesus; but he revealed himself to me as I went to persecute his followers. Blessed Jesus! You ask me how we should use our worldly property for him. I can only reply, we should give ourselves to him. We are not our own, being bought with a price. We should live with the utmost frugality, that we may have to give to Jesus and his cause. This has been the practice of his churches from the first. Those of Macedonia, even in a season of great distress and poverty, still did not relax in this duty. They denied themselves in many things, but they did not abate anything of their contribution to uphold the truth of Christ. I was taught by the Spirit to inculcate the same duty strongly on the rich church at Corinth, and I did so. And, in a word, I have left this for the permanent rule of the Christian Church to the end of time,—"On the first day of the week, let every one of you lay by him in store, as God hath prospered him." This is the amount of my testimony.

ALL THE SAINTS arose as soon as the Apostle of the Gentiles ceased. Jews and Gentiles united their testimony. At the erection of the Tabernacle, said the Jews, we gave cheerfully,—we all gave, men and women; we gave what we possessed, and we had to be restrained from giving. At the building of the Temple we did in like manner. Our kings, our nobles, and our people, rivalled one another in the offerings of gratitude and love. The Gentiles claimed to say that they had not fallen behind their brethren the Jews. They adopted their Scriptures for their guide, and conformed their conduct to their requirement, not merely joyfully devoting their tenth, but whatever else beside their circumstances enabled them to do or give. Widows were there—the widow of Sarepta, and she who had cast in her all to the treasury of the Lord. They were in great honour that day, as those who had best expounded the law by obeying it.

THE BIBLE, when these witnesses had spoken, was laid on the table. This, said the Judge, is the rule by which you are to determine. Mark its precepts, note its warnings, consider its promises, and enter into the spirit of its predictions. With these before you, my charge to you is to declare what you believe to be its doctrine on the subject of religious contribution—especially, what proportion of his income a believer in revelation should give to the cause of God? And whether it is your opinion that in the judgment of this book he can consistently give less than a tenth, or whether he should not give more,—in some instances much more?

JESUS CHRIST presented himself when the Judge concluded, and said—" Behold the Lamb of God, which taketh away the sin of the world." "How much owest thou unto thy Lord?"

To all who own themselves the followers of this divine Redeemer we now say, " Consider of it, take advice, and speak your minds." " Behold, ye are all children of Israel; give here your advice and counsel." In the light of the evidence adduced we demand an answer to the question, Does the Bible require that every man shall give at least a tenth of his income to the cause of charity and of Christ? There can be only one answer—and there is not a demonstration in Euclid based on clearer or more satisfactory evidence—It does! As for those who dispute it, if there be any such, we refer them to the judgment-seat of Christ. We shall all meet there, and give account to one another and to him. Meantime let us inquire what is our present duty, considering what has been said, and so have done.

1. We cannot help saying, our first duty is to be convicted of sin. Well does it become us to say, "We are verily guilty concerning our brother, when we saw the anguish of his soul, and would not hear." The law of God has been in our hands, to a large extent, a dead letter. Under the perverse idea that the gospel has released us from the precise demands of the law, thousands bearing the Christian name and making a Christian profession have felt no obligation to devote a portion of their property to him. Either they have formed no opinion on the subject, or they have entertained an incorrect one. Some have given, but far more from impulse than principle. They have been solicited and contributed—but had they been let alone they would have given nothing. An opinion requires to be created in the Church on the subject. And that it should be so in this age of the world is full of guilt.

2. Let us confess our sin. As we have much need so have we also great encouragement to do it. "If we confess our sin, God is faithful and just to forgive us our sin, and to cleanse us from all unrighteousness." This gracious word, however, if not acted upon, will greatly aggravate our condemnation. Sin known and proved, but not confessed, although God waits to be gracious, is very aggravated. Let it not be ours. Let each confess his own sin so far as he sees he has not been careful to know what is the mind of the Lord, or to act upon it. Let every one weigh the matter well, in its unhappy influence and fearful consequences, until his spirit is stirred within him, as it ought to be. Let us confess the sin of others, of the community, of the Church, and especially so far as we may have contributed to it, either by our neglect or evil example. It were a good omen if a spirit of humiliation were given, and sin was freely confessed to the Lord. And until such shall be manifested there can be little hope of amendment.

3. We should amend our ways. Confession without amendment is hypocrisy. Humiliation is good as a means, but it is not an end. We should humble ourselves and turn unto the Lord. When Joshua abased himself before the Lord, as it was right he should do, because the people had been discomfited before Ai, on account of some sin which had not been detected, the Lord said unto him, " Get thee up, wherefore liest thou thus upon thy face? Up, sanctify the people—thou canst not stand before thine enemies, until ye take away the accursed thing from among you." The sin must be put away. This is the law of the Lord universally. As Joshua set on foot an investigation in the camp, and pursued it till the offender was detected and destroyed, so must we do. Let us try ourselves whether we have kept the law of our God in this matter or not. Have we given the tenth to him at least? If not, say how much owest thou unto him, and "pay what thou owest." Do not delay this duty. Do it now. You cannot have peace of mind till you do so. It may cost you a struggle, but the end will be peace. Having entered on the right path, pursue it. You have got hold of the right principle, and be sure you keep it. Say with David, " I thought on my ways, and turned my feet unto thy testimonies. I made haste, and delayed not to keep thy commandments." Act thus, and you may add, " Blessed are the undefiled in the way, who walk in the law of the Lord. Blessed are they that keep his testimonies, and that seek him with the whole heart. They also do no iniquity; they walk in his ways. Thou hast commanded us to keep thy precepts diligently." Be sure and determined that as you have seen what the will of the Lord is, you will conscientiously, faithfully, and perseveringly, abide by it.

4. It is our duty to endeavour to lead others also into right views and practices. "No man liveth to himself, and no man dieth to himself." We are accountable for all the influence we are capable of exercising. The education of the Church in right views of giving to the Lord is yet to be begun. For this purpose, the school, the family, the pulpit, and the press, ought to be brought into requisition. Every teacher of the young should imbue them early with just views of contribution, founded on the

word of God; every parent should train his household to habits of giving, causing them to know this is a duty which God has made to be as indispensable as any other; the minister of the gospel should lift his voice like a trumpet, and give no uncertain sound, showing to the people the sin of withholding, and the duty of giving; the press should teem with tracts and volumes until all would know what the mind of the Lord is. Until the public mind is thus learned, the present wretched penury in all that pertains to the cause of God cannot be overcome. Prayer and diligence, however, with the promised blessing, will accomplish it.

5. Finally, let us keep steadily in view the great end ever to be aimed at in the consecration of our property to God. The mere act of giving is good, for it is a useful exercise of mind. The habit is one of the most salutary which can be formed for our own benefit. Still this is not the ultimate object. That is the subjection of the world to Jesus. We give that he may be honoured. We pray, "Hallowed be thy name, thy kingdom come, thy will be done on earth as it is in heaven," and we use the means which Christ has appointed for the accomplishment of these desires. We have great encouragements and powerful inducements to employ them at the present time. "The field is the world," and God has opened it to his servants. Peace prevails upon the earth. As when Jesus came the temple of Janus was closed at Rome, to intimate that peace universally prevailed, and as it was by that arrangement of divine providence the apostles had access to the nations around them, so now again, in a greatly widened circle, men are at peace with one another, and the way is opened to the messengers of the cross, to whom God is saying, Enter ye in and possess the land. Who can tell how long it may so continue? If the opportunity is not embraced, it will no doubt be withdrawn. Then how bitter will be the remembrance of the lost opportunity! If it is embraced, how blessed the results! The gospel with its benefits will be conveyed to all men. "Judgment shall dwell in the wilderness, and righteousness remain in the fruitful field. And the work of righteousness shall be peace, and the effect of righteousness

quietness and assurance for ever. And my people shall dwell in a peaceable habitation, and in sure dwellings, and in quiet resting-places." The highest condition of earthly prosperity and the universal acclamation of honour to Christ shall encircle the globe. "There shall be an handful of corn in the earth upon the top of the mountains; the fruit thereof shall shake like Lebanon; and they of the city shall flourish like grass of the earth. His name shall endure for ever; his name shall be continued as long as the sun; and men shall be blessed in him: all nations shall call him blessed. Blessed be the Lord God, the God of Israel, who only doeth wondrous things. And blessed be his glorious name for ever; and let the whole earth be filled with his glory. Amen and Amen."

O Lord, wilt thou condescend to employ us to accomplish a consummation such as this? Wilt thou deign to accept our offerings? "The silver and the gold are thine." We give them to thee. We lay them on thine altar. May it sanctify the gift! "Of thine own have we given thee." Amen.

THE
Jewish Law of Tithe, a Guide to Christian Liberality.

BY THE

REV. ROBERT SPENCE, M.A.

"Speaking the truth in love."—Eph. iv. 15.

CONTENTS.

Chap. I. Introduction.
  1. Present liberality of the Church.
  2. Results of the liberality.
  3. Symptoms of decline.
  4. Means of revival.

II. Reasons for Liberality.
  1. The results of sin.
  2. What God has done to abolish it.
  3. Dependent for success on man.
  4. The work devolving on man.
  5. The motive for its performance.
  6. Effect of this motive.
  7. Need for a measure of liberality.

III. The Old Testament Measure of Liberality.
  1. Origin of tithe and divine sanction of it.
  2. The purpose of the Levitical tithe.
  3. Extent of Jewish liberality.
  4. The tithe a voluntary payment.
  5. The moral reasons for paying it.
  6. Guilt incurred by withholding it.

IV. The Old Testament Measure, a Guide to Christian Liberality.
  1. The New Testament gives no definite measure.
  2. The reasons for this.
  3. A measure nevertheless must exist.
  4. The early existence and divine sanction of tithe recommend it.
  5. The repeal of positive law, and the change of its reasons, may not terminate the duty.

CHAP. V. COMPARISON OF THE REASONS FOR LIBERALITY UNDER THE OLD AND NEW TESTAMENTS.

    1. Statement of the question.
    2. We are as able to give a tenth as the Jews.
    3. Our temporal obligations are as great.
    4. Our spiritual position is better than theirs.
    5. The claim of justice is as strong.
    6. The call for liberality as great.
    7. The results of liberality as encouraging.
    8. The conclusion to which these comparisons lead.

VI. CONSIDERATIONS CONFIRMATORY OF THE PREVIOUS ARGUMENT.

    1. Special danger of a covetous spirit.
    2. The New Testament often inculcates liberality.
    3. The general spirit of the gospel, and
    4. Our profession of faith requires it, and so do
    5. The world's contributions for its pleasures.

VII. ADVANTAGES RESULTING FROM THE GIVING OF A TENTH.

    1. Mode in which our contributions should be given.
    2. Temporal prosperity would follow.
    3. Spiritual effects upon the individual.
    4. Upon the Church.
    5. Upon the world.

VIII. OBJECTIONS TO THIS MEASURE OF LIBERALITY.

    1. Inability to comply with it, and others do not do it.
    2. It is neither commanded nor needful to salvation.
    3. Danger of formality, and of self-confidence for success.
    4. The true measure for Christian activity not hostile to this.

IX. CONCLUSION.

    1. System ought to exist in our liberality.
    2. By not being liberal we lose greatly.
    3. Illiberality is robbery of God.
    4. The time of labour brief.

CHAPTER I.

INTRODUCTION.

1. THE duty of liberality to the cause of Christ is frequently taught both from the pulpit and the press. Within the last half century considerable prominence has been given to this great branch of Christian activity; and the result has been most encouraging. Missionary Societies for home and foreign service have been formed in almost every section of the Church. These have been ably supported by Bible and Tract Societies. For the support of these different instrumentalities the Church of Christ in this country now contributes annually about half a million of pounds sterling. When to this is added all the money raised for the support of the Gospel at home, it will be found that the Christian Church is at present presenting on the altar of God not less than two millions yearly. This is a glorious free-will offering to God. It does afford cause, not for self-laudation, but for great thankfulness to the Head of the Church for the grace given to his people.

2. As is always the case, this spirit of liberality has been followed by a revived state of religion. Churches have been multiplied, and piety become more active. Sunday-schools, from which so great an amount of good has resulted to the Church and to the world, have been to a very large extent supported, and supplied with teachers, as a consequence of this generosity. Home and foreign service in Christ's cause go hand in hand. And so do genuine liberality and personal effort. For the man who truly feels for the benighted Indian cannot but feel for his near neighbour who is without the knowledge of God. And he who feels the love of Jesus prompting him to give of his substance for the conversion of souls, will assuredly be ready to

engage in personal effort for the same object as opportunity is afforded him. Thus what the Church has done for the world has been amply repaid in spiritual blessings. God has abundantly fulfilled his promise: "He that hath pity on the poor lendeth to the Lord, and that which he hath given will he pay him again."—Prov. xix. 17.

3. Nevertheless there begin to be symptoms of declining interest and diminishing liberality. The impetus which modern missions gave to the Church seems to have reached its highest point, and to be on the decline. There is a pause in the increase of the income of many of our Christian societies, if not an actual decrease. Men do not offer themselves as they did for the work of the Lord, and many calls from the heathen are necessarily refused. The question, "What is the cause of this?" forces itself on our attention. Has the Church reached its full measure of labour and generosity? Has it even over-exerted itself and now requires a period of repose? We do not believe it. Much as has been done, it has only been little compared with what the Church is capable of doing were all its energies systematically called forth and rightly employed. There is power in the kingdom of God, were every man to do his part loyally as under the eye of Him who walketh amid the golden candlesticks, to make all that has hitherto been performed only as the small drops before the heavy rain.

4. But how can this be secured? The utmost that can be done by powerful appeals to the gratitude and benevolence of the Church has been done, until they cease to produce the effects which they once did. Every feeling becomes deadened by constant exercise. The sensibility grows less and less powerful; until appeals, which would once have produced a most generous response, are heard without any emotion.

There is one feeling which is not, in the same degree as others, subject to this conformity,—love to Jesus. As the song of Moses and the Lamb is ever new in heaven, so in the truly Christian heart is the love of Christ ever fresh and ready for action. As manifested in humanity it of course partakes of the imperfections of all our feelings; but, as divinely implanted by the Spirit of the living God, it is superior to them. Let the duty of liberality be devolved more exclusively upon this. Let the claims of Christ be dwelt on more fully, and the claims of the heathen less, and more will be done for a perishing world. Instead of saying so frequently and vehemently the great truth, "The heathen are perishing," let the vastly greater truth, "Christ hath redeemed you," be more constantly and prominently insisted on. Let the text be, not quite so often, "Where no vision is the people perish," and much oftener, "Ye know the grace of our Lord Jesus." If this be done the happiest results will follow. It is true, this course has been very largely pursued, or the liberality of the Church would not have risen to what it is. But while this is gladly acknowledged, it must be remembered that the effects produced are, in spiritual things as in physical, as much dependent upon the proportions in which the truth is presented as upon the actual materials. Is there not reason to fear that the utilitarian spirit of the age has influenced the Church in its labours more than it ought? The salvation of men from the punishment of sin has been more thought of than the glory of Christ. The miserable condition and terrible prospects of the ungodly have been oftener exhibited as motives to Christian activity than the obligations under which we lie to our Redeemer. But the latter is the stronger and purer principle, for its origin is divine. When it is put first it is nobly seconded, and guided to action by the other. But widely different results follow the reversal of this order. For a time this may not be felt, but in due course it will make itself palpably manifest.

But this will not be enough. Appeals to feeling, even of the highest kind, will produce only a fluctuating result, for it is far from immutable. Something more must be done. Let, then, system be introduced in our working and giving for Christ. Instead of leaving our liberality to the temporary excitement of a missionary sermon or public meeting, we must learn to be liberal upon system. Every Christian must be taught that God expects him to lay by him in store from day to day and week to week what he is to present to him. Whatever be the proportion of income consecrated to religious objects, let it be a fixed sum entering into all our estimates of expenditure. It must be considered as essential a part of our expenses as providing for the returning wants of our households or the education of our children, and prepared for with the same care and forethought. We cannot but hope that the adoption of system in our liberality would be productive of the happiest results. God is the God of order.

When the question comes to be asked, which it soon will be if we give systematically, "What ought I to offer to the Lord?" let the Christian seek for guidance from God. Instead of asking what his neighbours give, and adopting their measure as his, let him seek counsel from the law of the Lord. "They who measure themselves by themselves are not wise." (2 Cor. x. 12.) As a help to the Christian in determining what proportion he ought to give to God, this Essay directs his attention to the ancient law of tithe. It is for every reader to determine whether it does at all show what the Most High expects of him. We do not think that the Mosaic law is still in force, but we do believe that very considerable assistance may be derived from it in the performance of a duty which Christianity enjoins. In this belief we commend the following argument to the earnest and prayerful attention of the reader, and seek for it the blessing of Him, without whom nothing is wise, nothing strong, and nothing successful.

CHAPTER II.

REASONS FOR LIBERALITY.

THESE are very numerous and varied. All of them, however, may be regarded as arising, amongst men, from the existence of sin. We only at present consider the chief of them, so that the question, "What ought I to give?" may be traced to its origin.

1. Sin is rebellion against the government of God, which it is the duty of every loyal subject to aid in suppressing. It deprives him of that glory and praise, of that satisfaction and

delight, which a holy and happy world would have given him. As he made mankind, this rebellion against his will is most flagrantly unjust, and every one should seek to terminate it. In the spread of the Gospel we use the only means which can succeed in inducing sinners to cast aside their unhallowed weapons and return to their God. In this consideration there is, to all holy beings, a sufficient reason for the most energetic activity in diffusing the truth.

But sin not only deprives the Highest of the service and love of his creature, it also utterly destroys those in whom it dwells. By it the soul is separated from him, in whom alone a portion suited to its immortal nature can be found, and sent for supply and enjoyment to objects inferior to itself. Iniquity turns the glory of man into shame. Instead of rejoicing in the love of God—instead of cherishing the affections of a son, the sinner retires from his service as a burden, and shuns his presence. The spirit of holy trust with which all sinless intelligences regard the great Creator is exchanged for that of bondage and fear, servility and hatred. The carnal mind is enmity against God. When estranged from God the soul soon becomes its own tormentor. The understanding is darkened, the conscience seared, the affections are given to vanity, the desires are in mutual conflict, and the will is vitiated. There is war within. The conscience and the understanding are arrayed in hostility against the affections and desires. The conflict often rages so fiercely that the mind becomes a little hell, and is frequently ended only by the searing of the conscience,—only when the voice of God is extinguished. Then the peace of death ensues, perhaps not to be broken until the knell of judgment is heard.

In consequence of the rejection of God's government over the soul, men come to pursue different ends. Having left the supreme centre of attraction, which would have held them all in unity and brotherhood, the tendency is to separate from each other until the race becomes a multitude of units. Every party and every man become selfish, and care only for their own things. The necessary result of this is, that in the pursuit of their several ends they come into collision with each other. In the struggle which ensues the strongest comes off victor. As the circles formed in a placid pool when a handful of peebles has been scattered over its surface act and react upon each other until the whole are broken, or the strongest one conquers all the rest, though itself sadly marred and despoiled of its beauty in the collision,—so do men's purposes interfere with each other. How different had been the result had these peebles formed one mass! Then each acting from the common centre would have contributed to the effect of the whole. And equally different had been the condition of mankind had the love of God been the one motive, and his glory the one object of all men. The want of this has occasioned hostility, enmity, war: "From whence come wars and fightings among you? Come they not hence, even of your lusts that war in your members? Ye lust and have not, ye kill and desire to have, and cannot obtain." (James, iv. 1, 2.) Hence, also, springs that fierce competition in business, which advances onward to the accomplishment of its own purpose, reckless of the misery it causes and of the number it tramples under foot in its progress. Thus, through the existence of sin man has often become the enemy of man, and the earth a wide-spreading battle-field instead of the happy family home which it was designed to be. How much of wretchedness and suffering has man experienced in this life from his rebellion against God!

But that which has been already endured is only the shadow of that which has to be revealed, only the slight punctures of the sting of that worm which will devour the impenitent sinner for ever. If in this state of probation such fruits have sprung from sin, what must be the horrors of the place where its full recompense will be given? There the worm dieth not. There the fire is not quenched. The wicked shall be turned into hell, and all the nations that forget God. Let it suffice for the terrible character of the future of the ungodly that the most awful descriptions of it are given by Him, who came to render our escape from it possible. His gospel, received into the heart, saves from the wages of sin and delivers from its power. Its circulation is therefore called for by every feeling of humanity in our nature.

2 To effect the deliverance of man from sin, the Most High hath done amazing things. As soon as transgression was committed, he revealed his purpose of mercy. In the hearing of our first parents, he declared that the seed of the woman should bruise the head of the serpent. Even afterwards, for four thousand years, he made preparation for the fulfilment of his promise. Dispensation after dispensation was established, and messenger after messenger sent to prepare the way of the Lord. "When the fulness of time was come, he sent forth his only-begotten Son, made of a woman, made under the law, to redeem them that were under the law." " For ye know the grace of our Lord Jesus Christ, that, though he was rich, yet, for your sakes, he became poor; that ye, through his poverty, might be rich." (Gal. iv. 4 ; 2 Cor. viii. 9.) THIS was God's contribution to his cause on earth. Who can understand it? None by searching can find out God, none can find out the Almighty unto perfection : who then can comprehend this great mystery of godliness, God manifest in the flesh? The more the amazing fact, that God did *so* love the world, is contemplated, the more amazing does it seem. Surely in no way could God more deeply show his love to mankind than in this ! What more fully proves a parent's interest in a cause than the giving up an only and dearly-beloved son to ignominy and death for its advancement? Surely nothing. And God has given up *his* only-begotten and well-beloved Son to the cruel and accursed death of the cross, that he might lay deep and strong the foundation of the sinner's hope. What a stupendous, incomprehensible, almost unbelievable fact !

Having in this astonishing manner shown his intense anxiety for the restoration of man, all other blessings necessary for its accomplishment were sure to be given. " He that spared not his own son, but delivered him up for us all, how shall he not with him also freely give us all things ?" (Rom. viii. 32.) Accordingly he has exalted the great High Priest of our profession, Christ Jesus, to his own right hand in the heavenly places, and made him head over all things to his Church, placing him far above all principality and power, and might and dominion, and every name that is named, not only in this world, but also in that which is to come; with the design that " at the name of Jesus every knee should bow, of things in heaven, and things on earth, and things under the earth, and that every tongue should confess that Jesus Christ is Lord to the glory of God the Father." Thus, as our Mediator, Jesus rules over all things, for he has been crowned with glory and honour, because he suffered death. In the exercise of this rule (Acts, ii. 33), he has sent forth the Holy Spirit, to convince the world of sin, of righteousness, and of judgment, and to guide those who have believed through grace into all the truth. He also employs the angels as ministering spirits, sent forth to minister to them that are heirs of salvation; and renders every event in time subservient to the accomplishment of that for which he died.

3. The great purpose for which the Son of God shed his precious blood, and for which he reigns in heaven, is in the course of realisation now in our world; and it needs the co-operation of the Church. God in his sovereign pleasure has arranged it so. This is a most amazing fact. We might have expected that a work of so much importance would have been done far more efficiently and quickly than by human instrumentality. Having sent his Son to make the gospel, the noblest of the hierarchy of heaven would have been honoured by being intrusted with its proclamation. We can scarcely understand how the Most High, having done so much for man's redemption, should have intrusted, in any measure or to any extent, the result to the weakness and the wilfulness even of partially-renewed men. Only think what is thus made dependent on the Church. That cause in which is involved the everlasting glory, or endless misery of innumerable millions—that cause for which He who was rich became poor— He who is infinite manifested himself in human flesh, and gave up his life in excruciating agony, and whose prosperity and triumph was the joy set before Jesus when he suffered on the cross, is under the present dispensation dependent upon Christian activity and benevolence. The toil, suffering, and death of the Son of God, the teaching and blessing of the Holy Spirit, and the accomplishment of the Father's purpose of love, all require, and hang upon, the action of the Church. This can scarcely be

believed, its utterance seems rank impiety, and yet it is the truth. For whatever position we assign the Church in the conversion of men, high or low, it is indispensable. God could easily have made a different arrangement; he could have employed the angels of heaven, or the stones of the field, to preach the truth. But we have nothing to do with what the Almighty could have done—we must consider what he has done. And, however marvellous it may be, it is true that he has put the treasure in earthen vessels, that the excellency of the power might be of God. Thus the action of the Church has been made by the Highest essential to the fulfilment of his scheme of mercy. And the experience of the past proves that, on the whole, according to the measure and character of this action will be the prosperity of his cause. The Holy Spirit works according to the condition of the instruments he employs. This truth cannot be too deeply impressed upon our minds. We must, according to the providence of grace, be co-workers with God in order to secure the blessing.

4. The work which the Church has thus to do is wholly instrumental. The sacrifice for sin has been offered and accepted, and it is the duty of the Church to call attention to it by saying with the Baptist of old, "Behold the Lamb of God that taketh away the sin of the world!" The fountain of life has been opened, and it belongs to those who have found it to be "a well of water springing up unto everlasting life," to cry, "Ho, every one that thirsteth, come ye to the waters; and he that hath no money, come ye, buy and eat, yea, come, buy wine and milk without money and without price." His gospel has been fully revealed, and it now devolves upon the disciples to proclaim it by life and word wherever they are. This duty is personal, resting upon every one who has tasted and seen that God is good. As, however, it is impossible that every believer can consecrate himself wholly to this great work, it becomes necessary that those who do so should receive temporal support from their brethren. That which they do belongs to the whole community, and not specially to them as individuals. But for the sake of order and efficiency the principle of division of labour is, to some extent, acted upon. For their support and for the employment of other kinds of instrumentality, as the circulation of the Bible and tracts, pecu-

niary contributions are needful, and become a by no means unimportant part of the duty of Christians. Some may refuse most sinfully to bear their part of the toil, but as the action of the Church is indispensable the work must be done by others. Let the Church cease to circulate the Scriptures, to employ missionaries and ministers, to teach the old and the young, and to spread the truth, and the success of the cross comes to a pause. The channels through which the blessing flows being broken off, the heavenly influence no longer descends.

5. Since God has devolved this work upon his people, it becomes a question of deep importance, "What means have been adopted to secure their attention to it?" No bond can be too great, no sanction too solemn, and no penalty too awful, for this purpose. And if in regard to individual salvation the command, " Believe on the Lord Jesus Christ," be accompanied with the tremendous sanction, " He that believeth and is baptized shall be saved, but he that believeth not shall be damned," how much more solemn will be the sanction enforcing that duty upon which depends the salvation of millions—the practical result of Christ's Messiahship! Yet, when we open the volume of inspiration, we do not find this wondrous trust hedged round with penalties or enforced by threatenings. It is reposed by the Saviour in the love of those whom he has redeemed. " Freely," he says, to his followers, " ye have received, freely give;" " If ye love me, keep my commandments." If his love to his people—a love so strongly expressed by his cross—do not suffice to make them instant in season and out of season in promoting the cause for which he died, they may be inactive and ungenerous. He condescends to no other motive, speaks in no other language. " Ye know *my* grace " is his highest appeal. Whether we are called upon to labour or to give in his cause, the love of Christ must be our supreme motive,—a love ever fed by the deep consciousness, " that if one died for all, then were all dead; and that he died for all, that they which live should not henceforth live unto themselves, but unto him which died for them, and rose again." (2 Cor. v. 14, 15.) Other feelings may be auxiliary to this that can never be placed on an equality with it.

What an honour has Christ done his people by reposing this

sacred trust in their love! If we estimate the honour by the value of the trust, how great is it! The Son of the Highest became incarnate and dwelt as a man on the earth, gave his life a ransom for many, and for the joy that was set before him endured the cross. And yet the cause for which he has done so much he has left dependent on his people's love! He has committed to them the securing of his reward. In effect he has said, " You see what I have done, and how dear the salvation of men is to me, yet, without hesitation, I leave it to your affection to determine whether I shall see of the travail of my soul and be satisfied, or be deprived of my inheritance and joy." Could Jesus have done a higher honour to his people? No! for this was the highest, noblest charge he could give them. In this his love to his people and his confidence in them attained their highest expression. Surely, then, love will prompt them to be always ready for his service. They will be in danger rather of injuring themselves by their strenuous exertions, and constant zeal, than the cause of their Master by inactivity and illiberality. Conscious that their Lord has committed his all to them on earth, they will be found worthy of the trust, or, at least, doing their utmost to be so.

6. The result has proved that Jesus knew what was in man when he reposed this confidence in his people's love. The affection of the Church has not proved worthy of the trust—for that it could not do—but it has done far more than any other feeling would have done. It has induced greater activity and self-denial, and sustained greater burdens, than any other principle. It has given birth to a heroism which has encountered every danger, and endured patiently the cruellest tortures which persecutors could devise. Filled with love to Jesus, his feeblest disciples have stood the wrath of their foes as if girt about with omnipotence, and passed through the flames without dismay. It has given rise to generous self-sacrifice for the welfare of others, with which there is nothing in the history of the world to compare. Glowing with love to Him who became poor that he might make many rich, his followers have devoted their lives to toil and privation, to suffering and death, that the lamp of life might shine

upon the benighted souls of men. The sentiment of Paul has been no uncommon thing, " The love of Christ constraineth me." The names of a Brainerd, a Martyn, a Williams, a Moffat, and many others who have followed closely in the footsteps of the apostles, are household words in the family of God. The example of these heroes is appreciated and loved even when it could not be followed, for the motives which animated them are common to the disciples Jesus. And there are many, equal to these men in devotedness and heroism, whose scene of labour has been private, and whose works will not be known until they are proclaimed by Him who will say, " I was an hungered, and ye gave me to eat." It has also occasioned a liberality greater than any other feeling has ever continuously produced. Thus, however far short of what it should have been, the Church has fallen, yet " wisdom is justified of her children," and its history has proved the wisdom of the Lord in committing this great trust to the honour of his people. For what is now being accomplished, as well as for what has been done, by love to Jesus, we feel bound to render devout thanksgiving to the Father of all mercies.

But, notwithstanding the testimony which we thus thankfully bear to the power of love to Jesus, we are deeply conscious that it is not sufficiently strong nor manifested as it requires to be. Every feeling whose existence points to action must, in order to its practical worth, embody itself in deed. It must plant itself in the soil of fact, and grow up a work; otherwise the purpose of its existence is not answered. But the act in which it results is in a very great degree dependent for its character and magnitude upon the prevalent expression of the feeling. In some cases, indeed, where there is unusual independence and originality of mind, the embodiment will depend almost wholly on the feeling itself. But this is not the general character even of renewed men. They are not the creators of much of their own course, but lean upon others for help and guidance. Thus it may happen, that in one circle the consecration of one per cent. of income to the cause of God is as manifest a proof of liberality as ten per cent. in another. Now, it is only too possible that the common embodiment of Christian liberality may be too small, and yet this not be perceived, because the love to Jesus, which is the motive to liberality, is consciously felt, and the expression of it in act is in conformity with the prevailing one. If the same amount were given in a circle where a larger proportion was usual, the deficiency would immediately be seen, and probably amended. We ought not, then, to determine what we will give to the cause of Christ by measuring our contributions with those of others, for they may be too little. We cannot determine it by the authority of the New Testament; for while in it we find the strongest motives to generosity, it does not decide for us what generosity is. We can easily infer, that that for which the example of Jesus is adduced—that which his love is to prompt, and which is to express our obligation to him, should robe itself in no mean attire, but go forth before the world in strenuous efforts and noble contributions. But still the question returns unanswered, How much ought I to give? And unless some guide to the solution be obtained, there is reason to fear that the embodiment of our Christian love in liberal contributions will be less than it ought. The Church requires to have its love increased, and it also requires some guide to the right expression of its affection. The latter must be had as well as the former, because without it liberality will not increase. A feeling prevails widely among Christians, that in regard to this grace we are before any age of the Church, and nearly at perfection. Now, when one becomes satisfied with his attainments, it is not likely that he will advance much farther. There is great need, consequently, of some other measure of liberality than our own by which we may estimate ourselves.

CHAPTER III.

THE OLD TESTAMENT MEASURE OF LIBERALITY.

1. It seems to us that a standard by which we may measure our liberality with great profit is presented in the Old Testament.

From it we learn that in various periods of the Church a tenth of income was the proportion given to the Lord. At what time tithe began to be paid we have no information. The first time it is mentioned, in regard to the gift which Abraham made from the spoil taken from Chedorlaomer and the confederate kings to Melchizedek, the priest of the Most High God, it is alluded to as if the proportion were the established one. "And he gave him tithes of all." (Gen. xiv. 20.) From this it would seem to have been a well-known rule even at that early period. But when, or where, or by what authority, it was instituted, we do not know. Perhaps, and we think most probably, it was selected by God himself. At all events, the proportion appears to have been the recognised one in the days of the patriarchs. We find Jacob, on the morning after he had seen in a dream a ladder between heaven and earth, vowing, that if God would be with him and cause him to return to his father's house in peace, he would devote a tenth of all his property to him. (Gen. xxviii. 22.) We know that, whatever was the origin of tithe, it was under the Mosaic dispensation enacted by the express command of God. In this, as in several other things, the Levitical Institute was simply a renewal of the patriarchal custom. It is of importance to observe this. It shows clearly that sufficient reasons for the payment of tithe existed before the Israelites left Egypt, and affords ground for inferring that others may be found after the abolition of the Judaic dispensation. The law of Moses regarding tithe occurs in Lev. xxvii. 30–32.

2. The purpose to which this tenth was devoted among the Jews was the maintenance of the ministers of religion, the priests and Levites: "The tithes I have given you from them for your inheritance." (Num. xviii. 24.) In consequence of the consecration of the tribe of Levi to the service of the Lord, they did not receive any portion of the land when it was divided among the others, except the Levitical cities and their suburbs, which were scattered over the country. It was necessary that they, as ministers of religion, should be accessible to the people, and hence they were released from the burden of secular duties, and located in places some of which were near every part of Canaan.

In order to recompense them for their services, and in place of their inheritance, the tithe was given to them. It was no matter of almsgiving and receiving, but the requirement of strict justice. The law is very explicit in regard to this (Num. xviii. 20–24).

3. This tithe was by no means the whole of the contributions which were required of the Jews. In addition, "all the first fruits, both of fruit and animals, were consecrated to God (Exod. xxii. 29 ; Num. xviii. 12, 13, &c.), and the first fruits of corn, wine, oil, and sheep's wool, were offered for the use of the Levites (Deut. xviii. 4). The amount of this gift is not specified in the law of Moses, which leaves it entirely to the pleasure of the giver; the Talmudical writers, however, inform us, that liberal persons were accustomed to give the fortieth and even the thirtieth; while such as were covetous or penurious gave only a sixtieth part." Besides these first fruits, and the tithes of the Levites, there was another tenth, "which was carried up to Jerusalem, and eaten in the Temple, at offering feasts, as a sign of rejoicing and gratitude to God. These are called second tithes." "Lastly, there were tithes allotted to the poor, for whom there was also a corner left in every field which it was not lawful to reap with the the rest (Lev. xix. 9 ; Deut. xxiv. 19); and they were likewise allowed such ears of corn, or grapes, as were dropped or scattered about, and the sheaves that might be accidentally forgotten in the field." (Horne's "Introduction," vol. iii. pp. 296, 297, 8th ed.) Concerning this last tithe there is some dispute. Josephus ("Antiq." iv. 8, 22) states expressly that it was a third tithe, but others are of opinion that it was only the special devotion of the second tithe every third year to the poor. However this may be, it is obvious that the Jew had to contribute about the fourth part of his income, at the command of God. Besides these direct gifts, there were numerous other expenses connected with his religion which had to be met. He had often to present sacrifices for ceremonial and other transgressions, and to lose a considerable portion of his time from various causes. On the whole, therefore, his religion could not cost him much less than a third of his income. And in addition to these regular charges we find at different times the most generous and noble efforts

made by the Israelites in support of God's worship, as in the erection of the Tabernacle and Temple. Notwithstanding the very great cost of these buildings and their furniture, it was cheerfully met, and more than met, by the willing generosity of a grateful people. But leaving out of sight those special donations, and the contributions for ceremonial and benevolent purposes, we still have a tenth devoted by God's command to the purposes of religion. Whatever was given in support of the poor and in other benevolent ways, was in addition to this.

4. It does not seem that any provision was made by the law of Moses for the recovery of tithe, if the people proved unwilling to pay it. "The rendering of what was due was simply a matter of religious obligation, and where this failed the claim could not be enforced by any constraint of law." (Fairbairn's "Typology," vol. ii. p. 336.) "The payment and appreciation of them [the tithes] Moses left to the consciences of the people, without subjecting them to judicial or sacerdotal visitations." (Horne, p. 298.) This is manifest from the absence of any allusion to the legal machinery which would have been requisite for its enforcement, from the silence of the historical parts of Scripture respecting the occurrence of such a case, and still more from the expostulations addressed to the Israelites when they withheld their tithe. These striking moral and religious appeals would have been inappropriate had there been any legal means for obtaining the tithe. Law deals with rougher weapons than persuasion. "The conscientious accuracy of the people with respect to the second tithe was secured merely by the declaration which the Israelite made every third year before God;" "I have brought away the hallowed things out of my house, and also have given them unto the Levite, and unto the stranger, to the fatherless and the widow, according to all thy commandments which thou hast commanded me; I have not transgressed thy commandments, neither have I forgotten them." (Deut. xxvi. 13.) Hence it is manifest that the great difference between the law of liberality under the Gospel and the Mosaic dispensation is, that the latter, while it devolved the duty upon the religious feeling in common with the former, specified in addition the pro-

MOTIVES FOR GIVING IT—GRATITUDE. 199

portion that should be given. It is of great importance that this should be observed. We are so accustomed to think of tithe as a legal claim which may be enforced by legal appliances, that we are apt to carry our associations to the records of the Old Testament. But, on attentive consideration, we shall find that tithe under the old economy was a voluntary subscription, sought for only on moral considerations, with a specification of the amount that ought to be given.

5. Since the duty of paying tithe thus rested upon the moral and religious feelings of the people, it may be well to look somewhat more attentively at them. The first feeling must have been that of gratitude for goodness received. The tithes were an expression of thanksgiving. In the vow of Jacob this appears most prominently. And the same feeling must have been largely experienced among the Hebrews. The land which they possessed—a land flowing with milk and honey—had been given by Jehovah to them and their forefathers. They had been strangers in a strange land—slaves in the house of bondage—until God, with a strong hand and a stretched-out arm, effected their deliverance, and, after guiding them through the sea and the wilderness, had planted them in the goodly country he had promised to Abraham. As they reaped their harvest, and gathered the fruit into barns, these facts must often have been before their minds. The scenes of their early history were, by express command, transmitted from generation to generation, by the father to his children; and the Levite that was within their gate, whose subsistence was so largely dependent upon the tithe, would, for his own sake, take care to remind the Israelites of these wonderful events. That they were deeply imprinted on the souls of the people is manifest from the continued references to them in their literature. With these facts in their mind, could they, when, by the good providence of their fathers' God, they had sown and reaped, and had wanted neither the former nor the latter rain, grudge to render the tenth part of that as a thanksgiving, which was all a gift from Him? Every nation looks back with feelings of admiration and gratitude upon its heroes and founders, elevating them where true religion is unknown into

gods, and in the case of the Israelites these natural emotions led them to honour the true God.

Conjoined with these emotions of gratitude were those of religious veneration. This seems to have been the feeling which influenced Abraham in giving tithes to Melchizedek. His regard to the Most High God was expressed by his liberality to his priest. And unquestionably the same feeling must have had a prominent place in the mind of every Israelite who felt that the highest glory of his race was their possession of the knowledge of the true God. Other nations might surpass the Jews in power, in arts, and in fame, but among them alone were the oracles of the living God. "He showeth his word unto Jacob, his statutes and his judgments unto Israel. He hath not dealt so with any nation, and as for his judgments they have not known them. Praise ye the Lord." (Ps. cxlvii. 19, 20.) All who really felt this must have been solicitous that the worship of the Most High should be sustained in honour and splendour. They would wish it to surpass in the costliness, magnificence, and solemnity of its ceremonies those of all other religions, just as the Christian desires that love to Jesus should produce better and more abundant fruit than any other principle. But this most natural wish, which expressed itself so triumphantly in the erection of the Temple, directed that the servants of God who ministered in his Tabernacle should be well supported. The reverence and affection towards God, which religion excites, since they could not manifest themselves directly towards him, would do so in regard for the ordinances and ministers of his worship. While these feelings continued vigorous, the liberality of the Jews might exceed, but would not fall below, the measure which had been enacted. "Their gratitude to God, and their continual remembrance of him, required to have an expression and a testimony, in the presentation to him, not only of the firstlings of the herd and fold, not only of the fruits of the earth, and the tithe of time, but of all treasures of wisdom and beauty, as in the Tabernacle and Temple with their furniture." (Ruskin's "Seven Lamps of Architecture,"—Sacrifice.)

But the Old-Testament dispensation was even more prospective than retrospective. It looked forward to Calvary more than backward to Sinai. Those, therefore, who understood it, and doubtless many did, as the shadow of good things to come, would feel themselves strongly moved to sustain it, because of that which they dimly saw arising out of it. Whatever was involved in the bruising of the serpent's head—in the blessing of the whole world through the descendants of their father Abraham —these blessings were in some way connected with the Levitical dispensation. Dimly as they might be seen, these prospects could not fail to aid the religious Jew in cheerfully bearing the expenses of his worship. When Haggai was urging the Jews to rebuild the Temple, one of the chief encouragements he adduced was the promise, "I will shake all nations, and the Desire of all Nations shall come; and I will fill this house with glory, saith the Lord of hosts. The glory of this latter house shall be greater than of the former, saith the Lord of hosts; and in this place will I give peace." (Hag. ii. 7, 9.) And the same feeling must in a considerable degree have animated the whole nation at every period of its existence in its attention to the ceremonial law. The hope of future glory, even when dimly perceived, is always a powerful incentive to the performance of those duties from which it is to spring. And in regard to the Jews, whose religion was so much one of promise, this must have been particularly the case.

The great reason, however, upon which the Almighty based the duty of tithe was that of justice. This must precede generosity. If a claim be just there is little liberality in settling it. Besides, the feelings of generosity and benevolence cannot so well form the subject of legislation as that of justice, since their value depends on their spontaneity. But the demands of justice are more palpable, and it is to these that the law refers. The Levites were to devote themselves wholly to the service of the Lord, and could not consequently provide for their own temporal necessities. As the people had the land of the Levites divided among them, and enjoyed the benefit of their services—services which, from their spiritual nature, no tithe could repay—it was only simple justice for them to support the ministers of religion.

They who served at the altar had a right to live by the altar, even as they who preach the Gospel have a right to live by the Gospel. (1 Cor. ix. 13, 14.)

6. If the Israelites, notwithstanding these reasons, failed in the performance of their duty, they incurred very great guilt. At various times this sin was committed. During the reign of Ahaz, king of Judah, under the jurisdiction of Nehemiah, and while Malachi was the prophet of God, this was the case. (2 Chron. xxxi. 4; Neh. xiii. 10; Mal. iii. 8.) In the latter case, the criminality of the course is most strongly asserted. The Most High had sent a famine upon the Jews because of their conduct, which was not to be removed until they had brought all the tithes into his storehouse. The withholding of these tenths is expressly called a robbery of God, "Will a man rob God? Yet ye have robbed me. But ye say, Wherein have we robbed thee? In tithes and offerings. Ye are cursed with a curse, for ye have robbed me, even this whole nation." This very awful aspect of their sin, thus presented to them by God's messenger, must have produced a far deeper effect, and a much readier obedience, in every Israelite whose conscience was not entirely dead, than any merely human terrors could have done.

Thus it appears that, under the Old-Testament dispensation, liberality to the cause of God was a moral duty, as it is now,—the difference being that then a tenth was stated to be the proportion which should be given, whereas now every Christian has to determine for himself what he ought to give.

CHAPTER IV.

THE OLD TESTAMENT MEASURE, A GUIDE TO CHRISTIAN LIBERALITY.

1. WE have already said that, numerous and weighty as are the motives to liberality in the New Testament—and they could not be either more numerous or more weighty—it yet affords no clue as to the actual amount which the Christian should give. Neither in its precepts nor in its examples do we find this. The

example of the church in Jerusalem at its origin is indeed definite, but that it was not intended to be a pattern to future ages is manifest, for it soon died out there. The giving of all their possessions was obviously the expression of a deep impulse not yet subordinated to sound judgment. We find the Corinthians exhorted by Paul to abound in the grace of liberality, but they were left to determine for themselves what abounding in liberality meant. This is the mode in all the New-Testament inculcations of the duty. Its only rule is, "Estimate your obligations to Jesus, who hath by his death redeemed you, and give as the Lord hath prospered you."

2. Nor is this want of a definite rule an unintentional omission. The law of the Lord is perfect. And however much a Christian may wish that there had been some guide to determine what he, under the influence of the love of Jesus, ought to give to his cause, there are abundant reasons why it has not been given. The New Testament contains the religion of the world. Its principles and motives are not to be confined to a race, or country, or period of time; they are designed for all countries and for all time. The rich man and the poor man—the civilized and the uncivilized —the Esquimaux and the Polynesian—are alike to be imbued and governed by them. Had there been given a fixed measure of liberality binding upon all people in all times, it might have imposed upon some a burden grievous to be borne, while upon others its pressure would have been nothing. It was, consequently, needful that it should be encumbered with no inflexible rule as to the embodiment of its principles, which might possibly have been unsuited to many. Christianity, moreover, is a religion of spirit and life, not of letter and death. Its purpose is to renew the heart, and thence to reform and rule the whole man. Men, on the contrary, naturally look more to the overt act than to its motive. This has been borne testimony to in all ages. Had Christianity, then, inculcated the giving of a fixed proportion of property, the consequence would have been that many would have attended to the letter of the law while they neglected the spirit. They would have given the percentage, and thought that in doing so they fulfilled their whole duty;

though the feelings of sympathy and benevolence were uncultivated. The Gospel seeks, too, to train up the individual man to be a law unto himself. Hence, as far as may be, it leaves the Christian to find out for himself, by the light which it gives, the way in which we ought to walk. Its work is, in regard to duty, rather to take the veil from the eyes, that the right way may be plainly seen, than to lead by the hand. And therefore it gives a general principle, whose application to practical life requires forethought and care, and not a catalogue of duties minutely detailed, which a child might walk by.

3. It may be thought, that if these reasons for the omission of a law of tithe in the New Testament are valid, they prove at the same time that our argument is not only needless, but injurious, as supplementary to that which is perfect. But it is not so.

It is sufficiently obvious that the point which revelation leaves thus undetermined must be determined, and is so, in fact, by every Christian. If he gives nothing, he determines it; if he gives liberally, he does so. There *is* a definite measure to every man's liberality, though what it is may not be known even by himself. Often, alas! this is the case. The believer does not know to what extent he is obeying his Master's commands. Chance or circumstance determines what it shall be. That this is the truth, a little attention to the list of subscriptions to our religious societies would soon make evident. However important the cause may be, and whatever may be the difference in the means of those who give, it will be found that all the *respectable* give very nearly alike, as a general rule. Yet, surely, what we are to do in compliance with our Saviour's commands deserves to receive our serious thought. He and his cause are worthy of receiving from our hands, not any service that happens, but the best we can give. And it is an insult to our God, an insult to the interests of the world, and an insult to our own religious life, to commit the determination of this point to any external circumstance. It is worthy of receiving our most attentive consideration. If it is, thus becomingly, to be determined, we present the present argument as a light to the Christian's path.

But this is a vastly different position from that which an apostolic command would have occupied. We ask no further assent than the reader's conviction declares to be right, while an inspired command would have been authoritative. Our argument is not, therefore, in opposition to the spirit of the New Testament. Since the proportion to be given to the Lord must be fixed upon, we think the following considerations recommend the law of tithe as a guide to us in this determination.

4. The fact that a tenth was the proportion given before the law of Moses was instituted will have some weight in leading to its adoption. The argument of Paul, that the promise which God made to Abraham could not be annulled by the abrogation of the law which was given four hundred years after the promise, finds here a legitimate application. (Gal. iii. 16–18.) Whatever of obligation or propriety the usage had in the days of the patriarchs, it must still, in similar circumstances, retain, unaffected by the abolition of the law.

Besides, though as a part of a temporary dispensation it was abolished in its positive form, it is yet recommended by its being enacted by Moses. That for a very long time a tenth was the divinely appointed measure of liberality, must secure for it attentive notice, and requires that we should have good reasons for abandoning it. With the Christian who is asking, What will the Lord have me to do?—the position in which every Christian ought to be—this will have very considerable weight. And it is to Christians in this happy condition we speak. The duty of liberality is, unlike many duties of the Mosaic code, as binding upon us as it was upon the Jews, and if we can get any light from their law as to what we should do in regard to it, we may fairly use it. We do not revive any of its obsolete observances, as sacrifice, and so append something to Christianity which would be highly to be condemned, we only extract what light we can from the past to guide us in the performance of our own duty.

5. Although a positive command is abolished, yet if the reasons for which it was enacted remain, the duty which it enjoined continues binding, but not on the same ground. A posi-

tive command may be based on moral reasons, and generally is
so. The person on whom it is laid may be unable to see these
reasons, or unwilling to comply with them. Hence the need for
a positive command founded on them. But if that incapacity or
perversity should be removed, the positive law may be abrogated
without interfering with the performance of the duty. It would
now rest on the moral reasons. These as truly require obedience
as the positive command, and would, in every right mind, as
surely secure it. Cases of the kind supposed are of frequent
occurrence. How often does a father give a command to his
children, based upon moral reasons, which they cannot comprehend. When they have grown up, and are no longer subject to
positive law, the same duty, nevertheless, continues binding on
them. It may be, for instance, the keeping of the Sabbath,
which is commanded. When manhood is reached the Sabbath
is still kept, because now the reasons on which the father's
authoritative law was based are seen and felt, and become the
son's own reasons for keeping that day holy. The same might
have been the case in regard to the payment of tithe. It is not
difficult to suppose that the ancient Hebrews could not comprehend all the reasons for this law, and that God consequently
enacted it positively. But if the people were at length able
completely to appreciate all the causes for it, and no longer
requiring a positive law it had been repealed, yet would not the
rendering of tithe thereby have ceased to be a duty. In such a
case the result might well be a more willing and cheerful contribution, since it had become a moral service, and not a mere
proof of submission to authority. At all events, if the positive
command had been founded on sufficient reasons, which continued
after the repeal of the authoritative precept, the duty would
continue the same outwardly as before. There would be a
flexibility in the purely moral law, which would meet the circumstances of every case far more perfectly than the positive
command could do. Some, deeply conscious of their obligations
to God, and endowed with worldly substance, would give more
than ten per cent, and others involved in deep distress and
poverty might feel justified in not giving so much. These

variations are connected with the working of a moral law, and are a part of its excellency, while their absence is one of the great evils inseparable from general positive commands. Yet if the positive law had been fairly made, and expressed the obligation of the moral reasons well, they themselves, when felt, would produce quite as large a result over the whole community. We may make another change, and suppose that not only the positive enactment has been repealed, but also the reasons for that law altered. Even in this case, if other reasons of equal force are substituted, the observance itself will not fall into disuse. Supposing that, for the moral reasons on which God rested his claim of tithe from the Jews, there had been substituted higher claims upon their gratitude and reverence, would they have been justified in withholding its payment? The very contrary would have been the case; it would have been more binding; and the amount should have been increased rather than diminished. This seems most obvious. If the less blessing deserve ten per cent as a thank-offering, surely the greater blessing cannot be rightly acknowledged by a smaller amount. Now we affirm that the reasons for liberality have not been decreased under the present dispensation, but increased very largely; and that, as a consequence, the Christian Church ought to give more to God and his cause than the Jews did, rather than less. If ten per cent was not too much for them to give, it surely is not too much for Christians if they can render it. Our gratitude demands as large an expression surely as theirs, and our sense of duty also.

CHAPTER V.

COMPARISON OF THE REASONS FOR LIBERALITY UNDER THE OLD AND NEW TESTAMENTS.

1. In instituting this comparison we are fully aware that the claims of God upon his people cannot be estimated by the rule of proportion. All that God gives he gives freely. Our being

permitted to offer him anything is a favour we owe to his love. Hence we are conscious how easily our argument may be turned into a piece of blasphemy, by putting it thus:—" The Jews paid for the favours they enjoyed at God's hand so much; now the Christian receives much greater blessings, what should he pay?" It is in a spirit very different from this that we make this comparison. Our mode of looking at the question is ;—" The Jews, for what God so generously gave them, presented this on his altar; shall not we, who have received so much more from our heavenly Father, equal them in love, and in every manifestation of it?" We would use their example to provoke the Christian Church to excel them in this grace as they excel them in privilege. With this remark, which what follows may seem to require, we proceed to the comparison.

2. There are no peculiarities, so far as we know, in the circumstances of Christians at present, in this land, which render them unable to give as liberally as the Jews. During the continuance of their economy, there were very great diversities in their temporal condition, but the law of tithe continued the same. Sometimes their prosperity was almost unbounded, especially during the reign of Solomon, when such was the abundance of silver that it was nothing accounted of. (1 Kings, x. 21.) At other times they were in the deepest distress. A more oppressive and galling state of bondage is scarcely conceivable than that recorded in 1 Sam. xiii., when their enemies the Philistines would not permit even the smiths necessary for the repair of agricultural implements to reside in Judea. The condition of the Jews in the age of Malachi was very far from prosperous. According to the best biblical critics, he prophesied during the time of Nehemiah, and stood in the same relation to that governor as the prophets Haggai and Zechariah had done to his predecessor Zerubbabel. We find the general condition of the Jews in that age detailed at considerable length in the fifth chapter of Nehemiah. The mass of the people were so poor that they were compelled to mortgage their lands and vineyards in order to procure food for their families, and money to pay heir taxes. Nehemiah, in compassion for their miserable state,

refused to take any portion of his own salary from them, which most strikingly shows his opinion of their circumstances. Indeed these were only such as might be expected among a people lately returned, after a protracted captivity, to a desolate land. But they were not held by God as any reason for not paying tithe. Those pointed questions, which we have already quoted, (Mal. iii. 8) were at this time addressed to the Jews, "Will a man rob God? Yet ye have robbed me—in tithes and offerings." Probably in consequence of these sharp remonstrances, arrangements were speedily made for the regular payment of tithe and other dues. (Neh. x. 35–39.) Thus the low condition of these Jews did not exempt them from the duty of paying tithe. They were held as robbing God in withholding it, notwithstanding their depressed circumstances. Nor, except in the most extreme cases, does this seem strange, even under His government, who detests oppression, and hates robbery for burnt-offering. For there are comparatively few in any state of society who could not spare a tenth of what they have—were it necessary to give it up. Unquestionably it would be seriously missed—but many others have to live upon as little as the remainder. The Jew had only to look round him to find a number whose income was less than his would be even after deducting a tenth.

The present position of our nation does not, by its inferiority in wealth, as contrasted with the average condition of the Jewish people, afford us any reason for giving less than they did to the cause of God. They were an agricultural and pastoral people, farming each his own plot of land; while we are a commercial, and, consequently, a wealthy people. Their institutions were expressly designed to keep the mass of the community in the condition of small farmers, while ours are for the accumulation of wealth. We are therefore certainly as able to give a tenth as they were, and more so. But it may be said the Jewish government was not so expensive as ours—what we would give in contributions is taken from us as taxes. The complaints of the Israelites after the death of Solomon do not favour the notion that they were lightly taxed. Prosperous as had been that reign, we find the people at its close speaking thus: "Thy father made

P

our yoke grievous, now therefore make thou the grievous service of thy father, and his heavy yoke which he put upon us, lighter, and we will serve thee." (1 Kings, xii. 4.) And it was because these financial grievances, instead of being removed, were, according to the foolish threat of Rehoboam, to be increased, that the cry, " To your tents, O Israel ! What portion have we in David?" which divided the nation into two, arose. The condition of the people in the time of Nehemiah we have just noticed. They had then not only to support their own government, but to pay a tribute to the King of Persia, which made it needful for some of them to sell their property in order to meet it. The reports of our taxation, instead of showing that we are not able to give a tenth to God, most emphatically prove the contrary. A very large portion of the revenue consists of taxes upon articles by no means necessary to existence or even comfort. These are self-imposed ; as the disuse of the things would exempt from the tax. According to the most accurate conclusions to which Mr G. R. Porter could arrive, the British people tax themselves for spirits, wines, beer (exclusive of that brewed in private families), and tobacco in its various forms, to the extent of 57,063,230*l*. per annum. Whatever advantages may result from the use of these articles, most certainly less than the half of this sum is sufficient payment for them. The nation would on the whole be much better to be wholly without them. When to this enormous sum we add the amount spent upon other unnecessary and frequently injurious objects, it must be manifest that this nation, or an average section of it, could spare a tenth of their income. The same conclusion follows, perhaps, still more manifestly from a comparison of our wealth with that of other nations. France, with a population about 10,000,000 greater than this country, has a national income estimated at 320,000,000*l*., while that of Great Britain is estimated in Poole's " Statistics of Commerce" at 800,000,000*l*. In other words, the average income of every person in these islands is fully three times as much as that of an inhabitant of France. Surely when God has thus placed us in wealth so far above our neighbours, it would not be impossible to render as a thanksgiving one-tenth of what he has bestowed upon us. At all events, *we* cannot plead inability to conform to the custom of the Jews. These observations are related to the subject before us, because Christians are on an equality in respect to their condition in this life with the rest of the population. There have been times frequent and protracted, and there are now many countries, in which this could not be said. Happily, in our land those sad days when the followers of Jesus were driven from their homes, and compelled to wander in sheepskins and goatskins, and to lodge in dens and caves of the earth, are ended; and they are now permitted to buy and sell and get gain like others. Probably Christians from their probity and moral restraint occupy a rather higher position in life than the average one; for character has an earthly reward, and godliness hath the promise of this life as well as of that which is to come. We therefore conclude, that there is nothing in the outward condition of British Christians which will justify a diminution of their contributions to God below the proportion presented by the Jews.

3. Still less is there anything in the obligations under which the Most High has placed us which would warrant such a course. There may not have been the same manifest interposition on our behalf as there was for the Jews, but it has been, even in regard to our earthly life, as real and efficacious. Moses has not been sent to lead us out of social and political bondage, and to guide us through a literal wilderness by miracles to our present position. But the Christian knows that our happy condition is due to the kindness of Jehovah. He has learned to trace all his blessings through their secondary causes to Him from whom cometh down every good and perfect gift. And in whatever we institute a comparison between ourselves and the Jews, the advantage will usually be found on our side. Our institutions, our laws, our government, is better. Receiving these things from God, we owe to him a thank-offering as much as the Hebrews did. As Christians we do this in two respects;—for the progress which under the divine blessing this nation has made. It is no small favour to have had our existence in this land, where quiet and tranquillity prevail, and where we enjoy so many comforts and advantages. And then we owe a thank-offering for our position

as Christians. We have the fullest liberty to worship God according to the dictates of conscience, and to share in every blessing of the community. When we consider our position in contrast with that of many others, surely it becomes us to say, "The Lord hath done great things for us, whereof we are glad." Our condition is as different from that of our forefathers and of our brethren in many other lands, as was that of the Israelites in the land of Canaan from what it had been in the house of bondage. If God then claimed the obedience and gratitude of the Israelites because he could say, "I am the Lord thy God, which have brought thee out of the land of Egypt, out of the house of bondage," he has still a greater claim upon ours. And if the Jew was influenced in some degree by the wonderful kindness of God to his nation when he gave a tithe, feeling that it was not too much to render him as a thanksgiving, do our high temporal mercies deserve less?

4. Our religious advantages contrast still more favourably with those of the peculiar people. "Among them," said our Saviour, "that are born of women, there hath not arisen a greater than John the Baptist. Notwithstanding he that is least in the kingdom of heaven is greater than he." (Matt. xi. 11.) This estimate of the privileges enjoyed under the Old and New Testament dispensations, even we, with our dull spiritual perceptions, cannot fail to approve.

The great redemption, which was only dimly apprehended by them through shadowy types and obscure prophecies, has become to us a matter of history. Earnestly did they ponder the prophetic messages which were given them, "searching what, or what manner of time the Spirit of Christ which was in them did signify, when it testified beforehand the sufferings of Christ and the glory that should follow." (1 Pet. i. 11.) They saw, through the shadows which were given them, the day of Christ, and were glad. But we *know* more fully in whom we have believed, for in the fulness of time God was manifest in the flesh. Amid the accusations of conscience, and the mysteries of life, when we would naturally flee from God, and dread him, we can say, "He that spared not his own Son, but delivered him up for us all, how shall he not with him also freely give us all things?" "God commendeth his love towards us, in that, while we were yet sinners, Christ died for us. Much more then, being now justified by his blood, we shall be saved from wrath through him." (Rom. viii. 32; v. 8, 9.) Thus stable is the foundation which God had laid for our peace with him. Vast as might have been the ideas of the patriarchs and prophets concerning the tender mercy of God, and great as their expectations of its manifestations, how little could they have known the height and depth, the length and breadth, of that love which God has disclosed to us? "God so loved the world, that he gave his only-begotten Son" for it, is a New Testament text. How great should be our peace, since it rests on this foundation! How great our love and gratitude to him who hath so loved us!

Our present position as far excels that of the Israelites, as our knowledge of the plan of salvation does theirs. The law was given by Moses, but grace and truth came by Jesus Christ. We are under the dispensation of the Spirit. No longer does the commandment come from Sinai, with its terrible sanctions to drive us to our duty—it is written upon the tablets of our hearts, or falls upon our path, from the example of Jesus, as the light of heaven. We are no longer under tutors and governors as children, but have become sons of God through faith in Christ Jesus. The spirit of bondage has given place to that of adoption. We have had given unto us by the divine power *all* things that pertain to life and godliness, through the knowledge of *him* who hath called us to glory and virtue, whereby are given unto us exceeding great and precious promises, that by these we might be partakers of the divine nature. (2 Pet. i. 3, 4.) God has fulfilled to his Church his ancient promise, "I will dwell in them, and walk in them, and I will be their God, and they shall be my people;" for we are the temple of the Holy Ghost. We have also an advocate with the Father, Jesus Christ the righteous, through whose intercession our feeble prayer rises successfully to heaven. "We *are* come, not to the mount that might be touched, and that burned with fire, and unto blackness and darkness and tempest, and the sound of a trumpet and the voice of words, but unto Mount Zion, and unto the city of the living God, the heavenly Jerusalem, and to an innumerable company of angels; to the general assembly and church of the first-born which are written in heaven, and to God the judge of all, and to the spirits of just men made perfect, and to Jesus the mediator of the new covenant, and to the blood of sprinkling, that speaketh better things than that of Abel." (Heb. xii. 18-24.) How would the Old-Testament saints have appreciated our high position! Many prophets and righteous men have desired to see those things which we see, and have not seen them, and to hear those things which we hear, and have not heard them. Blessed are our eyes, for they see; and our ears, for they hear. (Matt. xiii. 16, 17.) Eye had not seen, nor ear heard, neither had entered into the heart of man, the things which God hath revealed to us by his Spirit. (1 Cor. ii. 9.)

And our hopes for the future are as much superior to those of the ancient people of God in character and clearness, as our views of the plan of redemption and our present privileges. The lamp of Judaism flickered amid the exhalations of the tomb, and threw only a few feeble rays upon the world beyond. But Jesus hath brought life and immortality to light in his gospel. The dark passage which connects the seen with the unseen state has become only the valley of the *shadow* of death, by reason of the rays of glorious light which now issue from the throne of God—from the land beyond death. We are delivered through faith in Jesus Christ from the fear of death, by which so many are all their lifetime held in bondage. We can even claim Death as our servant, for "Death is yours," and in the hour of dissolution triumph over our ancient foe. "O Death, where is thy sting? O Grave, where is thy victory?" may be our song; "for the sting of death is sin, and the strength of sin is the law; but thanks be to God who giveth us the victory through our Lord Jesus Christ." Nor need we wonder at this challenge of the king of terrors by those who can say, "Henceforth there is laid up for me a crown of righteousness, which the Lord, the righteous judge, shall give me at that day." "We have been begotten again into the lively hope of an inheritance incorruptible, undefiled, and that fadeth not away"—an inheritance to be enjoyed and a crown to be worn in the society of the glorified Jesus and all his saints. We rejoice in the hope of the glory of God.

When we thus review the wondrous revelation which God has given us concerning himself—the amazing privileges which by his grace we enjoy—and the bright hopes of immortality which we cherish through the love of Jesus, we shall feel that the least in the kingdom of heaven is in these things greater than any that had been born of women before. Surely, then, we cannot present less to God as an expression of our gratitude than the Hebrew did, if our relative spiritual condition is to influence us at all.

5. The plea of justice, upon which so much of the burden of the law of tithe was laid, may likewise be used in urging the Christian to liberality. When the tenth was withheld by the Jew, the Priest and Levite were defrauded of their due. It was their portion; and they who serve at the altar have a right to live by the altar. As well might the Jew go into the house of his neighbour and help himself to his property as keep back the tithe. A similar sin is committed when the Christian is illiberal. They who preach the gospel have a right to live by the gospel. Yet there are many in the ministry to whom great injustice is done. Anxious thoughts, harassing cares, and sometimes pinching poverty, distract the minds of not a few, who have devoted themselves to the service of the Church, to the great hindrance of their work. They do not seek a recompense for their labour here— their reward is on high. But they have a right to expect that those who receive spiritual good at their hands will set them above the hardships of poverty. Had they devoted their talents, educated as they have been, to secular business, they would have equalled in temporal circumstances the companions of their youth. But because they have devoted themselves to the ministry of the word, they have put this out of their power. To support them liberally is not charity, it is scarcely generosity. Justice demands it, and a serious offence against its sacred rights is committed when the demand is not complied with. " Let him that is taught in the word communicate to him that teacheth in all good things. Be not deceived; God is not mocked; for whatsoever a man

soweth, that shall he also reap; for he that soweth to the flesh shall of the flesh reap corruption, but he that soweth to the Spirit shall of the Spirit reap life everlasting." (Gal. vi. 6–8.) In this very solemn manner does the Apostle present this duty.

There is one great difference between the old and new dispensations, however, in regard to the plea of justice. God of old determined the number of his ministers. He elected all the descendants of Levi for this office. *Now* there is no determinate number. The consequence is, that the number of those who are engaged in the ministry is reduced when the Church is illiberal. Thus our missionary societies do not starve their missionaries; but they cannot employ the number which the cause of Christ and the world demand. Whether this is an alleviation to the injustice of withholding more than is meet, every Christian can determine. Under the former dispensation the robbery was committed chiefly against the servants of God, under the present it is more directly committed against Jesus himself. But surely this affords no reason, but the contrary, for our doing less than the Jews in support of God's worship.

6. But though there may be ability in the Church to give a tenth, and higher motives to induce its presentation, than were formerly known, it may be asked, Is there as strong a call for it? In the present age this will not be deemed an irrelevant inquiry. Perhaps as Christians this ought not to have the prominent place it receives. True gratitude, such as the believer ought to feel, will find for itself a mode of expression even when for utilitarian purposes it is not required. We cannot believe that the happy Christians, who shall inhabit the earth in the "latter-day glory," will find no mode, except words, of giving utterance to their gratitude to God. That would be a serious drawback to the glories of the millennial day, and would tend materially to damp the spirit of gratitude itself. We may rest assured, that when love to Jesus has no room to express itself in labours and liberality for the salvation of souls, it will find some other channel. What that will be we need not inquire. At present the pressing claims of the world clearly show in what direction we should make manifest our attachment to our Master.

When we contrast the demands made upon Jewish and

Christian liberality, we find the difference very marked. The Jew had to support religion among his own people—to see that the Priests and Levites were duly maintained, and the services of the Tabernacle regularly kept up. Into the reasons for it we cannot enter, but the fact is obvious that the Mosaic dispensation was more a conservative than an aggressive one. It did not reject proselytes, but it inculcated no strenuous exertions to make them. It was essentially national, and when duly observed by the Jews its chief object was accomplished. But Christianity is of a widely different character. It binds every man who receives it to labour and pray that all men may submit to the truth as it is in Jesus. It charges every Christian, by his fealty to God, by his love to Jesus, by his enjoyment of the guidance of the Spirit, and by the welfare of immortal souls, to preach the gospel to every creature, either personally or by proxy, as opportunity is given. So long as one island remains unevangelised—so long as one soul is in the darkness of nature, it impels the believer to pray and labour, to give and work, that God may be glorified in its conversion. Recognising in one soul a greater value than in the whole world, it seeks to present *every* man before God perfect in Christ Jesus. Thus Christians have not only, like the Jew, to maintain the worship of God among themselves, but to spread the truth throughout the world. Never can the Church, if it regards the glory of its Head and the welfare of men, desist from this until the earth be filled with the knowledge of the Lord, as the waters cover the sea.

How much of this work, to which the Christian Church is pledged by the strongest of all bonds, yet remains to be done, even in the most highly-privileged countries! In our rural districts, what ignorance concerning all spiritual things is often to be found! In our towns, what vast numbers pay no respect to the Sabbath, and never enter any place of worship! To evangelise these dense masses our Home and City Missions would require to have their agents multiplied exceedingly, and to be aided by the personal efforts of every Christian. The work even in this highly-favoured land is not yet half accomplished. Then there are those germs of future kingdoms—our colonies—increasing in population and influence in all parts of the earth. Of what essential importance is it that in their youth they should be thoroughly imbued with the knowledge of the Lord! We might then hope, that as additions are made to their population, the energy and Christian life of the original germ would, by the blessing of God, assimilate these to itself. But if the first ages of their growth be permitted to pass without their being imbued with the gospel, there is reason to fear that the exertions which would now secure their influence for Christianity will fail in making any deep or lasting impression on them. It is with communities as with individuals. When the period of youth is neglected, there is comparatively little hope in attempting to train them. The painstaking and earnestness which would once have produced the happiest effects fail to secure any preceptible improvement. Hence, in regard to these rising powers, *now* is the time to labour. Present neglect and idleness cannot be compensated by future activity. Faithlessness or half-heartedness in the performance of the work necessary for their evangelical training is the most flagrant injustice to our Divine Saviour, and the grossest neglect of man's welfare, of which British Churches can, in this age, be guilty. This seems emphatically the *present* duty. If we look still more widely over the earth, upon the nations that are under the Man of Sin or follow the False Prophet, or upon those sunk in the darkness of idolatry, we see still greater reason for Christian activity and liberality. What mean these million-tongued voices from India and China? Do they tell us that we may relax our labours and cease our exertions? Do they say, "We have no need for more missionaries, the truth has taken deep root among us, and will now be self-supporting and self-extending?" Ah! no. It is not the cry, "The kingdoms of this world have become the kingdoms of our God and of his Christ," which greets our ears. Is it not rather earnest entreaties to every principle of humanity in our nature, and fervent appeals to our zeal for the glory of Him who died for us, to increase indefinitely our efforts and to augment greatly the number of those who "preach the gospel of peace and bring glad tidings of good things?" Surely, then, if in any measure we are to be guided in our liberality by the demands which God makes upon it, Christians cannot conscientiously give less to God than the Jews did.

7. Or, again, we may ask whether the result which was secured by the liberality of the Jew, as contrasted with that which follows Christian beneficence, would warrant a diminution. What did the former get for his tithe? The support of the ritual under which he lived. The evening and morning sacrifice were duly presented, the golden candlestick was regularly lighted, and the shew-bread changed in its season, by the proper officers. These and similar services connected with the shadowy dispensation were attended to by those who were supported by the tithe. When considered in their spiritual significance they were most important, worth infinitely more than the trouble and expense they cost—for the value of spiritual results, however small, can never be estimated by material wealth :—but how much inferior are they to those which Christian effort and liberality secure? Already, since modern missions commenced, many of the islands of the Southern Pacific have been evangelised, native churches have been formed in considerable numbers in the East and West Indies, and a noble army of confessors has borne witness to the truths amid persecution and death, as in Madagascar. The Bible has been translated into all the principal languages of men, and its truths proved suitable to the spiritual condition of all races, from the "shivering Esquimaux to the burning Hindoo." There is now before the throne of God and the Lamb, taking their part in that glorious song, whose music shall fill the universe for ever, a goodly company gathered from amid the heathen of many tribes and tongues. And there are many at present following in the footsteps of those who through faith and patience are inheriting the promises. The foundations of idolatry in various places are beginning to give way, and the fields are getting white unto the harvest. True, it is only a beginning that has been made, but how precious is that beginning! What a reward to have our liberality under God the occasion of turning souls from darkness unto light, and from the service of Satan to that of the living God! Who would not change his earthly property into jewels

of God? Can we compare these results with the keeping up even of the most appropriate ritual? Surely our liberality is much more productive than that of the Jews! The Christian cannot, therefore, on this ground, reduce his contributions below a tenth.

8. This is the conclusion we have reached from every comparison. Combining these conclusions together, what answer ought we to give to the question, "If God directed the Jew under the Mosaic dispensation to give a tithe of his income to religious purposes, does he expect the Christian to give less under the higher and better dispensation?" It seems as if the answer to this question must be, "certainly not less." It is almost demonstratively evident that the people who have the greatest ability, the strongest and highest motives, the most imperative calls, and the worthiest results from their liberality, cannot rightly give less than the others. And if God required from the latter a tenth, he expects as much from the former. Our argument would sustain a stronger conclusion, and it does certainly show that ten per cent is the minimum of Christian liberality. If God expects a tenth from his Church, in what position are those placing themselves who give less?

CHAPTER VI.

CONSIDERATIONS CONFIRMATORY OF THE PREVIOUS ARGUMENT.

THE foregoing argument in support of a tenth as the minimum of liberality receives corroboration from various sources, which of themselves would not suggest this proportion.

1. It may with safety be laid down as an axiom, that the prominence given by the Holy Spirit to any subject is indicative of its relative importance. Whenever, therefore, especial attention is directed to a sin in the sacred Scriptures, we may infer that we are particularly exposed to it. This axiom arises from the fact that error may be as successfully taught by the misarrangement of truths as by the inculcation of what is false, and perhaps

more so. If that which is subordinate be put in the foreground and continually insisted on, while that which is essential is kept in the shade or seldom mentioned, a most incorrect and distorted notion will be conveyed to the learner. But the perfection of Holy Writ precludes the possibility of this in it. A disciple will not be set by it to spend his strength in fighting with an imaginary sin, for that would be practically to encourage immorality. Just as if in a besieged castle the commander were to direct all his energies to the defence of points not exposed to attack, while he left, in consequence, the assailable points, on which the whole force of the enemy would be brought to bear, undefended, the fortress would as certainly become the prey of its foes as if the gates were thrown open and they were invited to enter. Now there is scarcely a sin so frequently and indignantly denounced in Scripture as covetousness. It is condemned often in express terms. It is portrayed before us in its horrible consequences. It is held before us for detestation in the example of a Balaam who loved the wages of unrighteousness, and for a reward seduced the Israelites into lasciviousness. It turned the house of God into a den of thieves. It made Ananias and Sapphira lie to God the Holy Ghost. It prompted the son of perdition to stretch forth his hand against the Lord's anointed, and for thirty pieces of silver Jesus was betrayed. This sin finds a place along with murder, adultery, theft, and lying, in the decalogue, which God's own finger wrote on the tables of stone, and is again and again ranked with these sins in the New Testament. By Paul it is explicitly called idolatry, and said to be the root of all evil. Thus, in various ways and innumerable places, is covetousness denounced in the word of God. Hence, by the axiom laid down, it is a sin to which men are very liable, and against which they require to be continually on their watch. It is not requisite that its character as "idolatry" should be dwelt upon by us in order to our argument. That to every Christian must be apparent.

From this exposure to covetousness which facts abundantly confirm, some inferences follow highly favourable to our argument. One of these is that we ought to oppose a fixed and steady front to this sin. A constant pressure is sure to overcome a recurring force, even of greater power. And the tendency to covetousness will as a rule be found to overcome the impulses to generosity which the Christian receives, and to give the tone to the character. Hence our wisest plan for conquering this sin is to crucify it constantly. Instead of trusting for deliverance from its terrible grasp to occasional appeals, we ought to consecrate a fixed proportion of income to our Master's service. Thus, by giving to the Lord daily, we may hope to rise above this sin. But if we neglect our defence we need not wonder though we become a prey to this adversary. Our own welfare calls upon us to adopt this method of constantly crucifying our tendency to too great love to the things of this world.

Another inference which we may draw from this tendency is, that in all considerations as to the extent of our liberality we ought to be suspicious of those arguments which would save our money. The probability obviously is that they are the result of our natural worldly spirit, and would be frowned upon by the Holy Ghost. If any Christian, then, should resolve upon setting apart a fixed proportion of his income for religious purposes, he would require in determining the amount to be very suspicious of the reasons which would lead him to give less than a tenth. They may be thoroughly good, but this should be admitted only upon strict scrutiny. To forget this is to overlook the great fact of our depravity. If the inquiry be made in this spirit we have no doubt of the result.

2. The Scriptures, also, in many places expressly teach, in a very striking manner, the duty of liberality. A few instances from the New Testament may be cited. The principle which Jesus taught, that "it is more blessed to give than to receive," and his commendation of the woman who cast the two mites into the treasury, show his estimation of liberality; and his affecting statement, "It is easier for a camel to go through the eye of a needle than for a rich man to enter into the kingdom of heaven," reveals his opinion as to the danger of a worldly spirit. In the writings of Paul we find many inculcations of generosity. "Charge them that are rich in this world," he says to his son Timothy, "that they do good, that they be rich in good works, ready to

distribute, willing to communicate." (1 Tim. vi. 17, 18.) In a passage already quoted (Gal. vi. 7), he enjoins the duty of supporting spiritual teachers in the most solemn manner. A considerable portion of his epistles is taken up with the inculcation of Christian liberality towards the poor saints in Jerusalem. In adducing reasons why the Corinthians should engage heartily in this, he brings forward with laudation the example of the Macedonians, whose liberality had abounded so greatly " to their power, yea, and beyond their power," that they had to urge the Apostle "with much entreaty" to accept their contributions. Yet, though giving almost too liberally, Paul praises them. He then alludes to the attainments in other Christian graces of the Corinthians, and hopes that in the *grace* of generosity they will also abound. Immediately after he points them to the example of Jesus, "Who though he was rich yet for your sakes became poor, that ye through his poverty might be rich." (2 Cor. viii. 1–9.) What Christian can think he imitates his Saviour who only gives of his superfluity to the Lord? Is he to be our example who gave himself for us, and are we following when we give only that which we never miss? In Phil. iv. 16, Paul mentions with praise the fact that the Philippians had sent once and again to his necessity while labouring in other places as a missionary. The beloved disciple, in an ever-memorable passage, places this duty in a most striking light: "But whoso hath this world's good, and seeth his brother have need, and shutteth up his bowels of compassion from him, how dwelleth the love of God in him?" (1 John iii. 17.) This passage makes it our duty to give so long as we have, if our brother have need. And if we are to be thus liberal in supply of his bodily wants, ought we not to be still more earnest to supply his spiritual need? We have somewhat of this world's goods, though our portion may be small,—our brother has need, —need, above all things, for the glorious Gospel to bring him back to God and save his soul from woe; and if we shut up our bowels of compassion and do not give what is required for this great work, how dwelleth the love of God in us? Let this question be pondered over by those who live in luxury and heap up riches for their heirs, while souls innumerable are descending to the grave without the knowledge of God. How dwelleth the love of God in him? Ah! it will be hard for many a member of the lower Church to answer this question in the great day of judgment. Will a tenth enable us to do so satisfactorily? is surely rather the inquiry, than How much less can we give?

3. The design of the Gospel as a whole may be said to be to destroy selfishness. It seeks to lift man out of the orbit of self, to make him a servant of God. God is enthroned in the soul of every believer, and the objects with which he comes into contact are viewed in relation to his glory and government. In comparatively few cases, perhaps, has sin effected a complete work by making men thoroughly selfish, but its tendency is ever in that direction. The Gospel, by casting out sin, destroys its effects. Only so far as the truth as it is in Jesus has implanted supreme love to God, and generous affection to men, in our hearts, has it effected its object in us. The Gospel is emphatically the dispensation of love. Its foundations were laid in love,—the love of the Father to his sinful creatures. Its glad tidings were created in love,—love manifested in the incarnation and death of the Son. Its truth is borne home to the heart by love,—the love of the Holy Spirit. Its proclamation is intrusted to love,—the love of the redeemed to their Saviour. And the object at which it aims is the supremacy of love in the souls of men. There is, therefore, no surer test of its success than the love which it produces. But what measure of influence has it in his soul who will rather suffer his neighbour to be without the word of life than abridge his own comfort and ease? Can much love either to him who gave himself for human redemption, or to the eternal welfare of men, exist in him? Can he, valuing thus practically his own ease and riches more highly than either of these, be indeed a Christian? If a Christian be not denying himself for the sake of his Master, he is in a critical and dangerous position.

There is reason to fear, that in many instances the native selfishness of the heart has prevented this view of the purpose of the Gospel from obtaining due prominence. Many seem able to see in the dispensation of grace very little beyond a means of safety from hell. In this is concentrated to them the whole beauty of the truth. Now, important as this aspect of the Gospel is, when it becomes the only one looked at, the effect must be injurious. The Gospel is prized almost solely because it *does* appeal to self-love. But it is nearly forgotten that Jesus gave himself for us that he might redeem to himself a peculiar people zealous of good works. Not merely *in* them by securing energetic labour in behalf of those schemes of usefulness which are in operation, but *of* them by making his people ever on the watch for new opportunities of doing good. This aspect of the truth is not denied, but it is often put so much in the shade that it has not that prominent development in the life which it ought. By its being put in its proper place, self-denial will become much more common. It will be felt that the Gospel delivers from the curse of sin that it may make those so delivered loyal subjects and loving sons of the Most High. Under either of these relations a tithe is not surely too much to devote to his cause.

4. Our profession of faith in Jesus testifies it is not. To be a Christian involves as much now as it did in the days of the Apostles. Then Paul could say of himself, "The love of Christ constraineth us, because we thus judge that if one died for all, then were all dead; and that he died for all, that they which live should not henceforth live unto themselves, but to him who died for them and rose again." (2 Cor. v. 14, 15.) To the Corinthians he could thus speak: "Ye are not your own, ye are bought with a price; therefore glorify God in your body and in your spirit, which are God's." (1 Cor. vi. 20.) Numerous passages of the same character are found in the New Testament. And are not these things true of us? Do not we now profess that we are not our own, having been bought with a price; and that we do not live to ourselves, but to him who died for us? Our soul, our body, our time, our property, all we have and are, we hold by the kindness of God, and in trust for him. This is our profession as Christians still. Or has that glorious designation lost somewhat of its import with the lapse of ages, and come to signify less than it did? Far from it. Every Christian is and must be one who is not his own, and who is ready at the intimation of his Master

Q

to sacrifice everything, even life itself. Does not this lay us under obligation to devote as much of our income as we can to our Master's cause? Will it, in most cases, consist with our profession to give less than a tenth? We have professed to be stewards of our property. Let us act in accordance with this when we give to God. Yet, alas! many may be found who take an enormous per centage for being stewards, and give far more cheerfully for their own pleasure and amusement than they do for Christ's cause. Not a few may be found who expend more in rivalling the world in fashion and appearance than in promoting the world's salvation. For the former large sums are cheerfully given; for the latter it is esteemed liberal to put half a sovereign into a missionary collection. These things ought not so to be. They do not agree with the declaration that we are the Lord's, and bring disgrace upon the cause of Jesus. The world estimates the value of religion largely by the efforts Christians make for it.

5. The contributions which the world makes for its enjoyments and religion should stir up the Church to increased liberality. If there happen to be in one of our large towns about the same time a missionary collection for some object of pressing need, and some interesting performance, say of a noted singer, which of them will produce the larger pecuniary results? On examination it may even be found that the comparatively few who contributed to both have themselves given more to the latter than all that was done for the former. The collection may amount to 50*l*., and it is thought liberal, while the product of the other assembly is perhaps 1000*l*. Have not many Christians mourned in secret often over such disparaging contrasts? Can any enjoyment be to the worldling what the extension and progress of Christ's cause is to the believer? And yet the former often gives more for his enjoyments than the latter does for the high pleasure of doing good. Is not this fitted to suggest the serious question to many, "Whether they have as much enjoyment in doing good as their adherence to the Church of Christ would imply?"

Often, too, we see generosity displayed in support of false creeds greater than what is usual on behalf of the true faith.

We have only to look at the gorgeous cathedrals of Romanism or the rich temples of Hindooism, in comparison with the churches and chapels of Protestantism, to see this. We mean not to say that the cathedral is more adapted to the worship of God than the humbler structure. We only point out that in its erection greater expense has been incurred than our Protestant liberality would enable us to meet. Is this because their motives to liberality are greater than ours? Oh, no, there is nothing in the shape of motive which can produce such abundant fruits as the love of Christ. In this we have a principle which, were it thoroughly in operation, would set at defiance all attempts at imitation of our labour, and zeal, and self-denial for the welfare of others. But if, by permitting this to grow weak within us, or by carelessness as to what its utterance demands, it happens that heathens, Papists, or Socinians, rival us in liberality and good works, or in the support of their religion, there is cause for us to be up and doing. We must make a new start in our Master's service, and, instead of measuring ourselves by ourselves, drink anew of the fountain of life, and fresh from communion with God consider what his cause demands of us. "By their fruits," said our Saviour, "shall ye know them." From this test we will not be permitted to shrink. Fidelity to our principles, and love to our Master, demand that in the comparison we not only come off victorious, but that we utterly distance all competitors in those things which are pure and lovely, and of good report. The time has come when the Christian Church must feel its first love and do its first works, if it would not be unfaithful to its trust. We have heard it rumoured in some quarters, not unfriendly to evangelical religion, that if a private person be met engaged in acts of benevolence, and intent on helping the poor and relieving the distressed, it may be most probably concluded that he is not a professor of orthodox Christianity. We do not give full credit to this, but it shows that Christians must be up and doing. It is not enough to say of these men, their motive is not pure. We must show that our pure motives produce more fruit than theirs, if we would do honour to the truth and our Master. He has said, "Herein is my Father glorified if ye bear *much* fruit"

Not fruit which others may equal, but *much* fruit, which will lead others to forget *us* in admiration of the grace given unto us. A moderate degree of fruit unto holiness may attract notice to ourselves, and secure us glory, but if we produce much fruit, glory will be given to our Master, and we will be comparatively unseen, since it will be felt that He alone could have prepared us for our work. It behoves us, then, to let our light *so* shine, that the world, seeing our good works, may glorify our Father who is in heaven. The state of the world and the Church demands that serious and prayerful attention should be given to this. Liberality and philanthropy have, by the spread of a part of Christianity, become fashionable in the world, and we must not fail in going beyond its highest ideal of them and of every excellence. If we rightly consider our position, we shall feel that our donations to the cause of God, and our labours for the welfare of men, ought to be largely increased.

When the considerations adduced previously to show the solemn responsibility under which the Christian lies to be instant in season and out of season in serving God, and the argument suggested by the comparison of the present and past dispensations in regard to the claims on liberality which they make, are united to the considerations now placed under notice, they cannot fail, we think, to convince every believer that he ought to give a tenth of his income to the Lord. The argument is cumulative, and though any one branch may be deemed inconclusive, if collectively they be found sufficient, the conclusion follows that the practice they recommend should be adopted.

CHAPTER VII.

ADVANTAGES RESULTING FROM THE GIVING OF A TENTH.

HAVING established, we trust, the duty of giving at least a tenth to the Lord, we now proceed to point out some of the advantages which would result from the adoption of this practice. These advantages may well form part of the argument itself. For that which would produce the following results is its own best argument.

1. A remark or two may be useful as to the mode in which the tenth should be given. The advice given by the Apostle to the Corinthians is here in point: "Upon the first day of the week let every one of you lay *by him* in store as the Lord hath prospered him, that there be no gatherings when I come." (1 Cor. xvi. 2.) A few rules may be inferred from this verse. (1.) That the liberality of the Church is not to be the result of temporary excitement. The modern practice of getting the most eminent preachers to address the people previous to a collection, is implicitly condemned in this passage. Had the Apostle entertained the prevalent opinion of this age he would have written, "Delay your collection till I come." Paul, then, did not approve of getting up an excitement, that the people might give under a temporary impulse. (2.) That whatever is done should be done steadily and perseveringly. The Christians were to bear in mind the poor saints in Jerusalem from week to week, and to lay by in store for them. This is a point of great importance. It requires more principle to accomplish a purpose by steady toil and preparation beforehand, than is needful to secure a sudden, spasmodic, and violent effort. (3.) A third rule is, that the money consecrated to the Lord is to be laid by in store in the possession of him who gives it. The injunction is not to bring it to a public treasury in the place of worship, but to lay it aside at home until it was wanted. This simple matter of detail is of considerable practical importance. Not a little of the benefit which would result from weekly contributions is lost in the practice of giving it every Lord's day to a public collection. That is productive of better results than the impulsive one which is commonly adopted, but is far inferior to this recommended by Paul. As to the measure of liberality, "As the Lord hath prospered thee," we now suppose that this will amount to not less than a tenth. If a man then resolve to give a tithe to the Lord, let him lay aside the amount regularly—as regularly as he makes provision for the payment of his debts or taxes; and when any special religious claim is made upon him for help, let him con-

sider what proportion of the sum in hand he ought to give to it. The results of adopting this course would soon be apparent in showers of blessing.

2. It would bring a large measure of temporal prosperity. This God has expressly promised: "Honour the Lord with thy substance, and with the first-fruits of all thine increase, so shall thy barns be filled with plenty, and thy presses shall burst out with new wine." (Prov. iii. 9, 10.) "Thou shalt surely give to thy poor brother, and thine heart shall not be grieved when thou givest to him, because that for this thing the Lord thy God will bless thee in all thy works, and in all thou puttest thine hand unto." (Deut. xv. 10.) "There is that scattereth, and yet increaseth, and there is that withholdeth more than is meet, and it tendeth to poverty. The liberal soul shall be made fat, and he that watereth shall be watered also himself." (Prov. xi. 24, 25.) "Bring ye all the tithes into the storehouse, that there may be meat in mine house, and prove me now herewith, saith the Lord of hosts, if I will not open you the windows of heaven, and pour you out a blessing, that there shall not be room enough to receive it. And I will rebuke the devourer for your sakes, and he shall not destroy the fruits of your ground; neither shall your vine cast her fruit before the time in the field, saith the Lord of hosts." (Mal. iii. 10, 11.) Under the New Testament dispensation, spiritual blessings are promised to liberality, without, however, repealing the promises of the old. Indeed they are confirmed, for we are taught that the meek shall inherit the earth, and that godliness hath the promise of the life that now is as well as of that which is to come. Still, we are now to look more for spiritual fruit from every Christian act than temporal; and the temporal is rather, in general, the effect of the spiritual and moral condition, than of the immediate action of God. Thus the meek are more likely to have friends than the harsh and obstinate. This is a general law. And it is chiefly under laws of this kind that God now gives temporal blessings to spiritual acts.

In accordance with this principle, were the mass of the working classes trained to habits of self-restraint, so that they could deny themselves present pleasures, in order to afford future necessaries, they would live in comparative comfort. This is a well-known fact in regard, especially, to our manufacturing population. Comfort and blessing would be found in many places where there are now wretchedness and misery. This habit would infallibly arise from the adoption of what we recommend. The man who could, from a conscientious motive, lay aside weekly the tenth part of his income, and see it accumulating to a considerable sum, without yielding to the many inducements to break upon it which would occur, would speedily find himself rising in the social scale. The self-control thus displayed would soon bring the blessing of temporal prosperity to his abode. Let those who now find it difficult to make their income equal their expenditure, religiously consecrate henceforth a tenth to the Lord, and keep it by them until a call is made for it, and their present difficulties will vanish like the morning dew. This will be found an effectual, if strange, mode of securing this result. "There are those who scatter, and yet increase." The religious principle—the highest and strongest of all principles in the Christian—will thus be brought to bear upon the formation of prudent and considerate habits, and the result will be such as to prove that the declaration, "Godliness hath the promise of the life that now is," is not a mere figure of speech.

3. A far higher and more direct result of giving a tithe to God will be the increase of spiritual blessings. "He who soweth bountifully shall reap also bountifully. God loveth a cheerful giver." (2 Cor. ix. 6, 7.) "To do good and to communicate forget not, for with such sacrifices God is well pleased." (Heb. xiii. 16.) "And whosoever shall give to one of these little ones a cup of cold water only in the name of a disciple, verily I say unto you, he shall in nowise lose his reward." (Matt. x. 42.) "Charge them that are rich in this world that they be ready to distribute, willing to communicate; laying up in store for themselves a good foundation against the time to come, that they may lay hold on eternal life." (1 Tim. vi. 17–19.) These passages, as well as many others, show the estimation in which a liberal mind is held by God. And he who loveth a cheerful giver will

not permit his gift to pass without a smile. He will render to him a hundredfold in this life, and in the world to come he will be received into "everlasting habitations." (Luke, xvi. 9.) Our blessed Saviour, also, in one of his most sublime descriptions of the day of judgment, brings into most prominent notice the position which will then be assigned to acts of generous self-denial in his cause. They are the only proofs of Christian character to which he will refer. "I was an hungered, and ye gave me meat: I was thirsty, and ye gave me drink: I was a stranger, and ye took me in: naked, and ye clothed me: I was sick, and ye visited me; I was in prison, and ye came unto me. Come, ye blessed of my Father, inherit the kingdom prepared for you from the foundation of the world." (Matt. xxv. 35, 36, 34) Surely there is in these blessings what is well fitted to make us ambitious of obtaining them. Can we think of God loving a cheerful giver without wishing to be partakers of his love, or of the complacent smile of Jesus being enjoyed by those who have done much in his service, without desiring to share in it? By liberality and self-denying zeal we may secure them.

There is in this mode of liberality that which tends to sustain godliness in vigour. It keeps prominently before the mind the object for which the sacrifice is made. As the Christian week after week laid aside his tenth, his obligations to Jesus would be brought before his mind. As he meditated how he would spend his income, his resolution to give the Lord a tenth would be in his view. And as he looked round upon his home and saw this luxury awanting, and, it may be, that necessary more scantily supplied than it might have been, but for his liberality to God, he would be brought to the remembrance of the reasons for his course. Amid the distractions of life, and the attention that must be given to providing things honest in the sight of all men, the believer is prone to lose his spirituality, and to sink into a worldly frame. It is then no little matter for him to be furnished with a rule which would frequently bring him into the presence of his Master even while attending to his earthly duties. Were our Master oftener present to our thoughts, our growth in spiritual things would be much more rapid than it is. As a help, therefore, to our progress in the divine life, this rule is worthy of our adoption.

But in this practice there is more to increase our spirituality than even the fact that it brings Jesus often before our minds. We have already spoken of our innate tendency to fall into a worldly and avaricious spirit. The regular giving of a tenth would not only crucify continually this propensity, and thus protect us against an imminent danger, but it would also bring "out of the eater meat, and sweetness out of the strong." This strong natural inclination would thus be yoked to the service of Christ, and rendered useful to our growth in grace. "Blessed is the man that *endureth* temptation, for when he is tried he shall receive the crown of life which the Lord hath promised to them that love him." (James i. 12.) The conflict, with such a strong tendency, and its subjugation to Christ, would deepen our attachment to the cause of our Master.

It is not only, however, in the struggle that this would be done. After the victory had been gained, the love of this world would be found a valuable auxiliary to our interest in the progress of the Gospel. As the strongest enemy becomes, when thoroughly subdued, the most powerful auxiliary, so would love to this world when brought under Jesus help most powerfully the advancement of his cause. Let every Christian regularly give a tenth of his income to God, and he would feel that he had capital invested in his cause. How differently does a merchant feel as he hears the howling of the tempest when he has a vessel of his own exposed to it, and when he has not. In the former case he is all anxiety as to every turn of the wind; in the latter he can contemplate the storm with philosophical composure. And in the same manner would the Christian feel interested in the storms and difficulties, in the progress and triumphs, of the Gospel, had he a tenth of his income invested in it. When we give to God as a charity we feel little interest in the result of our donation. But were we to invest a tenth in the cause of the world, we would be as much interested about it as regarding any other investment of equal amount. Thus to our religious interest in the cause of Christ would be added this very strong earthly feeling. Besides this, when a person has a certain amount of capital to lay out, he is far more anxious in inspecting the share-list, the securities of property, and the profitableness of an investment, than he would be in other circumstances. And so would it be with the Christian. Has he five, or ten, or a hundred pounds, the tenth of his income for the year, to lay out on the various schemes of usefulness which claim his support? He will assuredly seek to expend it in the most profitable manner. The claims which are submitted to him will be weighed, and the reports of the various institutions, instead of being laid aside as soon as they come to hand, will be read and studied, that he may determine in which of them, and in what proportion, he ought to invest his capital. Thus the Christian's knowledge regarding the operations of our religious institutions would be greatly increased, as well as his interest in them? Would not this be a most advantageous result! If Christians were as watchful over the proceedings of these societies, and as much interested in them, as they are in other associations where they have invested a portion of their property, it would be a sure augury of the triumph of the gospel. It would be the not distant echo of that glorious song, "The kingdoms of this world have become the kingdoms of our God and of his Christ." Then, instead of looking upon the collectors for religious societies as seeking to dun him out of his money, the Christian would regard them as come to propose to him an investment of his capital, and would treat them accordingly. The statements made to him would be candidly weighed. "I have," he would reflect, "a certain sum that I have consecrated to God; what proportion of it does this claim deserve?" No longer would we see our places of worship partly emptied on collection-days, that the fervent appeal may not compel a donation, but every one would then be present in his place to give to the Lord cheerfully what he had vowed. This state of mind would be a comfort and blessing to its possessor, and would bring down the favour of Heaven on him. Is not a practice which would thus make even our love to this world, so often hostile to Christ's cause, a powerful auxiliary to it, worthy of adoption?

Its observance would also increase the spirit of prayer, especially for the prosperity of the Gospel. Feeling that their contributions might as well be cast into the sea as given for the spiritual welfare of mankind, if the increase were not given by God, Christians would lift up their cry more frequently and importunately to Him, with whom is the residue of the Spirit, for his blessing upon the work of their hands. No longer would our monthly missionary prayer-meetings be, as, alas! they now often are, the most scantily attended of all our prayer-meetings. Then would our Saviour's command, "Pray ye the Lord of the harvest that he would send forth more labourers into the field;" and the Apostle's entreaty on behalf of himself and other labourers in the Christian vineyard, "Brethren, pray for us, that the word of the Lord may have free course and be glorified," be much more extensively and earnestly attended to than they are. For whatever increases the Christian's interest in the Lord's work, will increase his prayerfulness for its prosperity. And the consecration of a tenth to the Lord would augment the interest felt in Christ's cause. We are well aware that no outward duty will of itself keep up the spirit of prayer, and secure that progress in the spiritual life which results from that spirit; but if we are not utterly mistaken in our reading of the human heart, the practice here recommended would form a powerful help to its maintenance. We do not think it probable that any man will continuously give a tenth to God's cause who will not pray more than he previously did for its success. The very strength of the innate tendency to covetousness or worldliness guarantees this.

In addition to these spiritual results, there is a blessed feeling accompanying self-sacrifice for a worthy object which is its immediate reward, and which makes its object more valued. The mother loves the sickly child that has cost her days and nights of watchful anxiety more than any of her children. The father rejoices more over his reclaimed prodigal son than over those who have never lapsed from the path of virtue. The shepherd rejoices more over his strayed sheep, when he has found it, than over his whole flock. Yea, our Master has taught us, "That likewise joy shall be in heaven over one sinner that repenteth more than over ninety and nine just persons that need no repentance." (Luke, xv. 7.) When we give our toil, our labour, our suffering, and our thought to any cause, it insensibly, but surely, becomes dearer to us. In accordance with this the whole history of the Church shows that one of the strongest secondary ties which can bind it to its Head is its being called upon to deny itself and suffer loss in his cause. And, in its measure, this will hold good of those, who at the expense of some worldly loss and inconvenience to themselves, give liberally of their substance to the Lord. When they find themselves unable to bear an equality with others in appearance, or perhaps even suffering some positive evil on that account, they will feel their Master and his cause become more dear to them. Those who only give because they will not miss their contribution cannot be partakers of their joy who make real sacrifices for Christ. Was not Paul's love to Jesus increased by the suffering and anxiety he endured in prosecuting the work intrusted to him? Undoubtedly it was. And so will it be in the experience of every one. We are not now called to suffer the loss of property, or to surrender life, for our attachment to Jesus, and we cannot have the reward of those who were. But we may by labour and generosity undergo self-denial in our Redeemer's service, and abundant will be our reward. Who would not have the blessing of self-denial for Christ? If we really love him, the knowledge that he permits this manifestation of love will prompt us in some way to make it. The devotion of a tenth to the Lord would enable many to partake in this blessedness, as well as increase largely their interest in all that relates to the salvation of men.

These are some of the advantages which would result from the giving of a tenth to the individual who does so. Let no one then say, that while undoubtedly the advantage to the cause of God would be very great if this practice were generally adopted, yet it would be of no avail for one person to give a tithe. Many, we fear, will seek to exempt themselves from the duty we inculcate by saying, "Our little income, were the whole of it given to God instead of the tenth, would be of little use." Thus, alas! too often does the individual excuse his inactivity under the shadow of that of the society in which he is, forgetful that the society is composed of individuals, and that if some one do not move, the community must remain for ever in its torpid condition. But if only one should resolve to give a tenth to the Lord, he will himself receive a rich recompense. True, it may not be of that outward kind which secures the praise and admiration of men, which it might be were many to do so, yet will it be real and precious in the soul's joyous experience. It is in the power of every individual to secure His notice, who loves the cheerful giver, though it may require a society to move to attract the attention of men.

4. If happily a considerable number should resolve to give a tithe to religious objects, other results would follow besides the advantages which each would personally receive. A blessing would descend upon the whole Church.

The spirit of brotherly love would be greatly promoted. This is the universal result of interest in a common object when anxiety for its advance is stronger than the wish for personal distinction. As soon as ever the Church of Christ feels a sufficient interest in his cause to give cheerfully and steadily a tithe for its advancement, there will be a breaking down of petty differences and a blending of heart with heart to an extent hitherto unknown. What a large measure of fraternal feeling has the present generosity of the Church called forth! We feel that those who are assailing earnestly with us the kingdom of Satan are our brethren. And when we come to see them and they to see us denying ourselves in order to give to the Lord, our love must abound towards each other. For in the Christian enterprise, in which every true labourer seeks not his own aggrandisement but the glory of his Master, the success of our brethren is ours as well. It is for the object dearest to our hearts that they suffer hardships. If, then, we do not love them for their works' sake, we have reason to question the supremacy of our love to Jesus. Do we not in that case wish more our own glory by the success than the result itself? This union in labour and self-denial for the welfare of men, our Lord himself mentions in his intercessory prayer as one of the bonds of union among his disciples : " And the glory which thou has given me I have given them, that they may be one even as we are one." (John, xvii. 22.) For what was the glory which he had received of the Father excepting that of "manifesting the Father's name, declaring the Father's word?" And he has given to his people "the highest glory a creature can have, that of manifesting the glory of the All-glorious One, in his truth, which he puts into their hands and hearts, and in the influence of that truth upon their character and behaviour. The Father glorified him by appointing and qualifying him to glorify him; and the Father through him." (Dr. Brown's "Exposition," p. 142.) And this glory of doing good Jesus has given to his people for the very purpose of promoting their unity. Can there be then any doubt, that were the Church to seek for this glory as heartily as the proposed measure of liberality would imply, its unity and love would be very largely advanced? Is not this exceedingly to be desired, both for the sake of the Church and of the world? The unity of the Church will have a most powerful influence upon the conversion of men. Our Saviour in the immediate connexion of the passage just quoted prays, "That they also may be one as thou, Father, art in me and I in thee, that they also may be one in us, that the world may know that thou hast sent me." (John, xvii. 21.) But, irrespective of its results, surely that unity which formed the one burden of the prayer of Jesus for his whole Church deserves every effort to secure it. Never can it be secured, as it seems to us, except by Christians sharing largely in the glory Christ has given his people, by every believer proving to his brother where his heart is, by his efforts and self-denial for the cause of Christ. But this will secure it.

The giving a tithe would also tend to advance brotherly love among Christians by separating them from those around them. A difference between the world and the Church would at once arise from it. The worldling who now professes Christianity because it is fashionable and perhaps profitable, would not be so willing to enter a community where he would be expected to give a tenth of his income to God. Now, conformity to the world is one of the greatest evils under which the Church suffers. Were there only a broader line of distinction between the sinner and the saint, Christians would be brought more closely into union. This line of distinction ought only to be the result of greater devotedness and zeal on the part of believers. Whenever it is thus produced, it is of vast service in cementing together the body of Christ.

Indeed, a universal revival in the Church might be anticipated from the general adoption of this rule. Sympathy with the cause of Christ, which expressed itself in such generous contributions, would not permit personal idleness when God gave an opportunity to labour. It would be felt to be foolish as well as inconsistent to contribute largely of substance while any labour that could easily be performed to promote the welfare of men was neglected. And, as in a healthy person growth in one part is indicative of growth in all, the increase of the grace of liberality would be accompanied with the advancement of all other graces. Virtue would be added to faith, and knowledge to virtue, while temperance, patience, and godliness, would follow in the train. Greater spiritual results would flow from an increase of liberality than from the growth of almost any other grace, because it lays the axe to the root of much of the weakness of the Church,— love to the world. It, indeed, would indicate a revived state as well as help it onward. For the Church that gives liberally is, most probably, prompted to do so by love to Jesus.

The complaint that men of the upper classes do not often seek the office of the ministry and missionary is one frequently heard. Rich Christians consecrate their sons to trade, to any of the more lucrative pursuits of life, rather than to the service of the Lord. Generally, except where high rank and social status are attainable, the ministry is entered only by those to whom it offers a rise in the social scale. And even of this class, many of those who are possessed of peculiar ability, give themselves to literary and other pursuits rather than to the service of Christ in preaching his word. In consequence of this there is often a lack of the right men in the vineyard of God. Our theological colleges are not full, our missions are in want of suitable agents. These things do not correspond with the professions of the Church regarding the honour of being co-workers with the apostles; they are not in harmony with the idea of Christ when he said, "The *glory* which thou hast given me I have given them." Were it esteemed a glory,—the very glory of the Redeemer,—to preach the Gospel faithfully, how very much greater would be the number pressing forward to the work! Then, instead of College and Missionary committees being in a measure compelled to take whom they can get, they would be able to choose the best men. The adoption of the Jewish measure of liberality would, under God, be highly advantageous in wiping off this disgrace from the Church. Every Church would then be enabled to sustain comfortably its own pastors, and thus raise the office of the ministry above the dread of poverty. This has often deterred well-qualified men from undertaking it, because they did not think they were called upon to endure want for the spiritual benefit of comparatively wealthy Christians. It is not needful that the ministerial office should be an object for worldly and ambitious men, but it is requisite that it should be above the dread of poverty. Our rule would not only in this way remove obstacles to entrance into the ministry, but much more by the higher estimate which it would tend to produce throughout the Church of the moral dignity of that office. Wherever a tenth is given to the Lord there will be a high estimate formed of the importance of his cause, which will speedily manifest itself in a sufficiency of the right men seeking to be specially engaged in it. Then would the noblest of the members of the Church esteem it an honour to have their sons occupying this high position.

5. The Church would not alone share in these results. The world at large would greatly profit by them. Our mission is to the world. For the Christian to care only for his own things, and not for the things of others, is to be grievously unfaithful to his Master, and terribly cruel to his fellow-men.

The improved character of the Church could not fail to have a highly salutary influence upon those who are without. As the light of the world, its illuminating power depends upon the intensity of its own flame. The more of Christ's love and earnestness it reflects, the better is it fitted to do his work. To whatever extent, therefore, the adoption of this rule would improve the Church, it would render it the better fitted to disseminate the knowledge and spirit of the gospel. For, as in all other respects, so especially in regard to spiritual power, it is true that " as the man is, so is his strength."

There would also be a large augmentation in the machinery at work for the conversion of the world. The income of our various societies for Home and Foreign Service would be greatly increased, and the number of their agents consequently multiplied. The directors of these institutions would no longer be compelled to refuse invitations from promising fields of labour, whose claims they are now afraid even to consider. Ethiopia would no more stretch out her hands for help in vain; nor would the augmenting cry from the crowded regions of the East, " Come over and help us," cause regret and sorrow. Our Home and City missions, and all our varied schemes of usefulness, would have new life and energy breathed into them. Nor, as we have shown, would the additional labourers which the augmentation of income would require, be long awanting. Many, seeing the abounding liberality of the Church, and sharing in the feeling which gave birth to it, would, in answer to Jehovah's question, " Whom shall I send, and who will go for us?" joyfully respond, " Here am I, send me."

This increased instrumentality, sustained and blessed by the increased prayerfulness of the Church, would speedily tell with mighty effect upon the appearance of the world. The Most High, seeing his people in earnest in his work, and hearing their fervent and importunate prayer, would cause Pentecostal showers of blessing to descend upon his vineyard. Already in many places does heathenism totter to its fall—it is old and ready to vanish away; and were this new increase of liberality, effort, and prayerfulness, brought to bear upon it, we might soon hear the reviving shout, " The kingdoms of this world have become the kingdoms of our God and of his Christ." The increased success in all departments of Christian effort cannot be calculated by the increase of agency. That is but one thing, and not the greatest. The growth of the Church's interest in the Lord's cause, and, above all, its greater prayerfulness, would give to every agent ten times the power which is at present possessed. Then might we hope in no long time to see the wilderness become a fruitful field, and the fruitful field a forest. Then would that day of glory, which filled with ecstasy the seers of ancient Israel, and formed the joy of Him who endured the cross, despising the shame, begin to dawn—when men shall be blessed in Jesus, and all nations shall call him blessed. "Arise," then may we say, in the words of the prophet, to the Church, "Arise, shine; for thy light is come, and the glory of the Lord is risen upon thee. For, behold, the darkness shall cover the earth, and gross darkness the people, but the Lord shall arise upon thee, and his glory shall be seen upon thee. And the Gentiles shall come to thy light, and kings to the brightness of thy rising." (Isa. lx. 1–3.) In the anticipation of that day, who would not join the sweet Singer of old in saying, "Blessed be the Lord God, the God of Israel, who only doeth wondrous things, and blessed be his glorious name for ever; and let the whole earth be filled with his glory." Grant, Lord, but this, and our prayers, as well as those "of David, the son of Jesse, are ended." (Ps. lxxii. 18–20.)

Surely, if but only a small part of these advantages to the individual, the Church, and the world, were to result from consecrating statedly a tenth of our income to the Lord, there is not one Christian who would not cheerfully do it. Let, then, the trial be made earnestly and prayerfully, and we have no fear of the result. "God never forgets any work of faith or labour of love, and whatever it may be of which the first and best portions or powers have been presented to him, he will multiply and increase it seven-fold." (Ruskin's Lamp of Sacrifice.) He who of old said, "Bring ye all the tithes unto my storehouse, that there may be meat in my house, and prove me now herewith, saith the Lord of hosts, if I will not open you the windows of heaven, and pour you out a blessing, that there shall not be room enough to receive it," will to his New Testament Church fulfil his promise abundantly beyond all that it can either ask or think. "That which a man soweth, that shall he also reap; he that soweth to the Spirit shall of the Spirit reap life everlasting. Let us not then be weary in well-doing, for in due season we shall reap if we faint not." Let us only be earnest and active, liberal and prayerful, in our Master's service, and He whose word must stand, though heaven and earth should pass away, will more than fulfil all his promises and exceed our hopes.

CHAPTER VIII.

OBJECTIONS TO THIS MEASURE OF LIBERALITY.

IN looking at a few of the most probable objections to the adoption of the law of tithe as a guide to Christian liberality, it will be well to bear in mind that, as has been already stated, all reasoning in favour of our worldliness ought to be looked upon with suspicion. Its validity should not be admitted until after strict examination.

1. Probably the most common and powerful objection will be inability: "We cannot afford it." This, if true, is a sufficient excuse. God hates robbery for burnt-offering, and would not have his service made heavy and grievous: "Let every man give according as he purposeth in his heart, not grudgingly, or of necessity, for the Lord loveth a cheerful giver." (2 Cor. ix. 7.) That in some, perhaps many cases, it is true, we at once admit. But all Christians, even the poorest, who may be receiving their daily supply from the generosity of others, will find it very conducive to their growth in grace to do something for Jesus. They ought to be enabled by their richer brethren to do so. The widow's mite was a noble contribution, and the giving of it to God did her soul good. This excuse, however, will often be adduced where it ought not, as a cloak for covetousness; where, were the light of eternity beaming round the soul, and the love of Jesus warming the heart, a fifth would not be thought too much. Let us look at this excuse a little more minutely. We

would say to the believer, It is probably quite true that your income barely equals your expenditure already, and that even a very little addition to the latter would prove more than you could bear. But is it indispensably necessary that your expenditure should be quite so large as it is? Must you have these elegancies and luxuries? Is there no needless expense for unnoticed fineries and formalities? Must you have them even though your neighbour should in consequence want a Bible? You would miss them—would you? And is this the utmost of your attachment to Christ and his salvation, that you will give him what you will not miss? Was this the measure of his love to you? Miss them! Aye, and so you should. You can never know how precious Christ is to you until you deny yourself for him. What a warm gush of cheerful love would rise spontaneously within your heart, if you felt that you were making real sacrifices, not to fashion and custom, but to Christ! Perhaps you would not feel the loss so much as you think. There are many of the things which cause half the expense of life without the least use, and not a few which "destroy its comfort, manliness, respectability, freshness, and facility. I do not say that such things have not their places and propriety; but I say this emphatically, that the tenth part of the expense which is sacrificed in domestic vanities, if not absolutely and meaninglessly lost in domestic discomfort and incumbrances, would, if collectively offered and wisely employed, build a marble church for every town in England,"—were that wanted. (Ruskin, " Lamp of Sacrifice.") At all events it is worth trying to do without some of them, if thus only we can contribute liberally to the Lord. He will richly repay the sacrifice.

That it is possible to live comfortably upon an income one-tenth less than what we have, is manifest from the fact that very many do it. We have only to look around us to find many who must do so. Is it impossible for us to do the same? Were God in his providence to change our position we might require to be satisfied with even much less than that. If many can thus live comfortably upon less than we would have after giving our contribution to God, surely we also can do so, as a proof of our love to Jesus. There are, morever, some with means as limited as their brethren who give more than a tithe to the Lord. This proves, however few there may be, that it can be afforded, and that the will only is awanting in others to enable them to do so. It may also be found, on inquiry, that some who think they cannot afford a tenth are actually giving it. Not a few of God's people are, we believe, in this position, without being aware of it. In these cases the mode of giving should be changed from impulse to fixed and steady principle. The former mode hinders the enjoyment of many blessings.

There will be found only a very few members of the body of Christ who, by prudent forethought and economy, could not give a tenth, or even more, of their income to God. If they must equal their superiors, outstrip their equals, and dazzle their inferiors, by the glitter of fashion and burden of appearance, most probably it will be found a hard thing to spare anything for the Lord. But if they must be generous to his cause, come of these things what may, they will have to give to God. It may, consequently, be safely taken for granted that, in nine cases out of ten, the objection, " I cannot afford it," is essentially false. In form it may be true, but if by struggling and endurance of hardship—by feeling the evils of poverty, even somewhat more keenly, —and by severer labour we can do it—surely Jesus and his cause are worthy of it. Ah! were it some earthly good for future years which were to be thus secured, how many who now can give scarcely anything to the Lord would find out that they could spare far more than a tenth? And will not Jesus give a far richer recompense to his servants for their work of faith and labour of love than anything the world can give?

We have spoken as yet only to those whose incomes meet their expenditure with difficulty; but there are many Christians who are laying past wealth, and acquiring, if not a fortune, at least a competency. From them at least the objection, " We cannot afford it," ought not to come. It is true, if they give a little to God, they may have to continue in business a little longer, and to leave a less amount in legacies. But if they love Jesus they will not account these very great sacrifices for him. Upon this class we would especially urge the adoption of the system of tithe. It will be found, in general, that they do not give in the same proportion as their poorer brethren. A man who gives 5*l.* out of 50*l.* to God will be much more easily found than one who gives 30*l.* out of 300*l.* And yet the latter could more easily give 100*l.* than the other 5*l.* The scene which attracted our Saviour's attention as he sat over against the treasury and saw the people casting gifts into it has still numerous parallels. The rich cast in handsome donations—the poor widow put in two mites, but it was all she had. (Mark, xii. 41–44.) If those who are placed by God in positions of comfort and affluence weigh all their obligations to him for temporal and spiritual favours, and the urgent claims of his cause, they will perhaps conclude that even ten per cent is not all they ought to give. To this as a minimum it is certainly their duty to raise their contributions, for they can afford it.

We have said that perhaps, on inquiry, it may be found that some are unconsciously giving this amount. In reckoning whether this be the case, the sums given at the bidding of the law, even for benevolent and religious purposes, ought not to be included. The whole character of the contribution is altered if it can be legally enforced. Religious motives may influence a person in the payment of legal tithe, poor-rate, and other charges, but they *must* be paid. Their character as a free-will offering is gone. And it is this which gives to our donations their spiritual significancy, and makes them acceptable in God's sight. He loveth a cheerful giver. What he values is the spontaneity of the gift.

Another excuse which some will probably make is, that others do not give a tenth. But the obligation to benevolence does not rest upon a society, as such, but upon the individuals composing it. Jesus did not redeem men as churches, but as persons. Since our connexion with Christ—the reason for all Christian duty—is personal, so are our duties. It is, consequently, no argument for neglecting our personal duties that others are inattentive to theirs, but rather the contrary. If we see that any duty is neglected, it becomes us to attend to it the more earnestly that we may counteract, as far we can, the prevailing evil. Let the Christian remember that he lives for God, not because others do so, but because he himself has received life from God. It is not the part of a Protestant to wait for the action of the Church when he clearly sees his own duty. Besides, the consecration of a tenth to the Lord will not attract the attention of others so as to make us singular — a thing very much dreaded by many, though the dread of singularity in the path of duty is a cowardly and unchristian feeling. Add to your faith *virtue*.

2. Some may object to this measure of liberality, that it is not commanded in the New Testament. If we have succeeded in showing that it is expected and needed, this ought not to be objected. We are not under law, except to Christ, and if the promptness of our affection to him do not lead to all necessary activity, his external command never will. Must we have a positive command from him whom we love, before we do that which would be well-pleasing in his sight? This would be to roll back the history of the Church, and to put ourselves again under the law,—" The law came by Moses, but grace and truth by Jesus Christ." Were we, because of positive command, to attend to a duty, which our love to Jesus failed to secure, though we knew that he would approve of it, it would be utterly worthless in his esteem. It would not spring from affection to him, nor be the utterance of the life which he gives. It is the effect of our natural depraved principle of obedience,—the service of a slave, not of a son. It is a dead work, for it has not our own new life in Christ as its cause. Not commanded! Have we forgotten that we are upon honour to God? Have we again come under the yoke of external command, and ceased to be partakers of that free life which joyously anticipates all com mands? Those who adduce this objection are strangely forgetful of the whole nature of Gospel obedience. We ought, in our service of God, never to come within sight of the statute, or hearing of the law. " The law is not made for the righteous man, but for the lawless and disobedient." (1 Tim. i. 9.) We live for God as Christians, not because he commands us under awful sanctions, but because we have received life from him. Law is

not our motive to obedience—it is only our guide; and if the course which God would approve be known to us, our love should make us walk in it joyfully. We are God's sons, not his children under tutors and governors, and far less his slaves. Because we are his sons, we do not require the numerous positive precepts of the old dispensation. (Gal. iii. 26.) If we say in regard to any course, which would be well pleasing in our Father's sight, as a reason for not walking in it, "It is not commanded," we prove that the spirit of adoption is yet awanting in our heart. The son anticipates his father's commands : it is the slave who delays, not only till they are uttered, but until he hears the sound of the lash. Then he works as much, and only as much, as he thinks will exempt him from punishment.

Are there not many who use God's generous confidence in the love of his redeemed people as an excuse for saving their money? Our Father in heaven has intrusted the support of his cause entirely to the love of his Church, not giving any command as to the proportion of income which ought to be given; and because of this want of positive command—of this trust in the affection of his people, there are professors of Christianity who give less than they would have been required to give under the law. Is not this turning God's confidence in his sons into sordid gold, and taking advantage of the trust he has so generously put in their love and honour in order to rob him? Is this Christian? Is it not the most flagrant sin—the most abominable transgression which can be committed? Let those who excuse themselves from the performance of this service because it is not expressly commanded see if they can make anything else out of their conduct. The only use of an express command to the Christian is to make his path clear—not to compel him to walk in it, and if the path be clear without express command, his love should urge him on in it. Of course, when the Christian believes that he would offend God by giving a tenth to his cause instead of pleasing him, his duty is not to give it. But we are persuaded there are few in this condition. The more general feeling is, "Perhaps I ought to give more—certainly God would be pleased at my doing so, but he has not commanded it, and therefore I will not do it." When this is the feeling the sin of not giving is very great.

There are a few who will even allege as an excuse for not giving a tithe that it is not necessary to salvation. We hope that these are but a very few! There is an ambiguity about this excuse which requires to be noticed. If it is meant that this practice is not necessary as a ground of acceptance with God, the same is true of all Christian duties. The only ground of acceptance is the mercy of God abounding towards us in his Son. But if we are to adduce this fact as a reason for not performing one duty we may do it for all, and so turn the grace of God into licentiousness. If it is meant, however, that this amount of liberality is not needful to prove our vital union with Christ—our being born again—we say, that depends upon circumstances. Christ claims that the whole heart should be given to him, and that the outward character should evince that he, on the whole, rules within. Less than this he will not admit as evidence of union with him. If then God has given us ability, and at the same time light to see that a tenth would be acceptable to him (which it would not without the ability), and we from love to the world withhold it, do we not thereby say that we love the world more than God? In such a case the giving of a tenth and more *is* necessary to salvation, because it is needful to prove Christ's supremacy in our soul. To those halting thus between the love of the world and the love of their Master, Jesus would say, not, Give a tenth, but, "Go, sell what thou hast, and give to the poor, and come follow me." This was the command he issued to the rich young man who came asking him, "Good Master, what must I do to inherit eternal life?" (Matt. xix. 16.) Jesus must reign in his people's hearts; and if we are not prepared to do anything which would be well pleasing in his sight, though it should be to surrender all our property and our life itself, we have need to investigate the foundation of our hope in God. At every cost of property and ease, Christ must be proved the Lord of our soul, or we have no sufficient evidence that we believe on him. If there be any, then, who cling to their property, because it is not necessary to salvation to part with it, they may rest assured that it is necessary for *their* salvation. Liberal, indeed, must be their donations to the Redeemer's cause before they can assure themselves that their love to Jesus is stronger than their love to the world. And this must be proved, even in the outward life, when God gives opportunity, or we cannot enter into the kingdom of heaven. The test of our faith is the supremacy of Christ in our hearts. His reign is not an undisturbed and peaceful one over his people while on earth, but on the whole he does reign supreme. If the promptings of our love to him be held in check continually by the spirit of worldliness, so that the latter shows itself the stronger principle, we are none of his. Let every professor inquire whether his liberality will suffice to prove that he loves Jesus more than the world.

3. It may be said that the adoption of this practice would reduce the liberality of the Church to a mere form: " The tenth will be given regularly, and under the cover of this the spirit of generosity will be permitted to die away." Without doubt this will require to be guarded against—for it is a tendency in our nature to lose the spirit while we retain the letter. But the same objection may be brought against the habitual practice of any religious duty. Is there no danger of bending the knee regularly, morning and evening, and permitting the spirit of prayer to leave us? Is there no danger of breaking the bread and drinking the wine without commemorating the death of Christ? Ought we, therefore, to give up regular seasons for prayer and the observance of the Lord's Supper? The duty of liberality is less exposed to this objection than most others. A heartless professor is far more likely to continue formal in prayer than in generosity. It needs strong love to Christ to impel a man to be truly liberal and to sustain him in that course, and, if that become weak, the antagonistic principles will generally break down any form. There are thus, in regard to this duty, strong feelings to co-operate with our watchfulness against formality. No one, therefore, need be deterred, on this account, from habitually giving a tenth to the Lord.

Objection may be taken to our view of the advantages which would result from this practice as too "rational," and not in harmony with the truth that God alone can give the increase. But he gives the increase after the sowing and the watering, and generally in proportion to them. Only as means for securing the divine blessing do we look upon any work of the Church. But it may be objected, liberality is not the means for obtaining the increase from God. Prayer is the appointed instrumentality. And is there no prayer in generous contributions? Is there no prayer in self-sacrifice for the cause of Christ? Is there no prayer in earnest effort for the salvation of men? Aye! louder and more prevailing than in many eloquent supplications. God reads in them the expression of intense desire, and is not prayer the offering up of our desires to God for things agreeable to his will? And let these things be done by a Christian, and there will be no want, as we have shown, of earnest cries to God for his blessing. They will render fervent prayer a necessity to the Christian, to secure the success of that for which he has done so much. It is not the active, liberal believer, who overlooks the power of supplication. There has often been, in seeking for the revival of religion, the neglect of a great law of our nature. Action has been sought for as the result of emotion, and rightly so. But the power of action in securing right emotions has been too much overlooked, yet this is almost equally important with the former. Let a Christian not only seek to feel right in order that he may act right, but let him act right in order that he may feel right. The act may be done as a duty at first, but if persevered in it will come to be esteemed a privilege. Thus, in order to be earnest in zeal for the conversion of the world, a Christian should not only give himself to meditation on the value of the soul, and prayer to God, but also to abounding liberality. Let him, as a duty, give a tenth or a fifth of his property to the Lord, and he will begin to be far more interested in the world's welfare than he ever was. And so it is in relation to all Christian virtues. Emotion and action go hand in hand. The one helps the other. And when a Christian seeks in any way to advance in spiritual things, we accept it as a proof that the Spirit of Christ has been at work in his heart. The surest way, therefore, to secure a revival of God's work is not only to preach the word faithfully and call upon God's people to meditate devoutly and pray fervently, but also to engage every one of them in active labour and generous liberality. A Church that both prays and works, gives and thinks, will assuredly have God's blessing. Organisation for labour and liberality is thus as essential to the prosperity of a church as the faithful ministration of the truth. It is because of this that we believe that a very abundant blessing would follow the general adoption of giving a tenth. Let the following passage from the writings of that great teacher, President Edwards, be taken in corroboration of these views: "If God's people in this land were once brought to abound in such deeds of love, as much as in prayer, hearing, singing, and religious meetings, and conference, it would be a most blessed omen. Nothing would have a greater tendency to bring the God of love down from heaven to earth; so amiable would be the sight in the eyes of our loving and exalted Redeemer, that it would soon, as it were, fetch him down from his throne in heaven to set up his tabernacle with men on the earth, and to dwell with them. I do not remember ever to have read of any remarkable outpouring of the Spirit, that continued any long time, but what was attended with an abounding in this duty. We know it was so with that great effusion of the Spirit which began at Jerusalem in the apostles' days. And the remarkable blessing that God has given Mr. Whitefield, and the great success with which he has crowned him, may well be thought to be very much owing to his laying out himself so abundantly in charitable designs. And it is foretold that God's people shall abound in this duty at the time of the great outpouring of the Spirit that shall be in the latter days. Isaiah, xxxii. 5, 8 : ' The vile person shall no more be called liberal, nor the churl said to be bountiful. But the liberal deviseth liberal things, and by liberal things shall he stand.'" (Roger's " Edwards," vol. i. p. 429.)

4. The arguments we have employed, it may be said by some, prove too much. They would require, in order to be fully acted out, the Church to sell all its property, and to rush in a body into the vineyard of God, neglecting business and every earthly concern in efforts to promote the spiritual welfare of men. A

very little reflection will show that this is not the case. The rule for Christian action and liberality, is to do, on the whole, as much in Christ's cause as possible. No argument can lead to more than this without defeating its own object. But up to this point the Church should ever seek, that its efforts and liberality may be. Let us live for God, not during a day, but during our life, and let us leave our successors as able to serve God as we are ourselves. Acting upon this rule, we believe the contributions of the Church will not fall below ten per cent. Scarcely in any case would that cripple a Christian for future effort. To give up the whole of one's capital to religious purposes is not, except in very peculiar circumstances, to give to God so much as we might, for it would incapacitate us for further liberality. Just as to wear the body out in exhausting toil in his cause is not to do so much as if by husbanding our strength we spread our exertions over a longer period. We are to act as stewards for God, but a steward does not cut down all the wood on the estate and throw the estate into the market to secure at once a large return. Our motto is to be, "We are God's." This will prevent us from overworking ourselves, and at the same time secure our activity. We think that this rule would require every man to give at least a tenth.

This rule for Christian exertion will obviate another objection against the practice we recommend, that it would destroy the freedom of the Christian, and in regard to liberality reduce the Church to one dead level. The Christian would still be left free, and be himself responsible for doing according to the command of the New Testament, "To give as the Lord has prospered him." All that our argument seeks is to raise the minimum of liberality from nothing to ten per cent, and not to determine the exact amount which the Christian should give. That is a matter for the consideration of every individual Christian, and if attentively considered (as everything pertaining to the service of God ought to be), it will often be found very difficult to ascertain. There is, probably, little danger, considering our nature, that an error will be made on the side of excess. It belongs, however, to every Christian to say how he will best fulfil the law of doing as much as he can for God. But we think he will err if he fix his liberality at less than a tithe. The freedom of the Christian is not to be idle, but to determine for himself, seriously, what he ought to do.

5. There is still a reason, which in most cases will be found to underlie the avowed apologies for not giving a tenth,—the want of disposition, the love of this world, "the love of money, which is the root of all evil." To this we cannot reply. We can only take the Christian to the cross, and pointing him to his Saviour say, "Ye know the grace of our Lord Jesus, how that, though he was rich, yet for your sakes he became poor, that ye through his poverty might be rich," and ask him, "How much owest thou?" What will you give to secure the harvest of joy which Jesus had before him when he endured the cross, despising the shame? If the indisposition remain in sight of a crucified Redeemer, nothing else can be done to remove it. But let the professor who is not melted into generosity by that sight examine himself strictly to see if his peace and hope be well founded. There is abundant reason to fear they are not.

If, while under the shadow of the cross, any one should feel that he ought to give a tenth, let him resolutely carry out his conviction. When he mingles with the world, he may lose the deep impression he had, but this ought not to check his action. In these solemn moments when the heart is full, God often gives light regarding our way, which we do not see with equal vividness at other times. The neglect of these impressions, momentary though they be, is a very great sin, and deeply grieves the Holy Spirit. Were they complied with, they would become permanent, but when neglected they die out and may not be again renewed. Let every one beware, then, of tampering with these convictions of duty. And in regard to our feelings of duty respecting liberality obtained at these times, we must be especially careful, since there are so many tendencies in our nature, and influences from without, calculated to quench them. Let no one thus grieve and resist the Holy Spirit.

CHAPTER IX.

CONCLUSION.

1. Some of the advantages which would result from consecrating a tenth to the Lord would be secured by a change from the present desultory mode of giving to a well-arranged system. Were the Christian to estimate his present offerings to the Lord, and to deduct only a like amount regularly from his weekly wages, his quarterly salary, or his annual income, it would keep the cause of God and his own interest in it prominently before his mind. This is within the power of all, and were this only done it would be no little improvement. Worldly prudence as well as Christian wisdom require that it be done. We fear it would puzzle the great majority of Christians to say what proportion of their income they give to God. They do not know whether it is a tenth or less. This is not prudent even for this world. And in regard to God's service it is grievously unjust. Surely he deserves to be served in a regular and orderly manner. Our offerings to him should not be left to chance. What steward would serve an earthly master so? And shall we render to God the halt, the blind, the lame, or whatever comes first to hand? Shall the service of our Father not be a fixed proportion of our expenditure? We feel deeply convinced that the adoption of system and forethought in our offerings to God is demanded from us by the solemnity and importance of the work itself, and would be the introduction of a much better state of things in relation to God's cause. Let every Christian then ask himself, " Shall the progress of Christ's kingdom — one great object for which I am left in this world — be served by me in a steady, systematic manner, or shall I leave it to be determined by the fluctuating circumstances in which I am, and the mutable feelings which I experience, whether I shall do anything for it, and what that shall be?" Only let the answer which most certainly both heart and conscience give be embodied in action, and henceforth the

liberality of the Church and of every Christian will be a well-known proportion of their income.

When acting upon the above principle, Christians come to the deliberate consideration in God's sight of the proportion they will consecrate to him, few instances will be found in which less than a tenth will be determined on. The cause why less than this is so often given is the habit of giving upon impulse without due forethought. But if the resolution be come to, that henceforth the Lord shall be served with the first-fruits, and not with what may be left after every other claim of necessity and luxury has been met, there is no fear that the Christian will offer to God less than the Jew. Remembering *what* he has received, and *how freely* he has received it, his heart will prompt him freely to give.

2. Whatever of spiritual or temporal blessing to ourselves or the world would result from giving a tenth is, of course, awanting so long as it is not done. It is, then, at no small expense that we retain more than is meet. We have, perhaps, though that is far from certain, a little more wealth to spend in adorning and supporting our outward man, or to leave in our will, and for these high privileges we pay in a lean and beggarly spiritual condition, in a world lying in the wicked one almost undisturbed. Is not this "to gain a loss" in the most emphatic manner? It is more than supposition, it is absolutely certain, that illiberality causes us to lose both in time and eternity. The withholding of more than is meet does tend to poverty. Let us open our hands generously, and the Lord will pour us out an abundant blessing; let us refrain from giving, and the blight will continue to rest upon us. Are we Christians? Have we professed to esteem spiritual blessings above all others, so that the whole world would be well exchanged for peace of conscience, the love of God, or the salvation of one soul? Shall we not then be found large dealers in this market, in which Jehovah promises to make the liberal soul fat, and to give abundant temporal and spiritual blessings to those who honour him with their substance? Have we faith in God? Does our faith only embrace the promises which relate to the eternal world, and which are in no wise

dependent upon our action, while those whose sphere of fulfilment is on the earth, or which are given to the performance of duty, are accounted unworthy of our regard? Can we trust him when he says, "Believe on the Lord Jesus, and thou shalt be saved," and does our faith falter when he says, "Honour the Lord with thy substance, and with the first-fruits of all thine increase, *so* shall thy barns be filled with plenty, and thy presses shall burst out with new wine?" Do we give his word unhesitating confidence as we read, "There is therefore now no condemnation to those who are in Christ Jesus," but account it worthless when it testifies, "Bring ye all the tithes unto my storehouse, and I will pour you out an abundant blessing;"— "As a man soweth," liberally or otherwise, "so shall he reap?" If there is one thing more than another which brings religion into contempt, it is such partial faith as this. The dullest eye can see that if God's promises are good for eternity, they are good for time, and, consequently, the man who professes to have found peace with God through believing the former, if he be obviously an unbeliever of the latter, is at once set down as a hypocrite. There is such a palpable contradiction in his conduct, that it is impossible for him to be otherwise judged. We must, to be consistent, take God's promises for time as well as for eternity. If then we believe God's declarations, is it not most manifest that the illiberal man impoverishes himself and deprives himself of innumerable blessings? He pays dearly for his savings.

The influence of our liberality is not confined to time. It will have some influence upon our eternal position. "Make to yourselves friends of the mammon of unrighteousness," said our blessed Saviour, "that when ye fail they may receive you into everlasting habitations." (Luke, xvi. 9.) How then can we store up our wealth on earth, so as to have the benefit of it in heaven? It has been well observed, in reply to this, that the only portion of our substance we shall have for ever is that which we give to the Lord, and, in obedience to his command, to the poor. What we spend upon our bodies will become the prey of the worms—what we leave when we die we lose for ever; but what we give to the Lord, we lay up in heaven in store. Since the case is so, as the Scriptures abundantly teach, surely the way to use our property, so as to get the most use of it, is obvious. Treasure it up, not for time, but for eternity; lay it aside where neither moth nor rust doth corrupt, and where thieves do not break through and steal. Thus, that only which we lay up with the Lord will await us, if it be presented in the right spirit, in the kingdom of heaven, while all our other earthly possessions we must lose for ever. If we believe this, it will appear in our contributions.

3. The Jew, as has been noticed, was accounted a robber of God when he withheld the tithe. Can less be said of the Christian when he commits the same offence? Wealth obtained by robbery is never a very desirable possession,—but wealth obtained by robbing God! Who would have it? Let the illiberal Christian look over his accumulations and inspect his expenditure. As he sees his store a little larger in consequence of withholding what was meet, or this and the other comfort procured by the same means, let him congratulate himself, if he can, on the success which has attended his robbery of God. There is no use in his cloaking over his conduct with fine names,—of his calling it prudence and economy; God has already given it the right name, and will yet tear away the flimsy covering from his course, and exhibit it publicly before assembled worlds as robbery of himself. For according to that which a man soweth he shall also reap. Economy is a great virtue, but its best sphere of application is not in abridging our liberality. Let it be practised in our personal and family expenditure, but not in our offerings to the Lord. Yet it somehow often happens, that when economy and retrenchment are thought to be needful, it is first practised in the withdrawal or diminution of contributions to Christian and benevolent purposes. Let it be known that this is not economy, but robbery. Will a man rob God? Will you, my Christian reader?

It is bad enough to rob God by the withholding of our due contributions to his cause, even were this the end of the sin. Were our money contributions of no use except as an expression of our devotion to his cause, the sin of illiberality would be very great. And by illiberality we mean the giving less than a tenth. It was the giving less than this—the keeping back the full tithe, that Malachi denounced as robbery of God. But the sin does not end here. Through our robbing God, by not giving him what we ought, we rob Jesus of souls that might have been redeemed. "My word," saith God, "shall not return to me void." And can it be questioned, that were the liberality of the Church doubled, this word would be proclaimed in many places where it is not? Faith cometh by hearing, and hearing by the word of God. For how shall men believe in him of whom they have not heard? And how shall they hear without a preacher? And how shall they preach except they be sent? And how shall they be sent without money to support them? The conclusion, then, is obvious, that the withholding money which ought to be given to God's cause robs the Redeemer of the glory of saving souls—of the joy that was before him when he endured the cross. Divine Wisdom hath builded her house; she hath hewn out her seven pillars; she hath mingled her wine; she hath also furnished her table. The feast of fat things, of wines on the lees well refined, which God hath prepared in his mountain for all people is fully ready. The atonement for sin has been made; for Jesus has died, and the dispensation of the Spirit has come; but, alas! the salvation of the world is delayed by the illiberality of the Church. Shall we who have received eternal life in Christ rob him of his inheritance and defraud him of his possession, in order that we may have gilded ceilings and luxurious carpets,—in order that we may have the fame of dying rich? Shall we, in whose love our exalted Lord reposed such a generous trust, that he left the reward of his toil, and sufferings, and death, dependent on our exertions, prove unfaithful to him, and unworthy of his confidence? Shall we, because he has so highly honoured us as to put us in a position, in the providence of his grace, where our efforts and liberality are indispensably necessary to the securing of the full result for which he died, take advantage of this to stop the current of salvation or to stint its flow? Surely no Christian would thus rob Jesus? And yet does it, under the present dispensation, amount to anything less, when, through our illiberality, the cry, "Come over and help us," must be answered in the negative? Aye! whatever we withhold from God's cause, which the highest love would prompt us to give, is the preventing of the mediatorial diadem of Jesus from having some of those gems in it which it otherwise might have had. Christians, are there connected with your balance at the bankers, with your houses and lands, any lost souls? Is there on your gorgeous apparel and splendid appearance the blood of souls? If you had given more liberally than you have done, might any now have been in heaven who are in hell? Oh, terrible thought! awful reflection! But we speak not of the claims of our fellow-men, of their redemption from hell,—we speak only of the claims of Him who gave himself for us; and we ask you, Christian, Will you, can you, for the sake of your own ease in life and aggrandisement, rob the Saviour who bought you of any portion of his glory? We appeal not to your benevolence to interfere for the rescue of your fellow-men from endless ruin, but we appeal to your love to Jesus, to your fidelity to your Saviour, and ask you, Shall that bloody agony which he endured in the garden of Gethsemane,—shall that cruel mocking and scourging,—shall that accursed death by which you have life, be in any measure deprived of their reward by your withholding more than is meet?

Christian, what a solemn position is yours! what heavy responsibilities rest upon you as the divinely appointed keeper of your brother and the co-worker with God,—responsibilities from which you cannot escape, and which, if rightly fulfilled, your highest glory,—"The glory which thou hast given me I have given them." Oh, pray God, use every endeavour that you may be found in the day of the Lord to have discharged them aright. Take Christ as your example and motive in this glorious task; you know his grace, how freely he has given you eternal life. Let this thought rule you in your exertions and liberality in his behalf, and you will probably find that ten per cent of your income will not satisfy the promptings of your heart. Because he who was rich for your sake became poor, that you through his poverty might become rich, see that you abound in this grace of liberality.

4. The day of the Lord, in which we shall have to give an

account of our stewardship, is rapidly approaching; our time for service will soon be at an end. Then will it be found that he only who sowed bountifully shall reap bountifully, while he who sowed sparingly shall reap sparingly. What a reflection for a death-bed will it be! what a thought for eternity! "I wore a better dress, ate of richer food, occupied a more splendid house, and left behind me a larger sum of money, by my parsimony to the Lord's cause." How different will be his reflections who can look back upon his pilgrimage and see that he might have had to toil somewhat less severely, and made a little better show in the world, had he not given a tenth to the Lord! Will he then regret that toil? will he lament his liberality? No; he has sown to the Spirit, and shall of the Spirit reap life everlasting. He has made to himself friends of the mammon of unrighteousness, and will be received into everlasting habitations. These two courses are before us with their respective terminations, and we must choose between them. May God give to every reader grace and wisdom to weigh aright this most important matter, and to act in it according to his convictions of duty. Amen.

The Christian Weekly Offering;

OR,

THE SCRIPTURAL PRINCIPLE AND RULE

OF

SELF-ASSESSMENT IN THE DEDICATION OF PROPERTY.

BY THE

REV. JOHN ROSS.

"And ye are not your own, for ye are bought with a price."
—1 Cor. vi. 19, 20.

PREFACE.

THESE pages were written under mingled feelings of joy and trembling. The proposal for an Essay on this subject came upon the Author with an overwhelming power, crowding his mind with thoughts that had long burned in his breast, and annihilating, under a feeling of imperative duty, that sense of incapacity and dread of presumption which had made him proof against the stirrings of his own breast and the importunities of friends to publish thereon. He wrote because he dared not do otherwise, and to relieve his soul of its pent-up and almost consuming fires.

The Author has long felt it to be a subject of intense moment, involving the fearful alternative of the still further delay, or the early realisation, of the world's subjugation to Christ. What more can the all-wise and beneficent God bestow for this purpose than is already granted? The Son of God has purchased salvation, and now intercedes on high. The Holy Spirit is irrevocably given. The pages of Inspiration blaze with the predictions of Zion's glorious destinies.

What, then, is the cause of her present prostration? Is it not found in the general absence among Christians of a deep sense of sacred obligation, and in the want of a Scriptural system of pecuniary dedication?

How can there be happiness and prosperity in the Church

but in her entire and hearty dedication to God? Fidelity to principle in every department of action has its test, which may, however, vary with circumstances. The test of Abraham was the surrender of his home and of his beloved Isaac; that of the rich Ruler, the entire distribution of his wealth; that of primitive Christians, confiscations, torture, and death. With the peculiar facilities and evangelistic organisations of the present day, who can doubt that *our test* is the systematic dedication of property to the advancement of the divine glory?

If ancient Christians took joyfully the spoiling of their goods, and cheerfully forfeited life in honour of their Redeemer, can we as believers grudge to devote to the same noble end our *spared life, property, and influence?*

We cannot help admiring their devotedness! Have we no impulses of holy ambition and grateful love to imitate them in the less painful forms of earnest labour and cheerful sacrifice? Reader, if you wish to know your sacred obligation, and to be approved of God on this momentous subject, implore the guidance of the Holy Spirit for the profitable perusal of these pages, and with an humble and candid mind follow his guidance, accounting expenditure for the glory of Christ the best outlay, and that which sanctifies the whole. If you are destitute of such desire, and opposed to such instruction and dedication, be entreated not to read another word, lest it should only tend to aggravate your guilt and condemnation. Let this be to you a sealed book.

May the Divine Spirit employ these pages, with those of the coadjutors in this work, for the speedy realisation of all the prosperity the Church is taught to anticipate.

THE AUTHOR.

January 23, 1852,
Woodbridge.

CONTENTS.

INTRODUCTION.

CHAP. I. THE PRINCIPLE OF THE SUSTENTATION AND EXTENSION OF RELIGION AND BENEVOLENCE BY PECUNIARY CONTRIBUTIONS, ARISING FROM,—
 1. The Necessities of Man's Physical Nature and Moral Condition.
 2. The Discovery of a Method of Co-operation with God.
 3. The Institution of a Test of Man's Love and Devotion.

II. THE MANNER OF OBTAINING THE NECESSARY RESOURCES.

III. THE OBJECTS TO WHICH THESE FUNDS SHOULD BE DEVOTED.
 1. The Ministry, and the Necessary Requirements of Worship.
 2. The Assistance and Extension of the Church, and the Conversion of the World.
 3. The broad range of general Benevolence.

IV. THE CONSECRATED PROPORTION OF INCOME TO BE ASCERTAINED,—
 1. By the general Spirit of the entire Scriptures.
 2. By the unchangeable Nature of all Religious and Moral Obligation.
 3. By the Jewish Law of Tithe and Free-will Offerings.
 4. By the immense enlargement of the Field of Exertion under the present Dispensation.
 5. By the peculiar Prominence given in the New Testament to the Pecuniary Department of Benevolence. Some Objections obviated.

CHAP. V. CONSIDERATIONS WHICH CONSTRAIN AND ANIMATE TO THE PRACTICE OF WEEKLY SELF-ASSESSMENT.

1. Those which spring from sacred Obligation to God.
   (1.) The Fulness of Divine Love and Bounty.
   (2.) The Sacred Obligation thence arising.
2. Those originating in the Claims and Condition of Man.
   (1.) The vast Importance and Urgency of the Interests involved.
   (2.) The Improbability of any marked Progress on any other Principle.
   (3.) The happy Influence it would exert on the World.
   (4.) The Sufficiency of such Resources for all Requirements.
   (5.) Examples of eminent Devotedness in this respect.
3. Those included in the Glory of Christ, and in Christian Consistency, Influence, and Happiness.
   (1.) Every Man thus fixes the Stamp and Standard of his own Life and Destinies.
   (2.) Its happy Influence on the Heart and Character.
   (3.) Its Design and Tendency to assimilate to God in Principle, Action, and Bliss.
   (4.) The Opportunity of peculiarly glorifying God.
   (5.) The Certainty of Personal Sufficiency in a course of Faithful Devotedness.
   (6.) Its Influence on the Enjoyment of the Divine Blessing in Time.
   (7.) On Man's future Eternal Condition and Happiness.

CONCLUSION.

INTRODUCTION.

IN the latter half of the nineteenth century, a serious proposal is made to ascertain the Scriptural principle and measure of contribution for religious and benevolent objects. Where have the consciences and the hearts of Christians been during these many ages?

Sciences, whose first principles but yesterday saw the light, have quickly attained to certainty and vigorous maturity. But this divine science is as yet only in its infancy. Is there any mystery in the prostration and inefficiency of the Church of Christ up to the present hour?

Honest inquiry, with a view to the distinct apprehension and cordial practice of such a rule, has rarely existed. The use of the term *rule* will take many by surprise. They never imagined such a thing. Their *will* is their only law.

It is here humbly attempted, in dependence on the divine blessing to ascertain this rule, and to advance those data, which will enable every sincere inquirer easily to learn the measure of his obligation.

Appeal is here made to the true followers of the Saviour. If men of the world treat the subject with scorn and indifference, earnest and faithful Christians cannot.

It is of the greatest moment to perceive distinctly the reason and the reasonableness of this requirement.

Independent of all other considerations, it is as needful as it is beneficial even to the giver, tending to exercise and improve both his graces and his heart. Principles, as well as organizations, in order to vigour and expansion, must have free and constant exercise.

Without some such arrangement, how could the principles of benevolence and active love be cultivated? How could man's native selfishness be subdued, and his heart and character be formed for the joys of heaven, and the fellowship of holy and benevolent beings?

Here is a means of training men on earth for stations of honour and blessedness in heaven.

That which man obtains without thought or toil, prayer or sacrifice, he lightly regards, whatever its true value.

The proper motive of this rule of action is love to God, from a sense of boundless obligation; and love to man, from identity of nature and interests.

It should be performed as a sacred duty, which it were fraud and embezzlement to neglect; with ardent delight, as being in itself right and excellent; and with a joyful knowledge that, though a most imperfectly performed duty, it is received as if it were the gratuitous offering of spontaneous love and holy sacrifice.

Above all, it must be in entire self-renunciation and freedom from personal merit, and in simple dependence on the grace and intercession of Christ, under the conviction, "We are unprofitable servants. Of thine own, O Lord, have we given thee."

So far are they from the expectation of salvation through their own beneficence, that the Saviour represents the redeemed as if they had lost the remembrance of their services, and as if filled with wonder at their gracious approval by the great Judge of all. (Matt. xxv. 37.)

As where there is no fixed and invariable rule prescribed, the amount contributed may fairly depend on the nature and magnitude of the objects to be compassed, it is proposed to inquire into the principle of sustentation and extension of religion and benevolence by pecuniary contribution,—the manner of obtaining the necessary resources,—the objects to which they are to be devoted,—the rule of proportion to be adopted in their dedication,—and the considerations which should animate to its prompt and universal practice.

CHAPTER I.

THE PRINCIPLE OF THE SUSTENTATION AND EXTENSION OF RELIGION AND BENEVOLENCE BY PECUNIARY CONTRIBUTIONS.

THERE are two prominent features of the religion of the present day most painful and unsatisfactory,—the absence of any defined and adequate scale of contribution among Christians at large, and the general failure of dedication by men of wealth, of a duly augmenting proportion of their ever-increasing possessions. Happily some are seriously weighing this subject, with a view to the earnest and conscientious performance of their sacred obligations. May they multiply a thousandfold!

Reasons of highest moment may influence God in preferring human agency above every other at command. The following more than suffice to prove the wisdom and goodness of the choice:—

1. The necessities of man's physical nature and moral condition.

Expenditure arises from the necessities of man's nature and position, and contributes to his benefit.

Salvation is a gift. The grace of Christ, the energy of the Holy Spirit, pardon, justification, and heaven, are free. "Thanks be to God for his unspeakable gift;" "Take of the water of life freely." The means of their use, preservation, and extension among men, are costly. The bread of life is a divine boon; the water of life and the grace of the gospel are a rich gratuity; but the necessary means for their dispensation, enjoyment, and diffusion, require funds. The divine treasure is gratuitous; the casket of its preservation it is for man to provide. This God has wisely and kindly devolved on man, for the exercise of his powers, the cultivation of his heart, and to make him mainly the instrument of his own happiness and advancement.

It were as acceptable to God to be worshipped under the canopy of heaven, as in the most magnificent temple ever constructed by human art. It would better tend to foster just conceptions of his majesty, bounty, and condescension.

Offerings, and means of service, are appointed of God, as according with man's nature, and best adapted to promote his spiritual advantage.

The proclamation of the truth for the refreshment of the Church, and the evangelisation of the world, is the institution of God for *man's* present and eternal welfare. Let man's skill and industry rear the temple which *his* nature requires, and let *his* resources furnish the instruments and sustain the agencies which conduce to *his* benefit.

To the wants and woes of humanity all are liable: let the sympathies of our common nature induce those who possess a competency, to render a prompt and cheerful relief, and let others assist as their means may allow.

The observance of divine worship and the practice of benevolence, is the spirit of the entire Decalogue. The appointments of the Jewish economy were for the performance of those duties. Christianity also provides its own institutions for the same purposes.

2. The discovery of a method of co-operation with God.

The beneficent Creator has given to all some department of occupation, some field of labour, suited to their powers and worthy of their toil. On man he has conferred the peculiar, noble, and animating task of self-cultivation, and the improvement and spiritual recovery of his race.

He first welcomes man to the experience of holiness and piety, and then sends him to enlarge the kingdom of truth and mercy, by winning others to their participation. Surely it were honour enough for man, to co-operate with God in any department of labour! But to be permitted to do so in reference to the present and eternal interest of his species! What condescension in God! What a privilege for man!

3. The institution of a test of man's love and devotion to God.

Love to God and man, though justly demanded, is not universally cherished. On its *existence* depends man's eternal state. Its evidence should be clear and indisputable. This is best seen in the cheerful surrender of prized good. Property is highly valued among men, as the product of toil and enterprise, and as the representative of all material treasures. God has given proof unmistakeable of his intense love of man, in the gift of Him who was dearer to himself than all the treasures and tenants of the universe,—his Son, Jesus Christ. Ought not man to give proof of love to God beyond dispute? Few things could better supply this, than the constant, cheerful, and copious dedication of property to the service of God. Few things so much engage the ardent interest and pursuit of man, as property. Few can impel him to so much present hardship, privation, and suffering for its attainment; or induce its surrender without full recompense.

Probably, in most instances, next to the forfeiture of life, the full and adequate dedication of man's possessions to God, in daily acts of beneficence and piety, is the most searching ordeal to which his love can be subjected. To some men, without a large measure of grace, it would be a perpetual torture.

It is evident, that God has committed the sustentation of his cause and the enlargement of his spiritual kingdom on earth, to the care and agency of the Church. He did so to the Jews in the institutions of Moses. He does so to Christians under the dispensation of grace. Where this work has been duly sustained by them, it has prospered, and they have prospered also. Where it has been neglected, both have gone to decay together. (Haggai, i. 6; James, v. 1-3.)

CHAPTER II.

THE MANNER OF OBTAINING THE NECESSARY RESOURCES.

As a method of laying aside the dedicated amount, none will be found at once so simple, easy, and fraught with advantages, as that commended by Paul, "Upon the first day of the week let every one of you lay by him in store, as God hath prospered him." (1 Cor. xvi. 2.) Some may think this plan troublesome and impracticable in connexion with large business transactions, and

T

in a day of credit and commercial enterprise, however suited to a less active age.

The plans of Infinite Wisdom are suited to every age, and capable of adaptation to every condition. Surely it is wise and safe to adhere to this method, till a better be substituted for it by the same authority. Surely it is high time to return to it, seeing that all human expedients fail to realise the required means, while the claims of benevolence and religion become more extensive and urgent year by year. But is there nothing of the sanction of the great Lord of the Church in this injunction? The moral weakness of man, as every heart must witness, is palpably manifest, in his reluctance to part with property in considerable sums, even for the most approved objects. Frequently it is out of his power to do so with safety; consequently, his offerings rarely reach to a full proportion.

Did not the Divine Spirit enjoin the habit of a weekly dedication as its best corrective? Is not its neglect unwise, unsafe, and every way pernicious?

Let every Christian, whatever his condition, deposit in a private treasury on the holy Sabbath, when the mind forms the truest estimate of earthly and heavenly things, and when the soul realises its warmest emotions of gratitude and love, his free-will offering for the week. Whether the weekly income be ascertainable at once, or only to be known by taking the average of a more lengthened period, the rule, "as God hath prospered," should ever determine the amount consecrated.

Such dedication would be the virtual and divinely approved performance of the vow of Jacob (Gen. xxviii. 22), in the measure enjoined by the sacred Spirit (Prov. iii. 9), and at the seasons, and under the influence (1 Cor. xvi. 2), which his infinite wisdom deemed suitable and effective. The mode revealed 1 Cor. xvi. 1, 2, is enforced by the argument of 2 Cor. viii. and ix., commended by the tender and irresistible consideration and example of its close, "Thanks be unto God for his unspeakable gift." Who can dispute the obligation either of *measure*, "As God hath prospered thee," or of *time*, "On the first day of the week?"

Rules of conduct, forms of law, and statute-books, are essen tial among rational beings in every stage of moral imperfection. If for the purpose of higher moral development, and under more free and gracious economies, the forms often seem to be placed in abeyance, their *obligations* continue in force so long as the relations exist which originated them. Their silence is no proof of their abrogation, but only indicates that under higher cultivation the requirements of formal rules should be anticipated by a willing spirit.

Christianity is a system of loving constraint, rather than of positive command. Its obligations are implied and suggested, rather than formally demanded. It leaves to the ingenuity of love to infer what Judaism in the minimum measure specifically prescribed.

The employment of the tithal system in Israel for religious and benevolent purposes, Paul's entire silence respecting its obligation on Gentile converts, and his suggestion of the above method of weekly offering, seem to commend this as the one best and all-sufficient means of providing for the requirements of the Christian ministry—of poor believers—of the expenses of public worship—of the propagation of the truth—and whatsoever other demands might arise in future times.

This system seems to have been practised by the Church with more or less precision for ages, and when national tithes subverted it, they also for centuries were appropriated to the joint purposes of supporting the clergy, relieving the poor, and repairing the churches.

The system thus sufficing for relative action in the Church must be equally appropriate to every other demand, as having its vitality and expansive power in the numberless offerings of weekly consecration, and the exhaustless resources of personal and domestic gratitude.

Paul had urged the method of *weekly proportionate offerings* on the Church at Corinth a year ago. (1 Cor. xii. 1, 2.) "Now concerning the collection for the saints," &c.

As to season, "Upon the first day of the week." The Christian Sabbath-day, the day of the Lord's resurrection, and of spiritual invigoration and progress; to employ material treasures for the benefit of souls, and to transmute the gains of earth into the riches of heaven.

As to persons, "Let every one of you," old and young, rich and poor, all possessing any personal means.

As to method, "Lay by him in store." Place it in a sacred treasury, ready for occasions of use.

As to measure, "As God hath prospered him." In proportion to the realised gains and mercies of the week.

As to the pervading principle of this method, "That there be no gatherings when I come." That there be no need for appeal to inferior motives; no need for descent from the grand theme of the Cross, to matters of benevolence and economics; but that all may be provided beforehand, as of conscientious purpose and bountiful devotion; and consequently exceed in measure and moral worth, the combined results of all other methods; being the fruit of the loftiest principle, and the full aggregate of all that ought in justice to be so employed.

He now endeavours to establish and perpetuate this practice among them, by the proof of its wisdom and effectiveness afforded by the Churches of Macedonia, an implication of the context beyond all dispute (2 Cor. viii. 1-6.) He animates to a similar zeal and devotedness, from a principle of holy emulation, and as unquestionable evidence of sincere and ardent piety. (7, 8.) He seeks to constrain to it, from the infinite condescension and love of Christ on their behalf. (9.) He then proceeds to advise it as the most becoming, advantageous, and satisfactory mode of vigorously, pleasantly, and conscientiously carrying out their acknowledged convictions and purposes of pecuniary dedication. (10–12.) In ix. 1–7, he presses it as the only likely means of reaching that high measure of aid, and of consequent estimation by the Macedonian brethren, of which their circumstances and promises had justly excited hope, and of furnishing (12–15), both to God and man, clear and indisputable proof of their real subjection to the claims, interest in the grace, conformity to the spirit, and cordial appreciation of the love of God in the gift of his Son for their salvation.

What higher authority could a grateful, loving heart desire, than that which is thus furnished under the veil of apostolic suggestion, not to say command, for the consecration, on every Lord's day, of a fit proportion of the blessings of the week just mercifully concluded? Of the sum thus added weekly to the general consecrated fund, it were well, if practicable, to deposit the proportion adjudged for the advantages of personal and relative worship, and the diffusion of religion, in a treasury in God's house every Sabbath; the remainder being reserved for judicious application to the manifold demands of religion and humanity as they arise.

It may be far easier to conclude than to prove its impracticability in our case, more than in that of a Christian of apostolic times. The more frequent the dedication, where really impracticable weekly, the more satisfactory in every respect. Surely the Christian, anxious to fulfil his sacred trust, instead of rejecting, will rejoice to adopt a method of dedication so commended and enforced, so simple and effective.

If Paul, the inspired Apostle, enjoined it on the churches of Galatia and Corinth, can we lay a gracious claim to their privileges, and yet safely and conscientiously refuse compliance with this demand? Is it less binding on us than on them? If this is not obligatory, what is? Let the reader but make a fair trial of it in integrity; he will soon rejoice in its issue.

It is simple, quite easy, and effective. It rests on conscientious principle, and not on caprice, impulse, or example. The sum is easily withdrawn from the common stock. It is ready for use when worthy objects arise. It bears a fit proportion to the divinely-bestowed blessings of the week, and secures a benediction on what is retained. It sanctifies all the acts of time, and connects them with the interests of eternity. It simplifies all questions of finance; inducing a true estimation of property, and closer adjustment of affairs, as stewards of God, ever liable to the final summons. It gives new ardour to spiritual life. It produces lively interest in every good object. It imparts cheerfulness and animation to the soul. It is the constant transmutation of the treasures of time into the enduring riches of eternity. Its dedication on the Sabbath is the sanctification to holy purposes of all the hours and labours of the week; giving them affinity with the day of the Lord, and stamping the coin of earth with the superscription of heaven.

How like all God's plans of action is this! not spasmodic, arbitrary, and uncertain; not amazing and stunning, like the falling avalanche or the boiling cataract. It is silent, gentle, and gloriously effective; like the dew and showers of heaven, like the ever-gliding river, like the gradually expanding spring and fructifying summer; bearing with them the proofs of their presence and efficiency in their blossoms, and odours, and delicious produce. Here the poor and rich may present an offering of widely different and yet equal value, "As God hath prospered them;" each acting as a steward of divine bounty, and realising the constant blessing of the approving Source of all good.

CHAPTER III.

THE OBJECTS TO WHICH THESE FUNDS SHOULD BE DEVOTED.

It will greatly simplify the subject, to place all objects connected with religion and benevolence together on the Scripture method, leaving the apportionment to every one's judgment and conscience.

There need be no fear of deficiency of means, or that the claims of any worthy object would be overlooked. With piety to dedicate sufficiency for all, there would be no lack of skill for its wise distribution.

The range of objects comprehends three distinct classes—the ministry and its requirements, the assistance and enlargement of the Church and conversion of the world, and the entire field of general benevolence.

1. The ministry and the necessary requirements of worship.

The ministry was the first thing provided for in Israel; not as of bounty, but of justice. The same holds good under the present dispensation. It is included here for convenience and conciseness of action. Every Jewish family furnished one-tenth of its income for the priesthood; and another tenth twice in three years prior to works of benevolence, for purposes of worship; and the third year for benevolence. Nor less positive and emphatic, both as to rule and measure, are the injunctions of the economy of grace with regard to the ministry: "Even so hath the Lord ordained, that they who preach the gospel should live of the gospel." (1 Cor. ix. 14.) "Let him that is taught in the word communicate to him that teacheth in all good things." (Gal. vi. 6.)

The ministry is, then, to be sustained as befits its importance and influence, and so as to exempt from the cares of business, and allow of entire dedication to the work of God; and this, not as bounty or benevolence, but as an equivalent for services rendered. Paul urged on the Church at Corinth, on grounds of justice and analogy, the liberal support of the gospel ministry, affirming his right to that, which, to prevent suspicion of self-interest in his argument, he waived; and while receiving needful aid from others, craving indulgence for the injustice thus done those, whose support was never tendered: "I robbed other churches, taking wages of them, to do you service." (2 Cor. xi. 7-9.) "For what is it wherein ye were inferior to other churches, except that I myself was not burdensome to you? forgive me this wrong." (2 Cor. xii. 13.) Paul thus taught the Corinthians, they had small grounds for glorifying in gifts and refinements, while wanting in mere justice, in permitting their minister to be supported by poor and distant churches. How clear the inference of a church's dishonour, in a parsimonious support, much more denial of support, to the ministry! Surely the labours and benefits of the ministry of grace are as valuable and refreshing as those of Judaism! Connected with this, as a mere matter of justice, are the temple and needful expenditure of divine worship. These are a Christian's first obligations; and well will it be, both for themselves and for the world, when every one shall joyfully dedicate to the ministry and sanctuary of his choice, some near proportion to the offerings of an Israelite. Such a scale of contribution would, doubtless, yield sufficent resources for all the requirements of worship and ministerial support, leaving a surplus fully adequate to every demand of temporal and spiritual beneficence.

2. The assistance and extension of the Church and conversion of the world.

No being may or can live for itself. God, who alone can, will not. All are placed in a state of mutual relation and dependence. Mankind specially are a brotherhood; a family, with kindred minds, wants, and sympathies. Selfishness violates this bond; benevolence cherishes it. The distinguishing feature of Christianity is benevolence. It is, as a system, the embodiment of divine benevolence, and its adaptation to the necessities of man. The benevolence of God blessing the individual man, and then, moulding him after the divine character and spirit, inducing cheerful self-sacrifice for the good of others. Its first field of exertion is the soul and its deathless interests. What a range of enterprise and sacrifice here opens to view! It is our privilege to live in a day of increasing Christian activity, and demand for pecuniary consecration. There is the work of relieving the poor of our own fellowship, of helping other churches involved in calamity, or unable of themselves to defray the expenditure of religious worship—contributions for the erection of sanctuaries in destitute localities, for education of youth, for the support of Home and Foreign Missions, and for all the agencies employed for the evangelisation of mankind.

3. The broad range of general benevolence.

Christianity aims to relieve and bless man, both for present and future existence. It dispenses blessings material for time, and moral and spiritual for eternity. It instructs, cheers, and elevates him on earth, and trains and qualifies him for the felicities of heaven.

It has its funds for the assistance of needy kindred, educational institutions, local poor assessments, hospitals, infirmaries, and all the varied operations and appliances of a true human sympathy, and of an enlightened and cordial imitation of the gracious Teacher and Benefactor of our race, "who went about doing good." All acts of benevolence to man as God's creature, and from regard to Him, are received by Christ as done to himself, and will of grace be so rewarded. (Matt. xxv. 40.)

It would be always preferable to apply devoted property in increasing the privileges and comforts of the needy; by finding them employment, heightening their wages, and otherwise calling out their energies on their own behalf; rather than in gifts and palpable acts of charity. All that a Christian intentionally and conscientiously expends on his social position and general style of living, with this distinct design, may be fairly considered as consecrated property; due regard being first given to other worthy objects. Indiscriminate almsgiving to strangers, would seem to be positively pernicious; tending to encourage vagrancy, idleness, and deception.

What a field is here presented for the exercise of a large, wise, and fervent charity; ranging from the effort to relieve the wants and sorrows of time, to the instruction and salvation of the soul; from the performance of the feeblest service for the honour of God, to the attempt to fill the earth with the grace and glory of Immanuel!

In such a work, who that aspires to the hallowed name of a Christian, would not exercise his ingenuity to discover how *much* rather than how *little*, he can consecrate? Who would not use the utmost economy of personal expenditure and family provision, to increase the means disposable to such an object? Can any one, having a spark of divine love in his soul, fail to dedicate anything short of all that he can possibly spare, however narrow his means, to glorify his Saviour, and promote the comfort, enlightenment, and salvation of his species? Can any nobler object be found to which to devote the largest wealth; or for which to exercise the most rigid economy and self-denial?

CHAPTER IV.

THE PROPORTION OF INCOME TO BE DEDICATED TO THESE PURPOSES.

INCOME is the means of subsistence, arising from estates, funds, interest of shares of companies, landed property, and profits of business, &c., when all payments on borrowed monies, and all the necessary expenses of conducting such business, are subtracted. Every well-conducted, successful business, must bear a percentage of profit on the amount of its returns. The income of its proprietor is what remains, when all its losses and expenditure are deducted. Let the Christian first satisfy himself as to the just proportion which different amounts of income should yield in the form of self-assessment, for the purposes of religion and humanity—what of incomes of 50*l*., of 100*l*., of 200*l*. per annum respectively, and so on in the ascending scale? Next, let him learn the amount of his income, as nearly as circumstances and the uncertainty of times will allow. Then let him dedicate such proportion, according to the importance of soliciting objects. A candid mind and upright heart will soon surmount all imagined difficulties, in the way of ascertaining the proportion of income that each Christian ought to consecrate. If there be any suitable and practicable rule, it must be expressed or implied in the statute-book of divine truth. Such rule can be ascertained, by the examination of the general spirit of the entire Scriptures,—by the unchangeable nature of all moral and religious obligation,—by the Jewish law of tithe and free-will offerings,—by the immense enlargement of the field of exertion under the present dispensation,—and by the special pominence given in the New Testament to the pecuniary department of benevolence.

1. By the general spirit of the entire Scriptures.

That spirit is one of thorough, universal, incessant consecration to God. It admits of no end of being inferior to this. One passage from each part of the sacred testimony will suffice for this purpose: " Honour the Lord with thy substance, and with the first-fruits of all thy increase." (Prov. iii. 9.) Here is a broad, definite, final, and universal principle of action, restricted to no period or dispensation; a general rule for all time, giving scope, nevertheless, in regard to measure, to the exercise of choice and good-will. Different methods may be employed to carry it out at different periods; but the *law* is one. God may at one time enjoin a particular mode of its application, both for present use, and to furnish suggestive light for future guidance, as with the rule of tithe and sacrifice of old; or he may employ knowledge of former regulations as a trial of fidelity and affection. Either way, not to live supremely to him, is treason to his throne. Still more emphatic, if possible, is the tenor of the Gospel, " Whether, therefore, ye eat, or drink, or whatsoever ye do, do all to the glory of God." (1 Cor. x. 31.) Here all the functions of life, and all the motives and actions of being, are claimed, as a cheerful sacrifice to the God of love. Were this our rule of conduct, how bountiful would be our pecuniary offerings!

2. The unchangeable nature of all religious and moral obligation.

If it was ever the duty of one man to worship and glorify God, and to love and befriend his fellow-men, it is equally that of every man in every age. If God taught Israel to maintain the ordinances of divine worship, for spiritual instruction and enjoyment, and to relieve their poorer brethren, by a prescribed rule; shall we, who live under a nobler economy, claim freedom from these moral duties, because we are not under their ceremonial? The conduct and teachings of the Saviour afford no encouragement to such a conclusion, but, entirely to the contrary: "I am not come to destroy the law, or the prophets, but to fulfil." "Till heaven and earth pass, one jot or one tittle shall in no wise pass from the law." (Matt. v. 17, 18.)

Instead of finding a plea for the neglect of moral duties, in the abolition of mere ceremonial observances, should not we, who derive our best plans and designs of form, taste, and architecture, from the material works of God, and the pencillings of his hand, joyfully adopt his methods for the attainment of moral and religious ends, in assurance of their wisdom and effectiveness? Should not our superior advantages constrain to the loftiest devotedness?

3. The Jewish law of tithe and free-will offerings.

The first mention of tithe is concerning Abraham's presentation of a tenth of the spoils to Melchizedek. (Gen. xiv. 18–20.) The next, Jacob's promise of a tenth to God, should he return to his native country. (Gen. xxviii. 22.) The words tithe, and tenth, are synonymous. Jacob's expression is, "I will give tithes, or tenth." Paul uses these terms synonymously, Heb. vii. 2–9.

The dedication of the same proportion in these instances, and the injunction of this proportion on Israel, excite the conjecture, that the consecration of a tenth was among the unrecorded institutes of worship conveyed to Adam, as animal sacrifices seems to have been. And therefore not a part of the mere ceremonial of the Mosaic economy, but a divinely-appointed method of fulfilment of a moral principle, never to be set aside.

The payment of tithes was binding on all heads of families, not dependent for subsistence on personal service. (Lev. xxvii. 30–32.) Its detention caused deep poverty and calamity, and was branded as robbery of God. (Mal. iii. 8.)

The Pharisee boasted of his scrupulous performance of this obligation, "I give tithes of all that I possess."

In the allotment of the land of Canaan, the portion that would have fallen to the tribe of Levi, except their cities of residence, was divided among the other tribes, and they were required to bring the tenth of their whole produce for the sustenance of the Levites. (Num. xviii. 21–24.)

This was simply a recompense for service done on their behalf. Jehovah would have his worship and service in Israel. He would have it conducted with order, reverence, and piety. The duties of its offices should not be left to the venture of the hour, or to the performance of any who would undertake them.

A large and well-instructed body of persons, the men of an entire tribe, in full age and energy, were to give themselves to this work, in its various departments; to fulfil their term of service in the temple, and to be the general instructors of the nation. For these labours they were to receive the tenth of the national produce. This tribe abstained from the ordinary engagements of life, to perform the routine of public worship for the nation; and eleven tribes, possessing and cultivating their territory, brought its proceeds, as the just recompense of their services and necessary means of their subsistence. On receipt of the national tithe by this tribe, a tenth of the whole was presented to the family of Aaron, which alone performed the strict duties of priesthood. (Numb. xviii. 25-30.)

A second tithe was required of the nation for the feasts, services, and sacrifices of the Tabernacle. (Deut. xiv. 22-27.) Every third year this tithe was appropriated to the relief and benefit of the poor and afflicted. (Deut. xiv. 28, 29.)

Josephus mentions both these tithes. (Antiq. lib. iv. cap. 8, § 8.)

Beyond these items of expenditure to Israel, there was, as some think, the *annual* payment of soul-ransom, a half-shekel levied on all males from twenty years old and upwards. (Exod. xxx. 11-16.)

There were the offerings of first-fruits (Exod. xxiii. 19); offerings of trespass after sin, or ceremonial defilement (Lev. v. 2-10); voluntary peace-offerings (Lev. xix. 5); the gleanings of the vines and fields (Lev. xix. 9). Besides these were those of their three principal feasts, which all mature males were required to attend with an offering, the value of which was left to their own disposition and ability. (Deut. xvi. 16, 17.)

From these particulars, it is evident, that the cost of religion and benevolence to a Jew, ranged from a fifth of his income to what higher proportion he chose; while the poorest of the nation were expected to render such aid as their limited means would permit. (Lev. xii. 6-8; xiv. 22-30.)

The design of this arrangement, probably, was to make religion and brotherly-kindness a fundamental principle and essential element of their personal and national life. Its influence, undoubtedly, was to make the service of God to a carnal, selfish mind, unbearably irksome and oppressive; but to a holy spiritual mind, an ever-flowing stream of satisfaction and joy; the constant realisation of life in and labour for God.

Was not a household method of contribution, in which the poorest might participate, preferred to every other, with the gracious design, that provision might be made for God as an inmate, resident, and member of every family? Was it not intended to teach, that the great Lord of all would condescend to dwell with, bless, and succour those families, which cheerfully conceded his claims, honoured him as the head, and prized him as the best beloved?

The correct application of the question of tithe and offerings to the circumstances and obligations of Christians, requires the present introduction of the two remaining considerations, only premising, that whatever may be the literal regulations of human law, the scriptural obligation is only enjoined on an occupying *proprietor*, and on a people in a state of *religious uniformity*.

4. The immense enlargement of the field of exertion under the present dispensation.

Judaism was a national system, of limited and restricted character. Though it allowed the benefit of foreigners, it was by proselytising; a measure not likely, as man is constituted, to operate extensively. Its offerings were for the benefit of their own poor, and the preservation of religion as it was. Its aim and action were local, limited, and conservative.

Christianity, as a system, open its arms and heart to the world. It offers its benefits to universal man. It is in its very nature aggressive and diffusive. It seeks to put away from man — *every man* — wherever found, every evil of his earthly condition, and to bring him into the liberty and dignity of a child of God. It aims to benefit him both for this and the future world. As the delegated dispenser of the " common salvation," and the infinitely varied and precious blessings it comprehends, it demands and merits for its diffusion the tongues and hearts—yea, the entire influence, talents, and property of all its subjects.

With such a field of labour, and such an object, must not the means supplied greatly exceed those of a mere stationary and national system? To suppose that the principle of tithe has nothing to do with Christianity, by way of suggesting an easy and universal method of voluntary assessment for religious purposes in the absence of a specific injunction, is to imply that Infinite Wisdom was at fault, in demanding ample means for a small and inferior work, and leaving the vast and God-like without resources adequate to its support. Can it be believed that this detail of plan and sufficiency of means for a temporary system, had no designed bearing on that which, succeeding it, is of universal operation, and worthy of unspeakably loftier liberality, though enjoining no such definite rule of contribution?

5. The peculiar prominence given in the New Testament to the pecuniary department of benevolence.

It will be easy to prove that the obligations and motives of pecuniary consecration adduced in the Old, increase and intensify in the New Testament. Could any be justly entitled to the privileges and mercies of either dispensation without liability to its moral obligations? Are not these obligations the same in both cases? Are not the two Testaments corresponding parts of one great and glorious system of truth; one revelation of the duty of man and the mind and grace of God? Either is incomplete alone. Judaism was "a shadow of good things to come," the introduction of a grand system of truth and spiritual economics, on a limited scale, and by stipulated rule; to prove what can be effected by orderly and universal action under the reign of love.

Christianity instead of being opposed to Judaism, or the abolition of anything in it that is moral, holy, or benevolent, is its unlimited expansion, both in the range of its objects and the means of its support. It is the impartation of the motive of love to the organisation of rule; the infusion of life into the well-adapted body of order and system. If Judaism supplied the rule of action, Christianity furnishes the motives for its fulfilment. The former rears the temple and altar, and prescribes the sacrifice; the latter furnishes the worshippers bringing their grateful offerings. Judaism stood in relation to Christianity as a type, a system of training by visible forms and ceremonies. What is ritual in the former is peculiar to it. What is moral in either is common to both. Christianity confirms and perpetuates what is moral in Judaism, while it adapts and modifies to its use whatever is wise and practicable of method and agency.

The *law of tithe* in Israel was not a mere *ceremonial*, as the wearing of certain garments, or the mode of offering sacrifices. It was a divinely-chosen method of performance of the obligations of piety, justice, and benevolence; and therefore worthy of man's use under all the altered aspects of religion, till God himself shall substitute for it some new and better system. He has never done this; therefore its principle remains in force.

The life and teaching of Christ should elevate all moral and religious obligations to the highest possible point of human estimation.

Christianity does not abolish tithe, but, infusing into it the life of principle and the warmth of love, it seeks to employ it for the world's evangelisation. Moses and Elias, having first discovered the wisest method of contribution, reveal Christ as the fit object of both human and divine love, and bid men lay at his feet the offerings of their grateful homage.

The demands of Christianity as an all-pervading principle of benevolence, are frequent and urgent; Judaism furnishes the best method for their fulfilment. Moses furnishes the rule, Christ the vitalising principle and motive of its performance. If the Old Testament enjoins the practice of liberality of offerings, the New reiterates and intensifies the same. (Ps. xli. 1; cxii. 4, 5, 9: Prov. iii. 9: 1 Tim. vi. 18: Heb. xiii. 16.) If the Old Testament condemns a grasping selfishness, Christianity brands it with its special malediction. (Ps. x. 3: Isaiah, lvii. 17. Hab. ii. 9: James, v. 1, 2: Luke, xii. 20.)

The instructions of the New Testament in this respect *exceed* those of the Old. It is here we learn the relation of man to God as a *steward* of divine bounty, intrusted with *talents* for use and increase. Here, by the parable of the good Samaritan, we learn that the range of benevolent exertion is universal man. Here the principle of *self-denial* breaks forth with affecting power, discovering its necessity for our own safety and honour; its beneficent influence upon others, and its bearing on the glory of God; at the same time illustrating and commending its lesson by the great example and symbol of self-sacrifice, which it so strikingly exhibits to view. (2 Cor. viii. 9.) Here a principle is propounded concerning all just and worthy claims which every one can practise, whatever his condition. (Matt. vii. 12; 1 Cor. xvi. 2; Gal. vi. 6-10; 1 Peter, iv. 10.) Here liberality is based on the highest possible motive, the grace of God towards us; and our attempted resemblance to him in spontaneous and disinterested beneficence. (Luke, vi. 35.) Here special notice is taken of instances of liberality in circumstances of poverty,—the widow's mite, the box of ointment, and the abounding liberality in deep poverty of the Macedonian churches. If the Old Testament suggests a wise and safe use of property—("He that giveth to the poor, lendeth to the Lord," Prov. xix. 17)—the New discloses the blessed issue to which it conducts, and the infinite gain that shall flow from the same. (Matt. vi. 19-21; Luke, xii. 33, 34; 1 Tim. vi. 17.)

The comparison of these passages teaches, that on the lowest ground, it is inconceivably gainful to change the perishable and uncertain property of earth, for whose future possession there can be no certain guarantee, into the sure and unending treasures of heaven;—that to employ them for those who are the special charge and care of God, the poor and afflicted, is to be sure of a rich and glorious recompense, when the treasures of earth shall be no more;—and that man should esteem his soul of higher nature and value than to be contented with earthly good, and should anticipate the eternal enjoyment of the divine favour as its only satisfying portion and happiness.

The Old Testament predicts the arrival of a period, when the prescribed measure of tithe will be cast into the shade, by the more ample offerings of a self-prompting gratitude and loving homage. How are such predictions as those of Psalm lxxii. and Isaiah lx. to be fulfilled, but under a state of piety and devotedness superior to the demands and gifts of stipulated duty? Is there anything in the history of the early Christian Church, composed of those who in various climes had performed the rites of Judaism, to indicate that they felt themselves absolved by the abolition of their ceremonial, from the obligation of pecuniary consecration? Does not the lovely picture drawn in Acts, ii. 44, 45, iv. 32–37, prove, that they felt their obligations to be immensely increased, and that their all was a sacrifice quite inadequate to its expression. Circumstances required an entire and universal surrender. Love and devotion were equal to the demand; and thus succoured and glorified the cause. The deed was worthy of the occasion, it nobly met its exigencies, and revealed the moral power of love at the commencement of its reign.

Had a similar spirit possessed the universal Church in all subsequent ages, what a heaven-like world had earth been long ago! How glorious had been her triumphs, and how rich her bliss!

In less trying periods, the Christian may advantageously pursue his calling, and dedicate a liberal measure of its profits. But surely the offerings of a state of safety and peace, should at least approximate to those of a condition of oppression and adversity!

The method of weekly contribution commended by Paul, is the systematic appropriation of property to the proper ends of its bestowment, so as constantly to meet the claims of God and man, leaving a principal in hand for future use and increase. The wisdom, dignity, and happiness of the Church, will be found in a liberal self-tithing by *weekly* presentation.

The true bearing of the Jewish law of tithe on Christians seems to be, the commendation of a principle and method universally appropriate, practicable, and satisfactory; a principle capable of adaptation as to measure, according to the means possessed, the objects requiring aid, and the obligations of the giver.

If the Christian is free from the *ceremonial* of sacrifices and ablutions, which were mere *emblems* of what he enjoys in *reality* through the blood of Christ, is it just and gracious, therefore, to infer and practise *freedom* from pecuniary consecration ? Is not the fair inference rather, *increased* consecration ? It is universally allowed that responsibility enlarges with privilege : " Where much is given much shall be required." Can anything short of a higher rate of offering than that of a Jew be appropriate for a Christian ?

The stipulations of rule were for a *new system*, — for its preservation under a state of childhood and servitude. Their removal under a state of manhood is proof of confidence in the higher influence of holy willinghood, and the larger sacrifices of cordial affection. It is confidence in mental ability and moral integrity to *infer* the measure of obligation, and in the power of love and gratitude to secure its full dedication. *Shall human parsimony be permitted to disappoint these just and gracious confidings of Divine benignity ?*

If there is no formal injunction of self-assessment on the Christian as on the Jew, it is from the assumption that duty is sufficiently clear without it; and because it is impossible to frame a law better adapted to reach the widely different conditions of men than this does. Tithe, as an institute, seems to be fairly compatible only with a limited and local Church, with uniformity of worship, as in Israel, all being about on an equality, and proprietors. It is essentially formal in nature, and restrictive in tendency. Christianity is universal in spirit and aim; one in essence, though diverse in mode. It is a state of active willinghood, furnishing spirit and motive wide as the range of man's sympathies and resources. It refrains from the imposition of a duty, to leave scope for the freer and fuller operation of self-purposing love. It is the God of love, saving by sovereign grace and mercy the creature who could not be saved of desert; refraining from imposing conditions and formal rules of grateful service, as detracting from the value both of this boon and man's grateful offering; leaving it to the heart to infer its own obligations, and enjoy all the delight of their free dedication. It is as if God would furnish evidence, under the two dispensations of law and grace, of the superiority of the latter.

The dispensation of law failed to furnish the means merely of its own sustentation, and the voice of the last prophet dies away, lamenting and rebuking this failure, and giving promise of a coming change of system. (Mal. iii. 10, 18; iv.)

The principle of a loving free-will offering; of constant unconstrained self taxation, guided by the light of the legal economy, supplies its place; the *additional* instruction given is the weekly period. (1 Cor. xvi. 2.) The demand of law is hushed, to allow scope for the richer offerings of grateful ingenuity and adoring love. It is the substitution of the gift of a friend for the payment of a menial, — the service of a child for that of a hireling, — the homage of a loyal and loving subject for the reluctant surrender of an imposed tax,—the box of precious ointment which an affectionate heart provides ever and anon, to heal the woes of man, and to shed a grateful perfume in the presence of Him to whom it owes its every hope and joy. What scope is there for stipulations of measure of dedication where all is devoted in the first act of personal religion, "Ye are not your own?" Who can frame a fixed, invariable, and limited rule for the measure of loyal service, or filial love, or conjugal sympathy? The Christian holds all these relations to the Infinite God, through the work of his Redeemer. Shall he require a rule for his offerings? What demand can be made, short of all that remains after the necessary expenditure of life, — that exception being made, only to fit for renewed consecration?

Christians require no *formal* substitution of the present for the ancient Sabbath. They realise at once their duty and advantage, in celebrating on that day their Redeemer's triumph over sin and death. The *implications* of the Gospel on this point, more than suffice to fix the rule. Why should it not be thus in reference to what is equally evident,—the law of pecuniary offerings? Every Christian is called to work in the vineyard of his Lord, to serve in his great household, to fight under his banner. His whole being, faculties, and possessions, are to be dedicated to his honour, and his entire nature sanctified to his glory.

This he admits to be his sacred obligation. What room is there, then, for defining a rule of measure concerning that which is already dedicated?

The very heathen have adopted tithe for religious purposes.

The Arabian merchantmen dedicated the tenth of their odoriferous treasures. The citizens of Athens sustained by tithe the numerous shrines, which acquired for them a reputation for religious reverence and worship. The Romans presented to Hercules a tenth of the spoils of war. Many Hindoos and Chinese devote a much larger sum to the service of idolatry.

Shall the Christian, then, refuse or grudge to offer a due and definite proportion of his property, on the altar of his God and Saviour?

The presentation to the Deity of man's best possessions has ever been a prevalent practice.

In ignorance of the true God, men have set apart the noblest objects of creation for *worship*. The finest specimens of the animal tribes have bled on their altars. The temples of heathen deities have been most magnificent erections, and their shrines have groaned under the richest gifts which deluded millions could present.

Shall not the offerings of intelligent Christian love exceed those of pagan fear and superstition?

The dedication of the choicest objects to God was a law in Israel, and is full of instruction for us. God required for his service a tabernacle of the most valuable and durable materials, gems of the brightest lustre, vessels of the most precious metals, fabrics of the finest textures and richest hues, animals of perfect form, and priests free from personal blemish. The Temple of Solomon was most rich and magnificent, and all its appurtenances most precious. If God was served for ages under a typical system, with the most valuable that man could present, and himself offered up his well-beloved Son to atone for man's sin, and make his services and offerings valid and acceptable, can the Christian fail to recognise his infinite obligation? Can he be reluctant to dedicate his best possessions with warmest love?

If the sentiments advanced be correct, it follows, that the proportion of the Christian's offerings to religion and humanity should as much exceed the ratio of the law of tithe, as his obligations exceed those of a Jew; that he should proportion his offerings to the measure of his resources; and that he should conscientiously keep down expenditure and practise self-denial of the luxuries and elegancies of life, to have wherewith to devote in the fullest measure to the Saviour's glory.

What scope is there here for endless diversity of amount, yet all proportionate, and all equally pleasing to God! Did such a practice prevail in these days of large and rapid accumulations, Christians would be found devoting in every possible proportion, varying probably from a hundredth part, to four-fifths, or even nine-tenths, of their income. How rare, then, would be the present frequent anomalous sight, of Christians growin immensely rich, while the assistance they render for the benefit of perishing millions, bears no proportion to their *accumulations!* Oh, that the true end and worth of wealth were thus generally understood! Oh, that its ardent pursuit by religious men were for this purpose!

It has been shown, that under Jewish law, all heads of families inheriting land, furnished more than one-fifth annually of their income for religion and benevolence; that the tribe of Levi contributed a tenth to the family of Aaron, and that e en the poor were required to assist according to their ability, in all acts of personal worship. If not able to present a lamb, to offer a pair of turtle-doves. (Compare Lev. v. 7; xii. 6–8; and Luke, ii. 22–24.) In a word, it demanded the co-operation of *all*, and fixing the minimum, left every one at liberty to exceed it as he would.

The various details of the Jewish ceremonial, having each their own spiritual import, Christianity absorbs their forms in the clearer manifestation of their meanings. Even in the brightest days of the tithal system, as if to foreshadow the greater demands and more adequate and suitable methods of a superior coming age, recourse was had for extra requirements to the expedient of extra free-will offerings; as for the erection and decoration of the Tabernacle by Moses; of the Temple by Solomon; and of the restorations of Jehoida and Ezra: as if adumbrating the more pliant nature and more prolific power of the appendage than the rule; and the designed absorption of tithe in free-will offerings in a coming age as its natural fruit and superior system; even as the moral of the Passover is merged and more clearly revealed in the Lord's Supper.

Nothing is stated in the New Testament as to the abrogation of tithe, though from the nature of the case, its dedication by Christians must have contemplated Christian rather than Jewish objects. It may be doubted if the full capabilities of the Jewish Institute have ever yet been developed: for does not the unlimited free-will offering after tithe contain the principle of sufficiency for every necessity, and the germ of the highest realizations of even Christian consecration; as well as the element of its absorption in the larger offerings of evangelic love? For what was the spirit of the Jewish Institute, but the dedication to the glory of God and the relief of man of all that could wisely be spared from realized income? these objects constituting a grand item in deciding the scale of relative expenditure, and the costs of social station.

And what beyond this are the highest demands even of evangelic obligation, and the largest offerings of Christian love? A full free-will offering to the extent of ability absorbs and exceeds tithe. Such is the precise character of Gospel obligation, "as God hath prospered."

The first mention of the dedication of property in the New Testament, the presentation by the Magi of gold, frankincense, and myrrh to the Infant Redeemer (Matt. ii. 11), is under circumstances both novel and peculiar, seeming to supersede tithe, at least to pervade, animate, and supplement it with the divinely-approved method of free-will offering, as most befitting the genius of, and most adequate to the requirements of, the incipient dispensation.

Thus Christ, as their antitype, received the tithe of the Patriarchal and Jewish ages, in the persons of Melchisedec and Aaron, as a National Priest; and the voluntary tribute and fealty of Gentiles as a Universal King. In the person of Melchisedec as his type, Christ received tithe of Abraham for all under the dispensation of animal sacrifice, which his death completed. (Heb. vii. 8–10; and ix. 26.) And in the homage of these Gentiles, he sanctified to this dispensation the principle of spontaneous offerings.

The subsistence of Christ and his apostles seems to have been largely drawn from the grateful bounty of persons indebted to his healing power. (Luke, viii. 2; John, xii. 1-2.) The costly box of ointment, both of the penitent (Luke, vii. 37-38,) and Mary of Bethany (John, xii. 3), were prized by the Saviour, as being the spontaneous offerings of hearts, whose adoring love exceeded all adequate means of expression. The superlative value of the widow's two mites consisted, in their being the voluntary dedication of all to the service of her God. (Luke, xvi. 4.) The exhortation of the Saviour, "Make to yourselves friends of the mammon of unrighteousness," &c. (Luke, xxi. 9), plainly points to free acts of benevolence as proofs of true piety. The singular and urgent condition of the Pentecostal Churches called for some new and superior means of supply, for the new and unprecedented demands; no part of the national tithe flowing into their coffers. Resources equal to the emergency were found in the collective free-will offerings of the Christian brotherhood. (Acts, ii. 44-45; iv. 34-35.)

The solemn expostulation of Peter with Ananias and Sapphira, was for wilful falsehood, concerning pretended consecration of what was entirely at their own disposal. (Acts, v. 4.)

The teachings of Paul to Gentile converts lift up the rule and measure of Christian dedication to the highest possible principle and motive, that of the scale of privilege and ability, and of its agreeableness in the sight of God. (1 Cor. vi. 19-20; xvi. 1-2; 2 Cor. ix. 6-7; viii. 9; Phil. iv. 18; Heb. xiii. 6.) The wise and simple method enjoined by him on the Galatians and Corinthians, and so elaborately and cogently argued and illustrated, (2 Cor. viii. and ix.) leaves the measure to voluntary decision.

The feature in the most opportune and refreshing relief, sent once and again to Paul from Philippi, that most cheered and delighted him was, that these spontaneous gifts to the servant proved their cordial love and devotion to his divine Master. (Phil. iv. 17.)

The resources of Apostolic Churches were not stipulated tithe, but the love-offerings of *Gentile Believers*, not used to, though probably instructed and influenced by it.

No traces are found in the history of the early Christian Churches of their practice of tithe as the dictate of holy willinghood; and when in the fourth century it was imposed by Imperial authority, it was not so much to sustain the true Church of Christ, as the ecclesiastical power of princes under Christ's name.

It is a palpable fact, that in the adoption of tithe as a National Institute in every age and country, the true Church of Christ has had little to do with its funds, while they have often sustained in power and grandeur her bitterest enemies.

Respecting the conduct of Christians in more recent times, the original advertisement beautifully says:—" In reading the biography of the most eminently pious and useful in different ages, one must have been often struck with the fact, that almost all of them devoted a regular proportion of their income to the Lord in pious and charitable uses. We might mention many whose names are familiar, whose writings are venerated, and whose memory is precious; *e.g.* the Lord Chief Justice Hale, the Hon. Robert Boyle, Archbishop Tillotson, the Rev. Drs. Hammond, Annesley, Watts, and Doddridge; the Revs. R. Baxter, J. Wesley, T. Gouge, Brand, and R. Treffry, jun.; together with the excellent Countess of Huntingdon, Mrs. Rowe, and Mrs. Bury. None of these gave less than one-tenth of their annual income, while several of them gave much more, and some of them gave all they had away, beyond the scriptural provision,—' food and raiment.'"

The conclusion thus reached is,—*a single tithe* seems to have been devoted, if not the sacred obligation, in patriarchal times, where considerable means permitted. Abraham paid Melchisedec tithe of the spoils of war (Gen. xiv. 20), and Jacob vowed to dedicate it if restored to his paternal inheritance. (Gen. xxviii. 20–22.) A *twofold tithe*, with several other stipulations, and any possible expansion of voluntary offerings, was the duty of an Israelite. Some Christians have practised tithe as an inferred obligation. Others have greatly exceeded it. The Christian seems to be left to deduce his obligation, in love and integrity, from the precedents of Judaism—the superiority of his advantages — the ever enlarging necessities of the world — the higher claims of the Gospel—and the extent of his resources.

Surely it must be a feeble state of piety, and low sense of love to Christ, that can infer an inferior obligation to that of patriarchal times; unless with very limited means, or very large and imperative social demands!

Surely Christians in easy, and especially in affluent circumstances, assuming any hope or interest in Christ, will recognise a rule of sacred obligation *equalling, if not exceeding, that of an Israelite!!*

Talents, under every dispensation, whether few or many, must return a measure of increase corresponding with their number and worth. How just, safe, and effective would it prove in every case to devote the same on the " first day of the week!" Some Christians, eminent for piety and intelligence, consider the rule of tithe as a minimum rate, universally binding on poor and rich, alike in every age: in truth, as a moral obligation, apart from and prior to any ceremonial. Does not the ancient economy, illustrated by the principle, "As God hath prospered thee," favour rather, the dedication of a rate bearing proportion to means? Abraham gave a tenth; Jacob vowed a tenth; an ordinary Jew gave not less than a fourth, or even a third, of his income; a poor person brought a lamb; and if very poor, two young pigeons. The inference seems to be, a varying, mild, and practicable proportion rather than a uniform rate. A measure unburdensome to the poor, and yet reaching the height of sacrifice with all.

The same rate on all varieties of income must either press severely upon the poor, or involve little self-denial on the part of the rich. The punctilious self-tithing of the leisurely if not opulent Pharisee, though not condemned by Christ, must be attended with the exercise of the higher principles of "judgment, mercy, and faith." It must be a high rate of gift in the rich to equal in moral worth the small offering of the poor, on the principle indicated by the Saviour in regard to the widow's mite,—that the worth of an offering appears, rather from what is reserved than from what is given.

And, surely, the consideration that they are not their own, and the desire to avoid undue conformity to the world, may well reconcile,—yea, rejoice the rich, to refrain from the lavish expenditure of their worldly compeers, whose style they could rival, that they may have the more to devote to his glory who bought them with his blood. Surely they will not the less prize their affluence because of their large Christian obligations! For whose sake does the husband and father chiefly value his increase, but for the loved ones of his household? And for whose sake can the Christian chiefly prize wealth, but for that of his Saviour? Has not the stranger to this feeling yet to learn what religion is?

For a uniform and universal literal tithing, the genius of Christianity clearly does not ask; but for a reasonable and grateful proportionment of offerings, according to resources, the system of tithe aiding in its discovery.

Any conjectured rule, to obviate reasonable objections, should be framed on the lowest equitable starting-point. Each can exceed this rate as conscience and heart may dictate. Families of few or no children can increase or double it, and yet the principal or capital remain for employment—for commerce or prudent enterprise.

To construct a scale of contribution, at once just and satisfactory, three questions need decision. Some starting-point from which to calculate different rates of offering—a distinct proportion, the suitable amount of its offering—and some definite and equitable rate of increase, determining the extent of obligation. The case of Israel furnishes safe and appropriate guidance on the first two points. The condition of Jewish families when entering on the practice of tithe, was one of comfortable sufficiency with social industry. Each family occupied its own estate. All were about on equality of condition, easy, if not affluent. (Deut. xiv. 21-27.)

The imperative demand of at least a fifth part of annual income, to be increased at the will of the giver, of all heads of households, when settling as equal proprietors in Canaan; and of the least costly animals of such as should fall into poverty, interpreted by the rule, " As God hath prospered thee," favours the appropriation of a percentage of income according to amount, and ever adjusted to its increase or decrease, rather than, as some think, a literal tithing of equal proportion in all cases and circumstances. Instances of special offerings, as Numbers vii. and 1 Chron. xxix., have also this bearing.

1. Suppose a present condition of 600*l*. or 700*l*. per annum, allowing for the present lower value of money, to equal their condition, a starting-point is gained. The Roman denarius was a good daily rate of wages. In our times " forty pounds a-year" would not be esteemed " passing rich," by the humblest minister.

2. If the devotion of a fifth, for the maintenance of ministry and worship, and for works of piety and benevolence,—the lowest rate of Israel—be admitted as a fair minimum measure for such a condition, difficulty vanishes. Can Christians, possibly, contend for a lower rate?

3. The third point, involving the vast diversity of human condition, would be attained with safety and justice to all, by a threefold increase of offering with a twofold increase of income, till some other proportion be required.

The following scale, the result of much reflection, is tremblingly submitted, merely for assistance, till a better be presented:—

Annual Income.			Annual Offering.			Rate of Offering.	Left for Expenditure.		
£.	s.	d.	£.	s.	d.		£.	s.	d.
12	10	0	0	5	0	a 50th	12	5	0
25	0	0	0	15	0	34th	24	5	0
50	0	0	2	5	0	23rd	47	15	0
100	0	0	6	15	0	16th	93	5	0
200	0	0	20	0	0	10th	180	0	0
400	0	0	60	0	0	7th	340	0	0
800	0	0	180	0	0	4¼th	620	0	0
1600	0	0	540	0	0	3rd	1060	0	0
3200	0	0	1600	0	0	a-half	1600	0	0
6400	0	0	4200	0	0	two-thirds	2200	0	0
12800	0	0	9600	0	0	three-fourths	3200	0	0

This scale is low and practicable. Each gives and retains more than the former. It is now being practised in various degrees. Intervening amounts can easily be found. The small sums may involve much sacrifice.

Contributions known to the Author in 1851, *illustrating the proposed scale.*

A. An aged Widow, income 8*l.* per annum   £. *s. d.*
    In support of ministry   0 4 0
    Place and purposes of worship   0 4 4
    School, 6*d.*; Missions, 6*d.*   0 1 0
                                                  £0 9 4

B. A Labourer, 20*l.* income, one child.
    Ministry   0 10 0
    Worship   0 8 8
    Missions, 1*s.*; Sabbath-school, 1*s.*   0 2 0
    Sacramental collections   0 4 0
                                                  £1 4 8

C. A Mechanic, 50*l.* income, three children.
    Ministry   0 16 0
    Worship   0 8 8
    Missions   0 19 0
    Sabbath-school   0 4 0
    Poor-rate   0 16 0
    Sacramental collections   0 6 0
                                                  £3 9 8

D. A Tradesman, 100*l.* income, one child.
    Ministry   4 0 0
    Worship   0 10 0
    Missions   0 10 0
    Day and Sabbath-schools   0 15 0
    Poor-rate   3 10 0
    Tract Subscription   0 5 0
    Sacramental   0 6 0
                                                 £9 16 0

E. A Minister, under 200*l.* income, six children.
    For purposes of worship   2 12 0
    Foreign and British Missions   3 0 10
    Poor-rate   2 12 6
                Carried forward   £8 5 4

	£.	s.	d.
Brought forward	8	5	4
Sabbath-school, 14s.; Day-school, 1l. 6s.	2	0	0
Tract subscription, 10s.; Bible subscription, 10s.	1	0	0
Two chapel cases	0	15	0
Sacramental collections	1	4	0
Peace, sick friend, temperance, apprenticeship, and Dorcas subscriptions	1	5	0
A needy friend	2	0	0
Various collections	1	10	0
Small benefactions	2	4	0
	£20	3	4

F. A Tradesman, 230l. income, three children.

Ministry	10	0	0
Worship	5	4	0
Sacramental collection	1	4	0
Day and Sunday-school	2	5	0
Foreign and British Missions	5	0	0
Tract subscription, 5s.; Bible subscription, 10s.	0	15	0
Poor-rate	5	0	0
Small gifts	2	10	0
Poor friends	10	0	0
	£41	18	0

G. A Tradesman, 500l. income, two children.

Ministry	15	0	0
Worship	3	0	0
Sacramental collections	0	12	0
Foreign and British Missions	2	11	0
Day and Sabbath-schools	2	10	0
Poor-rate	5	0	0
Tract subscription, 5s.; Bible subscription, 10s.	0	15	0
Small gifts	2	10	0
Chapel case	1	0	0
Small collections	2	0	0
Needy friends	26	0	0
	£60	18	0

These offerings would be found far to exceed the average of pecuniary consecration. The aggregate result of such a rate of dedication by all true Christians would augment the resources of God's treasury beyond belief. Allowing the proposed rate to be correct, they illustrate the deplorable but too general fact, that the *preponderance of moral worth of offerings is in favour of the smaller incomes.* Waiving the item of children, the 9s. 4d. of the 8l. income, is more than threefold that of 60l. out of 500l.; and the dedication of 1l. 4s. 8d. out of 20l. is more than double that of 20l. out of 200l., *in relative value and real sacrifice.*

They further demonstrate the unfitness of the too frequent uniform amount of subscriptions, by persons in widely different circumstances. If G. can dedicate at such rates to the mentioned objects, from an income of 500l., H. can, with equal ease, from an income of 1000l. double the amount to each of these objects, and still retain a large fund for other approved purposes; and so on with higher incomes.

Full scope may thus be found for the pursuit of every man's chosen object, when every other just claim is satisfied. The inheritors of the spirit of a Howard and a Fry, may devote their extra treasures to the relief of human suffering;—of an Oberlin, a Neff, and an Allen, to man's social elevation and spiritual security; of a Wilson, a Peto, and a Smith, to the erection of sanctuaries that may prove both the nurseries and the banquet-rooms of souls, while others may labour to scatter the seed-corn of truth, the aliment of immortal spirits, by various agencies, among the millions of mankind.

Three of these persons put into a purse every Sabbath the conscientiously determined proportion of the fifty-second part of their yearly income, and meet all demands therefrom as they arise.

Doubtless there are many who devote their full proportion without rule, and without being aware of the fact.

This scale of contribution is submitted, in the hope that the Christian is deeply affected with a sense of obligation to divine mercy, and knows no object so worthy of the best affections of his heart and largest expenditure of his resources, as the glorification of his Redeemer in the salvation of mankind. It is further presumed, that he is honestly anxious to ascertain the measure it becomes him to consecrate, and that he would tremble and grieve over any disposition to infer inferior obligations to a Jew, as being a sure indication of the feebleness, if not falseness of his faith and piety. It is in the hope, that he joys in the opportunity afforded under this dispensation to make the greatest possible sacrifice of personal comfort and enjoyment, to advance a cause so noble and beneficent; and chiefly desires increase of means and influence further to advance this object.

It may be well at this stage to anticipate and answer some objections and difficulties often advanced.

The novel and startling character of these suggestions may originate, even in candid and upright minds, such inquiries as,—

Where is the need for self-assessment in England and other like countries, where the tithe of a national establishment should largely serve the purpose? Suffice it to say in reply, tithe does, in some measure, answer this end; where it does not, those are responsible who prevent it. That, however, does not free any Christian from the obligation of consecrating his full proportion, specially those who do not pay tithes. Religious duty is an affair of the individual man. No national arrangement can absolve from it.

Should it be asked, Where is the record of the injunction of tithe on Christians? it is answered, What need is there of the renewed injunction of that, *which, though not binding strictly in the letter and form, has, in spirit, never been abolished?* What can be clearer than that, in the transition from the services of Judaism to those of Christianity, the funds no longer needed for the former should be transferred to the latter? What but a spirit of covetousness and very contracted piety can have prevented the inference by all subsequent believers, that their richer privileges, and the more gracious character of the new dispensation, claim of them an augmented offering? Would not the spirit that requires the express imposition of every duty, and perceives no beauty in the confidence that leaves it to a state of spiritual manhood to infer its obligations, be the first to resist them if stated? If Christians acted wisely and gratefully, instead of desiring freedom from the law of tithes, they would rejoice that God had condescended to reveal to them, through the example of others, a method so easy and effective; and they would joyfully modify it to their circumstances and capabilities.

It may further be asked, If tithe be contended for, why press the claim beyond the stated measure? It is replied, It is not a formal tithe, but the spirit and principle of that institution, that is pleaded for. The Jew was not restricted to the prescribed offerings. These he must bring on pain of divine pleasure for refusal. Infliction for detention was at God's decision. Doubtless it was often administered unperceived by man. (Haggai, i. 6; Mal. iii. 9-12.)

It may be feared, similar conduct often brings on Christians similar visitations. Here, doubtless, is an explanation of many of these disasters.

The Israelite might offer as much more as he pleased, with the certainty of its approval, according to the fulness of the sacrifice, and the humility, self-renunciation, and loving gratitude of the giver.

Christianity reveals its demands to the heart of every one honestly desirous of knowing them. It honours with acceptance the sacrifice of those who joy to lay it on the altar of divine love; who know no other object so worthy of its devotement; and who scorn to store it up for possible future contingencies, when it might be diffusing light, joy, and salvation over the globe.

The greatly increased ratio suggested for the affluent, is alike the dictate of reason and revelation. "Where much is given, much will be required." It is the only way of escaping the most fearful criminality in the possession of property. There is a style of living and expenditure quite beyond Christian propriety, and forbidden of God. "Be not conformed to this world." Every man should fix his style on a scale of large dedication as a faithful steward. To store up treasures is as criminal as to spend them lavishly. (James, i. 1-3.) But some must so expend, or store them, so extensive are their possessions, unless they dedicate them in a very high ratio. The consecration of property, and the employment of talents for holy and benevolent purposes, is their safest investment for the final account.

It may be asked, Why include the poor in the list of helpers? God himself has included them, in the privilege and joy of participation in this work. There are those among them, who would account it their deepest calamity and dishonour to be so excluded. The warmest eulogy ever pronounced by the lips of incarnate Love, was on the offering of the widow's mite. Next only to this was the commendation, " She hath done what she could," bestowed on the love-offering of one by no means affluent. Many of God's poor do nobly, according to their means, and will do it. A widow gave the first five-pound note she ever possessed to Christian missions. Another presented the only piece of gold she had handled for years, left to her by bequest, towards a new sanctuary, which she never expected to, and never did, enter. The poorest are required to aid, and their small but grateful offerings are in the sight of God peculiarly precious.

In an age of vast capital and enterprise it may be urged, Is not extensive reservation of profits for expansion of commerce necessary and proper? May not all suitable provision be made, without infringing on the claims of religion and benevolence? Is speculation for gain, or even for development of art or manufacture, of equal importance to the positive requirements of sacred obligation? May not the plea of accumulation on this ground be, unconsciously, a mere covering for avarice and penuriousness? Would not the admission of this view lead to the eternal impoverishment of heaven and of souls, for the enrichment of earth, in that which will prove the fuel of the final conflagration?

Is it not high time for Christians to put forth something of the spirit of lofty enterprise, in reference to that cause which alone is lastingly worthy of it, seeing that this only will demonstrate to the world their sincere and devoted attachment to their principles?

The instances of a few living princely contractors, tradesmen, merchants, and manufacturers, clearly manifest the compatibility of large benevolent outlay in various channels, with the successful employment of large reserved profits and capital.

Of these the late excellent Samuel Budgett is a fine type.

Is it inquired, Are not parents justified in making provision for children? It is replied, Paul says, "Parents should lay up for children, rather than children for parents." (2 Cor. xii. 14.) Needful and just provision may be made, without materially reducing what should be dedicated to God. Whatever trenches on this is injustice to God and man, and can bear no blessing to the child. A larger dedication would secure a blessing from above, of infinitely higher worth to children than earthly good.

The conduct of many parents must be highly offensive to God. It is as if they had no confidence in divine providence, but feared that God's care and guardianship would close with their descent to the tomb. Many Christian parents act too much like Esau in reference to his birthright. The God of love has covenanted to bless their posterity with grace, and to add thereto all needful earthly good; if they are trained in his fear, and supremely to desire his mercy; but they, by too eager pursuit of earthly good for their offspring, induce in them indifference to that inheritance which enriches both for time and eternity. A smaller portion of the property of earth sanctified by the divine blessing, would prove far more valuable. A large fortune left to children is a great thing in the world's estimation, but it is an alarming item to come under the judgment of God, when accumulated by neglect of his cause.

Should any ask, How is the rate of contribution of a variable business to be ascertained? It is answered, It is a less difficult task than may at first appear. Every honest man gets near the truth in reference to the income-tax. Let him strike an average, to find his weekly offering. Nor let it seem trivial or embarrassing, to abstract the weekly sum from the capital stock. Some have found it easy and pleasant, who deemed it impracticable. There need not be the slightest interference with capital. The largest enterprises may retain all their vigour. It is *interest*, not principal, that is sought; a portion of realised profit, to be devoted to God and man; instead of being expended for subsistence or enjoyment, or endlessly accumulated. This need not prevent improvement of circumstances. Suitable economy and simplicity of Christian life will leave full scope for such advancement, after the deductions mentioned. Apart from this system, many have devoted even higher rates, meanwhile rising from indigence to affluence. The amount, placed in a common treasury, can be appropriated as judgment and circumstances may dictate.

It cannot be denied, that the love and retention of property are conspicuous among Christians generally. So evident is it, that they have yet to learn the nature and extent of their sacred trust. To a large degree, they manifest a spirit of grasping and self-idolising covetousness, to the fearful neglect of the claims of religion and benevolence. Covetousness is the plague-spot, the brand-mark of the Church's present condition. It is an all-consuming cancer in her soul, eating up the vitals of her piety and bliss. A deadly upas, specious and fair to the sight; but extending wide its branches, and destroying every principle that comes within the range of its influence. A fatal opiate; under whose benumbing and stupifying operation she has become insensible to her leanness, and foolishly dreams of progress without devoted consistency. It has almost stifled in her the throes of soul-travail; shrinking her sons into spiritual dwarfishness, and reducing the sunlight and fire-heat of divine love in her heart, to the chill and gloominess of a cloudy moonlight. Oh. that the deep conviction of sacred obligation, its clear apprehension, and the spirit of its cordial performance, may quickly descend from " the Giver of every good and perfect gift!" Oh, that the Holy Spirit of light, love, and generous devotedness, may at once breathe life, warmth, and sympathy, into every Christian heart!

CHAPTER V.

CONSIDERATIONS WHICH CONSTRAIN AND ANIMATE TO THE PRACTICE OF THIS WEEKLY SELF-ASSESSMENT.

BEFORE mentioning these, it may be well distinctly to state what are the objects sought, and the course of action recommended, for their attainment.

The objects sought are, the realisation of sufficient pecuniary means to promote the relief, instruction, and salvation of mankind,—the maintenance of the worship of God, and the extension of his kingdom in the world.

The method proposed for their attainment is, the weekly dedication of a proportion of the income of the period, according to the measure of divine bounty received.

The amount to be consecrated on the principle of stewardship; and to be determined according to means and privileges enjoyed; guided by the light of Jewish precedent, the genius of Christianity, and the obligations of redeeming love.

Among the reasons that should operate to induce this consecration, are those which spring from sacred obligation to God;—those arising out of the condition and claims of man;—and those involved in the glory of Christ; and in the Christian's personal consistency, influence, usefulness, and happiness.

1. *Reasons springing from sacred obligation to God.* It should never be forgotten that all authority is of divine appointment. The relations of peoples to governments are not parallel with those of men to God. Earthly governments are a means to an end, that end being the safety, order, and prosperity of the people. Under the rule of God men are the means to the end, that end the glory of God.

If a government should require subjects to live only for its advantage, and to devote all but the bare means of subsistence to its coffers, it would forget its design and duty. For God to demand this is simply his rightful requirement. The Saviour demands this of every Christian,—

(1.) On the ground of his own free and unutterable bounty and love. If the record of divine benefaction be commenced, where will it close? With what noble natures and lofty powers is man endowed! His home and field of exercise for time is a very paradise of beauty and fruitfulness. The tokens of gracious consideration for his comfort and safety are vast and various. His wants and appetites are supplied, and his tastes gratified, with no niggard hand. What he has forfeited by sin is restored to him by the charter of sovereign grace and mercy. The glorious Persons of the Godhead conjoin to save, bless, and dignify him.

The tenants of heaven are enlisted in sympathy and co-operation for his welfare. The resources of Deity unite with the machinery of Providence to secure for him immortal life and blessedness.

So truly and intensely did the Father love him, that to redeem and save him he gave his only-begotten Son to sorrow and death. So deep and disinterested was the compassion and regard of Christ, that, unsolicited, he endured all the horrors and agonies of the curse of sin. Such is the tender and benignant interest of the Holy Spirit, that he offers to dwell in man's heart, and work in him a perfect fitness for the fellowship and enjoyment of heaven. There is nothing that the love and resources of God can bestow, or that his power can effect, to enrich and dignify man, that he is not prepared to impart. And on whom is all this goodness lavished? Is it on a noble being, of holy nature, lofty origin, and devoted fidelity? The very reverse of all this! It is yourself, Christian,—a creature of yesterday, depraved in heart, rebellious in life, but recently an alien and an enemy. He permits you to return to him for pardon and salvation. He places you in the position of a child and friend. He exerts his infinite power and love for your good. All that Christ was required to bear if he would effect your deliverance from eternal misery he voluntarily endured. Nothing is deemed too precious for God to bestow on you; no position too noble to which to raise you. " Beloved, even now are we the sons of God, and it doth not yet appear what we shall be." (1 John, iii. 2.) Ought we not, then, to catch something of this gracious and bountiful spirit, and to exert our best influence and powers for him who has done so much for us? If Christ devoted his all to enrich and bless us, shall not we at his call devote property and life to his glory? " Ye know the grace of our Lord Jesus Christ, who, though he was rich, for your sakes became poor, that ye through his poverty might be rich." Ought we not to imitate his self-sacrificing, disinterested bounty, in our labours and offerings to pread the triumphs of his cross? Can any service be thought excessive, or any gift too large a sacrifice for such beneficence? Can you, Christian, contemplate Christ giving himself an offering and oblation to save you from eternal death and infamy, and to raise you to the very pinnacle of attainable honour and happiness, and not feel joyfully constrained to the dedication?

> "Were the whole realm of nature mine,
> That were a treasure far too small;
> Love so amazing, so divine,
> Demands my soul, my life, my all."

(2.) The sacred obligation arising from this love.

Privileges and duties are ever united and equal. Love and mercy manifested towards us impose obligations of grateful return to the full extent of our power. Such was Paul's judgment, and such his conduct: "For the love of Christ constraineth us, because we thus judge, that if one died for all, then were all dead; and that he died for all, that they who live should not henceforth live unto themselves, but unto him that died for them and rose again."

The work of honouring God in life, love, and service, is only a part of our sacred duty. It includes the extension of the reign of mercy, and the general improvement of the condition of mankind. By whom is this to be effected but by those who have a hallowed sympathy with God, and a true interest in his glory? Was it not for this, in part, that God manifested his love to you? Can injunctions be more clear and emphatic than are those that bear on this point? "As we have opportunity, let us do good unto all men" (Gal. vi. 10); "Distributing to the necessities of the saints, given to hospitality" (Rom. xii. 13); "Every one of you, on the first day of the week, lay by him in store, as God hath prospered him" (1 Cor. xvi. 2); "Freely ye have received, freely give" (Matt. x. 8). Here we recognise the injunction of universality, liberality, frequency, and regularity, in the performance of that which every principle of interest, fidelity, and love, claims on the most extended scale; the dedication for the specific service of God of a part of that, the whole of which belongs to him by inalienable right of creation and redemption.

Are we living in the knowledge and experience of the only means by which the nature of man can be changed, and his guilt forgiven,— the gospel of the grace of God? Do we know that Christ has made it the duty of every Christian to publish it by all possible agencies for man's salvation? and dare we withhold the means at our disposal for this object? Are we stewards of the grace of God,—servants of Jesus Christ; and can we honestly— can we safely refuse constant and faithful dedication of ourselves, faculties, and possessions, for the honour of our Lord? Are we styled followers of God, and of the gracious example of Christ Jesus, that incarnation of benevolence, and can we decline to consecrate that which his bounty gave and his grace has preserved to us, to manifest abroad his glory, and increase the trophies of his saving power?

If Paul, to secure the forgiveness of Onesimus, could plead with Philemon, " Thou owest unto me thine own soul," what terms shall define the debt of the Christian to his divine Deliverer for redemption from woe to eternal life? The Saviour reveals in these most affecting terms the extent of obligation, in the light of the means by which you became his; and demands your love and service on a corresponding scale of entireness and heartiness: " Ye are not your own; for ye are bought with a price: therefore glorify God in your body and in your spirit, which are God's." " Ye are redeemed with the precious blood of Christ." Is there in the universe a name of dignity and endearment equalling that with which God has inscribed his people, " The children of the living God?" Is there a price of worth approaching that of their redemption, " The blood of Jesus Christ his Son?" What, then, must be their suitable obligation? Do Christians generally thus estimate their relation and fulfil their solemn trust? Who stands self-acquitted here? Do you not grieve, Christian, over past unfaithfulness? Will you not seek forgiveness of your injured Lord? Will you not now make a full dedication to him? Will you not at once adopt a method that will render this service constant, easy, and delightful?

2. Considerations arising out of the claims and condition of man. Among these are,—

(1.) The vast importance and urgency of the interests involved. It is not for a trivial and common object this consecration is solicited. It is to remove the guilt and misery of untold millions of our fellow-creatures, by making the Son of God the loved and adored of their souls. Not one-third of the population of the globe are acquainted with the only method of mercy—the Gospel. Of this number, with how large a proportion is religion rather a profession than a power! These inconceivable multitudes have souls of such value that we know no term adequate to its expression but infinite. One of these souls passes to the world of spirits every moment. We believe they are all guilty and condemned before a holy God—that they can obtain forgiveness and eternal life only through faith in Christ; and that if they are not thus saved, they are for ever lost. We feel that the Gospel remedy of divine mercy must be conveyed to men for its reception and belief; and that the Redeemer has made it the sacred obligation of every Christian to sustain the agency required for this purpose. We know that the prayerful consecration of property to this object will be blessed through the labours of various agencies to the salvation of many; and that the Holy Spirit will give vitality and efficiency to those humble efforts and offerings which are devoted to this service.

But are these, verily, our convictions? And is it possible that we withhold the means in our possession required for this end? Is it possible that we part with as little as we can for it; and that we are not anxious to know our duty in this respect? Can it be that we expend far more on mere elegancies and indulgences than for so vast and commanding an object? Surely all heaven cries — Shame! shame!! Surely all hell echoes the sound! May God penetrate our hearts to feel such shame and compunction as shall raise us at once to the full exercise of our sacred trust. We live under brighter light and richer privilege than ever Christians did. What, more than we have, can we desire or possess? What but a strong heart-love, and a full steady purpose, do we need for large sacrifice and glorious success? Our agencies and means of action are easy and appropriate, tried and effective. We enjoy the light of past history, examples, and achievements. We are nearing the end of time; and advantages, opportunities, and obligations, new and unequalled, concur to demand of us instant, vigorous, and self-sacrificing devotion.

Behold, Christian! a bleeding and dying world, of millions upon millions of souls,—souls more precious than the material universe,—durable as eternity,—prostrate in spiritual ignorance, guilt, and wretchedness. You, Christian, know the great Almighty Deliverer, and hope for eternal life through him. You possess the means by which they may be brought into your happy condition, and your gracious Sovereign requires you to employ them for this end.

Will you not make spare of family and personal expenditure to meet their urgent necessities? Behold the millions of supplicants for your aid—the diseased, the famishing, the ignorant, the criminal, the miserable,—Afric's swarthy sons with Asia's teeming empires, Europe's unregenerated peoples, and vast America's unsaved multitudes. They all, with united cry, loud as many waters, call to you, "Help us speedily, or we are for ever lost." Your Saviour Prince from his heavenly throne says, "What ye do to them, ye do to me. What, then, will ye dedicate to glorify me among them, and to bring them to share in your eternal felicities and dignities?"

The question of every Christian should be, How large a proportion can I arrange to devote for the present relief and eternal happiness of such a multitude? If it were only a few requiring aid in reference to the interests of time,—if there were multitudes ready to perform this task without us,—or if our term of life were long and certain, so that we could overtake the indifference of the past by the ardour of the future, we might have some plea for our neglect. But where it is on behalf of hundreds of millions of imperishable and priceless souls, for whom few care to exert themselves, and seeing that opportunity to benefit them is brief and uncertain, how can we endure ourselves in anything short of an intense and all-consuming devotedness?

If it were at the demand of a stranger, who had no special claim upon us for the sacrifice of something essential to our present happiness, and for the attainment of a trivial result, there were some excuse for our reluctance. But what shall be said when the grandeur of the object exceeds description, where the surrender is required by our Saviour Lord for his own glory, and when he asks only the forfeiture of a few luxuries and enjoyments of the passing hour?

Shall we as Christians expend our all on our puny selves and tiny households, and leave a mere pittance for the vast and ever-growing crowd of humanity? Shall we continue to consume the loaf, and leave them only the crumbs? Has not this course been followed already too long; while myriads have through our indifference perished in guilt and endless despair? Shall we not henceforth rise to our high calling, and account it our joy to be as devoted as we have been criminally negligent?

Who, then, will enter on this course of action, even, if otherwise unattainable, by a future limitation of matters of taste, art, and refinement,—yea, even of long-prized enjoyments, for the eternal well-being of more than eight hundred millions needing their aid?

(2.) The improbability of any marked progress on any other principle. What is the state of the Church at the present hour? Within the last half century she has betaken herself to the long-neglected work of evangelising the world. The several institutions originated for this purpose prove to be wise and appropriate. Large means have been expended. The smile of Heaven has richly prospered them. Are these not nearly all stationary for want of funds? Results have quite exceeded outlay and expectation. How shall larger blessings be secured but by larger and more numerous offerings? And how can these be obtained but by a liberal and universal self-assessment of Christians?

Till ampler means are supplied, where is the apparatus by which enlargement can be effected? So long as the parsimony or inconsideration of the Church withholds the resources needful for this purpose possessed by her, where is that sympathy of heart and aim with God which is requisite for any extensive blessing? God can only bless and employ for his glory a Church in full harmony of mind and feeling with himself. Large spiritual blessings and successes are only consonant with devoted hearts and consecrated property and powers.

The world, too, is in no temper to be taught about heaven and salvation by those whose love of mammon, after all their assumptions of benevolence and spirituality, is as evident as its own. Those who would attract men heavenward must encumber themselves less with the "thick clay" of earth, and manifest more of the spirit and possess more of the power of Heaven, than is now general among Christians. No mere ordinary procedure will suffice for this case. It requires immense and constant enlargement; increase of heart principle, and vigorous purpose; and of property, as its certain result. No mere expedients and fitful impulses, serving but for momentary improvement, will longer avail. Such means are almost spent, have lost the charm of novelty, and lack confidence with many for consistency. Every consideration of honour, gratitude, piety, and benevolence, calls for the adoption of a course at once *conscientious*, engaging the heart and judgment in its operation; *systematic*, proceeding by a clearly defined and unmistakeable rule; *periodical*, securing the presentation of offerings at frequent stated seasons; *punctual*, the act becoming a regular, joyful, and necessary engagement of the occasion; and *universal*, enlisting the energies and co-operation of the whole brotherhood of the faithful,—the thousand offerings of the rich and the million of the poor.

Here is a heaven-taught plan; the body of Judaism animated with the soul of Christianity; the just and all-extending rule of the former charged with the life and heavenly power of the latter. Judaism teaching all to bring a large portion of the best as a stipulated demand, prior to personal enjoyment, yet leaving scope for the largest exercise of voluntary offering; and Christianity suggesting the weekly season for its consecration, giving almost universality to the range of benevolent operation, supplying the force of heaven-born motive, and securing a sacrifice proportioned to the object sought and means possessed. It is man replenishing the treasury of God and the board of human want, and then feasting on divine goodness with a joyful heart.

(3.) The happy influence it would exert on the world.

It cannot be otherwise than that the world is amazed and rendered sceptical by the want of manifest Christian consecration. Reading the description of Christianity in the word of truth, it looks for its embodiment in the lives of believers. Here is a test which it can understand and appreciate. It reads that the Christian is purchased from eternal sorrow and infamy by the agonies and blood of the Son of God, evermore to love, adore, and serve him. "The love of Christ constraineth us." (2 Cor. v. 14.) The justice of this argument none can deny. The world, therefore, looks to Christians for its living illustrations. Alas! how few furnish the same! Now and then solitary instances occur, but how "few and far between!" Not enough to exert any powerful conviction in reference to a lofty principle; but serving rather to brand the few with the weakness of benevolent fanaticism. Paul speaks of the warm benevolence and liberality of his day as a divine experiment to elicit and demonstrate the power of the gospel, and to provoke the gratitude and admiration of observers. (2 Cor. ix. 12, 13.) Is the evidence of this kind now supplied by the Church honourable and satisfactory?

Paul speaks further of the abundant liberality of the Churches of Macedonia in a state of deep poverty, and he joys in this, and in their affectionate beneficence, not so much for the comfort it afforded him in his privations and afflictions, as that it produced fruit abounding to their immortal honour and advantage. (Phil. iv. 15.)

It is the present puzzle of the world that there is so little self-sacrificing liberality among Christians, on behalf of a cause which they profess to hold infinitely dear. Where, it justly and significantly asks, is the proof of this love? It boasts, with too much truth, that it can find many nobler instances of benevolence on mere grounds of humanity than the mass of Christians furnish; and it consistently demands of us, either to lower our professions, or to elevate our actions. When men of pleasure, men of taste, and men of science, expend large treasures and make cheerful sacrifices for the gratification of a favourite passion, no wonder is felt; but when Christians, whatever their taste and cultivation in mere matters of embellishment and equipage, indulge in expenditure immensely exceeding what they devote to the relief of humanity, the evangelisation of the earth, and the glorification of Christ, every thoughtful mind must be filled with indignant surprise. Can such conduct fail to harden irreligious men in indifference and scepticism? Surely the rejoinder was as just as severe in reference to Christians generally, when one seriously urged to seek salvation replied, "You do not believe these things yourself. If I believed man to be in the condition you represent, and knew, as you profess to do, the only remedy, I would go all the world over to urge it on the attention of every man I saw."

The Son of God has acted out his belief of these great and solemn truths in the most emphatic and convincing manner. The life of Paul evinces his deep conviction and sincere devotion. Oh, that the followers of Christ would imitate their great Master! Whenever the Church shall practically manifest her belief of truth by large and prayerful sacrifices, and by earnest, affectionate, and untiring labours, a strong sense of the reality, importance, and grandeur of religion, will seize the minds of men; and the approving blessing of Heaven, with such a holy, dependent, and self-devoted host, will make the conquest of a world so convinced an easy and speedy task.

(4.) The sufficiency of such resources for all requirements. No one can doubt this who reflects on the results of the united offerings of a multitude. What vast funds have been realised by the quiet operation of personal periodical contribution, in the various departments of the pecuniary system of the Wesleyan body! Even with the present limited degree of conviction and dedication, how large the aggregate of means at the disposal of the whole Church! Consider the vast annual taxation of Britain; nearly 60,000,000*l.* sterling; and you may thereby be prepared to conceive of the immense and all-sufficient funds which the united and proportionate assessments of the whole body of believers would produce. Let there be but the constant enaction of the scene in Israel, when the people, one and all, prince and peasant, united in contributing the means required for the service of the sanctuary. (1 Chron. xxix. 6-9.) Let there be the large and fully-proportioned offerings of the thousands of merchant-princes of the spiritual Israel; those of the professional classes, and such as are retired on a competency; with the gifts of tradesmen, mechanics, and poorer members of this holy brotherhood, in equal ratio; and how vast beyond conception the aggregate of the Church's resources, and how convincing the evidence of her sincere and cordial devotion! Let such a fund but once exist, and how rich will be the increase ever flowing from its tens of thousands of springs! What finances of earthly potentate, under the brightest day of human prosperity and power, would approach the sum of the treasures thus laid at the feet of the King of kings?

(5.) Examples of eminent devotedness to the interests of humanity and religion.

The Sacred Volume furnishes some noble instances.

David, who joyfully dedicated vast treasures to the erection of a magnificent temple for the worship of God, though not himself permitted to build it: Nehemiah, who declined taking the income and provision of the governor, that he might not increase his people's poverty, and largely expended his own property to forward the work of God: the Macedonian Churches, whose liberality and general consistency called forth Paul's unqualified commendation and eulogy: the family at Bethany, whose welcome hospitality was often rewarded by the presence and cordially-manifested friendship of the Son of God. Besides these were Gaius, Onesiphorus, Lydia, and a host of worthies, whose sympathy and aid rendered to apostles and suffering saints were eminently valuable, and proved a grateful boon to the approving Saviour.

Instances of similar devotedness are not wanting in more modern times.

Harlan Page expended a large proportion of his limited earnings in an extensive correspondence and distribution of tracts. Mr. Cobb, Boston, U.S., commenced business, resolving never to be worth more than 50,000 dollars capital, and to give one-fourth of his net profits to religious and charitable uses if ever worth 20,000 dollars, one-half if 30,000 dollars, and three-fourths if 50,000 dollars. This resolution he kept through life, giving in one year 7500 dollars to a separate object, the amount his income had exceeded 50,000 dollars. He died in worldly prosperity and soul-happiness. The noble brothers Haldane consecrated a princely fortune and their personal itinerancies to the effort of saving souls. The magnanimous Buxton often devoted large sums to carry out the plans of human freedom, instruction, and salvation, to which he further consecrated the energies of his life. The Countess of Huntingdon sold her valuables, and adopted a retired and inexpensive life, to devote more largely to the Redeemer's glory. An eminent Christian, lately deceased, dedicated annually for years six thousand pounds out of eight to the cause of religion and benevolence. A negro slave, an ingenious mechanic, having saved 35l. by working over-hours, devoted it all to the erection of a temple for divine worship.

Time would fail to tell of those of earlier days, as Judge Hale, Baxter, Watts, Doddridge, and others, as well as many of more recent times, who regularly devoted a tenth, or more, of their income to these purposes. Instances, also, of extensive and systematic liberality of churches might be noticed; but few, it is believed, have yet approached their capabilities, if exercised on the system recommended.

Christian, will you not henceforth, in view of the untold millions of souls needing salvation, of the unutterable love of Christ to you, and the urgency of his claim upon you, adopt this principle of pecuniary offering? In consideration of the brevity of the period during which you can benefit man, of the mere earthly value of property if used only for time, and of its permanent and expanding worth if employed for eternity,— in view of the hell to which millions are hastening, of the cross which has rescued you from it, and of the heaven to which you are tending, will you not dedicate your property as a means to save them from misery, and raise them to endless glory and bliss?

3. Considerations included in the glory of Christ, and in the Christian's personal consistency, influence, and happiness.

(1.) Every man thus fixes the stamp and standard of his own character and destinies. There is a higher standard of character than that which falls under human observation. The *ultimate* voice of history is nearest the truth. The judgment of God will reveal the real character of all. Every man is now writing his own history, and fixing his own unchangeable condition. It is left to him to form the character he wishes to appear in for ever. It does not depend on circumstances, education, or property, but on the action of life, as originated by the principles of the heart. Christianity knows nothing of right principles of heart, without conduct of a corresponding nature. Vital religion is the wedded union of faith and works. These two joined by God, never to be separated on earth. Either of them is dead and useless without the other. Together they tend to convert earth into a paradise of peace and prosperity, and to people heaven with untold millions of her sons. There is a spurious Christianity which affects lofty piety and spiritualism, but is destitute of labour and sacrifice, which it stigmatises as " legality and self-righteousness," but " By their fruits ye shall know them." The principle of final decision is, " Men shall be judged according to their works," because works are the embodiment of the principles of the inner life. The summary of the judgment is, " Come, ye blessed, for ye did such and such things," or " Depart, ye cursed, for ye did them not."

There is no higher character for a man to attain than one of self-denial and voluntarily imposed indifference to outward circumstances of time, for the elevation of his spirit and the benefit of his race. How noble is Paul in his avowal, " I am instructed both to be full and to be hungry, both to abound and to suffer need." Here was a true hero, a conqueror of self. This hero affirmed, " I will very gladly spend and be spent for you." What possessor of earthly good ever reached so lofty a position as he did ? What company of self-indulging ones ever stood so high in the estimation of even the thoughtful worldling, as the poor but liberal Christians of Macedonia? (2 Cor. viii. 1–5.) Every man is now on trial, to discover how he would act if placed in circumstances of greater comfort and affluence. Whether, like God, he

Y

would delight to diffuse good, or selfishly prefer to retain all for personal enjoyments. The consequences of his disposition and conduct will be his eternal inheritance. Its review and results will afford him endless sorrow or satisfaction.

(2.) Its happy influence on the character and heart.

An instant effect of the adoption of this plan is to make man honest-minded and simple-hearted, to induce " a conscience void of offence towards God and man." He remembers that he is not a *proprietor*, but a *steward*, to employ what he can honestly accumulate for the honour of God. He feels that he cannot better exercise the talent of property than in relieving man's necessities, and winning him to the enjoyment of redeeming love. So long as he either negligently or wilfully refrains from so doing, he is a stranger to heart-ease, conscious integrity, and true happiness.

To refuse to act up to this stewardship is flagrant dishonesty, self-idolatry, and soul-cruelty, of the deepest dye. So long as this continues, feebleness of the life and joy of piety must exist. Want of honesty with God, and wilful detention from the purposes of his glory of that which we profess to have dedicated to him, cannot be favoured with the light of his loving approbation. But where the service of Christ is regarded as the highest aim of existence, and the soul is but too happy to expend its all of energies and resources for its promotion, the joy of conscious integrity and of divine approval abounds.

With such harmony of profession and conduct, happiness must be associated. It lifts every act of time to a loftier standard and platform than earth. It furnishes evidence of character and devotedness that none can gainsay or resist.

Where the heart opens to the guidance of the Holy Spirit, and is bent on wise and faithful dedication to the divine glory as the only object of pursuit, there is sympathy of spirit with God, and there true and satisfying communion with him is realised. Such a state of mind peculiarly prepares for the clear and joyful comprehension of revealed truth. It introduces to the knowledge of the secret of the Lord, and enables us to understand, as far as feeble mortals can, the glorious mysteries of redeeming love. Such a soul consciously lives in the gaze of the eye of infinite purity, realising the approval of its humble, but loving efforts. The rays of the great spiritual luminary, the Sun of Righteousness, animate it with the light and warmth of divine love. Such consistency is the best preparation for the instructions and consolations of the Holy Comforter. "If any man will do his will, he shall know of the doctrine." "The eye being single, the whole body is full of light." "The work of righteousness is peace, and the effect of righteousness quietness, and assurance for ever."

The faithful use of former gifts secures the bestowment of more, and true happiness, reputation, and usefulness, increase with advancing time. (Matt. xiii. 12.) Those who so act are the true nobility of mankind; doing real and hearty service now, and certain of divine commendation and love when earthly coronets and titles shall be forgotten. Such answer the scriptural idea of sincerity; transparency of character, and incorruption of motive; and this unity, simplicity, integrity, and energy of character, invest them with a mighty charm and influence for good. Oh, the dignity and importance which such conduct attaches to every action of life! Imparting the grandeur of eternity to the hourly events of time, and making the humble offerings and services of every passing day productive of consequences of everlasting advantage and delight.

How blessed, too, is its influence on the heart and life! How does it prompt to and facilitate in the toil of labour and the exercise of prayer! Giving begets labour. Both together beget prayer. The largest givers and workers are generally most earnest in prayer. Working shows the need for funds, and disposes the heart to supply them. The difficulty of toil, and the need of divine power being realised for the performance of such a stupendous work, the soul is filled with ardent desire, and presses to the footstool of Omnipotence for the bestowment of that blessing which alone can give success. Unquestionably, as a rule, prayer, labour, and sacrifice, strengthen each other. Labour lays the train of means and agencies supplied by benevolence, and prayer invokes the sacred spark, to prostrate the will of human obduracy and pride, and transform it to love.

Exertion constructs the line of influences of the means which intelligent affection consecrates, and believing prayer charges the battery, and attracts the electric power which connects the might of Omnipotence with the feebleness of humanity.

The combination of prayer, sacrifice, and labour, in the spirit of humility, imparts confidence, tranquillity, and satisfaction to the soul. It is only in such conduct that the heart derives any real and substantial joy from property.

There is no true pleasure realised in acquiring it for its own sake. The appetite enlarges with the supply. Desire fulfilled expands for a larger grasp. The fuller the realisation, the farther from contentment and satisfaction. But there is true bliss and lofty consistency where there is conscious integrity in limiting personal gratifications for enlarged dedication.

If the reader would enjoy self-respect, peace of conscience, and the complacent smile of his God and Saviour, let him adopt the system of offering now commended.

(3.) Its design and tendency to assimilate to God in principle, action, and bliss.

The highest dignity and happiness of being is resemblance to God in holiness and active benevolence. The loftier the powers possessed, and the nobler the nature, the larger the range of possible beneficence. God himself exists and operates by choice, for the benefit of all; and by the bestowment of heartfelt religion, he puts this pre-eminent honour on man, beyond the gift of personal salvation, of qualifying and employing him to dispense to his fellow-men blessings of infinite worth. Thus men become channels of God's bounty and mirrors of his character. How truly blessed must it be thus to sympathise with God; to have as our great aim the extension of his praise; to make the hourly earnings of time, the fruit of the exercise of the brain, of the hands, and of the lips, the instruments of his glory. Our heavenly Father would have us thus imitate himself in benevolence, usefulness, and happiness, and in finding our bliss rather in dispensing than enjoying. He who is above want gives in infinite profusion, and is intensely gratified in beholding the joy which his bounty imparts. He would have us rise superior to cravings after enjoyment, and to find our delight in the luxury of giving. In this view the Saviour wears the charm of indescribable loveliness, and feels the throb of purest pleasure. "He who was rich for our sakes became poor, that we through his poverty might be rich." His constant and boundless beneficence proved to his great and compassionate heart a source of unspeakable alleviation and comfort under his agonising travail, as "a man of sorrow." His ever-augmenting mental anguish in bearing the burden of the curse of sin, could not stifle the intense satisfaction of his spirit, in the consciousness that his own temporary agonies would effect the deliverance of millions from unending sorrow. And has this example no constraining influence on us to seek in the measure of our power resemblance to him?

The Saviour speaks of being "glorified in his people;" and Paul writes of "the life of Christ being manifest in their mortal body." And what is this, but that Christians are to live in as near imitation of Christ as possible, in purity; and in cheerful, self-sacrificing toil and beneficence; to perpetuate in every regenerated man, through time, some feeble imitation of the holy image and gracious labours of the Son of God? Who could wish to reach a higher position than to understand and practise the great maxim and principle of the life of Christ,—"It is more blessed to give than to receive?" God himself knows no higher joy than to give freely and abundantly what none but himself has to communicate. Be it yours, Christian, as far as possible, thus to resemble him!

(4.) The opportunity thus possessed of peculiarly and extensively glorifying God.

Man, as far as we know, is the only creature privileged to give, and to behold its happy effects. The inferior creatures know not the value of their services to man. Angels cannot benefit each other or man, as man can his brother. The field opened for the advancement of the divine glory in the moral elevation of man by means of property is beyond belief. It can sustain vast and multiform agencies for this object. Men of the world, with their views, may reasonably regard property as the *great good*, the end of all means, because the representative of all earthly possessions. They seek it as their portion, and desire, as they believe in, no equal good. With the Christian it is far different. The good of earth is only the inferior part of his inheritance, not to be prized for itself so much, as that it can be made subservient to the recovery of man to the image and favour of God, and the establishment on earth of the reign of righteousness and peace. What end like this can property secure? If used mainly for personal advancement and gratification, while a scanty pittance is doled out to religion, how poor and contemptible a thing is it! Thus employed, how does it weld upon the heaven-born soul those moral fetters which hold it fast to this perishing earth! But if it be diffused over the broad field of benevolent labour, its very character will be changed, it will pass through the alembic of a divine operator, and its fruits of honour to God and advantage to man will be rich and ever enduring. By the consecration of property it is given to man in a peculiar and palpable manner to manifest his love and gratitude to Christ. The act of dedicating to his glory that which all account precious, and only part with from necessity, magnifies him; and gives the offering a worth and power for good beyond conception. To employ the treasures of time for mere earthly purposes is for them to perish in the using. Their expenditure for the education of the human mind, the consolation of the afflicted, and the renovation of souls, is to exercise them in polishing the richest gems of God's universe, immortal spirits, for the enjoyment and honour of Christ. It is more. It is to store up for ourselves true and enduring riches of friendship and grateful love in the everlasting habitations of bliss, when the labours of life shall have finished, and the treasures of earth perished. (Luke, xvi. 9.)

After all that the Scriptures affirm to the contrary, it must be allowed that man in general, and even many professors of religion, regard property as the real and chief good. Neither is it less evident that accumulation intensifies desire for more. Here is the snare and peril of wealth. It is difficult to conceive of a means better adapted to prevent this God-dishonouring estimate and perilous accumulation by persons in prosperity, than by *the weekly dedication of a sum proportioned to increase.*

The method serves as a safety-valve for the dangerous condition of prosperity, proving as much a preservation to givers as a benefit to receivers.

How affecting, weighty, and significant the exclamation of Christ, " How hardly shall they that have riches enter into the kingdom of God!" How strongly does it indicate the probability of their unwise and selfish appropriation! God would make Christians, by the dedication of property and labour, the dispensers of every form of blessing. He would thus make the tenderness and disinterested goodness of Christ to operate in ever-varying forms of beauty and beneficence in every locality of earth, and towards every class of sufferers. He would have them so to employ present good as to secure from it an imperishable fund of glory and delight when it shall no more exist. Oh, for grace, wisdom, and fidelity, so to use the talents of property, speech, and influence, as to increase the redeemed of mankind, and add to the glory of the Son of God!

(5.) The certainty of personal sufficiency in a course of faithful devotedness.

Can the fear ever for a moment be harboured that devotion to God conduces to loss? To have, and not to give, is to make possession a burden and curse, rather than, as was intended, a pleasure and blessing. It is to miss the true end and present enjoyment of possession. It is to provoke God to withdraw it from us, as much in mercy as in judgment towards us.

To distribute in proportion to receipts is truly to enjoy and faithfully to use. It is to make it wise, safe, and delightful for the giver to bestow more. He who gives from love to God, the very God of love will communicate to him in full measure supplies which shall bear the legible signature of the Giver.

To give in proportion to receipts is to sanctify the remainder with a special excellence and value, the divine benediction giving it the power, like the widow's oil and the bread of blessing, of extending over the full range of your necessities. It is a kind of devotion of all, making your food holy and your attire sacred. Here is the path of true plenty, on the promise of the omnipotent and faithful God. **He who depends on this shall have sufficiency** when the supplies of others fail. "My God shall supply all your need, according to his riches in glory by Christ Jesus." Men often deceive themselves by purposing to do better under more prosperous circumstances. Man's obligation springs from present condition; for this alone is he responsible. Faithfulness therein leads to increase; resistance of the dictates of conscience often conducts to adversity.

An aged Christian gave his history thus :—" Early in life I improved my condition. I resolved at marriage to devote a fixed portion of my income, and to increase the amount should my means enlarge. I prospered, aud became comparatively wealthy. I thought of my resolution, but grudged to perform it; a crowd of disasters almost ruined me. I mourned my unfaithfulness, and determined never to act so again, if indulged with returning success. I again reached a state of comfort and plenty with the same unhappy results, and again came adversity. I bless God now for freeing me from the snare of wealth, seeing I have twice proved my unfitness to be trusted with it."

Whoever heard of faithful devotion bringing final disaster? Instances of its results in blessing might be adduced almost innumerable. How significant is it, that Solomon, whose father David made the largest offering to God, himself became, by the divine blessing, the wealthiest and wisest of men!

(6.) It would secure a rich and unwonted measure of divine blessing. Unquestionably the detention of property from God is one great cause of the absence of temporal and spiritual prosperity. The Church is unfit for either; it is therefore withheld in mercy.

If unfaithful in little, what would she be with much, without a thorough change, but more grasping, guilty, and miserable?

If the present covetousness of Christians were exchanged for true liberality and consecration, and their worldliness for lofty spirituality, what a surprising and delightful change would come over both her temporal and spiritual state! " Then would her barns be filled with plenty, and her presses burst out with new wine."

God employs in his spiritual kingdom agents cherishing true

sympathy of heart with himself. Probably the cases of Balaam among prophets, and Judas among apostles, and their fearful close, were designed to put in the strongest light the need of this true heart sympathy. The chief cause of its absence under their advantages was covetousness. Can it be doubted that the same element largely affects the present condition of the Church?

The prominent features of the early Christian Church were entire consecration and glorious success. Who can doubt the force of their mutual influence? Are not her present features the reverse of these? Can *their* mutual influence be any more doubtful? What does she now need to be as morally courageous and as spiritually victorious, but to be as thoroughly consecrated to her Lord? God waits for this. "Bring all the goods into the storehouse, and prove me now herewith, if I will not open the windows of heaven, and pour you out a blessing." With this conduct, straitness would give place to abundance, and plenty to overflowing fulness. "For brass I will bring gold, and for iron I will bring silver, and for wood brass, and for stones iron." (Isaiah, lx. 17.) The state of heart that should secure large temporal blessings, would also realise those of higher nature in copious measure. When once the love of the Church shall lay on God's altar a full and appropriate sacrifice, and believingly implore the blessing of the Holy Spirit to make it effective, a new and glorious path shall open before her. And why is this blessed state of things, so richly predicted, so long delayed?

The price of redemption is paid,—the promised Spirit is bestowed,—the power of the Gospel is evinced in its past triumphs. If such scenes as were then beheld attended the zealous consecration of a few, what unthought-of blessings shall the Church experience when all her members shall live supremely for this object! Whenever there shall be this universal, faithful, and earnest self-dedication in heart, energy, and property, emulating the first Christians in vigour and devotedness, and aiming to realise the experience of their triumphs; a heavenly power will attend her, and a spiritual radiance will invest her, bearing her onward to unearthly conquests and glory.

The page of prophecy sparkles with animating disclosures of her coming prosperity and dignity. But why is the *boon* so long delayed? Is not he who gave the promise both able and ready to grant it to *a prepared and an expecting Church?*

The consecration of herself to her Redeemer in the spirit of true devotion, and her earnest pleading for the fulfilment of prophecy, as the one desire of her soul, would be the dawn of the day of divine power. It would be as though Prophecy, unable longer to endure the delay imposed for ages by the apathy of the Church, would bound to speedy accomplishment!

As if Jehovah, unwilling longer to allow the taunts of sceptics and the prostration of his cause, would lift his Zion by the might of his love and power to the position she has in vain been taught to desire, to be henceforth the envy and admiration of the world! As if the Saviour, wearied with the long delay of his purchased reward, and the Spirit of his predicted conquests, would bring on the instant fulfilment of that glorious summary of prophecy, (Isaiah, lx.); and, as in a moment, make " the little one become a thousand, and the small one a strong people ! "

(7.) Its influence on our present and eternal condition and happiness.

God made man for happiness, and conferred on him the means of its enjoyment. Universal man desires and seeks it. The great question is, What is it, and where is it to be found? It is found in *being* like, and in *doing* like God. It springs from the state of the heart, and is little dependent on outward circumstances. It is not to be found in science, wealth, or luxury. Man lost it by selfish indulgence, and attempted independence of his Maker. God has arranged, of his own free cost and love, to recover man to the same. This is only possible by man's compliance with the requirements of his original condition; living gratefully and dependently upon God, and lovingly and kindly towards men,

It is the wise and gracious purpose of God, to make man the instrumental agent of the fact and measure of his own present and eternal felicity. This depends on the principles which he adopts, and the life he pursues on earth,

Personal happiness is realised in the exercise of faith in Jesus Christ; and in usefulness and holiness, after the example of his life. This may be the portion of rich and poor. To decline this faith and imitation of Christ is to reject the essentials of true bliss: to embrace the same is to find rest, safety, and purity. It is to live for God; and to make the duties and expenditure of life conduce to the honour of God, the good of men, and our own preparation for bliss. It is thus man qualifies for heaven; associates even now in spirit and labours with those who are its denizens, and stores up for himself without design an ever-satisfying and imperishable inheritance. Oh, to be welcomed to heaven by those we have allured and guided thither, or to whom, though to us unknown, we conveyed the means of their salvation! Oh, to traverse with them its wide range in endless joy and purest friendship, feeling that we were blessed to help them thither by the exertions and sacrifices of time! Oh, to have the joy of eternity savour of the bliss of participation by others whom we won thither, and of adoring gratitude to the glorified Saviour for the bestowment of such exalted honour!

Christian! in addition to other most weighty reasons, the fulness and perfection, the richness and intensity, of your eternal felicity, demand of you the dedication of property to the work of winning souls to God and heaven, rather than its expenditure to clothe your person in rich attire, or gratify your appetite with pleasant viands. By this means you will stud your Saviour's diadem with the ever-shining gems, and delight your own spirit with ever new and satisfying joys.

Conclusion.

Let us seriously reflect what would have been the present condition of the world had all Christians of former ages acted up to their full obligations, and what had been their higher satisfaction in the consciousness of their fidelity, and the recognition of its blessed consequences. While we lament the sad results of their deficiencies, let us rise with appropriate earnestness to this noble consecration.

What must be the effect of such remembrances as these in

eternity? Who shall say they have no existence? "I professed on earth to love Christ, and to live to his glory, yet I never seriously and prayerfully sought to know the proper principle and measure of pecuniary consecration. I laid my plans, and employed time, talents, and energies, chiefly to acquire earthly possessions. By the time I had gained a competency, its surrender was required of me; and that which might have been turned to unspeakable account in honouring God and benefiting man, I failed to render productive of any real and lasting good"

"I," reflects another, "put away the claims of humanity and religion with the smallest pittance I could for shame bestow. I expended my all to live in luxury and display. Now the foolish dream of indulgence is over, and the good I could have done with my resources has no place in the divine records of earthly beneficence, chiefly to my own infinite and irreparable loss."

"I," reflects another, "feared to leave my children to the care of a gracious and faithful God; and in observing my anxiety to grasp and retain for them the treasures of time, they reached the conviction that they were the best inheritance, and could be persuaded to seek no other."

"I," observes another, "saw no value in property equal to that of using it to glorify my Saviour in promoting the holiness and happiness of man. Now I find, to my unspeakable joy, that though myself saved entirely by grace, the glorious results of the labours and sacrifices of time remain to me in the forms of imperishable riches and eternal delights, repaying with infinite interest every service and voluntary privation of earth."

No conjecture as to the final condition of such representatives of great classes of men will be ventured. That is left to the judgment of the reader. That such cogitations are indulged, who can doubt, while he admits that memory, conscience, and sense of responsibility, are imperishable?

How thrilling and significant the picture sketched by the great Teacher of him, who, in the night of his self-gratulation over the fulness of his possessions, and of decisions for future sensual enjoyment, was summoned to his final account; and that also of him, who, having just closed a life of selfish luxury on earth, "in hell lift up his eyes, being in torments, seeing Abraham afar off, and Lazarus in his bosom!" "They nourished their hearts as in a day of slaughter, and heaped up treasures for the last days;" the witnesses of their unfaithfulness and inhumanity, and the sources of their immitigable anguish. Beware lest in any measure you imitate their conduct, and share their doom. Will any regret in eternity the practice of economy and sacrifice to increase the amount of their offerings? Will not many for ever bitterly lament its absence?

Oh, the joy and surprise of those whose humble, but faithful devotion, shall receive the welcome and commendation of their Lord: "*Well done, good and faithful servant; thou hast been faithful over a few things, I will make thee ruler over many things: enter thou into the joy of thy Lord.*"

Oh, the consternation that will seize the souls of that numerous class represented by him, who pleaded, in justification of his unfaithfulness, that he hid his talent in the earth, when they hear the sovereign Judge pronounce, in tones that shall *awake* them to the dread reality of their past unfaithfulness, and of their eternal infamy and poverty, while stripping them of the last vestige of communicated goodness, "*Take from the unprofitable servant the talent, and cast him into outer darkness.*"

It has been attempted to show that it is the sacred obligation of all Christians, poor and rich, to sustain and extend the cause of religion and the true interests of mankind — that the amount contributed should be decided by the means possessed, the relation of sacred stewardship, and the immense obligations and demands of the all-diffusing dispensation of grace—that the best method of its consecration is the weekly assessment of the gains or income of the period, and that considerations involving the glory of God, the welfare of men, and their own eternal honour and felicity, invite to the immediate, hearty, and conscientious exercise of this system.

Christian reader! seriously consider the solemn mandate of thy Lord; it may be but now thrilling thy very soul : " Give an account of thy stewardship!" Hast thou forgotten thy true position, and expended for past gratification, or accumulated for future contingencies, that which, both of original right and by purchase of blood, belongs to him,—that which thou hast vowed to use for his glory? Canst thou peacefully think of meeting thy Saviour Prince while indulging in such dishonesty? Wilt thou not at once ease thine heart, and honour thy Lord, by surrendering what thou hast so long withheld, in disregard of the crying necessities of a woe-stricken world? If thou wilt do this, thou mayest yet rise to happiness, usefulness, and honour, and prove to observing men that thy religion is more than an empty name; that it is a self-sacrificing, sublime, and heaven-born reality and power, pregnant with issues of unspeakable good.

If thou wilt not, beware lest he summarily close thy unfaithful stewardship.

If thou sayest, "I will do as I choose with my own," and dost still withhold thy property from his cause, dost thou not thereby prove thyself alien from Christ? Is not thy hope of religion a delusion?—a spark of thine own kindling?—an *ignis fatuus*, arising from the swamps of thy pride and self-sufficiency? leading thee under the promise of glory to endless darkness and despair? Be assured that the light of religion that is kindled at the altar of divine love has warmth of grateful affection, as well as clearness of mental perception; and cannot fail to move the heart of its possessor to deeds of loving devotion.

But if thou canst make no recompense for the past, what is thy solemn purpose for the future? Wilt thou put it aside as Utopian and impracticable? or wilt thou honestly seek to know thy condition and fulfil thy trust? Dost thou regard this plan as reasonable and feasible? Wilt thou then commence its practice in penitent and grateful love? Canst thou fairly and dispassionately invalidate it? or has it won thy mind with the force of conviction, and thy heart to the solemn purpose of self-devotion? With the urgent necessities of hundreds of millions of thy fellow-immortals, groaned forth in wailings of earthly misery, and in unaffected agony of soul-tremblings, and with the infinite claims of the self-sacrificing God-Man, demanding its instant and entire consecration; wilt thou, reader, henceforth systematically devote a due proportion of thy property, or wilt thou act without rule or principle, and abide by the consequences?

Motives of the most cogent nature impel to a faithful dedication of property to God, ranging from mere reason and self-interest to the loftiest benevolence, gratitude, and self-improvement, and the glorification and imitation of God himself.

Insensibility to taste, beauty, refinement, and enjoyment, is no dictate either of true manliness or Christian sobriety. Still it were well, if, on grounds of *reason alone*, men in general and Christians especially, would give more heed to the testimony of universal and ever-accumulating experience, that it is vain and degrading to attempt to satisfy the cravings of the human spirit with material good; and that it is beneath the dignity of man to be ardently devoted to, and lavish of expenditure on, matters of style and equipage; while the less-favoured multitude manifestly enjoy all the essential elements of happiness without them; and seeing that the means of their cost might be applied to objects so immensely superior.

On grounds of reason, who has not admired the sentiment of Paul? " When I was a child I spake as a child, I understood as a child, I thought as a child; but when I became a man, I put away childish things." To a disciplined and matured mind what are the pageantry of retinue, the luxury of sumptuous fare, the lustre of costly attire, or the relish of pleasurable excitement,—as the chief result of property and pursuit of life? If men of the world exercise no higher reason than this, surely it becomes those who are taught of God—the expectants of eternal glory—to moderate these indulgences by the higher appreciation and more ardent anticipation of glories and delights, in comparison of which the brightest splendours and the richest joys of earth are not to be named.

Reader, if you have any regard for personal responsibility, fidelity, honour, and safety, in a condition of most solemn trust; or if you feel any strivings of holy ambition to share in the task and triumph of bringing about the world's subjugation to Christ, unite in this dedication your intelligence and affection. If you possess a spark of love for Him who deemed not his life and blood too precious a gift to save and bless you,—if you would not render the gracious purpose of your creation, the reasonable expectations of the Divine Redeemer, and your own hopes of salvation, abortive,—or if there live in your breast any emotion of real compassion towards those who joy not in your safety and bliss, live to God.

If you retain the exercise of any *true sense, prudent forethought, and righteous self-love*, and would tremble so to live on earth as to find yourself homeless, friendless, and portionless in eternity; and if you would have the existence of time prove you to be a gracious, God-like being, worthy of elevation to a nobler future, without dishonour to your Benefactor; and not a creature of all-absorbing selfishness, insensible to every generous emotion, and incapable of improvement, be persuaded at once to commence a life of true and grateful consecration.

In view of man's necessities, your own consistency and bliss, and above all, of your Saviour's love, what is your solemn purpose? Form it! Let it stand for ever!

"Who is willing to consecrate his service this day unto the Lord?" Let him join the noble and ever-increasing band of those who, like their divine Lord, find higher satisfaction in promoting the elevation and salvation of man than in personal ease and enjoyment;—those who, cheerfully sharing with him the toils and sacrifices of earth, shall through grace also participate of his felicities and triumphs in heaven.

Divine Spirit! baptize the Church with a God-like liberality and devotedness, that she may speedily prove "a crown of glory in the hand of the Lord, and a royal diadem in the hand of her God." Then shall the anthem of earth's long-predicted jubilee, swelling from land to land the strengthening shout of human tongues, and waking up the response of heaven, unite earth and heaven in the triumphant chorus, "*Now is come salvation and strength, and the kingdom of our God, and the power of his Christ.*" "*Alleluia, for the Lord God omnipotent reigneth.*"

The Christian Steward.

AN ESSAY ON THE RIGHT APPROPRIATION OF INCOMES,

WHETHER DERIVED FROM BUSINESS, SALARIES, WAGES,
OR OTHER SOURCES;

WITH

SPECIMEN ACCOUNTS OF MONIES

DEVOTED TO RELIGIOUS AND BENEVOLENT OBJECTS.

CONTENTS.

	PAGE
INTRODUCTION	339
THREE OBJECTS TO WHICH A PERSON'S INCOME SHOULD BE APPLIED	341
I. A certain proportion is to be taken for defraying Personal and Family Expenses	,,
II. Another portion is to be allowed to accumulate as Capital	342
Some persons suppose it is sinful for Christians to lay up property	,,
Others think it is right for Communities to accumulate, not individuals	344
Benefit Societies and Savings' Banks	347
Deferred Annuities and Life Assurance	349
III. A proper share is to be devoted to God	350
Exposition—" Let every one of you "	,,
" Lay by him in store "	353
" On the first day of the week "	354
" As God has prospered him "	356
Two common cases of family mismanagement	358
What amount should be devoted to the service of God	362
The sin of Covetousness	365
" That there be no gatherings when I come "	367
REASONS FOR USING A FORM OF DEDICATION	368
DESIRABLENESS OF KEEPING ACCOUNTS	370
STATEMENT OF THE CLAIMS OF DIFFERENT OBJECTS	,,
The support of the Pastor	,,
Education of young men for the Ministry	375
Colleges	376
The Poor	378
Schools	379
Home, Irish, and Colonial Missions	,,
Our Colonies	380
The Jews	,,
The Heathen	381
THE INFLUENCES OF THE HOLY SPIRIT NECESSARY	382
THE PROPOSED ACCOUNT-BOOK, AND EXPLANATION OF THE ACCOUNTS	383
FORM OF DEDICATION, AND OBJECTS OF BENEVOLENCE, No. I.	387
SPECIMEN OF ACCOUNTS, No. I.	388
FORM OF DEDICATION, AND OBJECTS OF BENEVOLENCE, No. II.	392
SPECIMEN OF ACCOUNTS, No. II.	394
BLANK FORMS	399

THE CHRISTIAN STEWARD.

An immense weight of obligation lies on the professed disciples of the blessed Redeemer. They are His appointed instruments for extending his kingdom in the world. To do this, both men and money are required,—men to proclaim the glad tidings of salvation, and money to sustain them in their self-denying and arduous labours. But it is necessary that appropriate means be used to obtain both these requisites. To personal exertions we shall not advert, but it will be the aim of this Essay to point out what is considered to be defective in the present mode of *devoting property* to charitable and religious purposes,—to show what is the Scriptural rule, and to recommend its more general adoption.

Various able treatises have lately appeared on Covetousness, and the duty and privilege of liberality. The perusal of these works cannot be too strongly recommended, particularly "Mammon" by Dr. Harris, and "Covetousness" by Mr. Treffry. But there is a duty, even prior to that of *giving* liberally, which we think has not been sufficiently inculcated or practised,—we mean, the deliberate appropriation and setting apart of a certain portion of a person's income, to be ready for distribution as occasions arise. That this is a plain duty, incumbent on all, we gather from the exhortation of the Apostle Paul to the Corinthians (1 Cor. xvi. 2): "Upon the first day of the week, let every one of you LAY BY HIM IN STORE, as God hath prospered him, that there be no gatherings when I come." It will be one of the main objects of this Essay to impress on Christians the desirableness and importance of duly attending to this precept.

The present, compared with former times, is an age of much liberality, yet, still, great improvement might be effected in the *manner* and *motive* of giving to religious objects, as well as in the amount contributed.

With few exceptions, men give their property at present to benevolent institutions more from *impulse* than consideration, —more from *feeling* than principle. They do not sit down composedly and prayerfully to determine how much of their weekly or yearly earnings ought to be devoted to God. Neither do they calmly compare the relative claims of the different objects to which they are called to contribute, and apportion their donations accordingly. The consequence is, that too much is left to the spur of the moment, and hence a common inquiry addressed to a collector, is, " How much did I pay last?" Or a list of subscribers is asked for, that the inquirer, casting his eye over it, may be guided by what others give. Far too much of the support which all voluntary associations receive, depends on the qualifications of the person who is chosen as collector. A good applicant for subscriptions must possess fluency of speech, and tact in suiting himself to the character and disposition of those whom he addresses. These things ought not so to be, for men should give according to the *merits* of the object; and not because of the influence or persuasion of the individual who makes the collection.

Of course it is not meant that the choice of collectors is a matter of no importance. On the contrary, it is necessary that they be intelligent and judicious persons; able when required properly to advocate and explain the object of the Society they represent. All we condemn is, the great want of right motives, sufficient reflection, and just discrimination as to the claims of different objects on the part of subscribers generally.

It appears from the fore-cited and other verses in the two Epistles to the Corinthians, that the Apostle was very anxious that the Gentile Churches should make liberal collections to relieve the necessities of the poor and persecuted Christians of Judea. He had already counselled the Galatians to proceed in an orderly manner. The precise directions to them, however, have not been left on record; but under the inspiration of the Holy Spirit, and, doubtless, for the instruction and guidance of all future generations, he laid down the general rules contained in the verse quoted. Circumstances are somewhat altered since these directions were given. There were then no charitable institutions, such as Hospitals, Asylums, or religious Societies—the glory of our age—in operation, to which men might devote their property; but the objects to which the charity of the early Christians was directed, and those to which the pious of our day devote their attention, were in reality the same. They were twofold—the care of the body, and the salvation of the soul. This collection, which Paul carried to Jerusalem, is an instance of the relief afforded to the bodily wants of the poor; and in various passages in the New Testament it is laid down as the bounden duty, as it was also the practice of the early Christians, to support, by their pecuniary contributions and hospitality, those among the disciples who were especially set apart for administering the divine ordinances, conducting public worship, and extending the knowledge of the gospel around them.

Before, however, we proceed to the chief object of this treatise, —THE DUTY OF DEVOTING, LAYING UP, AND EXPENDING A CERTAIN PORTION OF INCOME FOR RELIGIOUS PURPOSES— it will be well to inquire, "What are the different ways in which a man or a woman's earnings or income, be it large or small, may be spent, so as to meet with God's approval?

It appears plain that there are three objects to which it should be appropriated:—

    1st. A certain proportion is to be taken for defraying Personal and Family expenses.
    2d. Another portion is to be allowed to accumulate as Capital.
    3d. A proper share is to be devoted to God.

No one will question, but that God requires the first of these objects to be duly attended to. Every one is to be housed, clothed, and fed out of the proceeds of his industry, or the accumulations of himself or of his ancestors. This need not be urged on our readers; the only danger is, that too much be taken for this purpose.

With regard to the second, there has been, and continues to be, considerable difference of opinion. Some persons go so far as to affirm, that it is sinful for Christians to lay up property. They say, it is a distrust of God's providence and care, to store up money for the future provision of themselves or their families. They attempt to support their opinions by the misapplication of such texts as these, "Lay not up for yourselves treasures upon earth;" "The love of money is the root of all evil;" "Woe to him that ladeth himself with thick clay;" "Go to now, ye rich men, weep and howl for your miseries that shall come upon you. Your riches are corrupted," &c.

The common sense of mankind, however, as well as Scripture, when rightly compared and interpreted, is so totally opposed to these views, that there are few persons who actually carry them into practice. Yet still, we have observed, that public speakers and writers, when advocating the liberal support of religious and charitable institutions, and denouncing covetousness, use expressions which savour too strongly of these notions. It would appear as if they thought, that for it to be said of a professor of religion that he died rich, was affirming something, which, if not quite incompatible with his Christian character, was, at least, inconsistent with it. But rightly to judge in such a case, it should be inquired, whether he gave an adequate proportion to God while alive. If he did, why should obloquy be cast upon his memory? Whom has he offended?

The persons, who, in their over-zeal for the cause they are advocating, use such language, would not deny, that it is very right and proper for men generally to accumulate property. In fact, they must do so, if the high pitch at which man, in his social relations, has arrived, is to be maintained. If some persons did not possess capital, we could not sustain or make any further progress in the comforts and conveniences of life. All advancement in civilisation must be stopped. Capital is indispensable to build ships, sink mines, make roads, and construct houses; in fact, without capital we must immediately retrograde. Science, literature, and art, would, of necessity, fall to decay; and mankind relapse into the depths of barbarism. Where civilisation is declining, it is a sure sign that morals and religion have sunk, and are still sinking; for there never has been, and never will be, any prevalence of true religion, without a corresponding advance in everything beneficial to the temporal welfare of man. Where men honour and obey God, there, in an eminent degree, will be found the enjoyment of the substantial comforts connected with civilised life.

But these advantages can only be obtained through the accumulation of money as the means; and it must follow, that if Christians are not to increase their property, and civilisation is to be maintained and be progressive, it must be left solely to the men of the world to promote it. There will then arise this absurdity, that Christianity is the great civiliser, but Christians must not help forward civilisation—that it is right to promote the well-being of the soul, but wrong to add to the comforts of the body.

Besides, how can the following precept, which is the natural order of things, properly be obeyed, unless parents make some provision for their offspring? "Children ought not to lay up for the parents, but parents for the children."* It must, therefore, be lawful for them to do this; and taking care not to defraud God of his due, it certainly is the duty of all who have the opportunity, thus to provide for the well-being of the rising generation. Those who have acquired sufficient property for accomplishing this object, would expend it, either in giving their children a good education, to fit them for professional or other avocations, or, as in a great majority of cases, in setting them up in business.

The great body of the people, however, it is obvious, could not act thus. Their duty is to lay out as much as other claims will allow, in giving their offspring the best education in their power, that, as they grow up to adult age, they may be able to turn the

* 2 Corinthians, xii. 14.

labour of their hands to the best advantage, and cultivate their own minds as facilities may arise.

The following passages will show, that there is Scriptural authority for this common-sense view of the subject. The clear import of which is, that property is, in itself, a blessing, and only becomes a curse if wrongly employed. "The hand of the diligent maketh rich;" "He that gathereth in summer is a wise son;" "The blessing of the Lord, it maketh rich, and he addeth no sorrow with it;" "And the Lord hath blessed my master (Abraham) greatly, and he is become great, and he hath given him flocks, and herds, and silver, and gold," &c.; "And Isaac sowed in that land, and received in the same year an hundred-fold, and the Lord blessed him; and the man waxed great, and went forward, and grew, until he became very great."

There are others who think that, though it be wrong for individuals to accumulate wealth, it is right for *communities* to do so, —that men should labour for the general good, and their earnings be thrown into a common store, to be distributed to them again as their necessities require. This plan has been long and extensively tried by very different classes of persons—religious and non-religious. The monastic institutions of Catholic countries are, in a great degree, founded on this principle. Among Protestants the system has been partially adopted by the Moravians. It has also been a favourite idea among sceptics and infidels, and many attempts have been made by them to establish societies on this basis.

But these unnatural, and, we may say, unscriptural organisations, have never been found to succeed so as to produce any marked beneficial results superior to what have been attained in the ordinary arrangement of society, where each individual mainly labours for his own advantage and that of his family. Wherever these experiments have been tried without religion, they have miserably failed. Where connected with a truly religious society, the piety of the sect has prevented any great degree of evil from resulting. But we have only to read the pages of history, and to look around us, to perceive that this system is neither productive nor preservative of religion,—usually the contrary; certainly it does not tend to promote the progress of civilisation. The minds of the members composing such societies appear to be stunted; all prospect of individual benefit, from extra mental exertion, being cut off, few and feeble efforts are made by such communities to advance the arts, science, or literature.

It is true, just after the ascension of our Lord, when everything was in a transition state—when Jewish rituals and ceremonies were being superseded by Christian institutions—the plan of having "all things common"* was sanctioned and acted upon for a short time by the apostles. This may be accounted for by the then peculiar and unsettled state of the Church at Jerusalem. The early Jewish converts were excommunicated and anathematised by the Jewish authorities; and many of them, probably, were compelled to give up their former employments, and seek new modes of gaining a livelihood. To what extent the community of goods was carried, we are not informed, but it is plain that such a state of things could not long continue; and, in fact, we soon find that dissatisfaction prevailed as to the existing arrangements: "And there arose a murmuring of the Grecians against the Hebrews, because their widows were neglected in the daily ministration,"† and it appears probable, that, from that time, the practice fell gradually into disuse; for, thenceforward, neither in the Acts of the Apostles, nor in the Epistles, do we find any allusion to such an organisation.

For every one to reap the fruit of his own industry, is, doubtless, the most beneficial constitution of society. This is the most potent stimulus to exertion, both mental and bodily. That men should reap as they sow, is the great principle running through all the Divine arrangements. Throwing all into one stock counteracts this natural order,—the idle and industrious must, in a great measure, be placed on a level.

Such a system cannot but be wrong, because it affords no room for the exercise of the benevolent and charitable dispositions of *individuals*. Any acts of generosity which such communities may perform must be provided for out of the common stock.

* Acts, ii. 44; iv. 32. † Acts, vi. 1.

The gift would be mainly that of the ruling powers, the deed would be *official*, and the thanks correspondingly *formal*. During the Irish famine what a difference was there in the feelings excited in the minds of both the givers and recipients, between the *spontaneous offerings* of the people of England and the *Parliamentary Grant!* How much greater was the moral influence of the former, though the latter offering was vastly superior in amount!

Further, there is an instinctive feeling in the hearts of all right-minded parents to prefer the welfare of their own children before that of others. They naturally and properly wish to see their offspring happy, useful, and prosperous in the world. But where children are brought up in communities (such as have been referred to), the exercise of this natural parental feeling, implanted by God, cannot rightly develop itself.

But it may be said, "What has all this that has been affirmed, of the advantage and propriety of the individual accumulation of property, to do with the mass of the people?—surely it can only be applicable to persons of wealth,—to those who are making considerable profits by business, or who have large incomes from fixed property?" The subject, however, is of primary importance to a very large part of the population,—to all who are just entering on the active concerns of life, and are beginning to earn money. It applies to the young universally, and, perhaps, with some exceptions, to all who are in full work, or in the receipt of income.

We believe it to be a duty, the beneficial result of which, both morally and temporally, it is almost impossible to overrate, for young persons of both sexes to begin life with a determination not to spend all their earnings, as they arise, for what they suppose to be their immediate wants. They should look a little into futurity. But how lamentable is it that this is so little considered! Still, we do think, notwithstanding the vast amount of improvidence and reckless expenditure in dress, drink, smoking, and other wasteful practices, which is exhibited all around, that provident habits are beginning more extensively to prevail. Yet there can be no doubt, but that the sad extent to which these pernicious customs are carried, is a main cause of the vast amount of misery which is everywhere to be found.

It would be hopeless to expect, that the great body of the labouring classes could ever amass sufficient property to secure themselves, in any good degree, from the casualties and vicissitudes arising from want of work, from sickness, and old age. What individuals, however, cannot do, may be effected by men united in societies on the principle of mutual assistance. This has been tried with regard to sickness and old age, with most beneficial results—we need hardly say, we refer to those institutions denominated "Benefit Societies," or "Clubs." Whether this principle can ever be applied to loss of work seems very doubtful, most probably it never will; and the labourer who nobly wishes to maintain an honourable independence of alms and parochial relief, will have to depend on savings accumulated when in full employment. It should, indeed, excite the liveliest gratitude to the Almighty, that with regard to those two evils, sickness and old age—to which all are exposed—and which no foresight can avert, he has led men to adopt expedients, by which, so far as pecuniary means are concerned, the sufferings incident to them may be greatly alleviated, if not entirely removed.

For men and women to connect themselves with such institutions, is the most beneficial way in which all, who have to depend on their labour, can accumulate capital. The best thing that can be said to such is, "Join a Club as soon as possible. If you are able to save more from your earnings than is required for this purpose, as very many can, by all means place the money in a Savings' Bank." But these institutions are far inferior to clubs in usefulness, for a single sickness may absorb the deposits of years, and leave the depositor destitute, or dependent on parish relief. The Almighty sends sickness or health to individuals as seemeth good in his sight. Every man or woman, in joining a Benefit Society, places himself at His disposal. So long as God appoints health, the depositor in a club cheerfully contributes for the support of those from whom this blessing is withheld, and when the decay of his bodily powers takes place, or disease assails him, then he, in his turn, receives aid from those who are in the vigour of their strength and faculties.

Most clubs have hitherto been established on wrong calculations as to the payments necessary to secure the benefits promised, or they have been badly managed. The inevitable consequence has been, that such societies have been broken up, and that, generally, just at the time when the members, from advancing age and infirmities, were expecting to reap the fruits of the providence of many previous years. Seeing that so much bitter disappointment and distress have arisen from these failures of clubs, it is extraordinary, and at the same time a pleasing proof of the increasing prevalence of prudential self-denying feelings, that so many of the labouring classes are still eager and ready to join new institutions of the same sort. We would strongly advise them, however, to be very cautious as to the Society they connect themselves with. They should carefully avoid enrolling themselves in such clubs as promise great advantages, with easy monthly or quarterly payments, for such must fail in the time of need. In making their choice, they cannot be expected to know whether the pay proposed is adequate, or the rules and regulations necessary and wise; but they may be guided in a great degree by the character of the persons who manage them. Let them join such only as are conducted by sober, steady, business-like, and, if possible, religious men. They should shun, as they would the plague, all societies connected with inn-keepers or public-houses.

The great mass of those who live by their daily labour, both men and women, particularly those who have families, can be expected to do little more, in making provision for futurity, than contribute to such societies as these; but the young of both sexes, who have not these cares and claims upon them, but are looking forward to marriage, or those who have a laudable ambition (and God approves of such a desire if kept within due bounds) of advancing their condition, and "getting up in the world," as it is called, must do more than pay their regular contributions into a club. It is necessary for them to lay by an additional amount; and to such, as we have before said, we would recommend Savings' Banks as a safe deposit for their accumulations.

The foregoing observations are equally applicable to those in better pecuniary circumstances. We more particularly allude to those possessing little or no property, but who are living on incomes derived from professions or salaries, or such as are in a small way of business. There is in this class, also, a great want of caution and provident forethought, both in trade and family expenditure. All such are inexcusable if they live up to their incomes, and do not make a provision for their declining years. Life Assurance Offices offer to such all that can be wished. They may in these institutions, by paying an annual sum, become entitled to a deferred annuity, which will enable them to meet the exigencies of advancing age ; and by effecting an assurance on their lives, they can make a comfortable provision for their widows and families.

We have frankly and fully declared our opinion on the propriety and necessity, not only of adequately providing for present wants and comforts, but also of accumulating property for commercial and useful purposes, and for the future wants of ourselves and families. Some persons may have hesitated to do this so unreservedly as we have done, fearing it might counteract or weaken the arguments to be used to enforce the *third object*, of which we are now about to speak, namely, the portion to be allotted to the service of God.

The true interest, however, of the cause we are advocating requires no such concealment. An unwise suppression of this sort frequently injures the best of causes. We have, therefore, endeavoured to place the truth before the minds of our readers in all its fair proportions, and trust they will not make a wrong use of what we have written, by appropriating too large a share to objects of time and sense, but will acknowledge, both in theory and practice, that all God's commands are to be equally obeyed.

The third object, as we have just said, to which property should be devoted, is, THE SERVICE OF GOD.

This is not mentioned last, because it is thought to be a less imperative duty than the two objects already discussed; or that it is only any *surplus* which may remain, after these have been fully attended to, that is to be appropriated to religious and charitable purposes. On the contrary, it is spoken of last, because it is the highest and most soul-elevating object of the three; and that the obligation rightly to perform it may make the deeper impression; for to neither of them is there so great a danger of a stinted share being allotted as to this. They should all be looked upon as equally deserving consideration and attention; because God requires a right apportionment of property to each. Of course it is not meant that our income should be *equally* divided between the three claims. No, the distribution must vary, according to the position and circumstances of individuals.

In order to elucidate this part of the subject, it will be well to examine the scope and spirit of the Apostle's injunction, as contained in the verse already quoted, and which we now repeat: " UPON THE FIRST DAY OF THE WEEK, LET EVERY ONE OF YOU LAY BY HIM IN STORE, AS GOD HATH PROSPERED HIM, THAT THERE BE NO GATHERINGS WHEN I COME." (1 Cor. xvi. 2.)

Let us take the clauses separately, though not in the exact order in which they stand.

" LET EVERY ONE OF YOU."

This is a general, if not an universal command, and is applicable both to young and old, to the rich and to the poor. No one doubts that it is the duty of the rich to give; many, however, will suppose that in this passage the poor must be understood to be exempted. But the plain import of the precept is, with the exception of those who have no money at their own disposal, such as children and the inmates of workhouses, that none are excused. This appears to be clear for the following reasons:—

Poverty and riches are such comparative terms, that it would be extremely difficult, if not impossible, to draw the line between them, and define who are rich and who are not. Every man appears poor to those above him in pecuniary circumstances, and rich to those below him. The man getting ten shillings a-week, is considered well off by those in the receipt of only five; yet the person earning twenty or thirty shillings a-week, would look upon him who only earned ten as in low circumstances. We nowhere read in the Scriptures that God has divided mankind into two classes,—one, the rich, whose duty it is to give; the other, the poor, whose *duty* it is to spend all their gettings on themselves and families, and give nothing to God, or their poorer neighbours. We use the word "*duty*" advisedly, for if God has exempted the poor from giving, because of their own personal or family claims, it is a duty in them to obey, and not to give. Such a command, however, would not be in accordance with the divine beneficence; for it would tend to make a large proportion of mankind selfish in the extreme, and banish much of those feelings of kindness and benevolence of heart, which every one should sedulously cherish. It would, in fact, be contrary to multitudes of Scriptural precepts. Surely the commendation which the blessed Saviour passed on the widow, who cast her two mites into the treasury, being "all her substance," that is, all the money she then possessed, is sufficient to show that contributing to the service of God is a duty incumbent on the poorest as well as on the richest of mankind.

Let us, however, not be misunderstood. It is not at all necessary that the poor should give largely, in order that their offerings may be as acceptable to God as those of the rich. The same benevolent feelings may be called into exercise, and God equally approve of and reward the donation of a penny as of a pound. Men intrusted with but few talents will receive, not indeed a deserved but a gracious reward, equal to those who have more, if they only improve their lesser opportunities in the same proportion. This is evident from the Parable of the

Talents,* in which he who had received two talents, and had gained other two, received the same commendation as he, who, having received five, had made them ten.

To show that the poorest may give something, without suffering any great privations, the following extreme case may be adduced. Perhaps there is scarcely any one so indigent as not to receive, in one way or another, three or four shillings a-week. Suppose such a person were to lay up in store a farthing a-week, this would be from the 150th to the 200th part of his income, and however sorry we should be to see the comforts of the poor diminished, we think such a trifling amount as this would not be missed. We are sure any self-denial it might occasion would be amply compensated by the pleasure which would be felt in having something to bestow on a friend or neighbour in distress, or in dropping a penny occasionally into a collecting-box. By saving a farthing a-week, a poor man or woman would have a penny a-month to bestow on any object, which he or she might think would most meet with the Almighty's approval.

That this duty appertains to the poor as well as to the rich, may also be shown by the beneficial results which naturally flow from its right performance.

1st. As it respects God. Our Creator and Redeemer ought to receive as much glory as his creatures have it in their power to render. He makes no distinction between rich and poor, in endowing their minds with those susceptibilities which prompt to benevolent actions, whether to the souls or bodies of men; and He is honoured by the frequent and free exercise of such feelings. But if it be not the duty of the poorer part of mankind to contribute, they must of necessity lose the opportunity of giving free scope to those generous and tender emotions; and God must be deprived of the glory accruing from the exercise of the moral qualities which he has himself implanted.

2d. As it regards the individual. God has been graciously pleased to promise an abundant future reward to those who cultivate right principles, and perform benevolent actions. But if the poorer classes are not to bestow, when it is in the

* Matt. xxv. 14.

power of their hands to do so, they must forego this eternal recompense. It is true, God accepts the willing heart, and will reward the wish and intention, where the means of giving expression to them are wanting; but we think we have shown, that, with few exceptions, all have something to give; and if they refuse or neglect to fulfil their obligation, even from erroneous impressions, it will be to their everlasting loss.

"LAY BY HIM IN STORE."

This clause, as we have before said, plainly declares it to be the duty of every one, not simply to give when he is asked, or as occasions arise; but to store up beforehand a certain portion of his gettings, to be in readiness at any time for distribution. The advantages of such a procedure are obvious. Things done without premeditation or consideration are generally ill done. So in this case, when there has been no deliberate comparison of the claims of different objects, or no settled purpose as to what sum to give, the amount must be left pretty much to chance, and to the impulse of the moment when subscriptions are asked. Under such circumstances, the payment is too frequently made so reluctantly, or with such an ill grace, as to hurt the feelings of the person who takes the trouble to collect, and make him almost ready to refuse the donation. Whereas, when all is arranged and ready beforehand, a person has nothing to do but to go to his store, and take therefrom the destined amount. This is handed cheerfully to the collector, and the parties separate, both equally pleased with the interview.

This passage is also evidently designed to teach, not merely that a certain sum should be mentally devoted to God's service; but that it should be actually set apart. The poor, and such as are unable or disinclined to keep accounts, should literally comply with this precept, and have a bag or box expressly appropriated to this purpose; but for all who are able to write, and cast up pounds, shillings, and pence, this would not be absolutely necessary. For such it would be required that they should have an account-book, in which to make regular entries of the money so set apart, and how it is expended. In most cases, however, it would be desirable that both these plans be conjoined, and a purse or box be kept, in which to deposit the money as it is set apart, with a book for keeping a regular account of the way in which it is distributed.

Nothing is more conducive to success in any undertaking than method and regularity. In business, it is almost impossible to succeed without these two acquirements; and they are more or less indispensable in every case where pecuniary transactions are to be recorded. So much is this want felt in the ordinary concerns of life, that account-books, ready-ruled, and adapted to their respective purposes, are to be had in abundance. Not only are persons engaged in business plentifully supplied with cash-books, ledgers, &c. &c., suited to the wants of every class of trader; but the housekeeper has her account-book for entering family expenses; and even the gambler finds a book of the sort necessary, successfully to carry on and record his nefarious transactions.

It is not a little remarkable, however, that, so far as we know, no attempt has yet been made to supply Christians with this desideratum. We have never seen any ready-ruled account-book, with directions for using it, in which charitable individuals might record the subscriptions, donations, and the various disbursements of the money, which they have devoted to religious and benevolent purposes. To recommend the use of such a book is one of the main objects of this Essay. A specimen will be found subjoined, by inspecting which, and reading the accompanying directions, the mode of using it will be clearly perceived.

"ON THE FIRST DAY OF THE WEEK."

This clause clearly shows that the Sabbath-day is an appropriate time for carrying out the foregoing injunction, to lay up in store a proper proportion of a person's gains for sacred purposes. Although it would appear from this expression, and indeed from the scope of the whole verse, that St. Paul had in view only one collection, for a single object, yet, doubtless, it has a general bearing on all collections for religious and charitable institutions, for the reasons which made it applicable to this case, would have the same force in all other instances. That such is a right view of the subject is confirmed by the fact subsequently mentioned in the second Epistle to the Corinthians, chap. viii., 6th and 10th verses ; from which it appears that the collection was not actually made on a single day, but was extended, at least, over twelve months ; and the apostle, in a subsequent verse, urged them to proceed with it.

The inference to be deduced from this passage is, that the practice of storing up for future distribution should be adopted as often as a person receives his or her wages or income, be it weekly, monthly, quarterly, or yearly ; and with respect to those who live by the irregularly accruing profits of agriculture, trade, or commerce, that this duty should be performed immediately after they have " taken stock" as it is usually called, and have thus ascertained how they are getting on in the world.

It will be observed, that we recommend nothing more to be done on the Sabbath than to " lay up in store." The verse does not affirm that this is a proper day for inquiring how much a person has prospered, in order that he may determine what to give. Such an occupation of the mind would be improper in every respect, and opposed to other passages of Scripture, which require the banishment of such thoughts from the mind on that · sacred day. But it is a suitable and praiseworthy action, and one which God approves, for a person to lay up, on the first day of the week, the portion so set apart to his service. For instance, were a labouring man or woman, with right motives and feelings, regularly as the Sabbath returns, to take the pre-determined portion from the previous week's wages, and place it in his or her depository, the individual would be blessed in the deed ; and whoever acted thus might find the approving smiles of their heavenly Father's countenance resting on them throughout the day.

The aforementioned seasons of " taking stock," or the receipt of yearly or quarterly income, are the most appropriate times for reviewing and re-determining the right proportion to be given to

God, and allotted to different objects. These questions, however, need not be opened every time that persons in the receipt of weekly, monthly, or perhaps quarterly incomes receive their wages or salaries; only it is recommended that this deliberation should be frequent. But as it regards those who receive their incomes yearly, and also such as take stock, it is strongly advised that both these matters should, if not oftener, certainly then be made subjects of serious consideration. As a general rule, it may be laid down, that the intervals between the recurrence of this investigation should be short, for there can be no doubt, if the scrutiny be performed in a right spirit, that God would be honoured, and men benefited, by the frequently returning mental exercise, and by the pious feelings which would be thereby excited.

"As God has prospered him."

This is the New Testament rule whereby the amount of our donations to God's treasury is to be determined. But it implies something preliminary, namely, that every one should periodically look into and ascertain the state of his affairs. This is easily done by persons in the receipt of weekly, quarterly, or yearly payments; and also by those out of business, and living on fixed incomes. It is more difficult, indeed, for individuals to do so who are living on the profits of business. The Scriptural precept, however, is not less incumbent on them, and the command of God coincides with their truest worldly interest; for a very large amount of the failures in business that take place, and the consequent losses and misery which are thereby entailed on the sufferers, their families, and creditors, may be traced to this omission. Whereas, regularity in stock-taking, and in ascertaining the yearly amount of profits or losses, is a marked characteristic of a prudent tradesman; and if not a certain preservative from the aforementioned calamity, is at least an early forewarning of the consequences of pursuing a losing trade. When a man's business is failing, it is a great thing to get him clearly to see, and persuade himself, that his property is slipping away from him. He is naturally reluctant to admit such an unwelcome truth. But the disclosures of figures cannot be evaded; and a wise man, as soon as he has satisfied himself that his accounts certainly show that his affairs are going wrong, will immediately stop; and thus prevent that waste or ruin of his own and other persons' property, which so frequently occurs. We would here just observe, that as stock-taking is of such essential importance to all persons engaged in trade, it should never be delayed longer than a year.

The first thing to be done, then, by those whose property is invested in business, is to find out what they have gained or lost since they last took an account of their stock. The next would be, to strike an average of the profits of the two or three or more preceding years. In some occupations the gains are so regular from year to year, that such a process would be needless; yet, in many trades the fluctuations are so great, from high to low profits, or from gains to losses, that an average of several previous years must be taken in order to ascertain the proper amount of profits on which to take a percentage for God.

It is obvious that this is the only way of meeting the difficulty; for it would not at all be proper to be varying stated subscriptions every year, as profits may rise or fall, and it would be still less expedient to stop them altogether in years when there may be losses, instead of gains; for, besides the injury which would accrue to Societies thus precariously supported, it would be exposing to the world the good or bad results of a person's pecuniary transactions, which every prudent man of business is careful to avoid.

A question will arise in the minds of many, to which it may be proper here to advert. It is this :—" Does this rule of giving, according as profits arise, extend to property acquired by bequest or inheritance?" Most probably it does not, and is only intended to apply to a person's ordinary income—that which arises from manual labour, the proceeds of business and professions, or rents and dividends; for we do not read in the Scriptures that any portion of property obtained from ancestors, relatives, or friends, was required to be set apart for the service of God. Of course, where property accrues in this way, a man's responsibility increases with it; and he should dedicate to benevolent purposes a correspondingly large amount of the annual income derived from it, on a scale commensurate with that to be recommended hereafter. (Page 364.) Still, those who think the command has the extent of requiring a portion of the capital thus acquired to be so devoted, should act accordingly.

A person, having decided what his average income is, after having looked up to the Almighty for direction, would then sit down calmly to consider how to apportion it between the three objects before specified—present wants—store for futurity—and pious and charitable uses. It would be foreign to the design of this little work, to dwell much on the first two of these objects. Nevertheless, it may not be amiss to offer a few remarks and suggestions on the subject. In order rightly to divide the sum to be thus appropriated, we think that persons should look more than they are accustomed to do to futurity, and less to present gratification, whether it regards their style of living or apparel. Not that we would have men or women to be needlessly parsimonious in their household expenditure, or to dress below their station in society. We would have them avoid prodigality and profusion; and let nothing be wasted, either by themselves or their domestics. This they should do, not only because it is a sin; but that they may be able to make a better provision for their families, give more to religious societies, and afford greater help to their poorer neighbours.

It may not be out of place here, just to advert to two prevalent practical errors, which produce much unhappiness to individuals and families; and the straitened circumstances thereby induced are too often thought to be a valid reason for giving neither to God nor man.

The one is, where persons having limited or fixed incomes when they first set out in life, either from inconsideration, miscalculation, or inexperience, or really from an extra expenditure being then required, spend more than their income, and get into debt. They have not the prudence or firmness, by a little economy for the next few years, to pay what they owe, and retain some money always in hand. The consequence is, that for a series of years, perhaps the best part of their lives, though they annually spend no more than their income, their expenditure is always in advance of it : it may not be more than half a year, still, they are always in debt, and are obliged to deal with those only who will give them credit. They are constantly harassed with applications for payment, and are often at their wits' end for expedients to put off the claimants. Now, such persons, if they have the inclination to be charitable, ought not in justice to be so while their debts are unpaid; whereas, by pursuing an opposite course, and keeping their expenditure a little in arrear of their income, they would be able to purchase for ready money, and therefore more cheaply, or pay every bill as it is presented. By a little temporary self-denial of this sort, they might have the satisfaction of being considered persons of sufficient or even ample means, and be saved a thousand anxieties and troubles. But this desirable change is not all that is to be effected; they must carry their economy still further, and give to the cause of God its due. Only by acting thus can they escape the doom of unfaithful stewards.

It is much to be lamented that the foregoing observations are not only applicable to the higher, but to a multitude also in the lower walks of life, and the evil results are much the same, though the causes leading thereto may somewhat vary. To picture a scene of but too frequent occurrence. A labouring man and his wife set out in life with fair prospects, having suitable furniture and comforts about them. But they live quite up to their income, and spend each week the earnings of the previous one. After a time, want of work, or sickness if they are not in a club, obliges them, for a few weeks, to live upon " trust," as it is called The indiscretion, however, does not end here. When they get work again, instead of saving a little every week out of their earnings, and paying by degrees the shopkeepers to whom they have become indebted, they still expend on their living as much as before, and the old score remains a constant burthen on them; or they pay off a part of it, and at the same time run into debt to an equal amount, by taking up victuals or goods from any other person who will trust them. After a time, adverse circumstances again overtake the family, but now the heads of it are less able to meet the calamity, their credit being stretched to the utmost, and, as an only resource, the best piece of furniture, or the Sunday apparel, must be pledged at the pawnbroker's, perhaps never to be redeemed. Thus they go on from year to year, just as much in debt at the end as at the commencement, and throughout the whole time are obliged to buy everything at the dearest rate; for the small shopkeepers who give them credit must charge in proportion to the risk they run. In this way, as in the class before-mentioned, the happiness and domestic comfort of many a working man's family are destroyed, for the want of a little prudence and self-denying economy.

Much rather would we cover than expose the failings of others, particularly those of the poor, knowing, as we do, the difficulties with which they are often surrounded, yet still we feel it to be the truest charity to speak plainly. Indeed, it is absolutely necessary to point out the cause of an evil, if we wish to have it removed. How much pain and wretchedness all classes might avoid, if they would but profit by the observation recorded long ago by Solomon, "The prudent man foreseeth the evil, and hideth himself, but the simple pass on and are punished."

The other case is this. Where parents have, by their own industry, or by any other means, acquired property, it is natural and proper, when the desire is kept within due limits, that they should collect comforts and conveniences about them, and adopt a higher style of living. But it is a far too prevalent idea with such, and the notion becomes impressed on the children also, that when the latter form marriage connexions, or leave their father's house, and set up separate establishments of their own, they must form their associations, and live in the same style as their parents have been enabled to assume only after years of toil. This erroneous impression produces, ofttimes, disastrous results; preventing alliances suitable in other respects, and causing sons, when they set out in life, to adopt a more expensive mode of living, and to form acquaintances in a higher grade of society, than is suited to their resources. Just to suppose a case. A newly-married couple begin the world with a thousand pounds; by perseverance and assiduity they gradually make additions to it, and retire upon an income of (say) four or five hundred a-year.

Suppose they have five children, and as a marriage-portion, or to set them up in business, they should give them each a thousand pounds,—just the sum they themselves commenced with. If the sons or daughters have been brought up with high notions, and a false estimate of the station they must occupy when they will have to enter on the active concerns of life, it will in too many cases be found, that if, out of the profits of the 1000*l*., they are able to make the "two ends meet," they will not be able to lay up anything against seasons of adversity, or old age, nor have aught to spare for others. Frequently the result is worse than this, and it is lamentable to behold how often one or more of the children of parents who have creditably got on in life, become reduced far below the level from which their fathers originally rose.

We are persuaded, that a great many of those calamitous cases, in which the children of pious parents, to use a common expression, "turn out badly," may be traced to a withholding from God his due, and an over-anxiety on the part of the parents to provide for the temporal welfare of their offspring. The money which ought to have been devoted to God, when laid out in apparel unbecoming their station, or in teaching them fashionable, frivolous, or useless accomplishments, unsuited to the sphere they are to occupy in life, carries not His blessing with it. Thus the means used to cause children to be noticed and applauded by the world, become their curse and ruin.

One of the most prevalent sins among professing Christians of the present day is conformity to the world, or compliance with its maxims and practices. In this commercial country, large fortunes are constantly being accumulated; and, as is natural, the men of the world will display their riches by luxurious living and splendid equipages—the pomps and vanities of this vain world. This excites the emulation, not to say the envy, of those who profess to have set their affections on things above. They must needs, they think, keep up the same appearances as their neighbours or acquaintances of the same property or standing in society. Thus their minds are captivated, far too much of their property is absorbed, and what should have been for the welfare of individuals and churches becomes their bane. Oh, when will professing Christians shun these glittering snares, and rather strive to be "rich in good works, ready to distribute, willing to communicate?"*

Let us now proceed to consider what AMOUNT ought to be devoted to the service of God. In the apportionment of a person's property to the two objects already considered, it is highly necessary that the Almighty should be looked up to for guidance to do it aright; but more fervent prayer for the divine direction is requisite in deciding what portion to devote to His service, since self-love, not to say selfishness, will naturally prompt a man to take sufficient care for the temporal wants of himself and his family; but *conscience alone* will have to say what portion should be reserved to promote his own eternal interests, and to benefit the souls and bodies of others. Every one, therefore, who wishes to enjoy the approbation of God and his own conscience, will set apart a stated and sufficient time for asking counsel of Him in this matter.

Abraham gave a tenth of the goods he had recovered from Chedorlaomer to Melchizedek, the type of Christ; Jacob at Bethel vowed to render the tenth of his increase to God; and, under the Mosaic dispensation, Jehovah was pleased to give to his people very minute injunctions as to what proportion of the provisions and worldly substance bestowed upon them, he required to be returned to him in the shape of first-fruits, tithes, and offerings. All these laws are now so far abrogated as not to be specifically binding, but their *spirit* and *essence* remain. Men are to give now as then; but a more generous law is laid down, more confidence is placed in them by God. Shame to them, that their response to it is no better! Our sovereign Lord and Master now says, "Give me what a grateful heart prompts,— a heart not anxious to retain an undue provision for self or family." It is God who bestows life, health, affectionate relatives, and kind friends. It is he also who is giving you a sufficiency of food and raiment, and is prospering you in your worldly calling. Above all, he has adopted many of you as sons, and is ready to receive every one who is willing to come to him

* 1 Timothy, vi. 18.

for salvation Remember that Jesus, after a sorrowful life, shed his precious blood for you, and is now interceding at God's right hand for all who commit their immortal interests to his keeping. Remember that the Holy Spirit is willing to fill every seeking soul with his blessed influences; waiting to stimulate it to every good word and deed, to give wisdom to the understanding, and light to the conscience; and, moreover, this blessed Agent stands prepared to sanctify each willing heart, and carry on the work of grace, till it be consummated in glory.

Considerations such as these, drawn in a great measure from the larger effulgence of gospel light which was thrown on the world when God became "manifest in the flesh," may well induce Christians of the present day to *greater* acts of self-denial and benevolence than were practised by the Jews of old; certainly God will not be satisfied with *less*. Assuming this principle to be indisputable, it will be the duty of many persons, men or women, who have no family or near relative claims, to devote to God's service a seventh, a fifth, or even a half or more of their income. A middle class, having these demands on their money, but being in the receipt of incomes sufficient to meet them, and also to supply themselves, not only with necessaries, but comforts, will appropriate a tenth; while it will not be required of others, particularly in the lower walks of life, that they give more than a twentieth or thirtieth part, or even a less proportion than this, as in the extreme case mentioned. (Page 352.) Every one should act according to the dictates of an enlightened conscience, the obligations he is under to God, and the circumstances in which he is placed. The expression of gratitude to God, and efforts to extend the Redeemer's kingdom throughout the earth, by pecuniary contributions, should, in a certain degree, be restrained and regulated by the family requirements just adverted to; but these, on the other hand, must not by any means be allowed to stint the appropriation of property to religious and benevolent objects.

Although, as we have said, there is in the New Testament no mention made of any precise amount to be given to God, yet we may be sure of this, as a general rule, that the more the Almighty prospers a man, the more he expects him to give. It is not simply meant by this, that he should give in the same proportion from his greater, as he did from his lesser gettings; that is, if, for instance, he gave a tenth of 100*l.* one year, that he should give a tenth only of 200*l.* the next, if his profits in the interval had doubled, but that as God is increasing his store, so he should give in a larger proportion. Having given a tenth, or 10*l.* out of 100*l.* one year, when he had earned 200*l.* in another year, he might give, not merely a tenth of that, which would be 20*l.*, but an eighth, or 25*l.*, and so he might go on to increase the proportion as he more and more prospered. Alas! how often the reverse of this is the case. How frequently is it found that as God is pouring abundance into a man's lap, filling his garners with increase, he becomes more and more reluctant to give! What melancholy spectacles such individuals are! Men sorrow, angels may be said to weep, at the sight. How sad is the thought, that, at the last day, accumulations of wealth thus kept back from God will prove to be heavy millstones round the necks of such men!

God, under the Levitical dispensation, promised his blessing to the Israelites, both as a nation and as individuals, if they duly paid their tithes, and presented their offerings; and a curse invariably followed when they neglected thus to do. So, under the Christian dispensation, there can be no doubt but that God's blessing will attend the right performance of this duty. Not that persons are to expect that God will always, or even generally, favour them in exactly the same way, that is, by an increase of their worldly store. This may not be good for them in other respects. Besides, if such a recompense usually followed acts of generosity, it would have a strong tendency to induce men to give from wrong motives. Instead of gratitude being the operating principle, they would give in order to receive as much or more again. Just in proportion, however, as this and God's other commandments are kept, will he bless the individuals who observe them, either in their temporal affairs or spiritually, or in both ways at once. Numerous passages may be cited from the Scriptures to prove that God has pledged himself thus graciously to reward acts of piety and benevolence. The following will suffice: " The liberal soul shall be made fat; and he that watereth others, shall be watered also himself;" "Blessed is he that considereth the poor; the Lord will deliver him in time of trouble. The Lord will preserve him, and keep him alive; and he shall be blessed upon the earth;" "There is that scattereth, and yet increaseth, and there is that withholdeth more than is meet, but it tendeth to poverty;" "Will a man rob God? Yet ye have robbed me. But ye say, Wherein have we robbed thee? In tithes and offerings. Ye are cursed with a curse, for ye have robbed me, even this whole nation. Bring ye all the tithes into the storehouse, that there may be meat in mine house; and prove me now herewith, saith the Lord of Hosts, if I will not open you the windows of heaven, and pour out a blessing, that there shall not be room enough to receive it."

If it be hoped and expected to obtain God's blessing on the use of the portions devoted to ourselves, no time should be lost in deciding on and setting apart the share belonging to God; for this ought to be done before either of the other portions has begun to be used. This we learn from the command of Jehovah to the Israelites with respect to first-fruits: "When ye be come into the land which I give unto you, and shall reap the harvest thereof, then ye shall bring a sheaf of the first-fruits of your harvest unto the priest, and he shall wave the sheaf before the Lord to be accepted for you. And ye shall eat neither bread, nor parched corn, nor green ears, until the self-same day that ye have brought an offering unto your God: it shall be a statute for ever throughout all your generations."*

Cogent reasons to induce persons rightly to perform the duty of giving liberally might be abundantly multiplied, but the necessarily contracted limits of this Essay forbid. We cannot, however, pass on without calling the reader's serious attention to the sin of covetousness, and its heinousness in the sight of God. This abounding form of selfishness is ordinarily in the New Testament classed with crimes of the deepest dye: "But now I have written unto you not to keep company, if any man that is called a brother be a fornicator, or *covetous*, or an idolator, or a

* Leviticus, xxiii. 10, 11, 14.

railer, or a drunkard, or an extortioner; with such an one, no not to eat;" "Nor thieves, nor *covetous*, nor drunkards, nor revilers, nor extortioners, shall inherit the kingdom of God." It is a peculiarly *dangerous* sin; and, from the disguises it assumes, easily avoids detection. It is so difficult to draw the exact line between a due and an excessive love of gain—between the expenditure proper to procure the comforts of life, and mean and parsimonious saving—between the claims of family, of time, and of sense, and the requirements of God—that it is no easy matter to persuade persons that they are chargeable with this offence. The *insidious* character of this sin is also shown by the difficulty of eliciting evidence, and bringing proof of its existence home to any one, how clear soever appearances may be against him. It is, therefore, next to impossible to pass a public judgment and censure on this violation of the divine law. From the verse before quoted, it appears that the Apostle Paul would have the covetous, equally with the other notorious sinners there mentioned, excommunicated from the Church. But when and where, in our churches, was there ever such an act of discipline enforced? It behoves every one, therefore, in the privacy of the closet, faithfully to examine himself whether he be not an offender against God in this respect. Let him do it the more carefully and impartially on account of the indistinctness with which the boundary line between right and wrong, in this instance, is marked out. The great prevalence of this sin, unheeded and unrebuked, the more requires each one to suspect it in himself, and to lay open his inmost thoughts, motives, and actions, before the great Searcher of hearts, that it may be detected; and when it is discovered, let him keep carefully at the greatest distance from it, just as a man would, who had to pass, in a fog or in the dimness of twilight, near a precipice or a pit. A volume would be required to expose the greatness, the insidiousness, and the danger of the sin of covetousness, but it must suffice that we urge on every one that they should read some work on this soul ensnaring evil—if possible, those we have already mentioned—above all, that they would ponder deeply the many passages in the Bible in which it is exposed and condemned.

May we be allowed to adduce, before concluding this part of

the subject, one other motive to increased liberality, drawn from the altered and happier circumstances in which we find ourselves, compared with those in which our ancestors were placed; and no better words can be used to express the sentiment than those of a recent writer, Mr. Stoughton: "We are not called to resist unto blood, as our fathers did. 'Twas theirs to suffer, 'tis ours to serve. Their lot was tears, ours toil. They had to *take* joyfully the *spoiling* of their goods, we are required to *employ ourselves* joyfully in the *bestowment* of our goods."

Can there be any doubt, that this course of procedure,—the laying up for and contributing to the relief of the temporal and spiritual wants of mankind, is as much a duty as that of "entering into the closet and praying to the Father who seeth in secret," or of waiting on him in the public assembly? Surely, neither of these can be attended to with such a clear conscience as to profit a man, if something within him says, that the command to set aside a certain part of his income has been neglected, or a just proportion of it withheld from God. Let every one, therefore, who has hitherto neglected this duty, strive to get his soul filled with enlarged and elevated emotions of love, gratitude, and obedience. He will then cheerfully and willingly set himself immediately to the conscientious performance of it. Under the delightful influence of these feelings, he will not say within himself, "How *little* can I give and keep a clear conscience?" but a generous heart will exclaim, "How *much* can I give, and conscience not accuse me of neglecting other claims?"

"THAT THERE BE NO GATHERINGS WHEN I COME."

This clause contains the reason that induced the Apostle to give the advice expressed in the former part of the verse. It is mainly applicable to the circumstances connected with the Apostle's intended visit to Corinth; but we may gather from it some general instruction. He doubtless wished the benefactions of the Corinthians to be begun and ended before he arrived, that the collection might be made more orderly and with greater deliberation. His opinion of their liberality was high; he felt that he might even "boast" of it; he therefore was naturally anxious

that the confidence placed in them should not prove to have been
in vain ; and he probably calculated, that if the benefactions were
commenced early, and carried on systematically, they would be
so much the larger. He had, also, subjects of far higher importance to impress on their minds during his sojourn among them.
But, perhaps, his principal reason for urging on the collection
was, that he had in prospect the unpleasant duty of correcting
and setting in order many things which he knew to be amiss in
the Church, and which would be likely to cause uneasiness in
one quarter or another. Paul, therefore, wisely and prudently
wished, that these pecuniary matters should be well over before
he arrived, lest the contributions for the poor Christians in Judea
should be diminished by any difficulties that might arise.

We may hence learn, that when benevolent designs are to be
set on foot, it is well to look forward, and select the must suitable moment for their commencement, and then to lose no time
in carrying them into execution.

We now come to speak of the "FORM" appended to this book
(pages 387 and 392) for recording a person's conscientious and
deliberate resolve as to the amount which he has devoted to God,
and actually, or in effect, laid up in store.

Every time an individual reviews his pecuniary affairs for the
purpose of considering what portion should be set apart for benevolent objects, it is strongly advised that he should at once commit the result of his deliberation to paper in the form alluded to,
or something similar, and sign his name to it.

One reason why it is recommended for a person to adopt this
plan, is, because it is well known that what is awarded merely in
purpose is apt to be neglected or forgotten; while temptations to
break such a resolution are more easily resisted.

But there is another reason of more importance. Contrary
to our hopes and expectations, it is a subject of deep regret, that
although much good undoubtedly has arisen from the very extensive circulation of the two Essays on Covetousness before mentioned, yet it must be confessed, that these publications, with
other powerful appeals since made from the platform, the pulpit,
and the press, have not produced such a spirit of liberality in

Christians as might have been expected. Reflections on the cause of this, and a wish to suggest a remedy, mainly occasioned the production of this Essay.* The writer was led to think, that the reason why these excitements to liberality have not yielded more abundant fruit is chiefly this, that the authors and speakers above referred to, omitted to propose a method by which men, while their judgments were convinced and their consciences were moved,—might be induced to take a decided step, and by an express and definite act, such as that now recommended, devote a proper portion of their incomes to God. There can be no question but that many persons, while reading or hearing the exhortations referred to, and perhaps for some time afterwards, fully determined to devote more of their property to pious and benevolent objects than they had hitherto done. The resolution, however, being vague and indeterminate—no specific amount being fixed upon at the time, nor any deliberate thought exercised as to what would be the most suitable objects on which to bestow their intended increased pecuniary contributions—the convincing reasons contained in the book, or adduced in the discourse, slowly faded from their memory; other objects and subjects also intervened to draw off their attention; and conscience, by degrees, ceased to incite to the performance of that extended liberality, not long before so fully resolved upon. The lamentable consequence of such indecision is, that these persons, to use the expressive words of Scripture, have again "settled on their lees," and become no more free to give than before, perhaps even less so. The best remedy for this failure of carrying good intentions into execution, appears to be the immediate action of laying up in store; or, at least, the recording in writing of the amount determined to be set apart for benevolent purposes.

Such a dedication is not to be looked upon as a vow, never, under any circumstances, to be abrogated, but simply as a firm resolution, not to be broken except under unforeseen circumstances, such as a large loss of property in the interval between one act of dedication and another—a calamity which would but seldom occur. The sum so devoted should be regarded as a debt,

* It was written some time before the offer of prizes appeared.

2 B

which every man of honour or honesty would feel it a duty incumbent on him to discharge, provided he could do so after having satisfied all other just claims. We need scarcely add, that the books in which this resolve and the accounts are recorded can be kept as secret as may be wished.

Following this form of Dedication is a *List* of particular objects of benevolence to which the person who has signed the Dedication may be disposed to contribute, with the sum allotted to each.

In addition to this, it is highly desirable, not to say necessary, to be orderly, and keep regular *Accounts;* that it may be seen when and how the money has been expended, and to make it satisfactorily apparent to the donor that his previous resolve has been faithfully carried out. We have therefore attempted to show how such accounts should be kept; and, as an example or two will do this more clearly than can be done by any written directions, we have subjoined (pages 388 and 394) two fictitious accounts, one supposed to be that of a person (male or female) in low, and the other in higher, circumstances.

Before closing this appeal, we have thought it right particularly to advert to some of the objects to be found in the list above referred to, in order to show the peculiar "*claims*" they have on the liberality of Christians, and to explain why we have placed them in a particular order. On turning to the lists (pages 387 and 392), it will be observed that one object—the support of the Minister—stands first, and the others in regular succession. This has been done, not as presuming that we have formed in each case a right estimate of its importance, but merely to show what is the general view we take of their relative claims.

Every member of a minister's flock will be ready to allow that, out of his own family circle, THE PASTOR ought to have the first place in his affections, prayers, and sympathies; and that equal care should be taken to see him comfortably supported. Yet it is to be feared, that in too many cases this latter duty, to say nothing of the former, is not sufficiently attended to. It may not be difficult to account for this, from the peculiar circumstances in which ministers are placed. They may duly enforce upon their congregations the duty of liberality and benevolence in general; but delicacy forbids them to touch on their own case. The whole Bible is open to them to preach from, except such texts as these:—" If we have sown unto you spiritual things, is it a great thing if we shall reap your carnal things? Who goeth a warfare any time at his own charges? Who planteth a vineyard, and eateth not of the fruit thereof? Or who feedeth a flock, and eateth not of the milk of the flock? For it is written in the law of Moses, Thou shalt not muzzle the mouth of the ox that treadeth out the corn. Doth God take care for oxen? Or saith he it altogether for our sakes? For our sakes, no doubt, this is written; that he that plougheth should plough in hope, and that he that thresheth in hope should be partaker of his hope. Do ye not know, that they which minister about holy things live of the things of the temple? And they which wait at the altar are partakers with the altar? Even so hath the Lord ordained, that they which preach the gospel should live of the gospel."*

It becomes, then, the duty of a Church, and more especially of the office-bearers, to cherish in themselves, and stimulate in others, the sentiments inculcated in these passages. The payment of the Pastor — and adequate payment, too — is as much a debt due to him, as to any other person whom the members of the church and congregation may employ, such as physician, lawyer, schoolmaster, &c.

But the writer, having lately met with an admirable epitome of the reasons why ministers should be properly supported, in Barnes's Notes on 1 Corinthians, chap. ix., thinks it better to quote from him, than feebly to attempt to support their just claims by sentiments and language of his own. Barnes thus paraphrases and comments on the first of these verses:—"If we," Paul says of ministers, "have been the means of imparting to you the gospel, and bestowing upon you its high hopes and privileges, 'Is it a *great* thing if we shall reap your carnal things?'

* Cor. ix. 11, 7, 9, 10, 13, 14.

Is it to be regarded as unequal, unjust, or burdensome? Is it to be supposed that we are receiving that for which we have not rendered a valuable consideration? The sense is, We impart blessings of more value than we receive. We receive a supply of our temporal wants. We impart to you, under the divine blessing, the Gospel with all its hopes and consolations. We make you acquainted with God, with the plan of salvation, with the hope of heaven. We instruct your children; we guide you in the path of comfort and peace; we raise you from the degradations of idolatry and of sin; and we open before you the hope of the resurrection of the just, and of all the bliss of heaven. And can it be made a matter of question, whether all these high and exalted hopes are of as much value to dying man as the small amount which shall be needful to minister to the wants of those who are the means of imparting these blessings? Paul says this, therefore, from the reasonableness of the case. The propriety of support might be further urged,—

" 1. Because without it the ministry would be comparatively useless. Ministers, like physicians, lawyers, and farmers, should be allowed to attend mainly to the great business of their lives and to their appropriate work. No physician, no farmer, no mechanic, could accomplish much if his attention was constantly turned off from his appropriate business to engage in something else. And how can the minister of the Gospel, if his time is nearly all taken up in labouring to provide for the wants of his family?

" 2. The great mass of ministers spend their early days, and many of them all their property, in preparing to preach the gospel to others. And as the mechanic, who has spent his early years in learning a trade, and the physician and lawyer in preparing for their profession, receive support *in* that calling, why should not the minister of the Gospel?

" 3. Men in other things cheerfully *pay* those who labour for them. They compensate the schoolmaster, the physician, the lawyer, the merchant, the mechanic, and they do it cheerfully, because they suppose they receive a valuable consideration for their money. But is it not so with regard to ministers of the Gospel? Is not a man's family as *certainly* benefited by the labours of a faithful clergyman and pastor, as by the skill of a physician or a lawyer, or by the service of a schoolmaster Are not the affairs of the soul and of eternity as important to a man's family, as those of time and the welfare of the body?

" 4. It might be added, that society is benefited in a *pecuniary* way by the service of a faithful minister to a far greater extent than the amount of compensation which he receives. One drunkard, reformed under his labours, may earn and save to his family and to society as much as the whole salary of the pastor. The promotion of order, peace, sobriety, industry, education, and regularity in business, and honesty in contracting and in paying debts, saves much more to the community at large than the cost of the support of the Gospel."

May we add a few remarks as an incitement to a more liberal support of the minister? He is expected to be an example in every good word and work; he is to be benevolent and exercise hospitality; but how can he be so if he be stinted to the necessaries of life? His congregation would be displeased if he and his family did not appear respectable; but if, to keep within his means, he is obliged to act otherwise, the discredit falls on them. They expect him, week after week, to bring forth out of his treasury things new and old; but to do this, his mind must have sustenance as well as his body; he must, therefore, be properly supplied with books. Meagre sermons will be the almost inevitable result of empty book-shelves. It will thus be seen, that it is not only the duty, but the *personal interest* of a congregation, to afford an adequate subsistence to their Pastor.

We do not think that any private property a minister may have should be taken into account when calculating what salary to give him. No one thinks of paying a medical or other professional man in proportion to the property he has; and where congregations are able to support their minister, it would be the height of injustice for them to save their own pockets, just in proportion as he has money in his. What is his own, no one has a right, either directly or indirectly, to deprive him of; and his family or friends are rightful heirs to it. Besides, were a congregation to act thus, when a minister having property is removed there would either be a strong temptation to make wealth at least one of the qualifications of his successor, or there would be the greatest difficulty in raising sufficient funds adequately to support a pastor having no pecuniary resources of his own. When such cases of parsimonious saving have occurred, we believe they have arisen more from inconsideration, and from not looking forward to the consequences, than from any positive disposition to act unfairly, and to withhold more than is meet. Indeed, they have been generally caused by the disinterestedness of ministers, in their caring more for the flock than the fleece, and from a wish rather to refrain from presenting their just claims than appear to act contrary to the declaration of the Apostle, when he said, "We seek not yours but you." Still, we believe there is in some minds an impression that ministers ought to be thus self-denying; but have there not been reasons enough adduced, (and more might be added), to show that such an idea is erroneous and unscriptural in theory, and, in practice, neither beneficial to the pastor nor to his charge?

The proper rule for a congregation to guide themselves by in this matter, is, to determine that their pastor should have enough comfortably to support himself and family in the same rank of life and mode of living as the great body of the respectable (using this word for want of a better) part of his congregation.

The proportion, out of the whole amount devoted to God, to be apportioned by each individual to his minister, will greatly vary, according to the circumstances of the Church with which he is connected. In small congregations the sum must be large, and so where the people are poor; but in great and wealthy congregations the amount may be small, and yet the pastor be suitably remunerated. For instance, suppose a church, giving 150*l*. to its minister, devotes to religious and charitable purposes generally 300*l*.; here, on an average, half of each subscriber's donations must go to pay the minister's salary. But in a congregation whose minister is paid 300*l*. per annum, and which raise 1200*l*. for general benevolent objects, one-fourth would suffice. Rich churches, such as these, should subscribe largely to Home Missionary Societies; or assist deserving pastors struggling with difficulties; or such as are raising churches in destitute districts, where, at first, they can expect but little remuneration for their disinterested and arduous labours. All pastors should be well paid — none overpaid. We do not think there should be an equality in salaries. They should vary according to place and circumstances; and for this reason, that ministers ought to be suited to the majority of their congregations, as it regards intellectual acquirements, habits, tastes, and modes of living; and the natural, and therefore the best way to attain this accordance, is by salaries being unequal; but then, as we have said before, the pastor must have enough to feel comfortable and appear respectable.*

Next in importance, after the *sustentation* of the Pastor, we have placed the EDUCATION OF YOUNG MEN DEVOTED TO THE MINISTRY. Much misapprehension and indifference prevail on this subject. Pastors must be educated men; how else are they to keep ahead of the growing intelligence of Churches? Should they fall behind them in this respect, they will be despised, and the more intellectual part of their congregations will leave them for ministrations better adapted to their mental acquirements. *Piety* is the first qualification of a minister, and woe be to that church or denomination that shall esteem it a secondary object! But *aptitude to teach* is perhaps the next requisite, and this faculty is much improved by intellectual training. It is this which teaches men how to think clearly, and reason conclusively, and gain a knowledge of the readiest modes of obtaining access to the human mind. Besides, a man must learn, before he can be fit to teach; and this axiom is as true with respect to religious, as it is with regard to any other kind of knowledge. What success in instructing others can be expected from a man ignorant of the floods of light which have been thrown on the Scriptures by the labours of learned and pious men? It is from a deep study of the word of God that a sound theology can be

* The writer would wish here to state that he is a layman, and neither personally nor relatively interested in advocating the proper support of ministers. He has been induced to write as he has done, solely by the consideration that it is a peculiar duty devolving on church office-bearers and laymen generally, to keep the attention of churches and congregations directed to this paramount obligation.

derived. Personal piety, and even much religious knowledge, is not sufficient to constitute an *able* minister of the gospel. He must also acquire secular learning, for it has its uses, and, to a certain extent, may be said to be indispensable in this age of knowledge; not only that a minister may keep up with his flock in general information, but because every branch of learning, whether derived from nature or art, from the word or works of God, at suitable times and in proper ways, should be brought to bear on the great ends of the ministry,—the glory of God, and the salvation of souls.

To give this education, COLLEGES are instituted. It is taking an erroneous and contracted view of their utility to consider them of little benefit, because there are many popular and highly successful ministers who have never passed through an academic course. These, however, cannot be called uneducated men. By the native energy of their minds, assisted by books or private instruction, they have educated themselves. Men of this class are the exceptions, not the rule. The great mass of ministers must have an intellectual training, or their minds will break down under the demand, from week to week, by intelligent congregations, for new or varied matter to be delivered from the pulpit. Even the usefulness of the persons alluded to, would probably have been much increased by a College course; many of whom, we know, perhaps all, deplore the want of it.

Are we wrong in supposing, that another cause of the indifference with which our Colleges are regarded by many in our congregations, is, that too much is expected from a collegiate education? Many persons are disposed to undervalue the benefit of such institutions, because some students have disappointed the hopes entertained of them, or have come forth not very well qualified to sustain the pastoral office. The best Tutors cannot new-make the young men who come under their charge. Every student has his own peculiar intellectual endowments, constitutional temperament, and habits, — peculiarities, perhaps, of many years' standing. The most assiduous training can do little more than assist in the development and cultivation of those mental qualities which tend to good, and apply correctives to those which are evil. When the utmost has been done by a

Tutor, it must entirely rest with the student whether he will attend to the instructions given, and profit by them. No collegiate institution is therefore to be condemned, if some, or even many, of its alumni, come forth unfitted, in many respects, to undertake at once the charge of a large or old-established church.

It will scarcely admit of a doubt, but that the lay members of our churches, and many pastors, have been too remiss in preparing and providing for the future ministry—too little concerned to keep up a true apostolic succession of competent and faithful pastors. We believe it to be a duty, peculiarly devolving on the churches, not only to procure an earnestly pious and zealous ministry, but to take care that those who have the oversight of them in the Lord be well educated. Our ministers must be thoroughly learned, if they are to cope with the various and subtle forms of error, both of doctrine and discipline, which are advocated with so much ability, and propagated with so much zeal, all around us.

Great responsibility, therefore, rests on the pastors and members of our churches in this respect. They should see that the right men are sought out, and sent to be educated. When unworthy or unsuitable persons gain admission to our seats of learning, more blame will probably attach to those who sent, than to the College authorities who received them.

Nor must too much be expected from the young men when they have finished their course of education, and undertake the oversight of a congregation. Great allowance should be made for their inexperience, in matters both of a spiritual and a temporal nature. The expression of captious or censorious feelings on the part of their hearers, should be sedulously avoided; they should rather be treated with great kindness and forbearance. A little judicious and seasonable advice and assistance is peculiarly needful and encouraging when they have just entered on the arduous and self-denying work of the ministry.

We put the object, then, for which we plead in this light. If we are to have able and educated ministers, they must be sought out, and induced to devote themselves to the necessary preparatory studies. Perhaps there are few congregations to be found that do not expect to get such an one to fill their pulpit, in the event of its being vacated. All ought, therefore, to bear an equitable share in the expense of maintaining the institutions provided for the intellectual training of those who are to be their future pastors. On these various grounds we present this object to the consideration of churches and individuals, next after the duty of providing for their own minister.

The POOR we have placed in the list immediately after these two objects. The needy, the widow, and the fatherless, are, in numberless passages, both in the Old and New Testaments, presented to our notice as objects of compassionate regard; and perhaps there are more blessings promised to the kind-hearted who care for the poor, than to any other class of persons. In heathen countries there are none of those legal enactments for the relief of the destitute which we call "Poor Laws." Even in Judea, though the duty of providing for the needy was plainly prescribed, and the sources pointed out from which relief was to be afforded, yet, as all these were free-will offerings, where benevolent feelings were wanting much destitution and misery would at times inevitably prevail; the consequence was, that the young, the indigent, the sick, and the aged, were left mainly to be supported by their relatives, if they had any, or by casual charity if they had not. In the early Christian Churches, too, bigotry and persecution threw additional burdens on the churches; for children ofttimes refused to support their parents when they became Christians, and relatives their kinsmen. This was the sad condition of the Churches in Judea. It made the Apostle anxious to carry relief to them, and caused him to occupy so much of the Epistles to the Corinthians with pleas on their behalf. Circumstances, however, are now changed; and in this country a legal provision is made for all who are really destitute, so that no one need starve, or be reduced even to extreme want. Still, in most of our Churches, there are objects of charity to whom pecuniary or other assistance is highly acceptable; and it is the incumbent duty of those who have the means, to afford them those little comforts and conveniences of which they often, but particularly in sickness, stand so much in need.

Christians are more " especially " to attend to the wants of the "household of faith:" but our charity is not to be confined to them. We are to "do good unto all men," as we have the means and opportunity; and an excellent mode of doing so is by supporting Hospitals, Dispensaries, and other similar institutions.

SCHOOLS are inferior only to the ministry in importance, and therefore claim a large share of attention and support. Of course we only refer here to those requiring pecuniary aid, such as Sunday-schools, Day-schools for the poor, and Normal schools or training establishments for masters and mistresses. On these institutions, in a great measure, the hopes of the Churches and the nation rest. As they are efficiently conducted, or otherwise, both as regards religion and literature, so will the next generation be the honour and safeguard, or the disgrace and trouble, of the community. This sentiment is become so universally acknowledged, that it would be a waste of space to attempt to prove it. It is the less necessary also as it regards training-schools, because what colleges are to the ministry, they are to the educational system; and the observations we have made on the one, will, in a great degree, apply to the other.

As to the question, whether aid should be afforded to schools receiving grants of money from the Government, or be confined to those wholly independent of it, and relying solely on voluntary contributions, we offer no opinion; every one will do as to himself seems right. Only this we would say, that much responsibility, as to the future destinies of our beloved country, rests on the course which evangelical Christians generally may pursue in this matter.

We place next in order HOME MISSIONARY operations. Our blessed Saviour, when he sent forth his disciples to preach the gospel to every creature, enjoined them to begin at Jerusalem, so we say, with reference to Missionary effort generally, our HOME population has the first claim upon our liberality. We therefore earnestly appeal to Christians of England, Ireland, Scotland, and Wales, for a due measure of support to all those societies which have for their object the evangelisation of the destitute districts, whether town or country, of their respective divisions of the kingdom.

But the command is only to "begin" at Jerusalem; our sympathies must not end there. The richer part of the nation should assist the poorer, therefore it is peculiarly incumbent on British Christians to help IRELAND. The sister island has long been a perplexity and cause of just reproach to England, and there is but little prospect of much social or moral improvement until a purer religion shall have begun to leaven the minds of the great mass of its superstitious and ignorant population.

Our COLONIES, in all parts of the world, must by no means be forgotten. They are the germs of mighty empires, and, just as British evangelical Christians assist them in this,—the crisis, the infancy of their existence, so will they grow up to be truly Christian nations or not. Roman Catholics will not neglect them, if we should be so supine and criminally forgetful. They are pouring in swarms of priests to pervert the minds of any ignorant or indifferent Protestants they may meet with; and shall we turn a deaf ear to the petitions which are wafted across the mighty ocean, from poor, feeble, and scattered Churches, praying us, with much entreaty, that we would assist them to extend the spheres of their operations among the benighted and careless colonists around them?

The JEWS should have a considerable place in our regards. They are that wonderful people, " whose are the fathers, and of whom, as concerning the flesh, Christ came." Patriarchs, Prophets, and Apostles, were all of that lineage. There are many reasons why Christians should attempt to evangelise the descendants of Abraham. They are God's chosen people, and an abundance of blessing is in store for them through the instrumentality of Christians. Besides, they are owed an immense debt of reparation, both spiritual and temporal, for the inexcusable neglect and bloody trials they have had to endure at the hands of nations calling themselves Christian. They are placed before the next object to which attention is asked—the Heathen—for this reason also; it appears from prophecy, that they are to have an important influence in the conversion of the Gentiles. Could they but be generally brought to a heartfelt faith and belief in Christ as the Messiah, the great work of Christianising the world would doubtless go on rapidly; for, having penetrated into every land, wherever a pious Jew was found, there would be a missionary station. And they would be the best kind of missionaries; for, being native-born, they would perfectly understand the language, and be at once able, in the most efficient manner, to proclaim the glad tidings of salvation to the Heathens, Mohammedans, or nominal Christians around them.

We shall conclude our observations on the different objects to which the benevolence of the Churches may be applied, by referring to THE HEATHEN; and we speak of them last, not that we think they should be the least cared for, but because we have been guided by what we considered the *proximity* to us of the various claims on our liberality.

Here the extent of the field, white to the harvest, is almost bewildering; and the difficulty is, not to find an opening for missionaries, but to determine whither first to send them, for all nations seem to be stretching out their hands, and saying, "Come over and help us." How sad it is to have to say to most of these perishing supplicants, "You must remain yet longer in your ignorance, debasement, and sin; for we have not the means wherewith to assist you!"

There are many societies, instituted for the purpose of ameliorating the spiritual or temporal wants of the great human family, at home and abroad, which deserve to be more or less aided. The limits, however, to which we are restricted, forbid our commenting on any more of them separately, but the names of a few will be found in the appended Lists and Accounts. Among them are those for the erection of Places of Worship, to which we would beg particular attention, for "church extension" ought, especially in the localities of increasing population, to be more systematically pursued than it is.

It will be observed, on reference to the Specimen Accounts, that we have several times used the expression, "Society or

Societies." The reason is this, we would not by any means wish to restrict the benevolence of the individuals composing our churches and congregations to objects purely appertaining to their own denomination. No, we would have them show a far more catholic spirit, and appropriate a part, be it more or less, of their donations to the aid of societies which are doing the work of the Lord in connexion with other communities of evangelical Christians.

We cheerfully leave it to our readers to apportion their contributions to each object as they may think best. Some will give in proportion to the relative *nearness* of the claims—most to the Pastor, and less and less as the objects recede from personal and home operations; others will be guided by what they consider the paramount *necessities* of the cases; while others, again, will give in proportion to the *extent* of the field. These last would allocate a large portion of their contributions to the Heathen and the Colonies.

May the Holy Spirit pour out on individuals and churches a spirit of grace and supplication for a large effusion of all His blessed influences. Without this, all means will be useless. Books may be written deprecating covetousness, and urging to liberality; and Account-Books may be prepared; but all will be of no avail without His gracious operations on the hearts of men. Oh, that this sentiment may be deeply impressed, and rightly operate on the minds of our readers. Let them fervently and perseveringly implore this blessing, and it will be granted. Earnest prayer for a greater spirituality of mind and conduct seems to be the chief want of the age. Every evangelical denomination is mourning a state of collapse or declension: and one great cause of it, we fear, is a growing anxiety for the accumulation of wealth, either as a good in itself, or that it may be spent in luxurious living. A grasping eagerness for worldly gratification or riches is sure to lead to spiritual poverty. Nothing but prayer will revive us, and bring about a better state of things. It is a cheering sign of the times that many holy, zealous men, both lay and clerical, are sensitively alive to the evil, and are pointing out and urging us to the never-failing remedy—the prayer of faith.

In drawing to a close, may the Author be pardoned for expressing a hope, that all those who may read this little work will bear about with them the impression, that they are leaving something undone which ought to be done— neglecting something that God requires—until they have prayerfully considered, decided upon, and, if they think fit, made an express dedication in writing of the amount to be given by them to God. Has any one, while perusing the book, felt the reproofs of conscience as to his short-comings with respect to this matter; or has he even been sensible of a something within which made him restless and uneasy? Oh, let him not stifle the impression, or by palliatives and excuses evade acting on the conviction, and suffer the barbed arrow to rankle and fester in the wound. No; let him instantly go to the throne of grace, and pluck it out, by saying from the heart, "Lord, what wilt thou have me to do?"— "What wilt thou have me to give?"—then will he be able, with joyous emotions, to adopt the words of the great " Poet of the sanctuary," and say,—

> "All that I have, and all I am,
> Be, Lord, for ever thine;
> Whate'er my duty bids me give,
> My *cheerful* hands resign."

THE PROPOSED ACCOUNT-BOOK, AND EXPLANATION OF THE ACCOUNTS.

IF the suggestion contained in the foregoing Essay, to publish an Account-Book, as a guide to, and a record of, a Christian's liberality, should meet with general approval, the writer would venture to submit the following plan for carrying the design into execution.

As to the book itself, he thinks it should be got up in a neat style, perhaps with a short Calendar to begin with, then an Address on the evils of covetousness and the duty of liberality.

to be followed by a Form of Dedication and the Specimen Accounts beforementioned, with blank ruled leaves for real accounts. The Address should be condensed, terse, and pointed; be printed in a type large enough to be read with ease by persons past the middle age; and the whole book ought not to exceed a penny in price. There might be either a general one published, framed on the same principle as the following Specimen Accounts, and suited to all denominations; or else each section of the Church Universal might have its own, in which prominence would be given to the various institutions and objects to which that body of Christians usually devotes the largest share of its contributions. In some Church organisations the book might be published by the constituted authorities; but in others it would be necessary that private individuals, or some enterprising booksellers, should do so. The reason is obvious. It might be difficult, in some cases, to give satisfaction, as to the position in which different societies should be placed. Some persons would wish this object to stand foremost; others, that.

Concerted measures should be adopted by each congregation to place these publications in the hands of every one, young or old, rich or poor, who has money at his or her disposal. To do this efficiently, it is recommended, either that money be provided out of the Church funds, or that the office-bearers do so by a private contribution among themselves; and there is certainly no more legitimate or useful mode than this, in which such persons could bestow part of the money they themselves may appropriate to benevolent objects.

Presuming this plan to be acted upon, it is hoped that these little manuals, during the first year of their trial, will be found, in some good degree, to have answered the end proposed—that of being a stimulus and guide to the liberality of Christians. In order, however, that the good effected by them may be durable and progressive, it will be necessary to publish, annually, a succession of a similar character. But something more than mere publication will be requisite. So many persons are forgetful and unsystematic, that if it be left for individuals to procure these Account-Books for themselves, the plan will be almost sure to fail. These little tractates must, therefore, be supplied gratis, year by year, to every individual willing to receive them.

Should this proposal be energetically begun, and regularly carried on, may we not humbly, yet confidently, expect the blessing of God to rest on the effort? If this be experienced, the results, in various ways, will be highly beneficial both to churches and individuals, and greatly promote the spread of the glorious Gospel.

The advantages of a Form of Dedication have been fully shown at page 368.

To those accustomed to book-keeping the following observations on the appended Specimens of Accounts will be needless. They are intended for females, young persons, and those not used to business, that they may better understand how to make the entries correctly.

The first account is supposed to be that of a person who has devoted a shilling a-week, or 2*l*. 12*s*. a-year, to the service of God. In keeping a real account, the individual who does so can either lay up the shilling weekly, or monthly, as he may choose; both modes will be observed on the left-hand, or Debtor side, of the sheet. And with respect to the weekly subscriptions, he can either enter them when he pays them, as is shown in the first two months of the Creditor, or right-hand side of the Account; or insert them at more distant intervals, as in the subsequent part of it.

In the second Account, the individual (supposed to be a female) has placed in store 1*l*. per week, or 52*l*. annually, in four quarterly sums of 13*l*. each, and the donations on the other side are correspondingly larger than in the previous account; besides which, there are many other objects set down as being supported by her, to which the bounty of the former donor could not extend.

It will not be very practicable, nor will it be necessary, to disburse, within the prescribed time, the exact amount which has been consecrated. Sometimes a little more, and sometimes less, will be spent. These alternations will constantly occur, and the Specimen Accounts are adjusted to show how these variations are to be managed. If the reader will turn to the first Account, he will observe that the supposed person did not quite spend the whole of the 2*l*. 12*s*.—the consecrated money—1*s*. 2*d*. remaining in hand at the end of the year; which sum is carried on and added to the next year's Account, and placed at the head of the left-hand side of it.

In the second Specimen, more than the 52*l*.— the devoted portion—is shown to have been expended. It will be seen, by looking at the left-hand side of the Account, how this was effected, —that 5*l*. was, so to speak, borrowed, and added to the store, from some other source; and it is set down, when repaid, on the right-hand side of the new year's book.

In addition to the ordinary subscriptions, it will sometimes occur that extraordinary donations are required for special objects, such as the enlargement or rebuilding of the church or chapel in which a person has been accustomed to worship, or the erection of a new one, to which he may be disposed largely to contribute. In such a case, the person would either take the money out of his capital or his income, whichever his judgment and conscience should determine to be right. If from the former, the entries on each side of the Account are very simple. A record of this sort will be found in the new-year's Account (pages 396 and 397). Should he determine to take the subscription from his income, and he could not well spare the amount from one year's receipts, then it might be taken at first from some other fund, and be ultimately spread over two or more subsequent years. A person adopting this course would set down the receipt, and payments in a manner very similar to the entries of the 5*l*. before mentioned.

To know at any time whether the Account has been kept correctly, it is only necessary to cast up both sides, and subtract the one from the other. If the Account is right, and all the payments accurately entered, the balance thus found will agree with the money remaining in the box or purse.

No. I.

Form of Dedication.

After, I trust, due deliberation and prayer, I do hereby record the resolution I have made, to lay up one shilling weekly, to be expended on benevolent and religious objects. Out of this sum I have determined to give to the undermentioned objects the amount attached to each.

John A——

	£	s.	d.	
For the support of my Pastor, and the maintenance of Public Worship	0	5	0	per quarter.
At the collection for the College at B——	0	2	0	
For the poor, at the Sacrament, and other cases, about	0	7	0	per annum.
At the collection for the Dispensary	0	1	0	
" " " Sunday School	0	1	0	
For Home Missions	0	0	0½	per week.

Here enter any Society or Societies having this object in view.

| For Irish Missions | 0 | 0 | 0½ | per week. |

Here enter any Society or Societies having this object in view.

| For Colonial Missions | 0 | 0 | 0½ | per week. |

Here enter any Society or Societies having this object in view.

| For Foreign Missions | 0 | 0 | 1 | per week. |

Here enter any Society or Societies having this object in view.

| At the collection for the L—— Bible Society | 0 | 1 | 0 | |
| " " " M—— Tract Society } or to be laid out in the purchase of Tracts | 0 | 1 | 0 | |

The remainder to be disposed of as cases may present themselves.

SPECIMEN No.

Dr. LAID UP IN STORE.

185 .

				£	s.	d.
Jan. 7	Weekly Consecration of Income			0	1	0
,, 14	,, ,, ,,			0	1	0
,, 21	,, ,, ,,			0	1	0
,, 28	,, ,, ,,			0	1	0
Feb. 4	,, ,, ,,			0	1	0
,, 11	,, ,, ,,			0	1	0
,, 18	,, ,, ,,			0	1	0
,, 25	,, ,, ,,			0	1	0
Mar. 25	Monthly Consecration of Income			0	4	0
Apr. 22	,, ,, ,,			0	4	0
May 27	,, ,, ,,			0	5	0
June 24	,, ,, ,,			0	4	0
July 29	,, ,, ,,			0	5	0
Aug. 26	,, ,, ,,			0	4	0
Sept. 30	,, ,, ,,			0	5	0
Oct. 28	,, ,, ,,			0	4	0
Nov. 25	,, ,, ,,			0	4	0
Dec. 30	,, ,, ,,			0	5	0

Amount carried over . . £2 12 0

SPECIMEN ACCOUNT.—EXPENDITURE.

I. ACCOUNT   EXPENDED.   *Cr.*

185 .

Date	Description	£	s.	d.
Jan. 3	C—— Missionary Society (Foreign) at 1d. per week	0	0	1
,, ,,	Home, Irish, and Colonial Missions at 1½d.	0	0	1½
,, 7	Poor at Sacrament	0	0	4
,, 10	C—— Missionary Society, and Home, Irish, and Colonial Missions	0	0	2½
,, ,,	Paid Mr D—— E—— a quarter's seat-rent for Minister's salary	0	5	0
,, 17	C—— Missionary Society, and Home, Irish, and Colonial Missions	0	0	2½
,, ,,	Collection for B—— College	0	2	0
,, 24	C—— Missionary Society, and Home, Irish, and Colonial Missions	0	0	2½
,, 28	Paid Mr F—— G—— donation for new chapel at H——	0	4	0
,, 31	C—— Missionary Society, and Home, Irish, and Colonial Missions	0	0	2½
Feb. 4	Poor at Sacrament	0	0	4
,, 7	C—— Missionary Society, and Home, Irish, and Colonial Missions	0	0	2½
,, 11	Collection for Dispensary	0	1	0
,, 14	C—— Missionary Society, and Home, Irish, and Colonial Missions	0	0	2½
,, 21	,, ,, ,, ,, ,,	0	0	2½
,, 28	,, ,, ,, ,, ,,	0	0	2½
Mar. 4	Poor at Sacrament	0	0	4
,, 18	Collection for Jews	0	1	0
,, 28	C—— Missionary Society, four weeks at 1d.	0	0	4
,, ,,	Home, Irish, and Colonial Missions, four weeks at 1½d.	0	0	6
April 1	Poor at Sacrament	0	0	4
,, 8	Collection for I—— Missionary Society (Foreign)	0	1	0
,, 9	Paid Mr D—— E—— quarter's seat-rent for Minister	0	5	0
,, 20	K—— Sunday School Anniversary	0	1	0
,, 25	C—— Missionary Society, and Home, Irish, and Colonial Missions, four weeks at 2½d.	0	0	10
May 10	Collection for L—— Bible Society	0	1	0
,, 23	C—— Missionary Society, and Home, Irish, and Colonial Missions, four weeks at 2½d.	0	0	10
June 27	,, five weeks at 2½d.	0	1	0½
,, ,,	Collection for M—— Sunday School	0	1	0
July 1	Paid Mr D—— E—— quarter's seat-rent	0	5	0

Amount carried over   £1   13   9

Dr. LAID UP IN STORE.

185 .

	£	s.	d.
Amount brought over . .	2	12	0
	£2	12	0

NEW

185 .

	£	s.	d.
Balance brought from the Old Book of last year . . .	0	1	2
Jan. 8 Weekly Consecration of Income, increased to . .	0	1	6

Expended.   Cr.

185 .

			£	s.	d.
	Amount brought over		1	13	9
Aug. 5	Collection at the Anniversary of C—— Missionary Society		0	1	0
„ 10	Donation to poor man, John Brown		0	1	0
Sept. 2	C—— Missionary Society (Foreign) one quarter		0	1	1
„ „	Home, Irish, and Colonial Missions „		0	1	7½
Oct. 6	Paid Mr. D—— E—— a quarter's seat-rent		0	5	0
„ 10	Donation to a widow, Mary White		0	1	0
Nov. 11	Laid out for religious tracts		0	1	0
Dec. 2	Poor at Sacrament, 8 months at 4d.		0	2	8
„ 5	C—— Missionary Society, 1 quarter		0	1	1
„ 5	Home, Irish, and Colonial Missions, 1 quarter		0	1	7½
	Balance carried on to next year, and New Book		0	1	2
			£2	12	0

BOOK.

185 .

		£	s.	d.
Jan. 3	Donation to New School-room at N——	0	5	0
„ 4	Paid Mr. D—— E—— a quarter's seat-rent, increased to	0	7	6
„ 7	C—— Missionary Society, increased to 2d. per week	0	0	2
„ 7	Home, Irish, and Colonial Missions, as before	0	0	1½

No. II.

FORM OF DEDICATION.

After, I trust, due deliberation and prayer, I do hereby record the resolution I have made to lay up fifty-two pounds per annum, to be expended on benevolent and religious objects. Out of this sum, I have determined to give to the undermentioned objects the amount attached to each.

MARY B——

	£	s.	d.	
For the support of my Pastor, and the maintenance of Public Worship	2	10	0	per quarter.
To the Aged Ministers' Annuitant Society	1	1	0	per annum.
To the College at C——	2	2	0	,,
,, Dorcas or Clothing Society	0	10	0	,,
,, D—— Hospital	1	0	0	,,
,, E—— Orphan Institution	1	0	0	,,
,, F—— Sunday-school	1	0	0	,,
,, G—— Day-school	1	0	0	,,
,, Normal or Training School at H——	0	10	0	,,
For Home Missions	2	2	0	,,

Here enter any Society or Societies having this object in view.

For Irish Missions	1	1	0	,,

Here enter any Society or Societies having this object in view.

For Colonial Missions	1	1	0	,,

Here enter any Society or Societies having this object in view.

For Missions to the Jews	1	0	0	,,

Here enter any Society or Societies having this object in view.

SPECIMEN OF DEDICATION.

	£	s.	d.	
For Foreign Missions	4	4	0	per annum.

<small>Here enter any Society or Societies having this object in view.</small>

| For Tract or Book Societies . . . . | 1 | 0 | 0 | ,, |

<small>Here enter any Society or Societies having this object in view.</small>

| To the H—— Bible Society . . . . | 1 | 0 | 0 | ,, |

&c. &c. &c.

Dr.   LAID UP IN STORE.

No.

SPECIMEN

185 .

		£	s.	d.
Jan. 3	First Quarterly Consecration of Income	13	0	0
Mar. 28	Second do. do.	13	0	0
June 27	Third do. do.	13	0	0
Oct. 2	Fourth do. do.	13	0	0
	Added to the Store, to be refunded next year	5	0	0

Amount carried over . . £57 0 0

II.

ACCOUNT.

Expended.   Cr.

185 .

			£	s.	d.
Jan. 7	Poor at Sacrament		0	2	6
„ 10	Paid Mr. J—— K—— first quarterly payment for Minister		2	10	0
	Paid Mr. L—— annual subscription to D—— Hospital		1	0	0
Feb. 4	Poor at Sacrament		0	2	6
„ 5	Donation to Mr. M—— N—— towards his loss by fire		1	0	0
	Paid Mr. O—— annual subscription to F—— Sunday School		1	0	0
„ 7	Paid Mr. P—— Q—— annual subscription to Aged Ministers' Annuitant Society, and P. O. O.		1	1	3
	Paid Mr. R—— annual subscription to E—— Orphan Institution		1	0	0
	Paid Mr. S—— T—— annual subscription to Total Abstinence Society		0	10	0
Mar. 4	Poor at Sacrament		0	2	6
	Mr. U—— annual subscription to H—— Bible Society		1	0	0
	Treasurer of the Mechanics' Institute, a donation		0	10	0
	Mr. V—— annual subscription to W—— Sailors' Society		0	10	0
April	Mr. J—— K—— second quarterly payment for Minister		2	10	0
	Mr. X—— annual subscription to Y—— Missionary Society (Foreign)		3	3	0
	Donation to Z—— Missionary Society (Foreign)		1	1	0
	Paid Mr. J—— donation to new chapel at A——		10	0	0
May	Paid Mr. B—— annual subscription to the College at C——		2	2	0
	Donation to five Shipwrecked Sailors		1	0	0
	Annual subscription to D—— Irish Missionary Society		1	1	0
June	Donation to Mrs. E——, a widow		0	10	0
	Mr. F—— donation to new church at G——		2	0	0
July	Mr. J—— K—— third quarterly payment for Minister		2	10	0
August	Mr. H—— donation to new chapel at K——, in France		1	0	0
	Annual subscription to L—— School for Ministers' Sons		1	1	0
	Do. M—— School for Missionaries' Daughters		1	1	0
	Donation to a new Chapel at N—— in Canada		1	0	0
Sept.	Annual subscription to Dorcas or Clothing Society		0	10	0
	Mr. O—— annual subscription to G—— Day-school		1	0	0
	Mr. P—— do. H—— Normal School		0	10	0

Amount carried over . . £42 7 9

Dr.   LAID UP IN STORE.

185 .

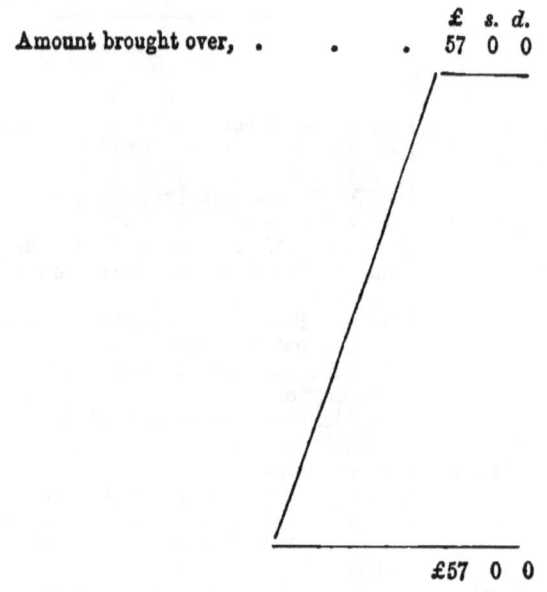

	£	s.	d.
Amount brought over, . . .	57	0	0
	£57	0	0

NEW

185 .

		£	s.	d.
	Balance brought from the Old Book of last year . .	1	1	3
Jan.	First Quarterly Consecration of Income, increased to .	15	0	0
	Cash taken from Capital, being a special Contribution towards the enlargement of my place of Worship	100	0	0

Expended. Cr.

185 .

		£	s.	d.
	Amount brought over	42	7	9
Oct.	Mr J—— K—— fourth quarterly payment for Minister	2	10	0
	Annual subscription to I—— Missionary Society to the Jews	1	0	0
	Annual subscription to K—— Missionary Society for the Colonies	1	1	0
	Ditto L—— Tract Society	1	0	0
Nov.	Donation for repairs of M—— Church	1	0	0
	Laid out for Tracts and Books, for gratuitous distribution	0	19	0
	Annual Subscription for Home Missions	2	2	0
Dec.	Poor at Sacrament, nine months at 2s. 6d.	1	2	6
	Sundry Collections at Public Worship	1	11	0
	Sundry small Donations to different objects and poor persons	1	5	6
	Balance carried on to New Book for next year	1	1	3
		£57	0	0

BOOK

185 .

		£	s.	d.
Jan.	Poor at Sacrament, increased to	0	3	0
	Mr J—— K——, first quarterly payment for Minister increased to	3	0	0
	Repayment of the advance of 5l. made last year	5	0	0
	Paid Mr M——, the first instalment for the enlargement of my place of worship	50	0	0

BLANK FORM FOR A REAL ACCOUNT.

Form of Dedication.

After, I trust, due deliberation and prayer, I do hereby record the resolution I have made, to lay up _____ * to be expended on benevolent and religious objects. Out of this sum I have determined to give to the undermentioned objects the amount attached to each.   †_____

	£	s.	d.

* Here insert the amount per year, or quarter, or week, you have determined to give.

† Here sign your name.

BLANK LEAVES FOR

Dr.   Laid up in Store.

		£	s.	d.

A REAL ACCOUNT.

EXPENDED.   *Cr.*

			£	s.	d.

INDEX.

ABILITY of the Church to give, 208
Account-books for business transactions, 354
  Christian purposes, 354
  the proposed, 383
Accounts, blank forms of, 400
  desirability and necessity of keeping, 370
  explanation of specimen, 385
  specimen, 388, 394
Agency of man indispensable, 190
  only instrumental, 191
Almsgiving, indiscriminate, injurious, 69, 281
Amount dedicated should be recorded, 368
  of a Jew's contributions in various forms, 197, 285
  of present liberality, 183
  to be devoted, intentionally left undetermined, 203, 247, 293, 362
Apportionment to various claims, 341, 370, 382
Avarice, awful effects of, in the church, 308
  tempts the curse of God, 328
Baptism, a proof of infant, 56, 111
Barnes on pastoral support, 371
Benefit societies, the importance and defects of, 347
  a privilege, 192
Benevolence a test of character, 273
  as beneficial to give as to receive, 269, 322
  assimilates man to God, 324
  indicative of man's state, 321
  examples of eminent, 319
  exerts a powerful influence on man's temporal and spiritual interests, 231, 240, 257, 328, 364
  on eternal happiness, 257, 330
  human merit discarded by Christians, 270
  love to God the proper motive of, 270
  needful for the world's conviction and conversion, 315
  never tends to poverty, 328
  peculiarly glorifies God, 325
  powerful influence of lofty, 317
  the best investment of property, 361
  urgent claims of the world on the churches, 314
Bequests, 357
Bible testimony concerning dedication of property, full and uniform, 170
Capital necessary for various purposes, 342
  not sinful to accumulate, 342
Christianity a religion of life and spirit, 201
  a system of loving constraint, 292
  contrasted with Judaism, 286
  elevates and vitalises Judaism, 288

Christianity increases obligations, 304
  makes man a law to himself, 204, 362
  not opposed to, but expansive of Judaism, 286
  the religion of the world, and, consequently, aggressive, 217, 286
Christians, objects of charity of early, 341
  should give at least as much as Jews did, 362
Collectors, importance and qualifications of, 340
Colleges, duty of pastors and churches to, 377
  importance and claims of, 376
Commerce, a manifold blessing, 168
Community of goods, disadvantages of a, 345
  in the early churches, 345
Condition of Jews, temporal, 208, 229
Confidence of Christ in his people, 192, 193
  how it has been met, 248, 316
Conscience, dictates of, to be obeyed, 383
Contributions to be laid by till wanted, 229, 353
Convictions, special, of the duty to be carried out, 254
Co-operation of man with God, 272
Covetousness, an insidious and perilous sin, 161, 365
  a test of, 81
  defects of works on, 339, 368
  necessity of constant opposition to, 221
  warnings against, 161, 222
  what it is, and what it is not, 50
Cross, the, the place for determining our gifts, 254
Decision and amendment, solemn call to, 333, 383
Decline of liberality, 184
Dedication, forms of, 387, 392, 399
  observations on, 368
  of property to God, 350, 353
Deficiencies, two prominent, among Christians, 271
Design of the Gospel, 224
  half views of, 224
Doctrines, important according to scriptural prominence, 220
Employment preferable to charity, 281, 345
Errors to be avoided must be exposed, 360
Excitement, giving from, 229, 316
Expenditure, excess of, in apparel and living, 346, 358, 360
Exposition of 1 Cor. xvi. 2, 275, 350
  2 Cor. viii. and ix., 276
  Genesis, iv. 3-7, 30
  Leviticus, xxvii. 30, 35
Famine in Ireland, 346

INDEX. 403

Feebleness, moral, of the church accounted for, 269, 315, 317
Forethought, duty and advantage of, 255, 340, 346
Free-will offerings Christian gifts must be, 246
    discretionary nature of, 38, 41
    expected of Christians, 59
    freely given by Christians, 60
    no merit in them, 42
    required in Christian more than Jewish times, 60
    stamped with special approval and pre-eminent worth, 227
Giving, defects in the mode of, 340
    predetermination should be exercised in, 353
    should be proportionate to means, 300, 351
    to be practised by all, 351
God, munificence of, 172, 207, 271, 273, 309, 310
God's goodness to Britain, 211
    promises for time to be credited, 257
Gratitude, a motive for paying tithe, 199
    a reason for giving now, 208
Harmony between feeling, work, and prayer, 194, 235, 250, 322
Heresy consists in self-chosen worship, 22
Honour conferred by being permitted to give, 192
Hope, a motive for paying tithes, 201
Hope of Christians, 214
Illiberality, results of Jewish and Christian, 216, 258, 305
Improvement to be reached by confession of past deficiencies, 174, 176
Income distinguished from property, 282, 357
    how to ascertain proportion of, to be devoted, 282
    of British nation, 210
    to be properly apportioned, 341, 358, 363
Indecision, danger of, 369
Inquiry, deficiency of, into Christian obligations, 269, 271
    into the doings of the wealthy, 151
Interest in Christ's cause promoted, 234
Justice, a motive for paying tithes, 201
    giving now, 215
    demands system in giving, 255
Liberality, amount of, required for salvation, 249
    calls upon the churches, 216
    dependent on our social circle and habits, 194
    duty of Christians, 367
    involved in a profession of faith, 225
    joyful spirit of, 41
    measure of, 363
    motives to, 367
    must be determined individually, 253
    of church predicted, 269
    of Jews not confined to tithes, 197
    of Pentecostal church, 290
    promotive of Christian union and increase, 237
    would largely tend to save the world, 241
Life Assurance, 349

Lord's day the proper time for setting apart property for religious and benevolent purposes, 127, 143, 303, 304, 354
Love of God, man's infinite obligation to the, 311
Manner of giving, 229
Measure of liberality, 363
    a test of devotedness, 201, 250, 252, 272
Melchizedek, 28
Ministers, necessary qualifications of, 375
    private property of, 373
Ministry, Christian estimation of the, 239
    necessity of an educated, 375
    obligations to support the, 215, 279, 370
Missions—Home, Irish, Colonial, Jewish, and Foreign, 379
Motives, order of, 184
Objections to tithe: "It will degenerate into form," 250
    "Not enforced in the New Testament," 247
    "Not necessary to salvation," 249
    "Others do not give a tenth," 236, 246
    "We cannot afford it," 243
    to weekly offering, 304—6
Objects of Christian liberality, 66, 280, 370
    Church Extension, 381
    Colleges, 376
    Ministry, 370
    Missions — Colonial, Home, Irish, Jewish, and Foreign, 217, 225, 379
    poor and schools, 378, 379
Obligation, Christian, implied rather than stipulated, 275
Obligations, religious, perpetual, and universal, 283
    the Christian's inferrible from the Jews, 297
Picture sketched by the Great Teacher, 332
Poor, duty of assisting the, 378
    Christians at Jerusalem, 340, 378
    not exempted from giving, 243, 246, 305, 352
    offerings of the, sometimes exceed all others, 303, 306
Position of British Christians, 210, 213
Positive law based on moral reasons, 206
Prayer, necessity of, 362, 382
Premeditation, importance of, 340, 353
Priesthood, origin of a, in Melchizedek, 30
Principle of Christian obedience, 247
Privileges of the Church, 213
Procrastination to be avoided, 365, 383
Profits and losses, 356
Progress, rapid, of human science, and slow, of Christian liberality, 269
Property, God disposes of his own, 9
    necessary, and in itself a blessing, 342
    the use of, left to man's discretion, under limit, 12—16
    when dedicated, to be "set apart," 353
Proprietor, God the sole, 5, 143

Provision, parental, for children, a duty, 343, 346
  when sinful, 306, 361
Prudence requires system, 255, 356
Reasons for a positive law may continue after it, 206
  for Christian liberality greater than Jewish, 207
  for not giving, suspicious, 222
  of Jews for paying tithe, 199
Reflections, solemn, on a death-bed, and in eternity, 261, 332
Regularity, importance of, in business, 354, 356
Responsibilities of the Christian, 253
  for extending the Gospel, 245, 339
Results of present liberality, 183, 219
Revival of religion, 239, 252
Riches, God to be remembered first in the use of, 64
  escape from the danger of, 63, 327
  insidious and increasing peril of, 62
Robbery of God, 202, 258
Romanism, contributions for, and Heathenism, 227, 293.
Rule in giving, rarely thought of, 85, 269
  the Scriptures, the only, of benevolence, 85
Sacrifice, Divine origin of, 17, 27
Savings' Banks, 349
Scale, a graduated, affords scope for endless diversity, 294
  illustrations of, 301
  submitted, 300
  the true Scriptural Rule, 298.
Scriptural examples and their respective lessons in order of treatment:
  Abraham, 90—6
  Jacob, 96—101
  Moses. Different tithes and offerings, 101—109
  Christian Church at Pentecost, 110—117
    in Macedonia, 118—121
    in Corinth, 121—126
  Erection of Tabernacle, 144—148
    Temple, 148—152
  The Widow of Sarepta, 152—154
  The Widow's Mite, 154—157
  Miscellaneous instructions, 157
    Precepts, 158
    Warnings, 161
    Promises, 164
    Prophecies, 166
Self-control, a result of giving, 230
Selfishness to be destroyed, 224
Separation of the Church from the world, 237
Sin, an act of rebellion against God, 186
  brings ruin and eternal destruction, 187
  makes men enemies, 187
Spiritual prosperity and liberality co-equal, 232
Steward, man a, of God's property, 7

widely different emotions of the faithful and unfaithful, 333
Stock-taking, necessity of, 356
Students, mental endowments and habits of ministerial, 376
Style of living becoming a Christian, 305
  errors in, 358, 360
Subscriptions should not be too frequently varied, 357
System in giving, 185, 255, 277, 353, 369, 384
Taxation among the Jews and ourselves, 209
Temptations of the present age, 361
Tithe, a divinely instituted mode of fulfilling a moral obligation, 17, 288
  Abraham's, 28, 196; Jacob's, 27; Jewish, 32, 216, 362
  antiquity of, 19, 195
  circumstances of injunction of, on Israel, 284
  freedom from, not license from benevolence, 290
  influence of, on Israel, 285
  instances of the practice of, by heathen, 293
  national, does not free from personal obligation, 304
  not abolished, but absorbed by Christianity, 295
  not a mere ceremonial institution, 34, 290
  obligatory on Christians in spirit, 44
  proper Christian inference from, 298
  recommended to Christians, 204
  various forms and uses of, 37, 196, 285
Weekly offerings, all-sufficient for every necessity, 318
  Divine origin of, 273—5
  ease, simplicity, and efficiency of, 277, 278
  generally, if not universally, practicable, 307
  purposes of application of, 279—81
  standing obligation of, 277
Work for Christ every man's duty, 191
  left to love, 192, 362
World, advantages to the, from liberality, 241
  contributions of the, for pleasure, 226
Worship defined by God, not to be chosen by man, 20
Worship, temples of, their cost man's charge, 272
  demand man's best offerings, 293
  exist for man's use, 271
  of heathen, very costly, 293
  penuriousness towards God's often entails a curse, 273
Young men should be sought for the ministry, 377
  ministers, kindness and consideration to, 377

BALLANTYNE AND COMPANY, PRINTERS, EDINBURGH.

www.ingramcontent.com/pod-product-compliance
Lightning Source LLC
Chambersburg PA
CBHW030600300426
44111CB00009B/1054